Nonviolent Communication
非暴力沟通

[美]马歇尔·卢森堡 Marshall B. Rosenberg, PhD / 著
刘轶 / 译　李迪　娅锦 / 审校

致广大读者

《非暴力沟通》中文简体版由华夏出版社出版十多年来,畅销百万册,深受广大读者的好评。随着越来越多的人学习、运用非暴力沟通,我们推出汉英对照版,遵照最新的英文原版内容和样式,传递马歇尔博士最直接的话语,以飨读者。

关于英文原文内容、本书新版中文翻译,如您有任何疑问、指正和建议,欢迎扫描二维码,反馈给我们。

扫码加"读者小助手"

进"正向改变"社群

在对与错的区分之外,有一片田野,
我将在那里遇见你。
——鲁米

中文版序

　　我们每一个人都渴望幸福，渴望生活在一个和平、稳定而又繁荣的社会当中。当人们的基本需要诸如食物和住所得到满足，决定我们生活品质的便是人与人的连结。这意味着，如果我和家人、亲属、朋友以及同事的关系在情感上是安全、滋养的；我可以表达我的想法并且得到理解、接纳、鼓励、同理；当美好的事情发生时能够庆祝……我便能掌握我的力量。这将在我生命遭遇困难时给予我信心、价值感和勇气。

　　而如果我与身边的人在关系中的状态是相互纠错、评判、指责，那么我会感到受伤、难过和孤独，我的生活也会充满压力。我相信，如果我们学习如何沟通、如何相互交谈和聆听、如何不带批评地诚实表达自己、如何带着同理心聆听……就会带来不同的关系品质。在本书中，马歇尔向我们展示了如何在日常生活中一步一步地做到这些，不论是在家庭中还是工作中，如此我们将拥有改变情境的力量，而不是让它变得更糟糕。

　　在这个如此多人共同生活的社会，即便我们拥有相同的愿景、梦想，要如何实现它们，每个人都可能有着不同的想法。这些不同常常引发群体内的冲突。新版中增加的章节为我们展现了如何通过非暴力沟通的调解来和平解决人与人之间的冲突。这种调解方式既能为一个安全而又和谐的社会做出贡献，也能时培育活力以及创造力以推进社会向前发展。

What People Are Saying About Nonviolent Communication™

Business:

"*Nonviolent Communication* is hands-down one of the best books I've read as a business owner, as well as a husband and father. This book is not a new title, but for me, it does much better than other books at unveiling key principles and practices of exceptional communication. It's also the first book Satya Nadella asked his leadership team to read, which is meaningful."

—Ben Peterson, BambooHR
Recommended by Forbes Human Resources Council as a must-read book for positive impact on how to approach work.

"One of the books I first recommended that everyone read, when I first got on, was *Nonviolent Communication*, which used to be able to say, look, let us make sure we are empathetic to each other's needs, because it requires that."

—CNBC Transcript, *Microsoft CEO Satya Nadella Sits Down With CNBC's Jon Fortt*

If empathy as a measure of emotional IQ is a predictor of success, then Nadella hit the nail on the head by inculcating the corporate giant with the trait from top to bottom. Why else is empathy important? Microsoft is both a services and a product company, and its offerings have to resonate with users. Nadella states: "You have to be able to say, 'Where is this person coming from? What makes them tick? Why are they excited or frustrated by something that is happening, whether it's about computing or beyond computing?'"

—HARRY McCRACKEN'S article in *Fast Company*

"I got to this book thanks to a recommendation by Satya Nadella (CEO of Microsoft). The book presents a simple technique and examples to empathize and connect with people's feelings. Instead of judging people by the message, the book helps you understand the needs behind and what feelings and emotions are driving them. Highly recommended."

—An online reviewer

"I love this book and have recommended it to several of my coworkers. A mentor recommended the book to me when I was having trouble giving direct feedback to people that I supervise without hurting their feelings. This book helped me to remove the judgment from my message and focus on the desired outcome. It's a relatively quick read and I can easily refer back to it when preparing for a tough conversation."

—An online reviewer

"This book was a life changer for me as I struggled in a dysfunctional workplace. It provided the skills I needed to gain respect and be able to work at my desired level of productivity. I highly recommend it for anyone who must work and live with others."

—An online reviewer

于我，从马歇尔那里学习到的重大收获是自我同理。通过自我同理，我对自己有了更多的理解和认识。例如理解自己为什么会去做那些让自己后悔的事情。这意味着，如果在行动之前就能懂得这些，我便不用如此行动。我学会了如何理解我的错误，我也学会了宽恕自己并理解这意味着什么。另外对我很有帮助的还有：如何充分地表达愤怒，让彼此加深理解并走向更深的连结；如何用不伤害关系的方式说"不"，因而我能更好地应对生活并且减少压力；在面对那些被我归类为"敌人"的人时，将他们作为"人"来看待，看到他们和我一样遭受着苦痛，他们和我一样在那一刻尽了自己最大的努力。

今日，我们正在共同面对由我们自己的思想和生活方式所造成的诸多问题，而此刻，世界召唤我们一起走向未知、绘制新的路径。当我们和自己内心最深处、最真诚的人类共同需要相连结时，我们便拥有了这份勇气。我相信中国正在朝着这个方向引领世界，而此书将带给人们一种看待世界的新方式以及新的思考和连结方式。

我也要祝贺我们在中国的第一位国际认证培训师刘轶，她亦是《非暴力沟通》新版的译者。我希望这本书能启迪更多的人，并且召唤更多认证培训师的出现。

凯瑟琳·韩·辛格
前国际非暴力沟通中心董事会主席

Communication:

"Nonviolent Communication can change the world. More importantly, it can change your life. I cannot recommend it highly enough."

—JACK CANFIELD, *Chicken Soup for the Soul* Series

"In this book, you will find an amazingly effective language for saying what's on your mind and in your heart. Like so many essential and elegant systems, it's simple on the surface, challenging to use in the heat of the moment, and powerful in its results."

—VICKI ROBIN, *Your Money or Your Life*

"Dr. Rosenberg has brought the simplicity of successful communication into the foreground. No matter what issue you're facing, his strategies for communicating with others will set you up to win every time."

—TONY ROBBINS, *Awaken the Giant Within* and *Unlimited Power*

"A way for people to speak in ways that foster greater connection, understanding, compassion. It is applicable to all areas of life: how we communicate with others in intimate partnerships, business, international relations, and also how we are with ourselves—are we our own best friend or are we beating ourselves up. Learning and practicing this process has enriched my life in myriad ways."

—An online reviewer

"Amazing. Empathy, active listening, compassion. This book will help you to raise the quality of your life, relationships with your colleagues, friends, family."

—An online reviewer

"I have found it to probably be the single most helpful book I have read in my life, and I have probably reread it ten times."

—An online reviewer

"I have never read a clearer, more straightforward, insightful book on communication. Amazingly easy to read, great examples, and challenging to put into practice—this book is a true gift to all of us."

—An online reviewer

"NVC is the language of enlightenment. So simple yet so difficult. Using NVC can change your life, bring clarity to your thinking, and transform relationships."

—An online reviewer

"If you want to be heard, and to hear what your loved ones are truly saying behind what they're saying, read this book! It will change your life."

—An online reviewer

译序

很荣幸在过去三年我能与马歇尔博士的《非暴力沟通》有如此亲密的接触，这本书可以说汇集了马歇尔对于"非暴力沟通"这套方法的所有精华内容。对于我来说，翻译的过程意味着不断深切感悟非暴力沟通的精神，体会其大道至简背后所蕴藏着的对人性深刻的理解。马歇尔博士其人、其事、其教诲让我获得许多滋养与感动。

回顾学习和实践非暴力沟通的这些年，我见证着自己的成长和蜕变。持续地为内心带去慈悲、关爱和理解不仅让生命变得柔软，也不断澄清着内心真正的渴望以及想要活出的状态。鲁米说，我们无须找寻爱，而只须消融内心爱的阻碍。非暴力沟通不仅是一座找寻爱的桥梁，更重要的是，它让我拥有爱的能力来支持生命中的各种关系。而在一个更广大的层面，非暴力沟通更是引领我走向世界，带着对人本自具足的信任与尊重，赋能更多人活出真我。因着这些年来的教学，我也得以见证许许多多的生命经由非暴力沟通走向越来越多的自由、力量、和平以及福祉，我深感赐福。

如今，自马歇尔博士开创非暴力沟通已经整整50年，非暴力沟通的影响力在全球持续扩大着，越来越多的人开始学习、实践并从中受益，这在我看来并不意外。走过风云变幻的50年，站在2020年所开启的更加多变、未知和动荡的时代前，非暴力沟通仍在向世界持续贡献着力量与活力。在这里，我想简单分享一下个人的实践和学习体会。

Conflict Resolution:

"Nonviolent Communication is one of the most useful processes you will ever learn."

—WILLIAM URY, *Getting to Yes*

"You'll learn simple tools to defuse arguments and create compassionate connections with your family, friends, and other acquaintances."

—JOHN GRAY, *Men Are From Mars, Women Are From Venus*

"It's a way to step out of the 'who's right, who's wrong?' conflict paradigm, and instead, to realize that people are always acting in a way to attempt to get their needs met. No one is wrong; it's just a matter of finding strategies to meet each other's needs."

—An online reviewer

"Like Noam Chomsky, Rosenberg's work is intrinsically radical, it subverts our whole status-quo system of power: between children and adults, the sane and the psychotic, the criminal and the law. Rosenberg's distinction between punitive and protective force should be required reading for anyone making foreign policy or policing our streets."

—D. KILLIAN, reporter, *On The Front Line, Cleveland Free Times*

"In our present age of uncivil discourse and mean-spirited demagoguery, the principles and practices of Nonviolent Communication are as timely as they are necessary to the peaceful resolution of conflicts, personal or public, domestic or international."

—MIDWEST BOOK REVIEW, *Taylor's Shelf*

"Rosenberg describes how, in numerous conflicts, once 'enemies' have been able to hear each other's needs, they are able to connect compassionately and find new solutions to previously 'impossible' impasses. If you want to learn ways of more skillful speech I highly recommend this clear, easy-to-read book."

—DIANA LION, Buddhist Peace Fellowship, *Turning Wheel Magazine*

"The best book I have read without a doubt. I have used all of the concepts covered in the book in my family violence intervention program and anger management classes. The people in class have loved the days we go over these ideas. I highly recommend this book to anyone who wants to find a healthier way to communicate and connect with other."

—An online reviewer

首先从个体层面来说，人不可能永无止境地被外在撕扯，这包括消费主义、碎片化的信息、竞争比较……我们作为宇宙之中承载着神圣使命的存在，重拾真我、完整、相互依存以及回归本质和意义，是人内心最深切也是最自然的渴望与召唤。如果人无法活出真我，人与人的相遇便无法真实，那"沟通"方法便会沦为操控与算计的工具。在这个层面上，我认为非暴力沟通提供的是人与人得以连结的底层逻辑，而这个连结首先从与自己开始，从对"认识自己"这样一个源头的探寻开始建立与自己的友爱关系，再推己及人，与他人建立带有尊重、理解和关爱的联系。

"你不能用创造问题的思维来解决问题。——爱因斯坦"

今天，越来越多的系统（不论是家庭、组织还是社会）开始关注一种不同于以往——能够赋能于人、激发内驱力和参与共创的方式来开展互动、发展自身。而行为的改变则需建立在意识、心智成长以及能力建设之上，在这个层面上，非暴力沟通的学习无异于一种从内向外的成长练习和生命教育。

写到这里，或许那些初识《非暴力沟通》的读者、学习者会满怀好奇甚至疑问：《非暴力沟通》难道不是关于人际沟通、好好说话的吗？我希望透过这一版的《非暴力沟通》为大家更清晰地呈现马歇尔在书名中所要展现的：一种生命的语言。"我想要与那美妙的生命之流保持连结。"马歇尔，这位喜欢在教学中拿起吉他弹唱的伟大老师曾这样歌唱道。经年累月的社会和文化制约透过某类语言（比较、评判、命令、推卸责任……）让我们疏离了与生命（人的需要）的连结，加深着与自己、他人和世界的对立，而通过非暴力沟通，马歇尔博士不仅带给我们一种使用语言的全新方式，更是用一种不同的心智模式和文化范式，引

"Emotions typically run high in conflict situations and when people don't have the language to articulate their feelings and what fuels them with accuracy and precision, which they often don't, it's like being on a stormy sea with no one at the helm; people get tossed about on the waves, sails get ripped and the relationship runs aground in a hurtful place that is a long shot from where it might have landed."

—RACHELLE LAMB, NVC Trainer

Education:

"Through compelling, real life examples, Rosenberg brings the NVC process to life. My college students, especially the older ones, share with me that reading this book has changed their lives. Trying to practice the steps myself in daily interactions, at meetings, and in the classroom, has also had a powerful effect on me."

—An online reviewer

"This book should be required reading in high school or college. The skill set of speaking our true needs taught in this book is priceless and practical. It is a must read."

—An online reviewer

Health/Healing/Self-Care:

"Marshall Rosenberg provides us with the most effective tools to foster health and relationships. Nonviolent Communication connects soul to soul, creating a lot of healing. It is the missing element in what we do."

—DEEPAK CHOPRA, *How to Know God* and *Ageless Body and Timeless Mind*

"Thought it was going to be a book on dealing with others, however the other surprise was on how it gave me the ability to see how I communicate with myself . . . all the self-talk that goes on within. Now I am kinder and more understanding to me which means . . . yes, I'm kinder and more understanding with others!"

—An online reviewer

"*Nonviolent Communication* is THE premiere how-to guide for improving your performance at doing empathy, which is one of the fundamental competencies of Emotional Intelligence."

—An online reviewer

"I enjoyed this chapter because it helped me translate my self-judgments into statements of my own unmet needs. I now see that when I am angry with myself it is because my actions were not in harmony with my values. Seeing things from this perspective helps me mourn my action and move into self-forgiveness by connecting with the specific need I was trying to meet when I used a strategy that I now regret."

—An online reviewer

领我们重新建立与生命的连结，创造和自己、他人以及世界之间基于生命的关系——伙伴关系。

马歇尔博士这一生，在世界各地奔走教学的同时，也去过许多充满着大大小小冲突的国家与地区：从美国的贫困社区到处在冲突中的中东，还有经历了大屠杀后的卢旺达，等等。在我看来，马歇尔并非所谓的身心灵成长导师，而是一位勇于面对人性、调停对立族群和帮派的和平使者。只因他全然相信，当人与人之间能够相互听见、理解、连结，心中的"敌人"自会消融。这便是"非暴力"的精神与力量：心无敌人。

"在一个充满冲突的世界中，为和平代言"，这是马歇尔，也是非暴力沟通前辈们以及我所完成的国际认证体系给我的教导和承诺。而面对今天的世界，我们比任何时候都需要强有力的内在资源——培养韧性、对人性的信任、对连结的信心以及对话的能力，并从自身开始成为和平、邀请和平、共创和平。

如今，非暴力沟通在中国也被越来越多的人了解、学习和实践着，要感谢许多人（华夏出版社、第一版的译者阮胤华先生、这些年来到中国分享非暴力沟通的国际中心认证培训师们以及无数有志于将非暴力沟通的精神内核分享给广大受众的践行者们）。作为其中的一员，我很荣幸能够以不同的形式贡献其中。

最后，我想感谢在这本书的翻译过程中给予支持的许多人。多年一起学习非暴力沟通的李迪和娅锦为审校付出了一年多的时间，精心打磨；数十位来自 NVC 中文学院的社群伙伴以及杨芮（Ruby Yeung）参与了校对工作，这份伙伴之间流动着的"由衷的相互给予"，给予了我许多温暖。陪伴和见证我这些年来成长的凯瑟琳老师（国际非暴力沟通

"This book has changed my life! What changed most was how I treat myself. Thank you Marshall!"

—An online reviewer

Intimate Relationships:

"In addition to saving our marriage, Nonviolent Communication is helping us repair our relationships with our grown children and to relate more deeply with our parents and siblings."

—A reader in Arizona

"I spent forty years of my life trying to receive empathy from my dad. After only reading half of this book, I was able to express myself in a way that he was able to finally hear me and give me what I needed. It was a gift beyond words."

—An online reviewer

"This book is essential reading for anyone seeking to end the unfulfilling cycles of argument in their relationship, and for parents who wish to influence their children's behavior by engendering compassion rather than simply achieving obedience."

—An online reviewer

Parenting and Family Communication:

"Nonviolent Communication allowed me to overcome my toxic conditioning and find the loving parent and person that was locked inside. Dr. Rosenberg has created a way to transform the violence in the world."

—A nurse in California

"What began as a search for a better discipline system for our six-year-old has turned out to be a philosophical approach and communication tool that is transforming how we relate to each other and ourselves."

—An online reviewer

Personal Growth:

"*Nonviolent Communication* by Marshall Rosenberg is a great book teaching a compassionate way to talk to people—even if you (or they) are angry."

—JOE VITALE, *Spiritual Marketing, The Power of Outrageous Marketing*

"A revolutionary way of looking at language. If enough people actually make use of the material in *Nonviolent Communication*, we may soon live in a more peaceful and compassionate world."

—WES TAYLOR, Progressive Health

中心董事会主席）、吕靖安老师（《非暴力沟通实践手册》作者）对于新的《非暴力沟通》中文版给予了殷切希望与谆谆指导；华夏出版社朱悦女士全程陪伴与支持；还有许多在这个过程中给予我鼓励和支持的伙伴们，感谢你们滋养和陪伴着我度过这段难忘又漫长的翻译历程。

  翻译的过程与我非暴力沟通实践和教学的过程可谓共生共长，新的理解和体悟随着生命的成长不断生发着，每一次校对都有新的发现，这也意味着翻译永远是一场遗憾的艺术，但或许又是某种开启。我诚挚地期待着透过这版《非暴力沟通》，与更多的人相遇、对话、共同成长。

刘轶

国际非暴力沟通中心中国大陆地区首位认证培训师

NVC 中文学院创始人

"This is the most concise, most clearly written manual on interpersonal communication I've ever come across. I've been challenged by this book to be the change I want to see in my world."

—An online reviewer

"I am one of those people who is highly critical of myself. This book is teaching me to love myself so I can truly care for others. It can pave the way for peace between people, different ethnic groups, countries, etc., and I believe our world really needs this."

—An online reviewer

"Very few books have changed my life, caused me to rethink who I am and how I present myself to the world."

—An online reviewer

Prison:

"For convicts immersed in an environment which intensifies and reinforces conflict, discovering this step-by-step methodology advocating compassion through communication is enormously liberating."

—DOW GORDON, NVC Trainer at Minimal Security Unit, Monroe Correctional Complex, Freedom Prison Project, Seattle, Washington

Spirituality:

"As far as nonviolence and spiritual activism, Marshall Rosenberg is it! Applying the concepts within these books will guide the reader toward fostering more compassion in the world."

—MARIANNE WILLIAMSON, *Everyday Grace* and honorary chairperson, Peace Alliance

Therapy:

"The quality of empathy I now am able to provide has enlivened my therapy practice. This book gives me hope that I can contribute to the well-being of my clients, and also connect deeply with my friends and family. The step-by-step empathy skills in this book are learnable by anyone."

—An online reviewer

"I have never read a clearer, more straightforward, insightful book on communication. After studying and teaching assertiveness since the '70s, this book is a breath of fresh air. Rosenberg adds the brilliant insight into the linkage of feelings and needs and taking responsibility and creates a true tool."

—An online reviewer

目录

016　序言
024　致谢

002　第一章　由衷的给予
030　第二章　疏离生命的语言
050　第三章　不带评论的观察
076　第四章　体会与表达感受
104　第五章　为自己的感受负责
142　第六章　提出请求，丰盈生命
188　第七章　以同理心倾听
230　第八章　同理心的力量
260　第九章　爱自己
288　第十章　充分表达愤怒
330　第十一章　化解冲突，调和纷争
380　第十二章　为了保护使用强制力
400　第十三章　解放自我，协助他人
428　第十四章　用非暴力沟通表达感激与赞赏
448　后记
454　资源

Contents

Foreword — 017
Acknowledgments — 025

1 Giving From the Heart — 003
2 Communication That Blocks Compassion — 031
3 Observing Without Evaluating — 051
4 Identifying and Expressing Feelings — 077
5 Taking Responsibility for Our Feelings — 105
6 Requesting That Which Would Enrich Life — 143
7 Receiving Empathically — 189
8 The Power of Empathy — 231
9 Connecting Compassionately With Ourselves — 261
10 Expressing Anger Fully — 289
11 Conflict Resolution and Mediation — 331
12 The Protective Use of Force — 381
13 Liberating Ourselves and Counseling Others — 401
14 Expressing Appreciation in Nonviolent Communication — 429
Epilogue — 449
Resources — 455
Bibliography — 462
About the Author — 465

序言

已故的马歇尔·卢森堡是最值得我们感激的人之一，他的一生就像他的一本书名：在冲突世界中为和平代言[①]。书中马歇尔告诫我们：你说出口的话将会改变你的人生。每个人从婴儿时期便开始用语言构建自己的生命故事，因此，马歇尔发展了基于语言的冲突解决方法，教导人们在对话时避免评判、指责和带有暴力意味的字眼。

晚间新闻中那些街头抗议者们的扭曲面孔，每每令人不安，它们绝非只是新闻画面而已。每一张脸、每一声呐喊、每一个手势都带着一段历史。每个人都紧紧抓着自己的历史，因为那关乎自己的身份。因此，当马歇尔倡导和平的语言时，他倡导的其实是一种新的身份认同，而他也很清楚这一点。在这个最新版本中，马歇尔在提到非暴力沟通以及调解人的角色时说："我们所做的改变是在尝试活出一种不同的价值体系。"

在马歇尔所憧憬的新价值体系下，冲突解决不再仰仗于叫人沮丧的妥协手法。相反，有争议的双方相互尊重，询问对方的需要，在没有义愤填膺和偏见的氛围中建立连结。凝视这个充满战争和暴力的世界，"我们还是他们"的思维早已深入人心，有的国家无视文明，犯下各种不堪的暴行。在这样的一个世界中，新的价值体系似乎遥不可及。在欧

---

① 此为直译，为了让读者有直观感受。此书的简体中文版译为《用非暴力沟通化解冲突》，由华夏出版社出版。

Foreword

Deepak Chopra, MD
Founder of the Chopra Center for Wellbeing and author of more than eighty books translated in over forty-three languages, including twenty-two *New York Times* bestsellers

No one deserves our gratitude more than the late Marshall Rosenberg, who lived his life just as the title of one of his books states: *Speak Peace in a World of Conflict*. He was keenly aware of the maxim (or warning) that's contained in the subtitle of that book: *What You Say Next Will Change Your World*. Personal reality always contains a story, and the story we live, beginning from infancy, is based on language. This became the foundation of Marshall's approach to conflict resolution, getting people to exchange words in a way that excludes judgments, blame, and violence.

The contorted faces of protestors on the streets that make such disturbing images on the evening news are more than images. Each face, each shout, each gesture has a history. Everyone clings to their history with a vengeance, because it anchors their identity. So when Marshall advocated peaceful talk, he was advocating a new identity at the same time. He fully realized this fact. As he states about Nonviolent Communication and the role of the mediator in this new third edition, "We're trying to live a different value system while we are asking for things to change."

In his vision of a new value system, conflicts are resolved without the usual frustrating compromises. Instead, the contending parties approach each other with respect. They ask about each other's needs, and in an atmosphere free of passions and prejudices, they reach a connection. Gazing on a world rife with

序言

洲召开的一次调解人大会上,有人批评马歇尔用的方法属于心理治疗,认为他不过就是让人们把过去摆在一边,握手言和。这种做法不要说在战争面前,就是对于离婚案,恐怕也太不切实际。

价值体系体现在我们对世界的每一个看法中。人们不仅无可避免地受其影响,甚至还以此为傲。例如,千百年来全世界都在同一时期出现尚武或恐武的价值思想。荣格学派的心理学家认为,战神的原型存在于每个人的潜意识中,因而冲突和侵略乃无可避免的现象,这是人类与生俱来的恶。

然而,马歇尔在本书中则激昂地传递了另一种人性观,并叫我们务必仔细思考,因为这是我们唯一的希望。马歇尔认为,我们并不等同于我们的观念(故事)。这些观念只是我们自己创造出来的虚构故事,因为习惯、群体胁迫、旧有的制约以及缺乏自觉而被完好地保留着。然而,即使是最好的故事也会助长暴力。例如,你想用强制力保护家人、自我防卫、打击不法、防止犯罪,可哪怕你参与的是所谓的"正义之战",你也可能被暴力所蛊惑。而如果你决定退出,很可能会受到来自社会的抨击和惩罚。简而言之,人类要找到一条出路并不容易。

在印度,有一种古老的非暴力生活方式,被称为"Ahimsa",这也是非暴力生活的核心思想。"Ahimsa"通常的意思是"非暴力",后来经由甘地的和平运动及史怀哲(Albert Schweitzer)对生命敬畏的思想而得到了很多拓展。"Ahimsa"的首要宗旨是:不伤害。让我对刚刚过世不久、享年80岁的马歇尔博士钦佩不已的是,他把握住了"非暴力"的两方面:行动和意识。

"非暴力沟通"的过程很好地说明了"非暴力Ahimsa"的行动层面,在此我不再赘述。而活出"非暴力Ahimsa"的意识则是更有力量

war and violence, where us-versus-them thinking is the norm, and where countries can break all bonds of civilized existence to commit unbearable atrocities, a new value system seems far away. At one European conference for mediators, a skeptic criticized Marshall's approach as psychotherapy. In popular language, isn't he asking us to simply forget the past and just be friends, a remote prospect not just in the war-torn areas but in any divorce case?

Value systems are packed in the luggage of every worldview. Not only are they inescapable, but people are proud of them—there's a long tradition around the world of prizing and fearing warriors at the same time. Jungians tell us that the archetype of Mars, the volatile god of war, is imbedded in everyone's unconscious, making conflict and aggression inevitable, a kind of inherent vice.

But there's an alternative view of human nature, eloquently expressed in this book that must be considered, because it's our only real hope. In this view, we are not our stories. These stories are self-created fictions that remain intact through habit, group coercion, old conditioning, and lack of self-awareness. Even the best stories collaborate in violence. If you want to use force to protect your family, guard yourself from attack, fight against wrongdoing, prevent crime, and engage in a so-called "good war," you have been co-opted by the siren song of violence. If you decide to opt out, there's a sizable chance that society will turn on you and exact retribution. In short, finding a way out isn't easy.

In India there's an ancient model for nonviolent living known as Ahimsa, which is central to the nonviolent life. Ahimsa is usually defined as nonviolence, although its meaning extends from Mahatma Gandhi's peaceful protests to Albert Schweitzer's reverence for life. "Do no harm" would be the first axiom of Ahimsa. What so impressed me about Marshall Rosenberg, who passed away at eighty, just six weeks before I write this, is that he grasped both levels of Ahimsa, action and consciousness.

The actions are well described in the following pages as principles of Nonviolent Communication, so I won't repeat them here. To be in Ahimsa consciousness is much more powerful, and Marshall possessed that trait. In any conflict, he didn't choose

序言

的，马歇尔本人就呈现出这样的状态。无论身处何种冲突，他都不会偏袒任何一方，甚至不太会把关注点放在各方的说辞上。他认为所有的说辞都会有意无意地造成冲突，所以他将焦点放在连结上——搭建人与人之间一座心灵的桥梁。这样做和"非暴力 Ahimsa"的另一个宗旨相吻合：重要的不是你做了什么，而是你注意力的品质。以离婚为例，尽管从法律角度，双方已经完成了财产分割，但双方在情感上所受到的影响则远没有结束。用马歇尔的话来说，太多说出口的话早已让两人的世界发生了改变。

敌对意识深入我们的"小我"（ego）中，每当面对冲突，我们的注意力就会被"我、属于我的"这样的想法所占据。表面上，我们的社会崇尚圣贤，景仰他们放下自我、臣服神明的精神，但事实上，我们所拥护的价值观却和所作所为之间存在着一道巨大的鸿沟。而人们通过"非暴力 Ahimsa"可以拓展自己的意识，从而消弭鸿沟。解决所有暴力的唯一道路便是放下自己的执见。人若在世界上仍带有私利便无法开悟——这或许是"非暴力 Ahimsa"的第三个宗旨，虽然这些话听上去有些像耶稣在"登山宝训"中的激进教导：温柔的人有福了，因为他们必承受土地。

不过，不论是"非暴力 Ahimsa"还是耶稣的教导，说的都是改变你的意识而非行为。为此，你必须从一种生活（满足"自我"无止境的欲求）走向另一种生活（无私的状态）。坦白说，没有人真的喜欢无私的状态，从"小我"的角度来看，这样的状态听上去可怕而又难以企及。既然"小我"只在意得失，你若废黜了"小我"，会有什么结果呢？一旦没有了"小我"，你是否会像一具只有精神的懒骨头消极地坐在那里？

sides or even care primarily what their stories were. Recognizing that all stories lead to conflict, either overtly or covertly, he focused on connections as a psychological bridge. This is in keeping with another axiom of Ahimsa: It's not what you do that counts, it's the quality of your attention. As far as the legal system is concerned, a divorce is over once the two parties settle on how to split their assets. But this is far from the result that's reached emotionally between the two divorced parties. Too much has been said, to use Marshall's wording, that changed their world.

Aggression is built into the ego system, which totally focuses on "I, me, and mine" whenever conflict arises. Society pays lip service to saints and their vow to serve God instead of themselves, but there's a huge gap between the values we espouse and the way we actually live. Ahimsa closes this gap only by expanding a person's awareness. The only way to resolve all violence is to give up your story. No one can be enlightened who still has a personal stake in the world—that could be the third axiom of Ahimsa. But this seems like a teaching as radical as Jesus in the Sermon on the Mount when he promises that the meek shall inherit the earth.

In both cases, the point isn't to change your actions but to change your consciousness. To do that, you must walk a path from A to B, where A is a life based on the incessant demands of the ego and B is selfless awareness. To be frank, nobody really desires selfless awareness; from the viewpoint of looking out for number one, it sounds at once scary and impossible. What's the payoff if you depose the ego, which is all about payoffs? Once the ego is gone, do you sit around passively like a spiritual beanbag?

The answer lies in those moments when the personal self falls away naturally and spontaneously. These occur in moments of meditation or simply deep contentment. Selfless awareness is the state we're in when Nature or art or music creates a sense of wonder. The only difference between those moments—to which we can add all experiences of creativity, love, and play—and Ahimsa is that they flicker in and out while Ahimsa is a settled state. It reveals that stories and the egos that fuel them are illusions, self-created models for survival and selfishness. The payoff for

序言

答案就在"小我"自动消融的时刻。这样的时刻会出现在冥想或处于深度满足时。当我们体验到经由大自然、艺术或者音乐所创造的美妙时，就能体验到"无我"的状态。这样的时刻（包括当我们体验到创造力、爱和玩耍时）和"非暴力 Ahimsa"状态的区别在于，前者时有时无，忽隐忽现；"非暴力 Ahimsa"却是稳定的状态。由此可见，所有的念头（故事）以及那个喂养念头的"小我"都只是幻想，是人们为了生存和利己所创造出来的。"小我"会不断升级虚幻，驱使我们追求更多的金钱、财产和权力，而"非暴力 Ahimsa"则让你真正活出你自己。

用高层意识来称呼"非暴力 Ahimsa"太过于高调了。事实上，在这个"社会规范"已经毫不正常、甚至近乎病态的世界里，称其为"正常意识"更加恰如其分。在我们今天的世界里，用几千颗核弹对准敌人，恐怖主义被视为受推崇的宗教手段——这些情况已经不只是"普通"情况了，而是成为了"社会规范"，生活在这样的世界里并不正常。

对我而言，马歇尔对后世的影响并不在于他颠覆了调解人的角色，尽管这很重要，而是在于他所活出的新价值体系，而这样的价值体系古已有之。由于人性被"和平"和"暴力"所撕裂，因而每一个时代都召唤着"非暴力 Ahimsa"。卢森堡博士已经证明，进入这样一种被拓宽的意识状态不仅是真实不虚的，也能行之有效地用来化解争端。他留下了让我们得以追随的足迹。如果真正关心自身的福祉，我们就会跟随这足迹。在这个亟需智慧指引，祈望消弭战争的世界，这是我们唯一的选择。

迪帕克·乔普拉（Deepak Chopra），作家 & 医生

Foreword

Ahimsa isn't that you upgrade the illusion, which is what the ego is always striving to do with more money, possessions, and power. The payoff is that you get to be who you really are.

Higher consciousness is too lofty as the term for Ahimsa. Normal consciousness is more accurate in a world where the norm is so abnormal that it amounts to psychopathology. It's not normal to live in a world where thousands of nuclear warheads are aimed at the enemy and terrorism is an acceptable religious act—they are merely the norm.

For me, the legacy of Marshall's lifelong work doesn't lie in how he revolutionized the role of the mediator, valuable as that was. It lies in the new value system he lived by, which in truth is quite ancient. Ahimsa has to be revived in every generation, because human nature is torn between peace and violence. Marshall Rosenberg gave proof that entering this state of expanded awareness was real and, when it came to settling disputes, very practical. He leaves footprints that the rest of us can follow. If we have true self-interest at heart, we will follow. It's the only alternative in a world desperately seeking wisdom and the end of strife.

—Deepak Chopra

致谢

感谢卡尔·罗杰斯（Carl Rogers）教授，当他正在研究"有益于人际关系的要素"这一课题时，我有幸向他学习并与他共事。这项研究的结果在我发展"非暴力沟通"的过程中至关重要。

我亦将永远感谢迈克尔·哈基姆（Michael Hakeem）教授，他让我看到，我所接受的基于病理学的应用心理学专业训练不仅在科学上是有局限的，对社会和政治也会有危害。正是因为看到了现有理论的局限以及对生命有了更多的认识，我渴望探索一种不同的心理学方法。

此外，我也很感谢乔治·米勒（George Miller）和乔治·艾比（George Albee）。他们努力地提醒心理学家们要找到比心理学更好的方法，他们让我看到，面对这个充满困难的世界，我们要找到比临床心理学更加有效的方式和更有帮助的技能。

我还要感谢吕靖安（Lucy Leu）女士负责编辑此书，并加以完稿；感谢瑞塔·赫尔佐格（Rita Herzog）以及凯西·史密斯（Kathy Smith）协助编辑工作。感谢许多人提供的帮助。

最后，我要感谢我的朋友安妮·穆勒（Annie Muller）。她鼓励我更清晰地呈现非暴力沟通的精神基础，这不仅让非暴力沟通更加扎实，也让我的生命变得更加丰盈。

Acknowledgments

I'm grateful that I was able to study and work with Professor Carl Rogers at a time when he was researching the components of a helping relationship. The results of this research played a key role in the evolution of the process of communication that I will be describing in this book.

I will be forever grateful that Professor Michael Hakeem helped me to see the scientific limitations and the social and political dangers of practicing psychology in the way that I had been trained: with a pathology-based understanding of human beings. Seeing the limitations of this model stimulated me to search for ways of practicing a different psychology, one based on a growing clarity about how we human beings were meant to live.

I'm grateful, too, for George Miller's and George Albee's efforts to alert psychologists to the need to find better ways for "giving psychology away." They helped me see that the enormity of suffering on our planet requires more effective ways of distributing much-needed skills than can be offered by a clinical approach.

I would like to thank Lucy Leu for editing this book and creating the final manuscript; Rita Herzog and Kathy Smith for their editing assistance; and, for their additional help, Darold Milligan, Sonia Nordenson, Melanie Sears, Bridget Belgrave, Marian Moore, Kittrell McCord, Virginia Hoyte, and Peter Weismiller.

Finally, I would like to express gratitude to my friend Annie Muller. Her encouragement to be clearer about the spiritual foundation of my work has strengthened that work and enriched my life.

语言是窗(或者是墙)

你的话像是对我的审判,
我仿佛见弃于人,备受责难,
在离开以前,我想问,
这真的是你的意思吗?
在我愤然自我辩护前,
在我带着痛楚或恐惧斥责前,
在我用言语筑起心墙前,
请告诉我,我真的听见你了吗?
语言是窗,或者是墙,
它审判我们,或令我们自由,
当我说话、当我聆听,
请让爱的光芒经由我闪耀。
我心里有话要说,
那些话对我意义非凡,
如果言语无法传递我的心声,
请你帮我获得自由,好吗?
如果你认为我想责难你,
如果你感到我不在乎你,
请尝试透过我的语言,
聆听我们共有的情感。

——鲁斯·贝本梅尔(Ruth Bebermeyer)

Words Are Windows
(or They're Walls)

I feel so sentenced by your words,
I feel so judged and sent away,
Before I go I've got to know,
Is that what you mean to say?

Before I rise to my defense,
Before I speak in hurt or fear,
Before I build that wall of words,
Tell me, did I really hear?

Words are windows, or they're walls,
They sentence us, or set us free.
When I speak and when I hear,
Let the love light shine through me.

There are things I need to say,
Things that mean so much to me,
If my words don't make me clear,
Will you help me to be free?

If I seemed to put you down,
If you felt I didn't care,
Try to listen through my words,
To the feelings that we share.

—Ruth Bebermeyer

第一章

由衷的给予

> 我渴望我的生命活出善意和慈悲（Compassion）①，
> 由衷的给予在你我之间流动。
> ——马歇尔·卢森堡，博士

---

① 译者按：在英语中 Compassion 一词由两部分组成，前缀 com 意为共同、一起，passion 的拉丁词根 passio 意为苦痛，compassion 直译过来是：与苦痛同在。非暴力沟通的核心过程"同理"的状态也如此：与他人或自己当下的经验同在。故马歇尔·卢森堡博士也将非暴力沟通称作 Compassionate Communication。在中文中最能够传递 compassion 的词为"慈悲"，"慈"的意思与"由衷给予"一致，而"悲"意为同感其苦，则与同理的状态一致。在繁体版的《非暴力沟通》中，Compassionate Communication 被译为"善意沟通"。故在本版中，译者将用慈悲和善意交替呈现英文中的 Compassion。

在中文中，"慈悲"一词最早由佛教翻译而为大家所知晓，而这个词实际所承载的意思却是普世、一般化、超越宗教与信仰的，这也正是马歇尔博士在非暴力沟通中所要带给大家的——与我们的源头相连，与生命相连。

Giving From the Heart

The Heart of Nonviolent Communication

*What I want in my life is compassion,
a flow between myself and others based
on a mutual giving from the heart.*

—Marshall B. Rosenberg, PhD

Introduction

Believing that it is our nature to enjoy giving and receiving in a compassionate manner, I have been preoccupied most of my life with two questions: What happens to disconnect us from our compassionate nature, leading us to behave violently and exploitatively? And conversely, what allows some people to stay connected to their compassionate nature under even the most trying circumstances?

My preoccupation with these questions began in childhood, around the summer of 1943, when our family moved to Detroit, Michigan. The second week after we arrived, a race war erupted over an incident at a public park. More than forty people were killed in the next few days. Our neighborhood was situated in the center of the violence, and we spent three days locked in the house.

When the race riot ended and school began, I discovered that a name could be as dangerous as any skin color. When the teacher called my name during attendance, two boys glared at me and hissed, "Are you a kike?" I had never heard the word before and

第一章　由衷的给予

导言

我相信，由衷的相互给予是我们天性所乐见的。因而，我将大部分生命投入对这两个问题的探寻之中：

是什么让我们悖离了天性中的善，做出暴力与毁灭性的行为？

又是什么使得有些人即使在极度恶劣的环境下，依然与天性中的善相连？

当我还是孩子的时候，我开始有了这样的疑惑。大约在1943年的夏天，我们家搬到了密歇根州的底特律。两周后，公园里发生了一起由种族冲突引发的暴力事件，之后的几天中40多人遇害。我们居住的社区正位于冲突的中心。整整3天，我们紧闭家门，足不出户。

骚乱结束后，学校复课了。我却发现人名可以和肤色一样带来危险。当老师点到我的名字时，有两个男孩瞪着我，嘘声说："你是犹太鬼子（kike）？"我从未听过这个词，更不知道它是某些人对犹太人的蔑称。

放学后，那两个男孩拦住我，他们把我摔倒在地上，拳打脚踢。

从此，我就一直在思索那两个问题：

是什么赋予我们力量，使我们在最恶劣的情况下依然与天性中的善相连，就像艾提·海勒申（Etty Hillesum）那样的人，纵然面对德国集中营的恶劣条件，也依然保有慈悲之心？她在日记中这样写道：

> 我并不那么害怕，不是我勇敢，而是因为我清楚，站在我面前的是人，我想要尽我所能去理解任何人做的任何事，就像

1 Giving From the Heart

didn't know some people used it in a derogatory way to refer to Jews. After school, the same two boys were waiting for me: they threw me to the ground and kicked and beat me.

Since that summer in 1943, I have been examining the two questions I mentioned. What empowers us, for example, to stay connected to our compassionate nature even under the worst circumstances? I am thinking of people like Etty Hillesum, who remained compassionate even while subjected to the grotesque conditions of a German concentration camp. As she wrote in her journal at the time,

> I am not easily frightened. Not because I am brave but because I know that I am dealing with human beings, and that I must try as hard as I can to understand everything that anyone ever does. And that was the real import of this morning: not that a disgruntled young Gestapo officer yelled at me, but that I felt no indignation, rather a real compassion, and would have liked to ask, 'Did you have a very unhappy childhood, has your girlfriend let you down?' Yes, he looked harassed and driven, sullen and weak. I should have liked to start treating him there and then, for I know that pitiful young men like that are dangerous as soon as they are let loose on mankind.
>
> —Etty Hillesum in *Etty: A Diary 1941–1943*

While studying the factors that affect our ability to stay compassionate, I was struck by the crucial role of language and our use of words. I have since identified a specific approach to communicating—both speaking and listening—that leads us to give from the heart, connecting us with ourselves and with each other in a way that allows our natural compassion to flourish. I call this approach Nonviolent Communication, using the term *nonviolence* as Gandhi used it—to refer to our natural state of compassion when violence has subsided from the heart. While we may not consider

> 在今天早晨，一位心情不佳的年轻盖世太保冲着我大骂，我并未生气，油然而生的是一份真切的慈悲之情。我甚至想问他：'你的童年过得不开心吗？女友的言行令你失望了吗？'他看上去那么烦躁、紧张、阴沉且虚弱。我早该善意地对待他，这般可怜的年轻男子一旦放纵自己将有多么危险。
>
> ——艾提·海勒申日记一则 1941-1943

我一直在探究到底是什么因素能让我们保有善意，在此过程中，我深刻意识到语言及我们使用语言的方式所扮演的重要角色。后来，我发现了一种具体的沟通方法：它包含表达与聆听，能让我们由衷地给予，与自己和他人建立连结，并充分展现天性中的善意。

我称这种方法为非暴力沟通。这里借用甘地曾使用的"非暴力"一词，来指代当暴力从心中消融，天性中的善自然呈现的状态。尽管我们可能并不认为自己的说话方式是"暴力"的，但我们的言语却时常引发他人或自己的痛苦。这种非暴力沟通方法也被称为"善意沟通"。

转变注意力的焦点

非暴力沟通建立在语言以及特定的沟通方法上，让我们即使是在逆境中，也有能力活出人性的光芒。非暴力沟通并没有任何新知。它所整合的内容早已被人们知晓了千百年。非暴力沟通意在提醒我们早已知道的：人与人之间相互连结是人类的天性。非暴力沟通以一种具体的方式帮助我们活出天性。

the way we talk to be "violent," words often lead to hurt and pain, whether for others or ourselves. In some communities, the process I am describing is known as Compassionate Communication; the abbreviation *NVC* is used throughout this book to refer to Nonviolent or Compassionate Communication.

> **NVC: a way of communicating that leads us to give from the heart.**

A Way to Focus Attention

NVC is founded on language and communication skills that strengthen our ability to remain human, even under trying conditions. It contains nothing new; all that has been integrated into NVC has been known for centuries. The intent is to remind us about what we already know—about how we humans were meant to relate to one another—and to assist us in living in a way that concretely manifests this knowledge.

NVC guides us in reframing how we express ourselves and hear others. Instead of habitual, automatic reactions, our words become conscious responses based firmly on awareness of what we are perceiving, feeling, and wanting. We are led to express ourselves with honesty and clarity, while simultaneously paying others a respectful and empathic attention. In any exchange, we come to hear our own deeper needs and those of others. NVC trains us to observe carefully, and to be able to specify behaviors and conditions that are affecting us. We learn to identify and clearly articulate what we are concretely wanting in any given situation. The form is simple, yet powerfully transformative.

As NVC replaces our old patterns of defending, withdrawing, or attacking in the face of judgment and criticism, we come to perceive ourselves and others, as well as our intentions and relationships, in a new light. Resistance, defensiveness, and violent reactions are minimized. When we focus on clarifying what is

> **We perceive relationships in a new light when we use NVC to hear our own deeper needs and those of others.**

第一章　由衷的给予

非暴力沟通帮助我们重新构建表达自己和聆听他人的方式，使我们的言语不再只是出于习惯的自动化反应，而是牢固地建立在觉察感受和需要的基础上，做出有意识的回应。我们既能诚实、清晰地表达自己，也能带着尊重与同理心关注他人，从而在任何交流中听见自己和他人心灵深处的呼声。非暴力沟通还训练我们仔细观察，具体地指出什么样的行为和事件对我们造成了影响，学会了解我们当下的需要并清晰地表达出来。如此简单的形式，却能带来强有力的改变。

当面对别人的评判或指责时，我们通常报之以防卫、回避或攻击。而一旦我们将注意力聚焦在彼此的观察、感受和需要，而不是去诊断和评判，我们就能发现内心深处的善意。随着旧有的反应模式被非暴力沟通所取代，我们便能以一种全新的眼光来看待自己和他人，并且对自己的初心和人际关系保有觉察，进而抗拒、防御和暴力的回应得以减轻或减少。通过强调深度聆听自己和他人，非暴力沟通能够培育我们对他人的尊重、觉察与同理心，并愿意发自内心地相互给予。

尽管我称非暴力沟通是一种"沟通过程"或是"善意沟通"，它却不止于此。在一个更深的层面，它是持续的提醒，让我们更好地专注于自己的生命意义和方向。

有个故事讲述了一名男子在路灯下四处找东西，一位路过的警察见状问他在做什么。

"找我的汽车钥匙。"这位看上去有些醉意的男子回答道。

警察询问他："你把钥匙丢在这里了吗？"

"不是这里，"男子回答，"我把钥匙落在巷子里了。"

见到警察很困惑，男子急忙解释："但这里的光线要亮得多呢。"

1 Giving From the Heart

being observed, felt, and needed rather than on diagnosing and judging, we discover the depth of our own compassion. Through its emphasis on deep listening—to ourselves as well as to others—NVC fosters respect, attentiveness, and empathy and engenders a mutual desire to give from the heart.

Although I refer to it as "a process of communication" or "a language of compassion," NVC is more than a process or a language. On a deeper level, it is an ongoing reminder to keep our attention focused on a place where we are more likely to get what we are seeking.

There is a story of a man on all fours under a street lamp, searching for something. A policeman passing by asked what he was doing. "Looking for my car keys," replied the man, who appeared slightly drunk. "Did you drop them here?" inquired the officer. "No," answered the man, "I dropped them in the alley." Seeing the policeman's baffled expression, the man hastened to explain, "But the light is much better here."

I find that my cultural conditioning leads me to focus attention on places where I am unlikely to get what I want. I developed NVC as a way to train my attention—to shine the light of consciousness—on places that have the potential to yield what I am seeking. What I want in my life is compassion, a flow between myself and others based on a mutual giving from the heart.

> Let's shine the light of consciousness on places where we can hope to find what we are seeking.

This quality of compassion, which I refer to as "giving from the heart," is expressed in the following lyrics by my friend Ruth Bebermeyer:

第一章 由衷的给予

我们都对人生拥有渴望。然而我发现，主导我们的文化却可能带我们偏离了方向。为此，我开发了非暴力沟通。它作为一种训练注意力的方式，让我们可以把注意力放在真正要去的地方。我渴望的是，在生命中活出慈悲之心，让由衷的相互给予，在你我之间流动。

那份慈悲心，也是我所说的"由衷的给予"，在我的朋友鲁斯·贝本梅尔（Ruth Bebermeyer）的这段歌词中得到展现：

> 你取之于我，是对我最好的馈赠。
> 请你知道，这种给予带给我快乐。
> 我给予绝非冀盼你偿还，
> 只因我想活出对你的爱。
> 也许，你的欣然接受，
> 就是对我的最佳馈赠。
> 我无法将两者分开。
> 你施与我，我给予我的接受；
> 你取之于我，是对我最好的馈赠。
>
> ——"馈赠"（1978）来自鲁斯·贝本梅尔
> 唱片集《馈赠》

每当我们想要丰盈他人的生命，由衷给予他人时，我们是出于心中油然而生的喜悦之情。给予者和接受者都会从中获益。当给予是由衷的，而非出于害怕、内疚、羞愧或是渴求回报，接受者才能心无挂碍地享受这份馈赠。与此同时，给予者因为看到自己为他人的幸福做出了贡献，也会收获更多的自我肯定。

1 Giving From the Heart

I never feel more given to
than when you take from me—
when you understand the joy I feel
　　giving to you.
And you know my giving isn't done
　　to put you in my debt,
but because I want to live the love
　　I feel for you.
To receive with grace
may be the greatest giving.
There's no way I can separate
　　the two.
When you give to me,
I give you my receiving.
When you take from me, I feel so
　　given to.

—"Given To" (1978) by Ruth Bebermeyer
from the album *Given To*

When we give from the heart, we do so out of the joy that springs forth whenever we willingly enrich another person's life. This kind of giving benefits both the giver and the receiver. The receiver enjoys the gift without worrying about the consequences that accompany gifts given out of fear, guilt, shame, or desire for gain. The giver benefits from the enhanced self-esteem that results when we see our efforts contributing to someone's well-being.

The use of NVC does not require that the persons with whom we are communicating be literate in NVC or even motivated to relate to us compassionately. If we stay with the principles of NVC, stay motivated solely to give and receive compassionately, and do everything we can to let others know this is our only motive, they will join us in the process, and eventually we will be able to respond compassionately to one another. I'm not saying that this always happens quickly. I do maintain, however, that compassion

第一章　由衷的给予

我们使用非暴力沟通，并不要求沟通的对方也懂得它，甚至无须对我们保有善意。只要我们遵循非暴力沟通的原则，发自内心地给予，并尽我们所能让对方知道这是我们唯一的动机，他们也会加入我们，最终双方必然能以善意相待。当然，这一切不一定会很快发生，但我相信，只要我们坚持非暴力沟通的原则与方法，友善之花终将在你我心中盛开。

非暴力沟通过程

要达到让双方都能发自内心地相互给予，我们需将注意力聚焦在四个方面——它们是非暴力沟通模式的四个要素。

首先，我们观察实际上发生了什么。不论他人的言行是否有益于我们，我们只是去观察。要做到清晰表达所观察到的，我们的挑战在于不夹杂任何评判。不论喜欢与否，我们只是说出人们做了什么。第二步，表达出我们看到这些行为时的感受：是感到伤心、害怕、喜悦、有趣，还是心烦呢？第三步，表达出我们的感受与什么需要相关联。通过对这三个要素的觉察，我们清晰和诚实地表达出自己的状态。

例如，一位母亲想和正值青春期的儿子用非暴力沟通的方式来说话，她可以这样来表达以上三个要素："菲利克斯，看到咖啡桌下的两团脏袜子和电视机旁边的三团脏袜子，我很生气，因为我希望在我们共用的空间里能多些整洁。"

紧接着，她可以表达非暴力沟通的第四个要素——一个具体的请求："你愿意把你的袜子放在你房间或放进洗衣机里吗？"我们借助这

inevitably blossoms when we stay true to the principles and process of NVC.

The NVC Process

To arrive at a mutual desire to give from the heart, we focus the light of consciousness on four areas—referred to as the four components of the NVC model.

First, we observe what is actually happening in a situation: what are we observing others saying or doing that is either enriching or not enriching our life? The trick is to be able to articulate this observation without introducing any judgment or evaluation—to simply say what people are doing that we either like or don't like. Next, we state how we feel when we observe this action: are we hurt, scared, joyful, amused, irritated? And thirdly, we say what needs of ours are connected to the feelings we have identified. An awareness of these three components is present when we use NVC to clearly and honestly express how we are.

> **Four components of NVC:**
> 1. observations
> 2. feelings
> 3. needs
> 4. requests

For example, a mother might express these three pieces to her teenage son by saying, "Felix, when I see two balls of soiled socks under the coffee table and another three next to the TV, I feel irritated because I am needing more order in the rooms that we share in common."

She would follow immediately with the fourth component—a very specific request: "Would you be willing to put your socks in your room or in the washing machine?" This fourth component addresses what we are wanting from the other person that would enrich our lives or make life more wonderful for us.

Thus, part of NVC is to express these four pieces of information very clearly, whether verbally or by other means. The other part of this communication consists of receiving the same four pieces of information from others. We connect with them by first sensing what they are observing, feeling, and needing; then

第一章　由衷的给予

个要素提出对他人的期许，希望他（她）怎么做来满足我们的需要，让我们的生命更加美好。

非暴力沟通的一部分是对这四个要素的清晰表达，表达的形式也不拘泥于语言。而另一部分则是从对方的表达中了解这四个要素。我们通过感知对方此刻的观察、感受和需要，与他们建立连结，进而聆听他们的请求，来找到通过什么方式让他们的生命变得更丰富。

当我们将注意力持续聚焦在以上几个方面，并协助对方也这样做，我们便在彼此的沟通中创造了一种流动，如此你来我往，最终双方都能自然而然地展现善意：我此刻的观察、感受和需要是什么；为了让我的生命更美好，我的请求是什么；你此刻的观察、感受和需要是什么；为了让你的生命更美好，你的请求是什么？

在使用非暴力沟通时，我们既可以先表达自己，也可以先同理倾听他人。在本书的第三至第六章，我们还将深入地学习如何倾听与表达每一个要素。很重要的一点是，牢记非暴力沟通不是固定公式，人们可以根据不同的情境，以及不同的个人和文化习惯做出调整。为了叙述方便，我将非暴力沟通称为一种"方法"或是"语言"，当然它的实现不一定借助言语。因为，非暴力沟通的精髓在于对这四个要素的觉察，而非在交流中具体说了什么。

非暴力沟通的运用

无论在自我对话、与人互动还是团体交流中，非暴力沟通能让我们在心中怀有善意。因而，人们可以将它有效地运用在不同层面的沟通和

we discover what would enrich their lives by receiving the fourth piece—their request.

As we keep our attention focused on the areas mentioned, and help others do likewise, we establish a flow of communication, back and forth, until compassion manifests naturally: what I am observing, feeling, and needing; what I am requesting to enrich my life; what you are observing, feeling, and needing; what you are requesting to enrich your life . . .

NVC Process

The concrete actions we *observe* that affect our well-being

How we *feel* in relation to what we observe

The *needs*, values, desires, etc. that create our feelings

The concrete actions we *request* in order to enrich our lives

---

When we use this process, we may begin either by expressing ourselves or by empathically receiving these four pieces of information from others. Although we will learn to listen for and verbally express each of these components in Chapters 3–6, it is important to keep in mind that NVC is not a set formula, but something that adapts to various situations as well as personal and cultural styles. While I conveniently refer to NVC as a "process" or "language," it is possible to experience all four pieces of the process without uttering a single word.

Two parts of NVC:
1. expressing honestly through the four components
2. receiving empathically through the four components

第一章　由衷的给予

多样的情境中，包括：

- 亲密关系
- 家庭
- 学校
- 组织与机构
- 心理辅导与咨询关系
- 外交与商业谈判
- 任何性质的纠纷与冲突

有些人在亲密关系中用非暴力沟通创造了深度的连结与关爱：

> 当我通过非暴力沟通学会了如何接收（聆听）和给予（表达），我不再觉得受伤和忍气吞声，而能聆听并且领会话语背后的感受。我发现，这个与我结婚28年的男人，内心原来如此痛苦。在参加"非暴力沟通"工作坊前的那个周末，他向我提出了离婚……长话短说，今天我们得以一起来到这里，要感谢非暴力沟通为我们带来的美好结局……我学会了聆听感受，表达我的需要，接纳我并不乐意听到的回答。我们都无需讨对方的欢心，而是学着成长、接纳和爱。
> ——一位在美国加利福尼亚州圣地亚哥参加工作坊的学员

有的人在工作中用非暴力沟通创造了更高效的关系：

> 我在特殊教育班级中应用非暴力沟通已经一年了，它同样

The essence of NVC is in our consciousness of the four components, not in the actual words that are exchanged.

Applying NVC in Our Lives and the World

When we use NVC in our interactions—with ourselves, with another person, or in a group—we become grounded in our natural state of compassion. It is therefore an approach that can be effectively applied at all levels of communication and in diverse situations:
- intimate relationships
- families
- schools
- organizations and institutions
- therapy and counseling relationships
- diplomatic and business negotiations
- disputes and conflicts of any nature

Some people use NVC to create greater depth and caring in their intimate relationships:

> When I learned how I can receive (hear), as well as give (express), through using NVC, I went beyond feeling attacked and 'doormattish' to really listening to words and extracting their underlying feelings. I discovered a very hurting man to whom I had been married for twenty-eight years. He had asked me for a divorce the weekend before the [NVC] workshop. To make a long story short, we are here today—together, and I appreciate the contribution [NVC has] made to our happy ending. . . . I learned to listen for feelings, to express my needs, to accept answers that I didn't always want to hear. He is not here to make me happy, nor am I here to create happiness for him. We have both learned to grow, to accept, and to love, so that we can each be fulfilled.
>
> —a workshop participant in San Diego, California

第一章 由衷的给予

适用于那些有着表达迟缓、学习困难和行为问题的学生。我的班级里有一位学生,当有人靠近他的课桌时,他会吐口水、骂人、尖叫、用铅笔戳他们。我提醒他:"请换一种方式表达,使用你的长颈鹿语言①。"(我在课堂中使用长颈鹿玩偶作为示范非暴力沟通的辅助教具。)他立刻笔挺地站起来,看着那个让他生气的学生,平静地说:"当你靠我那么近时,我感到生气。可以请你离我的桌子远点吗?"另一名学生也许会回答:"抱歉,我忘了你不喜欢这样。"

我也开始思考如何应对这个孩子带给我的挫败感。我想探索,除了和谐与秩序,我还有什么需要。我意识到,自己投入了许多时间备课,可为了管理课堂纪律,我无法施展我想要实现的创造性与贡献,也没能照顾到其他孩子的学习。当这个孩子再次在课堂中发生不当行为时,我就告诉他:"我希望你能注意听我讲。"也许一天中要提醒他100次,但他听到后通常都会重新参与到课堂中。

——美国伊利诺斯州芝加哥市的一名教师

一位医生写道:

我越来越多地在医疗工作中使用非暴力沟通。有的病人问

---

① 译者按:马歇尔博士在介绍非暴力沟通时使用了两个动物作为比喻,用长颈鹿来代表非暴力沟通,豺狗来代表疏离生命的语言。

Others use it to build more effective relationships at work:

> I have been using NVC in my special education classroom for about one year. It can work even with children who have language delays, learning difficulties, and behavior problems. One student in our classroom spits, swears, screams, and stabs other students with pencils when they get near his desk. I cue him with, 'Please say that another way. Use your giraffe talk.' [Giraffe puppets are used in some workshops as a teaching aid to demonstrate NVC.] He immediately stands up straight, looks at the person toward whom his anger is directed, and says calmly, 'Would you please move away from my desk? I feel angry when you stand so close to me.' The other students might respond with something like, 'Sorry! I forgot it bothers you.'
>
> I began to think about my frustration with this child and to try to discover what I needed from him (besides harmony and order). I realized how much time I had put into lesson planning and how my needs for creativity and contribution were being short-circuited in order to manage behavior. Also, I felt I was not meeting the educational needs of the other students. When he was acting out in class, I began to say, 'I need you to share my attention.' It might take a hundred cues a day, but he got the message and would usually get involved in the lesson.
>
> —a teacher in Chicago, Illinois

第一章　由衷的给予

我是否是心理医生，因为医生通常并不关心患者的生活方式和对疾病的态度。非暴力沟通帮助我理解病人的需要以及特定时刻他们想要听些什么。我发现这对治疗白血病和艾滋病感染者格外有用，由于他们带着强烈的愤怒与痛苦，医患沟通通常存在极大的阻力。有一位女性艾滋感染者在过去五年中接受我的治疗，最近，她告诉我，我努力帮助她寻找生活的乐趣，是她得到的最大帮助。非暴力沟通功不可没！而在过去，当我知道病人得了不治之症，便满脑子只想着病情会如何发展，而很难真诚地鼓励他们好好生活。通过非暴力沟通，我发展了新的语言模式，同时也获得了新的意识状态。它与我的医疗工作相辅相成，令我惊喜不已。将非暴力沟通运用到工作中，让我感到精力充沛并乐在其中。

——一位来自法国巴黎的医生

还有些人在政治领域使用非暴力沟通：

法国的一位内阁部长在探望她的妹妹时，注意到妹妹和妹夫之间的沟通与从前很不一样。听了他们对非暴力沟通的介绍，她深受鼓舞，随即提到下周她将要参与的一场谈判会议，涉及法国与阿尔及利亚之间有关收养程序的敏感话题。尽管时间紧迫，我们还是派了一位说法语的培训师前往巴黎协助这位内阁部长工作。后来她将此次谈判的成功归功于新学到的非暴力沟通方法。

在耶路撒冷，有着不同政治立场的以色列人共同参加了一次工作坊，他们用非暴力沟通的方式对有高度争议的约旦河西岸问题发表意见。许多在西岸地区安家的以色列人相信他们的行为是在行使宗教所赋

1 Giving From the Heart

A doctor writes:

> I use NVC more and more in my medical practice. Some patients ask me whether I am a psychologist, saying that usually their doctors are not interested in the way they live their lives or deal with their diseases. NVC helps me understand what patients' needs are and what they need to hear at a given moment. I find this particularly helpful in relating to patients with hemophilia and AIDS because there is so much anger and pain that the patient/health care-provider relationship is often seriously impaired. Recently a woman with AIDS, whom I have been treating for the past five years, told me that what has helped her the most have been my attempts to find ways for her to enjoy her daily life. My use of NVC helps me a lot in this respect. Often in the past, when I knew that a patient had a fatal disease, I myself would get caught in the prognosis, and it was hard for me to sincerely encourage them to live their lives. With NVC, I have developed a new consciousness as well as a new language. I am amazed to see how much it fits in with my medical practice. I feel more energy and joy in my work as I become increasingly engaged in the dance of NVC.
>
> —a physician in Paris, France

Still others use this process in the political arena. A French cabinet member visiting her sister remarked how differently the sister and her husband were communicating and responding to each other. Encouraged by their descriptions of NVC, she mentioned that she was scheduled the following week to negotiate some sensitive issues between France and Algeria regarding adoption procedures. Though time was limited, we dispatched a French-speaking trainer to Paris to work with the cabinet minister. The

第一章 由衷的给予

予的权利。因此他们不仅深陷与巴勒斯坦人的冲突,还与那些认可巴勒斯坦人在这一地区享有国土主权完整的以色列人陷入对立。在工作坊的一个环节中,我与一名培训师示范了用非暴力沟通的方式来同理倾听,然后邀请参与者们轮流以对方的立场做角色扮演。20分钟之后,一位西岸的定居者宣布,如果她的政治对手能像这样聆听她的心声,她愿意考虑放弃在西岸的土地产权,搬迁到国际认可的以色列领土。

在世界各地,有些地区面临着激烈的暴力冲突。对于剑拔弩张的族群、政治或宗教关系,非暴力沟通为冲突调解提供了有效的支持。看到非暴力沟通培训的普及以及人们使用它来调解在以色列、巴勒斯坦地区、尼日利亚、卢旺达、塞拉利昂和其他地区的冲突,我倍感欣慰。有一次我与工作伙伴们在贝尔格莱德紧张地工作了3天,培训在那里为和平工作的市民们。他们的国家深陷于波斯尼亚和克罗地亚之间的一场残酷战争中。我们刚抵达时,绝望之情在他们的脸上清晰可见。随着培训的推进,他们在发言中有了笑声,分享自己找回了渴望已久的力量,并为此深感喜悦和感激。接下来的两周,在克罗地亚、以色列以及巴勒斯坦的工作坊中,我们不断见证着——通过非暴力沟通,那些饱受战争摧残而绝望的人们重获了力量与信心。

能有机会在世界各地教授非暴力沟通,见证它为人们带来力量和喜悦,我深感幸运。此刻,我为能通过此书与大家分享非暴力沟通的丰富内容而感到十分欣慰。

minister later attributed much of the success of her negotiations in Algeria to her newly acquired communication techniques.

In Jerusalem, during a workshop attended by Israelis of varying political persuasions, participants used NVC to express themselves regarding the highly contested issue of the West Bank. Many of the Israeli settlers who have established themselves on the West Bank believe that they are fulfilling a religious mandate by doing so, and they are locked in conflict not only with Palestinians but also with other Israelis who recognize the Palestinian hope for national sovereignty in the region. During a session, one of my trainers and I modeled empathic hearing through NVC and then invited participants to take turns role-playing each other's position. After twenty minutes, a settler announced that she would be willing to consider relinquishing her land claims and moving out of the West Bank into internationally recognized Israeli territory if her political opponents could listen to her in the way she had just been listened to.

Worldwide, NVC now serves as a valuable resource for communities facing violent conflicts and severe ethnic, religious, or political tensions. The spread of NVC training and its use in mediation by people in conflict in Israel, the Palestinian Authority, Nigeria, Rwanda, Sierra Leone, and elsewhere have been a source of particular gratification for me. My associates and I were once in Belgrade for three highly charged days training citizens working for peace. When we first arrived, expressions of despair were visibly etched on the trainees' faces, for their country was then enmeshed in a brutal war in Bosnia and Croatia. As the training progressed, we heard the ring of laughter in their voices as they shared their profound gratitude and joy for having found the empowerment they were seeking. Over the next two weeks, during trainings in Croatia, Israel, and Palestine, we again saw desperate citizens in war-torn countries regaining their spirits and confidence from the NVC training they received.

I feel blessed to be able to travel throughout the world teaching people a process of communication that gives them power and

小结

非暴力沟通帮助我们与他人和自己建立连结,使我们得以流露与生俱来的慈悲之心。它指引我们通过将注意力聚焦在观察、感受、需要和请求这四个要素,来重新构建表达和聆听的方式。

非暴力沟通培育深度倾听的能力,让我们带着尊重和同理心对待他人,并且发自内心地相互给予。用非暴力沟通的方式,有的人学会了爱自己,有的人在人际关系中创造了更深厚的连结,有的人在工作或政治领域中建立了更有效的关系。在世界各地,非暴力沟通还被用来调和各个层面的纠纷和冲突。

非暴力沟通实例

本书的"非暴力沟通实例",旨在让读者体会非暴力沟通在实际生活中的应用。不过,非暴力沟通并不只是一种语言或是一套说话的技巧。人们也能通过静默、临在的状态以及面部表情和肢体语言来表达意识和用意。这里的实例是实际对话的摘要和删节版。在实际交流中,无声的同理倾听、讲故事、幽默的语言、姿态……都能让双方的连结更自然。

joy. Now, with this book, I am pleased and excited to be able to share the richness of Nonviolent Communication with you.

Summary

NVC helps us connect with each other and ourselves in a way that allows our natural compassion to flourish. It guides us to reframe the way we express ourselves and listen to others by focusing our consciousness on four areas: what we are observing, feeling, and needing, and what we are requesting to enrich our lives. NVC fosters deep listening, respect, and empathy and engenders a mutual desire to give from the heart. Some people use NVC to respond compassionately to themselves, some to create greater depth in their personal relationships, and still others to build effective relationships at work or in the political arena. Worldwide, NVC is used to mediate disputes and conflicts at all levels.

NVC in Action

Interspersed throughout the book are dialogues entitled NVC in Action. These dialogues intend to impart the flavor of an actual exchange in which a speaker is applying the principles of Nonviolent Communication. However, NVC is not simply a language or a set of techniques for using words; the consciousness and intent that it embraces may be expressed through silence, a quality of presence, as well as through facial expressions and body language. The NVC in Action dialogues you will be reading are necessarily distilled and abridged versions of real-life exchanges, where moments of silent empathy, stories, humor, gestures, and more would all contribute to a more natural flow of connection between the two parties than might be apparent when dialogues are condensed in print.

第一章 由衷的给予

"杀人犯！凶手！杀孩子的刽子手！"

我曾在伯利恒一处难民营的清真寺里，向170多位巴勒斯坦穆斯林男子介绍非暴力沟通。演说中，我突然注意到听众席中传来一阵低声的骚动。"他们在暗暗说你是美国人！"我的翻译刚警告完我，一名男子就从台下冲到他跟前，径直面向我使劲喊道："杀人犯！"瞬即，许多人大声附和道："凶手！""杀孩子的刽子手！""杀人犯！"

幸好，我努力让自己全神贯注地体会那名男子当时的感受和需要。来难民营的途中，我看到许多前一天晚上射入难民营的催泪弹弹壳，每只弹筒上"美国制造"这几个字清晰可见。我理解难民们对美国向以色列供应催泪弹和其他武器满怀愤怒。

我向那个称我为杀人犯的男子回应道：

马歇尔：你很生气，是因为你希望我的政府能改变使用资源的方式是吗？（我并不知道我的猜测是否准确，但重要的是，我诚恳而努力地体会着他的感受和需要。）

男　子：天杀的，我当然生气！难道你认为我们需要催泪弹？我们需要排水管，而不是催泪弹！我们需要房子！我们需要有自己的国家！

马歇尔：所以，你很愤怒，你希望得到支持来改善你们的生活条件，并且获得政治独立，是这样吗？

男　子：你知道我和家人、孩子还有所有人在这里住了27年是什么滋味吗？你能想象这对我们意味着什么吗，哪怕只是一点点？

马歇尔：听起来，你感到非常绝望，你想知道，我或者别人是否能够真

1 Giving From the Heart

"Murderer, Assassin, Child-Killer!"

I was presenting Nonviolent Communication to about 170 Palestinian Muslim men in a mosque at Dheisheh Refugee Camp in Bethlehem. Attitudes toward Americans at that time were not favorable. As I was speaking, I suddenly noticed a wave of muffled commotion fluttering through the audience. "They're whispering that you are American!" my translator alerted me, just as a gentleman in the audience leapt to his feet. Facing me squarely, he hollered at the top of his lungs, "Murderer!" Immediately a dozen other voices joined him in chorus: "Assassin!" "Child-killer!" "Murderer!"

Fortunately, I was able to focus my attention on what the man was feeling and needing. In this case, I had some cues. On the way into the refugee camp, I had seen several empty tear gas canisters that had been shot into the camp the night before. Clearly marked on each canister were the words *Made in U.S.A.* I knew that the refugees harbored a lot of anger toward the United States for supplying tear gas and other weapons to Israel.

I addressed the man who had called me a murderer:

MBR: Are you angry because you would like my government to use its resources differently? *(I didn't know whether my guess was correct—what was critical was my sincere effort to connect with his feeling and need.)*

Man: Damn right I'm angry! You think we need tear gas? We need sewers, not your tear gas! We need housing! We need to have our own country!

MBR: So you're furious and would appreciate some support in improving your living conditions and gaining political independence?

Man: Do you know what it's like to live here for twenty-seven years the way I have with my family—children and all? Have you got the faintest idea what that's been like for us?

第一章　由衷的给予

正理解这样生活的滋味，对吗？

男　子：你想来理解吗？告诉我，你有孩子吗？他们有学上吗？他们有玩耍的操场吗？我的儿子病了！他在水沟里玩耍！他的教室里没有课本！你见过没有课本的学校吗？

马歇尔：我听到，在这里抚养孩子，对你来说是多么痛苦。你希望我知道，你所要的是每一个父母都想给孩子的——好的教育、玩耍的机会、健康的环境……

男　子：是的，就这些基本的东西！你们美国人不是说这是人权吗？何不让更多的美国人来这里看看，你们把什么样的人权带到了这里！

马歇尔：你希望更多的美国人意识到这里的人们所忍受的煎熬，并能更深地认识到我们的政治行动对你们造成的影响，是吗？

　　我们的对话就这样进行了20多分钟，他一直在表达痛苦，而我持续地聆听每一句话背后所包含的感受和需要。我不表达认同或不认同，也不将他的话当作攻击。在我看来，这是一份来自人类同胞的礼物：这个人和我分享的，是他的灵魂以及他深深的脆弱。

　　当他感受到被我充分理解后，他开始愿意听我解释来难民营的目的。一小时后，这位原本称我为杀人犯的男子邀请我到他家中享用了一顿丰盛的斋月晚餐。

MBR: Sounds like you're feeling very desperate and you're wondering whether I or anybody else can really understand what it's like to be living under these conditions. Am I hearing you right?

Man: You want to understand? Tell me, do you have children? Do they go to school? Do they have playgrounds? My son is sick! He plays in open sewage! His classroom has no books! Have you seen a school that has no books?

MBR: I hear how painful it is for you to raise your children here; you'd like me to know that what you want is what all parents want for their children—a good education, opportunity to play and grow in a healthy environment . . .

Man: That's right, the basics! Human rights—isn't that what you Americans call it? Why don't more of you come here and see what kind of human rights you're bringing here!

MBR: You'd like more Americans to be aware of the enormity of the suffering here and to look more deeply at the consequences of our political actions?

Our dialogue continued, with him expressing his pain for nearly twenty more minutes, and me listening for the feeling and need behind each statement. I didn't agree or disagree. I received his words, not as attacks, but as gifts from a fellow human willing to share his soul and deep vulnerabilities with me.

Once the gentleman felt understood, he was able to hear me explain my purpose for being at the camp. An hour later, the same man who had called me a murderer was inviting me to his home for a Ramadan dinner.

第二章

疏离生命的语言

你们不要论断人,免得你们被论断。
因为你们怎样论断人,也必怎样被论断。
——《圣经·马太福音 7:1》

Communication That Blocks Compassion

*Do not judge, and you will not be judged.
For as you judge others, so you will yourselves be judged . . .*

—Holy Bible, Matthew 7:1

In studying the question of what alienates us from our natural state of compassion, I have identified specific forms of language and communication that I believe contribute to our behaving violently toward each other and ourselves. I use the term *life-alienating communication* to refer to these forms of communication.

> Certain ways of communicating alienate us from our natural state of compassion.

Moralistic Judgments

One kind of life-alienating communication is the use of *moralistic judgments* that imply wrongness or badness on the part of people who don't act in harmony with our values. Such judgments are reflected in language: "The problem with you is that you're too selfish." "She's lazy." "They're prejudiced." "It's inappropriate." Blame, insults, put-downs, labels, criticism, comparisons, and diagnoses are all forms of judgment.

The Sufi poet Rumi once wrote, "Out beyond ideas of wrongdoing and right-doing, there is a field. I'll meet you there." Life-alienating communication, however, traps us in a world of ideas about rightness

> In the world of judgments, our concern centers on "who is what."

第二章　疏离生命的语言

是什么使我们难以体会天性中的慈悲和善意？在研究这个议题时，我发现，某些语言与表达方式造成了人们对自己和他人的暴力。我将这些表达方式称为"疏离生命的语言"。

道德评判

道德评判是其中的一种。当他人的行为与我们的价值观不符，我们便认为这个人是错的或是恶的。例如：

"你的问题就是太自私了。"
"她很懒。"
"他们有偏见。"
"这样做不恰当。"

指责、侮辱、贴标签、批评、比较、分析都是评判的形式。
苏菲派诗人鲁米曾写道："在对与错的区分之外，有一片田野，我

2 Communication That Blocks Compassion

and wrongness—a world of judgments. It is a language rich with words that classify and dichotomize people and their actions. When we speak this language, we judge others and their behavior while preoccupying ourselves with who's good, bad, normal, abnormal, responsible, irresponsible, smart, ignorant, etc.

Long before I reached adulthood, I learned to communicate in an impersonal way that did not require me to reveal what was going on inside myself. When I encountered people or behaviors I either didn't like or didn't understand, I would react in terms of their wrongness. If my teachers assigned a task I didn't want to do, they were "mean" or "unreasonable." If someone pulled out in front of me in traffic, my reaction would be, "You idiot!" When we speak this language, we think and communicate in terms of what's wrong with others for behaving in certain ways or, occasionally, what's wrong with ourselves for not understanding or responding as we would like. Our attention is focused on classifying, analyzing, and determining levels of wrongness rather than on what we and others need and are not getting. Thus if my partner wants more affection than I'm giving her, she is "needy and dependent." But if I want more affection than she is giving me, then she is "aloof and insensitive." If my colleague is more concerned about details than I am, he is "picky and compulsive." On the other hand, if I am more concerned about details than he is, he is "sloppy and disorganized."

> Analyses of others are actually expressions of our own needs and values.

It is my belief that all such analyses of other human beings are tragic expressions of our own values and needs. They are tragic because when we express our values and needs in this form, we increase defensiveness and resistance among the very people whose behaviors are of concern to us. Or, if people do agree to act in harmony with our values, they will likely do so out of fear, guilt, or shame because they concur with our analysis of their wrongness.

第二章　疏离生命的语言

将在那里遇见你。"然而，疏离生命的语言却让我们陷入充满评判的对与错的世界中。这时我们关注的往往只有好与坏、正常还是不正常、负责任还是不负责任、聪明还是愚蠢，等等。

我从小就学会了以一种看似不带个人色彩的方式说话，以免泄露自己的内心世界。遇到不喜欢或无法理解的人和行为，我会认为是他们有问题。如果不想做老师布置的作业，我就会说他们"刻薄""不可理喻"；如果塞车时有人插队，我会脱口而出："你这混蛋！"

使用这类语言时，我们满脑子想的都是别人哪里做得不对。同样的，要是达不到自己的期待，我们也会这样批评自己。我们一心都在分析和追究自己和他人有什么问题，却不曾思索自己和他人有什么需要没有得到满足。

如此这般，如果我的伴侣想要多一些体贴，我就会说她"要求太多、太黏人"；可如果我想要多一些体贴，我就会说她"太冷漠、太麻木"。如果同事比我更在意细节，我就会说他"挑剔、有强迫症"；反之，如果我比他更在意细节，我就会说他"做事懒散、不严谨"。

在我看来，当我们在分析和评判时，其实都是在表达自身的价值观和需要，但这样的表达方式却是悲剧性的，引发的是对方的防卫与抗拒。就算他人遵从了我们，很有可能是出于恐惧、内疚或羞愧，而非发自内心。而同时，人们这样做其实意味着他们接受了我们的评判，真是两败俱伤。迟早有一天，我们会发现对方不再那么友好，因为由于内部或外部压力而屈服的人们一定会心怀怨恨，他们由此失去尊严，在情绪上付出代价，更不可能怀着善意回应我们的需要和价值观。

在这里，重要的是不要把"价值判断"与"道德评判"混为一谈。每个人都会对生命中自己所珍视的品质做出价值判断。例如，我们也许

2 Communication That Blocks Compassion

We all pay dearly when people respond to our values and needs not out of a desire to give from the heart, but out of fear, guilt, or shame. Sooner or later, we will experience the consequences of diminished goodwill on the part of those who comply with our values out of a sense of either external or internal coercion. They, too, pay emotionally, for they are likely to feel resentment and decreased self-esteem when they respond to us out of fear, guilt, or shame. Furthermore, each time others associate us in their minds with any of those feelings, the likelihood of their responding compassionately to our needs and values in the future decreases.

It is important here not to confuse *value judgments* and *moralistic judgments*. All of us make *value judgments* as to the qualities we value in life; for example, we might value honesty, freedom, or peace. Value judgments reflect our beliefs of how life can best be served. We make *moralistic judgments* of people and behaviors that fail to support our value judgments; for example, "Violence is bad. People who kill others are evil." Had we been raised speaking a language that facilitated the expression of compassion, we would have learned to articulate our needs and values directly, rather than to insinuate wrongness when they have not been met. For example, instead of "Violence is bad," we might say instead, "I am fearful of the use of violence to resolve conflicts; I value the resolution of human conflicts through other means."

The relationship between language and violence is the subject of psychology professor O.J. Harvey's research at the University of Colorado. He took random samples of pieces of literature from many countries around the world and tabulated the frequency of words that classify and judge people. His study shows a high correlation between frequent use of such words and frequency of incidents. It does not surprise me to hear that there is considerably less violence in cultures where people think in terms of human needs than in cultures where people label one another as "good" or "bad" and believe that the "bad" ones deserve to be punished. In 75 percent of the television programs shown during hours when American children are most likely to be watching, the hero

第二章　疏离生命的语言

会珍视诚实、自由、和平。价值判断反映着我们的信念——我们如何全然地活出自己的生命的本性。对于那些不符合我们价值观的人和行为，我们常常会做出道德评判。例如，我们也许会在和平的价值观受到冲击时说："暴力是不好的。杀人者很邪恶。"但如果从小学习非暴力沟通，我们就能够清楚而直接地表达出自己的需要和价值观，而不是指责他人。我们可以说："对于通过暴力来解决冲突，我很担心，我希望能选择其他方式来化解纷争。"

科罗拉多大学的心理学教授哈维（O.J.Harvey）专门研究了语言和暴力的关系。他从许多国家的文献中随机抽取了若干样本，统计出那些涉及道德评判的词语使用频率。研究结果显示，这类词语的使用频率越高，暴力事件就越频繁。相较于那些将人分为好和坏、认为坏人应当受到惩罚的文化，在那些关注人的需要的文化中，暴力事件也会少很多。对此我一点也不感到意外。在美国，在儿童最有可能观看电视的时段中，有75%的节目在播放英雄们杀人或暴打他人的情节。而这些暴力场面往往被视为节目的"高潮"。观众之所以看得津津有味，正是因为文化教导让他们相信"坏人应当被惩罚"。

不论是发生在家庭成员、种族、国家间的语言暴力，还是心理或肢体暴力，这些暴力的根源都是人们在遇到冲突时，认为那是对方的错，也因而看不到彼此的脆弱。我们可以从冷战中看到这种思维的危险性。美国的领导人将苏联视为势必要摧毁美国式生活的"邪恶帝国"，苏联领导人则将美国人称为试图征服他们的"帝国主义压迫者"。双方都没有意识到这些标签背后隐藏的恐惧。

2 Communication That Blocks Compassion

> Classifying and judging people promotes violence.

either kills people or beats them up. This violence typically constitutes the "climax" of the show. Viewers, having been taught that bad guys deserve to be punished, take pleasure in watching this violence.

At the root of much, if not all, violence—whether verbal, psychological, or physical, whether among family members, tribes, or nations—is a kind of thinking that attributes the cause of conflict to wrongness in one's adversaries, and a corresponding inability to think of oneself or others in terms of vulnerability—that is, what one might be feeling, fearing, yearning for, missing, etc. We saw this dangerous way of thinking during the Cold War. Our leaders viewed the U.S.S.R. as an "evil empire" bent on destroying the American way of life. Soviet leaders referred to the people of the United States as "imperialist oppressors" who were trying to subjugate them. Neither side acknowledged the fear lurking behind such labels.

Making Comparisons

Another form of judgment is the use of comparisons. In his book *How to Make Yourself Miserable*, Dan Greenburg demonstrates through humor the insidious power that comparative thinking can exert over us. He suggests that if readers have a sincere desire to make life miserable for themselves, they might learn to compare themselves to other people. For those unfamiliar with this practice, he provides a few exercises. The first one displays full-length pictures of a man and a woman who embody ideal physical beauty by contemporary media standards. Readers are instructed to take their own body measurements, compare them to those superimposed on the pictures of the attractive specimens, and dwell on the differences.

> Comparisons are a form of judgment.

This exercise produces what it promises: we start to feel miserable as we engage in these comparisons. By the time we're as depressed as we think possible, we turn the page to discover that the first exercise was a mere warm-up. Since physical beauty

做比较

评判的另一种形式是做比较。在《如何让自己活得很悲惨》一书中，作者丹·格林伯格（Dan Greenburg）诙谐地揭示了"比较"的心态是如何暗中对我们产生作用的。他建议读者，如果真的想让自己的生活变得悲惨，就去学着与他人做比较。在一个练习中，他展示了两张男人和女人的全身像，他们都拥有时下媒体眼中的"完美"身材，接着，他请读者们测量自己的身材尺寸后与照片上的数字做比较，同时用心体会两者之间的差距。

一旦我们开始比较，就会感到郁闷！此练习的效果绝对百发百中。当人们以为这样已经足够郁闷时，翻到下一页的练习，便会发现刚才只是热身罢了。由于形体美相对来说是表面的，格林伯格接着请人们针对他们更在乎的事情——"成就"来做比较。他从电话簿中随机选出几个人名让读者比较自己和那些人的成就。他称电话簿中的第一个名字是莫扎特，随即列出了莫扎特擅长的语言和他在十多岁前完成的主要作品。接着他要求读者们想一想自己现在的成就，并和莫扎特12岁时的成就做出比较，用心体会两者之间的差距。

想必，读者们就算不做上述练习，也能看到比较是如何切断我们对人对己的善意。

is relatively superficial, Greenburg next provides an opportunity to compare ourselves on something that matters: achievement. He turns to the phone book to give readers a few random individuals to compare themselves with. The first name he claims to have pulled out of the phone book is Wolfgang Amadeus Mozart. Greenburg lists the languages Mozart spoke and the major pieces he had composed by the time he was a teenager. The exercise then instructs readers to reflect on their own achievements at their current stage of life, to compare them with what Mozart had accomplished by age twelve, and to dwell on the differences.

Even readers who never emerge from the self-induced misery of this exercise might see how powerfully this type of thinking blocks compassion, both for oneself and for others.

Denial of Responsibility

Another kind of life-alienating communication is denial of responsibility. Communication is life-alienating when it clouds our awareness that we are each responsible for our own thoughts, feelings, and actions. The use of the common expression *have to*, as in "There are some things you have to do, whether you like it or not," illustrates how personal responsibility for our actions can be obscured in speech.

> **Our language obscures awareness of personal responsibility.**

The phrase *makes one feel*, as in "You make me feel guilty," is another example of how language facilitates denial of personal responsibility for our own feelings and thoughts.

In her book *Eichmann in Jerusalem*, which documents the war crimes trial of Nazi officer Adolf Eichmann, Hannah Arendt quotes Eichmann saying that he and his fellow officers had their own name for the responsibility-denying language they used. They called it *Amtssprache,* loosely translated into English as "office talk" or "bureaucratese." For example, if asked why they took a certain action, the response would be, "I had to." If asked why they "had to," the answer would be, "Superiors' orders." "Company policy." "It was the law."

第二章 疏离生命的语言

推卸责任

每一个人都对自己的思想、情感与行为负有责任,若无法意识到这一点,沟通也会疏离与生命的连结。我们习惯使用"不得不"这样的表达方式来淡化对自己行为所负的责任。例如"有些事不管你喜不喜欢,都不得不做"。另一个习惯表达是"让人感到"。例如"你让我感到内疚"。借由这样的说法,我们也回避了为自己的感受和想法所负的责任。

在《艾希曼在耶路撒冷》一书中,作者汉娜·阿伦特(Hannah Arendt)记录了审判纳粹军官阿道夫·艾希曼(Adolph Eichmann)的过程。审判中艾希曼否认自己对屠杀负有责任。对此,阿伦特发现军官们有一套卸责的语言,引用艾希曼的话,这是他们在执行"命令"(德语原文:Amtssprache)。例如,如果他们被问到为何要采取某个行动时,他们就会回答:"我不得不那么做。"若被追问为什么"不得不那么做",他们就会说那是"上级的命令"或"公司政策""法律规定"。

当我们将行动的原因归咎于外部因素时,我们便在试图推卸自己的责任。诸如:

- 模糊的外部因素:
  "我打扫我的房间,因为我不得不做。"
- 个人状况、医疗诊断结果、身体或心理病史:
  "因为我有酒瘾,所以我喝酒。"
- 他人的行为:
  "我的孩子冲上了马路,所以我才会打他。"

2 Communication That Blocks Compassion

We deny responsibility for our actions when we attribute their cause to factors outside ourselves:

- Vague, impersonal forces—*"I cleaned my room because I had to."*
- Our condition, diagnosis, or personal or psychological history—*"I drink because I am an alcoholic."*
- The actions of others—*"I hit my child because he ran into the street."*
- The dictates of authority—*"I lied to the client because the boss told me to."*
- Group pressure—*"I started smoking because all my friends did."*
- Institutional policies, rules, and regulations—*"I have to suspend you for this infraction because it's the school policy."*
- Gender roles, social roles, or age roles—*"I hate going to work, but I do it because I am a husband and a father."*
- Uncontrollable impulses—*"I was overcome by my urge to eat the candy bar."*

Once, during a discussion among parents and teachers on the dangers of a language that implies absence of choice, a woman objected angrily, "But there are some things you have to do whether you like it or not! And I see nothing wrong with telling my children that there are things they have to do, too." Asked for an example of something she "had to do," she retorted, "That's easy! When I leave here tonight, I have to go home and cook. I hate cooking! I hate it with a passion, but I have been doing it every day for twenty years, even when I've been as sick as a dog, because it's one of those things you just have to do." I told her I was sad to hear her spending so much of her life doing something she hated, because she felt compelled to, and I just hoped that she might find happier possibilities by learning the language of NVC.

I am pleased to report that she was a fast learner. At the end of the workshop, she actually went home and announced to her family that she no longer wanted to cook. The opportunity for some feedback from her family came three weeks later when her two sons arrived at a workshop. I was curious to know how

第二章　疏离生命的语言

- 权威的命令：
  "我欺骗客户，因为老板叫我这么做。"
- 群体压力：
  "朋友都抽烟，所以我也开始抽烟了。"
- 机构政策、章程、规定：
  "因为你的违规行为，所以我不得不勒令你停学，这是学校的制度。"
- 性别角色、社会角色或年龄角色：
  "我厌恶上班。我去工作，因为我是一名丈夫和父亲。"
- 无法抑制的冲动：
  "我一时没克制住，就把那根棒棒糖给吃了。"

有一次，我与一群家长和老师们讨论，如果语言中暗示别无选择，会带来什么危险。结果有一位女士气愤地反对道："有些事情不管你喜不喜欢，你就是非做不可！并且我认为，告诉我的孩子们有些事他们也必须做并没有什么不对。"于是我问她："有什么事情是你非做不可的？"她立刻回答："这太容易了！今晚离开这里回到家后，我就必须要做饭。我讨厌做饭！讨厌到了极点！20 年来，每天我都不得不做饭，哪怕有时累得像条狗也一样。因为，这些事情就是非做不可。"我告诉她，听到她花了那么多时间做自己不喜欢的事情，只是因为她认为必须要这么做，我很难过。我希望她在学了非暴力沟通后能找到让她更开心的选择。

所幸这位女士的学习能力很强。工作坊结束后，她就向家人宣布，她不想再做饭了！三个星期后，她的两个儿子也来参加我的工作坊，我

2 Communication That Blocks Compassion

they had reacted to their mother's announcement. The elder son sighed, "Marshall, I just said to myself, 'Thank God!'" Seeing my puzzled look, he explained, "I thought to myself, maybe finally she won't be complaining at every meal!"

Another time, when I was consulting for a school district, a teacher remarked, "I hate giving grades. I don't think they are helpful and they create a lot of anxiety on the part of students. But I have to give grades: it's the district policy." We had just been practicing how to introduce language in the classroom that heightens consciousness of responsibility for one's actions. I suggested that the teacher translate the statement "I have to give grades because it's district policy" to "I choose to give grades because I want . . . " She answered without hesitation, "I choose to give grades because I want to keep my job," while hastening to add, "But I don't like saying it that way. It makes me feel so responsible for what I'm doing."

"That's why I want you to do it that way," I replied.

I share the sentiments of French novelist and journalist George Bernanos when he says,

> We can replace language that implies lack of choice with language that acknowledges choice.

> We are dangerous when we are not conscious of our responsibility for how we behave, think, and feel.

> I have thought for a long time now that if, some day, the increasing efficiency for the technique of destruction finally causes our species to disappear from the earth, it will not be cruelty that will be responsible for our extinction and still less, of course, the indignation that cruelty awakens and the reprisals and vengeance that it brings upon itself . . . but the docility, the lack of responsibility of the modern man, his base subservient acceptance of every common decree. The horrors that we have seen, the still greater horrors we shall presently see,

第二章　疏离生命的语言

好奇地询问他们如何看待母亲的决定。大儿子叹了一口气说："马歇尔，当时我心想，真是谢天谢地啊！"看到我一脸困惑的表情，他解释道："她终于不用在每次吃饭时发牢骚了！"

还有一次，我在某个学区担任顾问。我请老师们练习如何在课堂中使用非暴力沟通语言，借此提升学生们的意识，学会为自己的行为负责。一位老师随即表示："我厌恶打分。我认为这对学生没什么好处，反而为他们带来焦虑。但我不得不打分，这是学区的规定。"于是，我建议那位老师练习将"我不得不打分，因为这是学区的规定"转换为"我选择打分，因为我想要……"她脱口而出回答："我选择打分，因为我想保住这份工作。"然后，她又连忙补充道："但我不喜欢这样说，因为这会让我觉得要为我所做的事情负责。"我回答她："所以我才希望你这样说呀！"

法国作家和记者乔治·贝尔纳诺斯（George Bernanos）有段话颇能引发我的共鸣，他说：

"我常想，若有一天日渐强大的摧毁性技术使人类从地球上灭绝，真正要对此负责的远非是技术本身（当然技术暴行会唤醒人们，招来人们对技术的反击与仇视），而是现代人的唯唯诺诺、缺乏责任感、毕恭毕敬地服从每一个司空见惯的规定。我们所看到的悲剧以及即将来临的更大悲剧，并非是世界上反抗、不服从的人增多了，而是唯命是从、听话的人越来越多。"

——乔治·贝尔纳诺斯

are not signs that rebels, insubordinate, untamable men are increasing in number throughout the world, but rather that there is a constant increase in the number of obedient, docile men.

—George Bernanos

Other Forms of Life-Alienating Communication

Communicating our desires as demands is yet another form of language that blocks compassion. A demand explicitly or implicitly threatens listeners with blame or punishment if they fail to comply. It is a common form of communication in our culture, especially among those who hold positions of authority.

My children gave me some invaluable lessons about demands. Somehow I had gotten it into my head that, as a parent, my job was to make demands. I learned, however, that I could make all the demands in the world but still couldn't make my children do anything. This is a humbling lesson in power for those of us who believe that, because we're a parent, teacher, or manager, our job is to change other people and make them behave. Here were these youngsters letting me know that I couldn't make them do anything.

> **We can never make people do anything.**

All I could do was make them wish they had—through punishment. Then eventually they taught me that any time I was foolish enough to make them wish they had complied by punishing them, they had ways of making me wish that I hadn't!

We will examine this subject again when we learn to differentiate requests from demands—an important part of NVC.

The concept that certain actions merit reward while others merit punishment is also associated with life-alienating communication. This thinking is expressed by the word *deserve* as in "He deserves to be punished for what he did." It assumes "badness" on the part of people who behave in certain ways, and it calls for punishment to make them repent and

> **Thinking based on "who deserves what" blocks compassionate communication.**

其他疏离生命的沟通形式

当我们以"要求"的方式来表达我们的诉求时,实际上是在或明或暗地指责或惩罚那些不配合我们的人。这样的沟通方式在我们的文化中司空见惯,特别是来自那些有着权力地位的人。

关于"要求",我从孩子们那里学到了许多宝贵的教训。不知从何时起,我有了这样的观念——作为家长,我有责任要求孩子们做什么。家长、老师、管理者……许多掌握权威的人同样相信,他们的工作就是去改变他人、让他人守规矩。是孩子们让我明白,我无法要求他们去做任何事。是的,我可以通过惩罚,让他们服从我的要求或让他们后悔没有照着我的话去做,但他们终将让我明白,用惩罚的方式强迫他人是多么愚蠢,而我真希望自己不曾用那样的方式来对待他们。这是一次关于谦卑的学习。

在第六章中,我们将再次探究非暴力沟通中的这一重要主题:区分"请求"与"要求"。

疏离生命的语言还与"奖惩"思维有关,即有的行为应该受到奖赏,而有的行为就该受到惩罚。人们常用"活该"这样的字眼来表达这种思维。诸如,"他活该为自己的所作所为受到处罚"。这样的表达其实隐含着一种假设:做出某些事情的人必定是"坏人",他们应当受到处罚,他们应该忏悔并且做出改变。然而,我相信所有人都渴望改变,那是因为人们明白改变能为自己带来益处,而不是因为不想受到惩罚。

我们大多数人在贴标签、做比较、要求和评判的语言环境中长大,

change their behavior. I believe it is in everyone's interest that people change, not in order to avoid punishment, but because they see the change as benefiting themselves.

Most of us grew up speaking a language that encourages us to label, compare, demand, and pronounce judgments rather than to be aware of what we are feeling and needing. I believe life-alienating communication is rooted in views of human nature that have exerted their influence for several centuries. These views stress humans' innate evil and deficiency, and a need for education to control our inherently undesirable nature. Such education often leaves us questioning whether there is something wrong with whatever feelings and needs we may be experiencing. We learn early to cut ourselves off from what's going on within ourselves.

> Life-alienating communication has deep philosophical and political roots.

Life-alienating communication both stems from and supports hierarchical or domination societies, where large populations are controlled by a small number of individuals to those individuals' own benefit. It would be in the interest of kings, czars, nobles, and so forth that the masses be educated in a way that renders them slavelike in mentality. The language of wrongness, *should*, and *have to* is perfectly suited for this purpose: the more people are trained to think in terms of moralistic judgments that imply wrongness and badness, the more they are being trained to look outside themselves—to outside authorities—for the definition of what constitutes right, wrong, good, and bad. When we are in contact with our feelings and needs, we humans no longer make good slaves and underlings.

Summary

It is our nature to enjoy giving and receiving compassionately. We have, however, learned many forms of life-alienating communication that lead us to speak and behave in ways that injure others and ourselves. One form of life-alienating

鲜少被鼓励去觉察自己的感受和需要。我认为，疏离生命的语言植根于影响了我们数千年的性恶论，这一人性观强调人性本恶，认为人们需要通过教导来压制某些卑劣天性。但这样的教育时常让我们对自己的感受和需要心存疑虑，于是我们早早地就学会了与自己的内心隔绝。

疏离生命的语言既源于等级制度或霸权社会，又反过来巩固它们。在这类社会中少数个体通过控制大部分人为自己牟利。对国王、沙皇、贵族阶层来说，将臣民的心智模式训练成奴隶般顺从听话，最符合他们的利益。诸如"错误""应该""不得不"的语言是完美的工具。人们越是被教育用道德评判来区分对错、好坏，就越是习惯向外、向权威寻求判断的标准。一旦我们开始聆听自己内心的感受和需要，便不再是好奴隶、好随从。

小结

由衷地给予和接受，是人类天性所乐见的。然而我们习得了太多疏离生命的语言形式，导致我们的说话和行为方式给他人和自己带来伤害。其中的一种形式是道德评判，即认为那些不符合我们价值观的人是不对的、不好的。另一种形式是做比较，让人们难以升起对人对己的善意。疏离生命的语言还会使我们无法认清：每个人要为自己的想法、感受和行为负责。此外，还有一种形式是用要求来表达我们的诉求。

communication is the use of moralistic judgments that imply wrongness or badness on the part of those who don't act in harmony with our values. Another is the use of comparisons, which can block compassion both for others and for ourselves. Life-alienating communication also obscures our awareness that we are each responsible for our own thoughts, feelings, and actions. Communicating our desires in the form of demands is yet another characteristic of language that blocks compassion.

第三章

不带评论的观察

去观察,就像信仰一样重要。
——弗雷德里克·布希纳(Frederick Buechner)

Observing Without Evaluating

> OBSERVE!! There are few things as
> important, as religious, as that.
>
> —Frederick Buechner, minister

*I can handle your telling me
what I did or didn't do.
And I can handle your interpretations,
but please don't mix the two.*

*If you want to confuse any issue,
I can tell you how to do it:
Mix together what I do
with how you react to it.*

*Tell me that you're disappointed
with the unfinished chores you see,
But calling me "irresponsible"
is no way to motivate me.*

*And tell me that you're feeling hurt
when I say "no" to your advances,
But calling me a frigid man
won't increase your future chances.*

*Yes, I can handle your telling me
what I did or didn't do,
And I can handle your interpretations,
but please don't mix the two.*

—Marshall B. Rosenberg, PhD

第三章　不带评论的观察

我欣然接受你告诉我,
我做了什么或者我未做什么。
我也欣然接受你的评论,
但请不要将两者混淆。
如果你想把事情搅乱,
我可以告诉你如何做到:
将我做的事情
和你的反应混为一谈。
当你见到做了一半的家务活,
可以告诉我你感到失望。
但说我不负责任,
绝无可能让我做得更多。
当我对你的表白说"不",
请告诉我你感到伤心。
但说我冷酷无情,
并不能给你带来更多机会。
是的,
我欣然接受你告诉我,
我做了什么或者我未做什么。
我也欣然接受你的评论,
但请不要将两者混淆。

——马歇尔·卢森堡博士

3 Observing Without Evaluating

The first component of NVC entails the separation of observation from evaluation. We need to clearly observe what we are seeing, hearing, or touching that is affecting our sense of well-being, without mixing in any evaluation.

Observations are an important element in NVC, where we wish to clearly and honestly express how we are to another person. When we combine observation with evaluation, we decrease the likelihood that others will hear our intended message. Instead, they are apt to hear criticism and thus resist whatever we are saying.

NVC does not mandate that we remain completely objective and refrain from evaluating. It only requires that we maintain a separation between our observations and our evaluations. NVC is a process language that discourages static generalizations; instead, evaluations are to be based on observations *specific to time and context*. Semanticist Wendell Johnson pointed out that we create many problems for ourselves by using static language to express or capture a reality that is ever changing: "Our language is an imperfect instrument created by ancient and ignorant men. It is an animistic language that invites us to talk about stability and constants, about similarities and normal and kinds, about magical transformations, quick cures, simple problems, and final solutions. Yet the world we try to symbolize with this language is a world of process, change, differences, dimensions, functions, relationships, growths, interactions, developing, learning, coping, complexity. And the mismatch of our ever-changing world and our relatively static language forms is part of our problem."

> **When we combine observation with evaluation, people are apt to hear criticism.**

A colleague of mine, Ruth Bebermeyer, contrasts static and process language in a song that illustrates the difference between evaluation and observation:

第三章　不带评论的观察

非暴力沟通的第一个要素是区分观察与评论。我们要清楚地观察有哪些所见、所闻和所触，正影响着我们幸福，而不夹杂任何评论。

在非暴力沟通中，当我们想要清晰且诚恳地向他人表达我们的状态时，"观察"是一个重要的要素。如果我们在观察中夹杂着评论，人们便不那么容易真正听见我们想要表达的内容，反而会听到批评，甚至产生抗拒心理。

非暴力沟通并不要求我们保持完全客观，不做任何评论。它只是强调，我们要区分观察与评论。非暴力沟通是一个动态的语言，它不鼓励一成不变、一概而论的陈述。语义学家温戴尔·约翰逊（Wendell Johnson）指出，用静态的语言来表达或捕捉瞬息万变的现实世界，会带来许多问题。他说："我们的语言年代久远，是有缺陷的工具。它反映着泛灵论的思想，倾向于谈论稳定与恒常，谈论相似性、常态和分类，神奇的转变、立竿见影的疗效、简化的问题以及终极解决方案。然而，我们尝试用语言符号化的这个世界，却包含了无穷无尽的过程、变化、维度、变数、关系、功能、互动、发展、学习、应对和复杂性。不断变化的世界与我们相对静态的语言形式并不匹配，我们的许多问题正是因此产生。"

我的同事鲁斯·贝本梅尔在这段歌词中对比了静态语言与动态语言，由此来展现评论与观察的区别：

> 我从未见过什么懒汉，
> 我见过的他，有时在白天睡觉，
> 在某个下雨的日子呆在家里。
> 但他不是个懒汉。

3 Observing Without Evaluating

I've never seen a lazy man;
I've seen a man who never ran
while I watched him, and I've seen
a man who sometimes slept between
lunch and dinner, and who'd stay
at home upon a rainy day,
but he was not a lazy man.
Before you call me crazy,
think, was he a lazy man or
did he just do things we label "lazy"?

I've never seen a stupid kid;
I've seen a kid who sometimes did
things I didn't understand
or things in ways I hadn't planned;
I've seen a kid who hadn't seen
the same places where I had been,
but he was not a stupid kid.
Before you call him stupid,
think, was he a stupid kid or did he
just know different things than you did?

I've looked as hard as I can look
but never ever seen a cook;
I saw a person who combined
ingredients on which we dined,
A person who turned on the heat
and watched the stove that cooked the meat—
I saw those things but not a cook.
Tell me, when you're looking,
Is it a cook you see or is it someone
doing things that we call cooking?

What some of us call lazy
some call tired or easy-going,
what some of us call stupid
some just call a different knowing,

第三章　不带评论的观察

请在说我胡言乱语之前，
想一想，他真的是个懒汉，还是
他的行为被我们贴上了"懒惰"的标签？
我从未见过什么傻孩子；
这个孩子有时做的事，
我不理解或始料不及，
这个孩子的看法与我不同，
但他不是个傻孩子。
请在你说他傻之前，
想一想，他是个傻孩子，还是
他知道的事情和你不同？
我使劲看了又看，
却从未看到一个厨师；
我看到的是一个人，为我们的餐食调配食材，
那个人点燃灶火，看着炉子上正烹饪着的菜肴，
我看到的只是这些，而不是厨师。
请告诉我，当你看的时候，
你看到的是位厨师，还是
有个人做的事情被我们称之为烹饪？
有些人所说的懒惰，
另一些人却说那是淡泊人生；
有些人所说的愚蠢，
另一些人称之为看法不同。
因此，我得出结论，

so I've come to the conclusion,
it will save us all confusion
if we don't mix up what we can see
with what is our opinion.
Because you may, I want to say also;
I know that's only my opinion.

—Ruth Bebermeyer

While the effects of negative labels such as "lazy" and "stupid" may be more obvious, even a positive or an apparently neutral label such as "cook" limits our perception of the totality of another person's being.

The Highest Form of Human Intelligence

The Indian philosopher J. Krishnamurti once remarked that observing without evaluating is the highest form of human intelligence. When I first read this statement, the thought, "What nonsense!" shot through my mind before I realized that I had just made an evaluation. For most of us, it is difficult to make observations, especially of people and their behavior, that are free of judgment, criticism, or other forms of analysis.

I became acutely aware of this difficulty while working with an elementary school where the staff and principal had often reported communication difficulties. The district superintendent had requested that I help them resolve the conflict. First I was to confer with the staff, and then with the staff and principal together.

I opened the meeting by asking the staff, "What is the principal doing that conflicts with your needs?"

"He has a big mouth!" came the swift response. My question called for an observation, but while "big mouth" gave me information on how this teacher evaluated the principal, it failed to describe what the principal *said or did* that led to the interpretation that he had a "big mouth."

When I pointed this out, a second teacher offered, "I know what he means: the principal talks too much!" Instead of a clear observation

第三章　不带评论的观察

> 如果不在所见中夹杂我们的观点，
> 我们便可以避免混乱。
> 可能你还有困惑，
> 因而，我还想说的是：
> 我知道这只是我的看法。
>
> ——鲁斯·贝本梅尔

使用诸如"懒惰""傻"这类负面标签所带来的影响或许显而易见。但即使是像"厨师"这样所谓正向或者看上去中性的标签，也会妨碍我们全面地看到一个人。

人类智力的最高形式

印度哲学家克里希那穆提（J. Krishnamurti）曾经说："不带评论的观察是人类智力的最高形式。"第一次读到这个观点时，我的脑海中立马闪现出一个念头："简直是胡说八道。"它快到以至于我都无法意识到自己正在做出一个评论。对大部分人来说，观察他人而不做任何评判、批判或分析是很困难的。

有一次我为一所小学提供咨询服务，对此有了深刻的体会。这所学校的教职员工与校长时常反映彼此之间很难沟通。于是，学区负责人请我为他们化解冲突。我首先和教职员工交谈，接着邀请校长加入会谈。

会谈开始时，我先询问教职员工："校长做了什么不符合你们的需要？"

of the principal's behavior, this was also an evaluation—of how much the principal talked. A third teacher then declared, "He thinks only he has anything worth saying." I explained that inferring what another person is thinking is not the same as observing his behavior. Finally a fourth teacher ventured, "He wants to be the center of attention all the time." After I remarked that this too was an inference—of what another person is wanting—two teachers blurted in unison, "Well, your question is very hard to answer!"

We subsequently worked together to create a list identifying *specific behaviors,* on the part of the principal, that bothered them, and made sure that the list was free of evaluation. For example, the principal told stories about his childhood and war experiences during faculty meetings, with the result that meetings sometimes ran twenty minutes overtime. When I asked whether they had ever communicated their annoyance to the principal, the staff replied that they had tried, but only through evaluative comments. They had never made reference to specific behaviors—such as his storytelling—and they agreed to bring these up when we were all to meet together.

Almost as soon as the meeting began, I saw what the staff had been telling me. No matter what was being discussed, the principal would interject, "This reminds me of the time . . . " and then launch into a story about his childhood or war experience. I waited for the staff to voice their discomfort around the principal's behavior. However, instead of Nonviolent Communication, they applied nonverbal condemnation. Some rolled their eyes; others yawned pointedly; one stared at his watch.

I endured this painful scenario until finally I asked, "Isn't anyone going to say something?" An awkward silence ensued. The teacher who had spoken first at our meeting screwed up his courage, looked directly at the principal, and said, "Ed, you have a big mouth."

As this story illustrates, it's not always easy to shed our old habits and master the ability to separate observation from evaluation. Eventually, the teachers succeeded in clarifying for the principal the specific actions that led to their concern. The principal listened earnestly and then pressed, "Why didn't

第三章　不带评论的观察

"他是个大嘴巴！"有人马上回答。我提问的是观察——校长说了什么或做了什么，而"大嘴巴"却是这位老师对校长的评论。

当我指出这一点后，另一位老师响应道："我知道他的意思了。校长的话太多！"这仍不是一个清晰的观察，而是对校长说多少话的评论。随后，第三位老师说："他认为只有他想说的话是重要的。"我进而向他们解释，推断他人的想法和对他人行为的观察是两码事。随后，第四位老师大胆地说："他总是想成为人前的焦点。"当我指出这也是推断时，两位老师不约而同地说道："你的问题太难回答了！"

接着，我们一起拟了份清单，明确列出校长有哪些具体行为令他们感到不满，并确保不掺杂评论。例如，在全体教师会议上，校长会讲述他的童年和战争经历，有时导致会议超时 20 分钟。我问老师们是否曾经和校长沟通过他们的不满，他们说曾经试过，但都用具有评论意味的言辞向校长提出批评，而从未提及任何具体行为，例如校长在会议中讲述自己的故事。最后，老师们同意在与校长会谈时将这一点提出来。

会谈刚一开始，我便目睹了老师们所描述的情景。不论讨论的主题是什么，校长都会插话说："想当年……"接着开始讲述他的童年或战争经历。我等着老师们表达他们的不满。然而，他们并没有运用非暴力沟通的方式，而是无声的抗议。有的人开始翻白眼，有的人故意打着哈欠，还有个人一直盯着手表。

直到我按捺不住问他们："没有人有话要说吗？"迎来的是一阵令人尴尬的沉默。接着，之前会谈中率先发言的那位老师鼓起勇气，直视着校长，然后说出："艾德，你真是个大嘴巴！"

就像这个故事所展现的，从我们的旧习惯中挣脱出来，并有能力熟练地区分观察与评论并不容易。最终，老师们终于可以明明白白地告

3 Observing Without Evaluating

one of you tell me before?" He admitted he was aware of his storytelling habit, and then began a story pertaining to this habit! I interrupted him, observing (good-naturedly) that he was doing it again. We ended our meeting by developing ways for the staff to let their principal know, in a gentle way, when his stories weren't appreciated.

Distinguishing Observations From Evaluations

The following table distinguishes observations that are separate from evaluation from those that have evaluation mixed in.

Communication	Example of observation with evaluation mixed in	Example of observation separate from evaluation
1. Use of verb *to be* without indication that the evaluator takes responsibility for the evaluation	You are too generous.	When I see you give all your lunch money to others, I think you are being too generous.
2. Use of verbs with evaluative connotations	Doug procrastinates.	Doug only studies for exams the night before.
3. Implication that one's inferences about another person's thoughts, feelings, intentions, or desires are the only ones possible	She won't get her work in.	I don't think she'll get her work in. *or* She said, "I won't get my work in."
4. Confusion of prediction with certainty	If you don't eat balanced meals, your health will be impaired.	If you don't eat balanced meals, I fear your health may be impaired.
5. Failure to be specific about referents	Immigrants don't take care of their property.	I have not seen the immigrant family living at 1679 Ross shovel the snow on their sidewalk.

诉校长，他们对他的哪些行为感到不满。校长认真地听完后郑重地说："为什么从没有人告诉我呢？"他承认他有讲故事的习惯，接着就开始说与这个习惯有关的故事了！我见状打断了他的话，婉转地提出他在重蹈覆辙。会议最后，我们商量了一些办法，以后当老师们不想听校长回忆往事时，就用温和的方式提醒他。

区分观察和评论

在以下列表中，我举例说明如何从混杂着评论的句子中区分出观察。

表达方式	混淆观察和评论	区分观察和评论
1. 未对自己的评论负责。	你太大方了。	当我看到你将午餐的钱都给了别人，我认为你这样做太大方了。
2. 使用的动词暗含评论。	道格爱拖延。	道格只在考试前一晚学习。
3. 推断他人的想法、感受、意向或愿望时，暗示这是唯一可能。	她无法完成工作。	我不认为她能完成工作。或她说："我无法完成工作。"
4. 把预测当作确定的事实。	如果你的饮食不均衡，健康就会出问题。	如果你的饮食不均衡，我担心你的健康会出问题。
5. 指代不具体。	这户移民家庭照顾不好自家的院落。	我没有看到过住在罗斯路1679号的那户移民家庭铲路边的雪。

3 Observing Without Evaluating

Communication	Example of observation with evaluation mixed in	Example of observation separate from evaluation
6. Use of words denoting ability without indicating that an evaluation is being made	Hank Smith is a poor soccer player.	Hank Smith has not scored a goal in twenty games.
7. Use of adverbs and adjectives in ways that do not indicate an evaluation has been made	Jim is ugly.	Jim's looks don't appeal to me.

Note: The words *always, never, ever, whenever*, etc. express observations when used in the following ways:
- Whenever I have observed Jack on the phone, he has spoken for at least thirty minutes.
- I cannot recall your ever writing to me.

Sometimes such words are used as exaggerations, in which case observations and evaluations are being mixed:
- You are always busy.
- She is never there when she's needed.

When these words are used as exaggerations, they often provoke defensiveness rather than compassion.

Words like *frequently* and *seldom* can also contribute to confusing observation with evaluation.

Evaluations	Observations
You seldom do what I want.	The last three times I initiated an activity, you said you didn't want to do it.
He frequently comes over.	He comes over at least three times a week.

第三章　不带评论的观察

续表

表达方式	混淆观察和评论	区分观察和评论
6. 在描述他人能力时，并未表明那只是自己所做的评论。	汉克·史密斯是个糟糕的足球运动员。	汉克·史密斯在20场球赛中未能进一个球。
7. 使用含有评论意味的形容词和副词。	吉姆长得难看。	吉姆的长相对我没有吸引力。

注意：总是、永远、从来、每次之类的词语在以下用法中表达的是观察：

- 每次我看到杰克打电话，他都至少打半小时。
- 我记得你从来没有写信给我。

然而有时，这些词是言过其实的表达，混淆了观察和评论：

- 你总是在忙。
- 在需要她的时候，她永远都不在。

这样的表达经常会引发他人的逆反心理，而非慈悲之情。

"经常""很少"这样的词也可能混淆观察和评论。

评论	观察
你很少配合我。	上一次当我提议一项活动时，你说你不想做。
他时常来访。	他上个月每周至少有三次来访。

Summary

The first component of NVC entails the separation of observation from evaluation. When we combine observation with evaluation, others are apt to hear criticism and resist what we are saying. NVC is a process language that discourages static generalizations. Instead, observations are to be made specific to time and context, for example, "Hank Smith has not scored a goal in twenty games," rather than "Hank Smith is a poor soccer player."

NVC in Action

"The Most Arrogant Speaker We've Ever Had!"

This dialogue occurred during a workshop I was conducting. About half an hour into my presentation, I paused to invite reactions from the participants. One of them raised a hand and declared, "You're the most arrogant speaker we've ever had!"

I have several options open to me when people address me this way. One option is to take the message personally; I know I'm doing this when I have a strong urge to either grovel, defend myself, or make excuses. Another option (for which I am well-rehearsed) is to attack the other person for what I perceive as their attack upon me. On this occasion, I chose a third option by focusing on what might be going on behind the man's statement.

MBR: *(guessing at the observations being made)* Are you reacting to my having taken thirty straight minutes to present my views before giving you a chance to talk?

Phil: No, you make it sound so simple.

MBR: *(trying to obtain further clarification)* Are you reacting to my not having said anything about how the process can be difficult for some people to apply?

Phil: No, not some people—you!

第三章　不带评论的观察

小结

非暴力沟通的第一个要素是区分观察与评论。当我们在观察中夹杂着自己的评论时，他人往往会认为我们在批评他们，并因而产生抗拒的心理。非暴力沟通是一种动态的语言，它不鼓励人们做静态、一概而论的陈述，而是提倡我们在描述观察时，清楚地说出特定的时间和情境。例如"汉克在过去20场球赛中未进一球"，而非"汉克是名糟糕的足球运动员"。

非暴力沟通实例

"我们遇到过的最傲慢的演讲者！"

以下对话来自我主持的一场工作坊。在讲解了约半小时后，我停下来请学员谈谈他们的心得。这时，有人举起手说："你是我们遇到过的最傲慢的演讲者！"

当听到有人这样说我，我的回应方式可以有几种选择。其中一种是认为这确实是我的问题。我知道，一旦我想讨好对方、为自己辩护或开脱，就可以将错误归咎到自己身上。另一种方式是认为对方在攻击我而

3 Observing Without Evaluating

MBR: So you're reacting to my not having said that the process can be difficult for me at times?

Phil: That's right.

MBR: Are you feeling annoyed because you would have liked some sign from me that indicated that I have some problems with the process myself?

Phil: *(after a moment's pause)* That's right.

MBR: *(feeling more relaxed now that I am in touch with the person's feeling and need, I direct my attention to what he might be requesting of me)* Would you like me to admit right now that this process can be a struggle for me to apply?

Phil: Yes.

MBR: *(having gotten clear on his observation, feeling, need, and request, I check inside myself to see if I am willing to do as he requests)* Yes, this process is often difficult for me. As we continue with the workshop, you'll probably hear me describe several incidents where I've struggled . . . or completely lost touch . . . with this process, this consciousness, that I am presenting here to you. But what keeps me in the struggle are the close connections to other people that happen when I do stay with the process.

第三章　不带评论的观察

开始反击，这也是我过去时常选择的方式。而这一次，我选择了第三种方式，既没有辩解也没有指责对方，而是将注意力放在他言语背后发生了什么。

马歇尔：（猜测他的观察）你这么说，是针对我连续讲了半小时才给你们机会发表意见吗？

菲　尔：不是，你把事情说得太简单了。

马歇尔：（请他澄清）那是不是因为我没有提到非暴力沟通对有些人来说用起来会很困难？

菲　尔：不，不是有些人，而是你！

马歇尔：所以，你这么说是因为我没有提到，有时我也很难运用非暴力沟通，是吗？

菲　尔：正是。

马歇尔：你感到不高兴，因为你希望我能告诉你们，我自己在使用这个方法时会遇到的困难？

菲　尔：（犹豫了一会儿）没错。

马歇尔：（当我能体会到他的感受和需要时，我感到放松了许多，我开始关注他的请求）你是不是希望此时我能够承认，我自己在运用这个方法的时候，也会遇到一些困难？

菲　尔：是的。

马歇尔：（当我清楚地了解了他的观察、感受、需要以及请求后，我问自己是否愿意满足他的请求）是的，这个方法对我来说也是不容易的。在接下来的时间里，你也许会听到我讲述那些抓狂的时刻，有时甚至完全做不到。而当我真的能够运用非暴力沟通

Exercise 1

OBSERVATION OR EVALUATION?

To determine your proficiency at discerning between observations and evaluations, complete the following exercise. Circle the number in front of each statement that is an observation only, with no evaluation mixed in.

1. "John was angry with me yesterday for no reason."
2. "Yesterday evening Nancy bit her fingernails while watching television."
3. "Sam didn't ask for my opinion during the meeting."
4. "My father is a good man."
5. "Janice works too much."
6. "Henry is aggressive."
7. "Pam was first in line every day this week."
8. "My son often doesn't brush his teeth."
9. "Luke told me I didn't look good in yellow."
10. "My aunt complains when I talk with her."

Here are my responses for Exercise 1:

1. If you circled this number, we're not in agreement. I consider "for no reason" to be an evaluation. Furthermore, I consider it an evaluation to infer that John was angry. He might have been feeling hurt, scared, sad, or something else. Examples of observations without evaluation might be: "John told me he was angry," or "John pounded his fist on the table."
2. If you circled this number, we're in agreement that an observation was expressed without being mixed together with an evaluation.

第三章 不带评论的观察

时，就可以和他人建立紧密的连结。因此，尽管有许多困难，我依然愿意坚持尝试这个方法。

练习一：观察还是评论？

请完成以下练习，看看你是否可以熟练区分观察和评论。请标出那些只是描述观察而不带有评论的句子。

1. "昨天，约翰无缘无故冲我发脾气。"
2. "昨天晚上，南希一边看电视一边咬指甲。"
3. "会议上我没有听到桑姆询问我的意见。"
4. "我的父亲是个好人。"
5. "詹尼斯花在工作上的时间太多了。"
6. "亨利很强势。"
7. "这周，潘每天第一个来排队。"
8. "我的儿子经常不刷牙。"
9. "卢克说，我穿黄色衣服不好看。"
10. "姑姑和我说话时一直在抱怨。"

以下是我对练习一的回应：

1. 如果你认为这句话是观察，我们的意见不同。我认为"无缘无故"是评论。此外，我认为说约翰"发脾气"也是评论。他也许感到受伤、害怕、伤心……不带有评论的观察可以是："约翰告诉我他在生

3 Observing Without Evaluating

3. If you circled this number, we're in agreement that an observation was expressed without being mixed together with an evaluation.
4. If you circled this number, we're not in agreement. I consider "good man" to be an evaluation. An observation without evaluation might be: "For the last twenty-five years, my father has given one-tenth of his salary to charity."
5. If you circled this number, we're not in agreement. I consider "too much" to be an evaluation. An observation without evaluation might be: "Janice spent more than sixty hours at the office this week."
6. If you circled this number, we're not in agreement. I consider "aggressive" to be an evaluation. An observation without evaluation might be: "Henry hit his sister when she switched the television channel."
7. If you circled this number, we're in agreement that an observation was expressed without being mixed together with an evaluation.
8. If you circled this number, we're not in agreement. I consider "often" to be an evaluation. An observation without evaluation might be: "Twice this week my son didn't brush his teeth before going to bed."
9. If you circled this number, we're in agreement that an observation was expressed without being mixed together with an evaluation.
10. If you circled this number, we're not in agreement. I consider "complains" to be an evaluation. An observation without evaluation might be: "My aunt called me three times this week, and each time talked about people who treated her in ways she didn't like."

第三章　不带评论的观察

气。"或者是："约翰用拳头砸了一下桌子。"

2. 如果你认为这句话是观察，我们的意见一致，这是一个不带评论的观察。

3. 如果你认为这句话是观察，我们的意见一致，这是一个不带评论的观察。

4. 如果你认为这句话是观察，我们的意见不同。我认为"好人"是评论。不带评论的观察可以是："过去 25 年来，我的父亲将他收入的十分之一捐给了慈善事业。"

5. 如果你认为这句话是观察，我们的意见不同。我认为"太多"是评论。不带评论的观察可以是："这周詹尼斯在办公室工作了 60 小时以上。"

6. 如果你认为这句话是观察，我们的意见不同。我认为"强势"是评论。不带评论的观察可以是："亨利在妹妹切换电视频道时撞了她一下。"

7. 如果你认为这句话是观察，我们的意见一致，这是一个不带评论的观察。

8. 如果你认为这句话是观察，我们的意见不同。我认为"经常"是评论。不带评论的观察可以是："本周我的儿子有两次没有在睡觉前刷牙。"

9. 如果你认为这句话是观察，我们的意见一致，这是一个不带评论的观察。

10. 如果你认为这句话是观察，我们的意见不同。我认为"爱发牢骚"是评论。不带评论的观察可以是："这周我的姑姑给我打了 3 次电话，每次她都会说起别人用她不喜欢的方式对待她。"

3 Observing Without Evaluating

The Mask

Always a mask
Held in the slim hand whitely
Always she had a mask before her
face—

Truly the wrist
Holding it lightly
Fitted the task:
Sometimes however
Was there a shiver,
Fingertip quiver,
Ever so slightly—
Holding the mask?

For years and years and years I
wondered
But dared not ask
And then—
I blundered,
Looked behind the mask,
To find
Nothing—
She had no face.

She had become
Merely a hand
Holding a mask
With grace.

—Author unknown

面具

总有一副面具
由纤细白皙的手举着,
在她的脸前。
那轻握面具的手腕
甚是老练。
然而,是否有时,
会有颤抖的一刻,
举着面具的指尖
略微地松动呢?
年复一年,我不禁好奇,
但不敢问
终于
无意中
窥见了面具背后
却什么也没有。
她没有脸孔。
她已成了
优雅地
举着面具的手。
——佚名

3 Observing Without Evaluating

The more we use words that in any way imply criticism, the more difficult it is for people to stay connected to the beauty within themselves.

第四章

体会与表达感受

Identifying and Expressing Feelings

The first component of NVC is to observe without evaluating; the second component is to express how we are feeling. Psychoanalyst Rollo May suggests that "the mature person becomes able to differentiate feelings into as many nuances, strong and passionate experiences, or delicate and sensitive ones as in the different passages of music in a symphony." For many of us, however, our feelings are, as May would describe it, "limited like notes in a bugle call."

The Heavy Cost of Unexpressed Feelings

Our repertoire of words for calling people names is often larger than our vocabulary of words to clearly describe our emotional states. I went through twenty-one years of American schools and can't recall anyone in all that time ever asking me how I felt. Feelings were simply not considered important. What was valued was "the right way to think"—as defined by those who held positions of rank and authority. We are trained to be "other-directed" rather than to be in contact with ourselves. We learn to be "up in our head," wondering, "What is it that others think is right for me to say and do?"

An interaction I had with a teacher when I was about nine years old demonstrates how alienation from our feelings can begin. I once hid myself in a classroom after school because some boys were waiting outside to beat me up. A teacher spotted me

第四章　体会与表达感受

非暴力沟通的第一个要素是不带评论的观察；第二个要素则是如何表达内心的感受。心理治疗师罗洛·梅（Rollo May）认为："成熟的人能捕捉到感受的细微差别，不论是强烈热忱的，还是微妙细腻的，就好像聆听交响乐的不同乐章。"然而对许多人来说，我们所能体会的感受就如他所描述的，"像军号上的音符一样单调"。

压抑感受的代价

相比形容感受的词汇数量，我们用来评论他人的词汇通常要多得多。我在美国上了21年学，却想不起有什么人问过我的感受。人们认为感受是无关紧要的，重要的是各种权威所界定的"正确思考方式"。我们被训练成以他人为导向，而非聆听自己。我们逐渐习惯于考虑："人们期待我怎样说话和做事？"

我们是如何开始与感受渐行渐远的呢？回想起我9岁那年，有一天放学后，我躲在教室里，想要避开在校外等着打我的几个男生。一位老师发现了我，让我离开学校。当我告诉她我很害怕时，她斩钉截铁地对

4 Identifying and Expressing Feelings

and asked me to leave the school. When I explained I was afraid to go, she declared, "Big boys don't get frightened." A few years later I received further reinforcement through my participation in athletics. It was typical for coaches to value athletes willing to "give their all" and continue playing no matter how much physical pain they were in. I learned the lesson so well I once continued playing baseball for a month with an untreated broken wrist.

At an NVC workshop, a college student spoke about being kept awake by a roommate who played the stereo late at night and loudly. When asked to express what he felt when this happened, the student replied, "I feel that it isn't right to play music so loud at night." I pointed out that when he followed the word *feel* with the word *that*, he was expressing an opinion but not revealing his feelings. Asked to try again to express his feelings, he responded, "I feel, when people do something like that, it's a personality disturbance." I explained that this was still an opinion rather than a feeling. He paused thoughtfully, and then announced with vehemence, "I have no feelings about it whatsoever!"

This student obviously had strong feelings. Unfortunately, he didn't know how to become aware of his feelings, let alone express them. This difficulty in identifying and expressing feelings is common, and in my experience, especially so among lawyers, engineers, police officers, corporate managers, and career military personnel—people whose professional codes discourage them from manifesting emotions. For families, the toll is severe when members are unable to communicate emotions. Country singer Reba McEntire wrote a song after her father's death, and titled it "The Greatest Man I Never Knew." In so doing, she undoubtedly expressed the sentiments of many people who were never able to establish the emotional connection they would have liked with their fathers.

I regularly hear statements like, "I wouldn't want you to get the wrong idea—I'm married to a wonderful man—but I never know what he is feeling." One such dissatisfied woman brought her spouse to a workshop, during which she told him, "I feel like I'm

第四章　体会与表达感受

我说："男孩子不要胆小怕事！"几年后，作为运动员，我的感受更显得微不足道。教练们评估运动员的方式是他们是否拼尽了全力，即使身体疼痛，也在继续迎战。有一次我的手腕骨折，我没有接受任何治疗，依然忍痛坚持了一个月的棒球训练。

在一次工作坊上，一位大学生提到他的室友在夜晚将音响开得很大声，一整夜他都无法入睡。我询问他对此事的感受，他说："我觉得晚上把音乐放得这么大声是不对的。"我提醒他，虽然他用了"觉得"这个词，但他所表达的是他的想法，而非感受。我请他再次试着表达感受。这一次，他说："我觉得，那样做会打扰到别人。"我向他解释，这依然是一个想法而非感受。他想了想，激动地大声说："我对这件事情没有任何感受可言！"

很明显，这位学生有着强烈的感受。遗憾的是，他体会不到感受，更不用说表达了。对许多人来说，体会和表达感受并不容易，对律师、工程师、警察、企业经理人、军人尤为困难，流露情感与他们的职业形象相冲突。而在家庭中，家人之间无法交流情感，是很悲哀的。乡村歌手瑞芭·麦克英特尔（Reba McEntire）在父亲过世时写了一首歌，名为《我未曾认识的伟大人物》。许多人渴望与父亲建立情感连结，却从未能做到，她表达的正是这样一份感伤。

我经常听到这样的说法："请别误会我的意思，我的先生是个很棒的男人，只不过我从来不知道他有什么感受。"有一次，一位女士将先生带到了工作坊中，上课时，她对他说："我觉得我就像嫁给了一堵墙。"而这位先生的反应真的像极了一堵墙，他坐在那里一动不动、一言不发。恼羞成怒的太太转向我大声说："你看！他永远都是这样，坐在那里，一句话也不说。我真的像在和一堵墙过日子。"

4 Identifying and Expressing Feelings

married to a wall." The husband then did an excellent imitation of a wall: he sat mute and immobile. Exasperated, she turned to me and exclaimed, "See! This is what happens all the time. He sits and says nothing. It's just like living with a wall."

"It sounds to me like you are feeling lonely and wanting more emotional contact with your husband," I responded. When she agreed, I tried to show how statements such as "I feel like I'm living with a wall" are unlikely to bring her feelings and desires to her husband's attention. In fact, they are more likely to be heard as criticism than as invitations to connect with our feelings. Furthermore, such statements often lead to self-fulfilling prophecies. A husband, for example, hears himself criticized for behaving like a wall; he is hurt and discouraged and doesn't respond, thereby confirming his wife's image of him as a wall.

The benefits of strengthening our feelings vocabulary are evident not only in intimate relationships but also in the professional world. I was once hired to consult with members of a technological department of a large Swiss corporation; they were troubled by the discovery that workers in other departments were avoiding them. When asked, employees from other departments responded, "We hate going there to consult with those people. It's like talking to a bunch of machines!" The problem abated when I spent time with the members of the technological department, encouraging them to express more of their humanness in their communications with co-workers.

In another instance, I was working with hospital administrators who were anxious about a forthcoming meeting with the hospital's physicians. The administrators were eager to have me demonstrate how they might use NVC when approaching the physicians for support for a project that had only recently been turned down by a vote of 17 to 1.

Assuming the voice of an administrator in a role-playing session, I opened with, "I'm feeling frightened to be bringing up this issue." I chose to start this way because I sensed how frightened the administrators were as they prepared to confront the physicians on

第四章　体会与表达感受

"你是不是感到孤单，想要和先生有更多情感上的交流？"我回应她。在她表示认同后，我尝试让她理解，类似"我觉得我就像嫁给了一堵墙"这样的话，不太可能让她的先生明白她的感受与渴望，反而更容易认为她在批评他。并且，这类话语最后往往会真的应验，也就是说，当先生听到太太批评他"像一堵墙"时，会感到委屈和气馁，因而不愿意做出回应。这样一来，先生像是一堵墙的印象便会在太太心中进一步得到强化。

提升表达感受的能力不仅有利于促进我们的亲密关系，对职场关系也会有帮助。一次，我为一家瑞士大公司的技术部门做咨询。他们面临的困扰是，其他部门的同事不愿和他们打交道。在接受访问时，其他部门的同事表示："和他们说话就像对着一堆机器，所以我们不喜欢找他们咨询问题。"于是，我鼓励技术部门的成员在与同事们沟通时更多地表达他们的感受，之后情况就改善了。

还有一次，我应邀为一所医院的行政管理层担任顾问。他们有一个计划需要医生的支持，但在不久前，医生们以 17:1 的投票否决了该计划。对于接下来和医生的对谈，管理层非常焦虑，期盼着我能向他们展示如何使用非暴力沟通来取得医生的支持。

在模拟管理层与医生的对话时，我首先扮演了一名行政管理人员来开启谈话："再一次提出这个计划，我感到非常惶恐。"之所以选择了这样的开场白，是因为我体会到管理层对于和医生重启协商有着诸多害怕。但我还没来得及往下说，一位负责人便打断了我并抗议道："这太不切实际了！我们决不能告诉医生们我们有多么害怕。"

当我问他为何不能承认自己的感受时，他毫不犹豫地答道："一旦我们示弱，他们会将我们批得体无完肤。"对于他的回答，我并不意外。

4 Identifying and Expressing Feelings

this topic again. Before I could continue, one of the administrators stopped me to protest, "You're being unrealistic! We could never tell the physicians that we were frightened."

When I asked why an admission of fear seemed so impossible, he replied without hesitation, "If we admitted we're frightened, then they would just pick us to pieces!" His answer didn't surprise me; I have often heard people say they cannot imagine ever expressing feelings at their workplace. I was pleased to learn, however, that one of the administrators did decide to risk expressing his vulnerability at the dreaded meeting. Departing from his customary manner of appearing strictly logical, rational, and unemotional, he chose to state his feelings together with his reasons for wanting the physicians to change their position. He noticed how differently the physicians responded to him. In the end he was amazed and relieved when, instead of "picking him to pieces," the physicians reversed their previous position and voted 17 to 1 to support the project instead. This dramatic turn-around helped the administrators realize and appreciate the potential impact of expressing vulnerability—even in the workplace.

> Expressing our vulnerability can help resolve conflicts.

Finally, let me share a personal incident that taught me the effects of hiding our feelings. I was teaching a course in NVC to a group of inner city students. When I walked into the room the first day, the students, who had been enjoying a lively conversation with each other, became quiet. "Good morning!" I greeted. Silence. I felt very uncomfortable, but was afraid to express it. Instead, I proceeded in my most professional manner: "For this class, we will be studying a process of communication that I hope you will find helpful in your relationships at home and with your friends."

I continued to present information about NVC, but no one seemed to be listening. One girl, rummaging through her bag, fished out a file and began vigorously filing her nails. Students near the windows glued their faces to the panes as if fascinated by what was going on in the street below. I felt increasingly more uncomfortable, yet continued to say nothing about it. Finally, a

第四章　体会与表达感受

对许多人来说,在工作中表达感受是无法想象的事情。不过,让我感到颇为欣慰的是,有一位负责人还是决定鼓起勇气尝试表达他的心情、袒露他的脆弱。于是,他没有像惯常那样理性又冷静地陈述观点,而是选择了表达他的心情,说明他为何希望医生们能改变立场。会议最后,医生们非但没有将他"批得体无完肤",还改变了之前的立场,并且投票通过了该计划。这戏剧性的转变让管理层意识到,即使在工作中展现脆弱也是有积极影响的。

最后,我想分享我亲历的一场冲突事件,它让我明白压抑感受可能会带来的后果。那时我正在为市中心贫民区一所学校的学生讲授非暴力沟通。第一天,我一走进教室,学生们停下热火朝天的交谈,突然安静下来。"早上好!"我向他们打招呼。依然是一片沉默。我开始感到不自在,却又不好意思说出来。于是,我保持着职业形象继续上课。"本节课中,我们将要学习一种沟通方法。我希望它能促进你们的家庭和睦,增进朋友间的友谊。"

我继续介绍着非暴力沟通的内容,但似乎没有人在听课。有个女生翻了一通她的包,掏出一把指甲刀,开始起劲地修起了指甲。靠窗的学生则转脸趴在玻璃窗上,好像街上有特别吸引人的事。我越发觉得不自在,但还是什么都没说。终于,有位学生(他显然比我更勇敢)突然大声说道:"你讨厌黑人,不是吗?"我吃惊地愣了一下,却很快意识到,我试图隐藏我的不安导致了学生们对我的看法。

"我确实很紧张,"我告诉他们,"但并不是因为你们是黑人,而是因为我和大家是初次见面,当我走进教室时特别希望能得到你们的接纳。"当我表达了自己脆弱的一面,学生们的态度便有了明显的改变。他们开始问问题,介绍他们自己,并开始对非暴力沟通表现出好奇。

student who had certainly more courage than I was demonstrating, piped up, "You just hate being with black people, don't you?" I was stunned, yet immediately realized how I had contributed to this student's perception by trying to hide my discomfort.

"I *am* feeling nervous," I admitted, "but not because you are black. My feelings have to do with my not knowing anyone here and wanting to be accepted when I came in the room." My expression of vulnerability had a pronounced effect on the students. They started to ask questions about me, to tell me things about themselves, and to express curiosity about NVC.

Feelings versus Non-Feelings

A common confusion, generated by the English language, is our use of the word *feel* without actually expressing a feeling. For example, in the sentence, "I feel I didn't get a fair deal," the words *I feel* could be more accurately replaced with *I think*. In general, feelings are not being clearly expressed when the word *feel* is followed by:

1. Words such as *that, like, as if*:
   "I feel *that* you should know better."
   "I feel *like* a failure."
   "I feel *as if* I'm living with a wall."

   > Distinguish feelings from thoughts.

2. The pronouns *I, you, he, she, they, it*:
   "I feel *I* am constantly on call."
   "I feel *it* is useless."

3. Names or nouns referring to people:
   "I feel *Amy* has been pretty responsible."
   "I feel *my boss* is being manipulative."

Conversely, in the English language, it is not necessary to use the word *feel* at all when we are actually expressing a feeling: we can say, "I'm feeling irritated," or simply, "I'm irritated."

> Distinguish between what we feel and what we think we are.

区分感受与想法

我们使用语言的习惯时常会引发这样一个混淆,在使用"觉得/感到/感觉"这类词时,我们实际上并没有在表达感受。例如,在"我觉得没有得到公平对待"这句话中,将"我觉得"换成"我认为"也许更恰当。在以下例子中,说话者在使用"觉得"时都并未准确地表达自己的感受。

1. 在"我感到/觉得"后加上一句话或类似"就像""好似"这样的词:

"我觉得你应该更懂事。"

"我觉得自己就像个失败者。"

"我觉得好像在和一堵墙生活。"

2. 在"我感到/觉得"后带上"我、你、他、她、他们、它"这些人称。

"我觉得自己一直在被使唤。"

"我觉得这样做是没有用的。"

3. 在"我感到/觉得"后加上指代他人的名称或者名词。

"我觉得艾米挺负责的。"

"我觉得我的上司很爱控制人。"

相反,实际在表达感受时,我们甚至可以完全不使用"感到/觉得"这个词。我们可以说"我觉得很恼火",也可以简单地说"我很恼火"。

4 Identifying and Expressing Feelings

In NVC, we distinguish between words that express actual feelings and those that describe *what we think we are*.

1. Description of what we *think* we are:
   "I feel *inadequate* as a guitar player."

   In this statement, I am assessing my ability as a guitar player, rather than clearly expressing my feelings.

2. Expressions of actual feelings:
   "I feel *disappointed* in myself as a guitar player."
   "I feel *impatient* with myself as a guitar player."
   "I feel *frustrated* with myself as a guitar player."

   The actual feeling behind my assessment of myself as "inadequate" could therefore be disappointment, impatience, frustration, or some other emotion.

Likewise, it is helpful to differentiate between words that describe what we think others are doing around us, and words that describe actual feelings. The following are examples of statements that are easily mistaken as expressions of feelings: in fact they reveal more *how we think others are behaving* than what we are actually feeling ourselves.

> **Distinguish between what we feel and how we think others react or behave toward us.**

1. "I feel *unimportant* to the people with whom I work."
   The word *unimportant* describes how I think others are evaluating me, rather than an actual feeling, which in this situation might be "I feel *sad*" or "I feel *discouraged*."

2. "I feel *misunderstood*."
   Here the word *misunderstood* indicates my assessment of the other person's level of understanding rather than an actual feeling. In this situation, I may be feeling *anxious* or *annoyed* or some other emotion.

第四章　体会与表达感受

在非暴力沟通中，我们需要区分：我们是在表达自己的感受，还是在表达对自己的想法。

1. 想法：

"我觉得作为一名吉他手，我弹得不够好。"

在这个句子中，我在评价自己作为吉他手的弹奏水平，而没有表达自己的感受。

2. 感受：

"想到我的吉他弹奏水平，我感到失望。"

"想到我的吉他弹奏水平，我感到着急。"

"想到我的吉他弹奏水平，我感到沮丧。"

当我认为自己"弹得不够好"时，背后的感受可能是失望、着急、沮丧或是别的情绪。

还有些表达被误认为是感受，实际上却是我们对他人的想法，以下是一些例子：

1. "我觉得我的同事看不起我。"

"看不起"是在描述想法，即我认为别人如何看待我，背后的感受也许是难过、挫败。

2. "我感到被误解。"

"被误解"是在描述想法，即我认为他人不了解我，背后的感受也许是焦虑、不快等。

3. "我感到受到了冷落。"

这句话同样是在对他人行为做出诠释。当我们正想一个人呆着时，"受到冷落"也许会让我们感到如释重负；但有时，如果我们很希望融入他人，则会感到伤心。

4 Identifying and Expressing Feelings

3. "I feel *ignored*."

   Again, this is more of an interpretation of the actions of others than a clear statement of how we are feeling. No doubt there have been times we thought we were being ignored and our feeling was *relief*, because we wanted to be left to ourselves. No doubt there were other times, however, when we felt *hurt* when we thought we were being ignored, because we had wanted to be involved.

Words like *ignored* express how we *interpret others*, rather than how we *feel*. Here is a sampling of such words:

abandoned	distrusted	put down
abused	interrupted	rejected
attacked	intimidated	taken for granted
betrayed	let down	threatened
boxed-in	manipulated	unappreciated
bullied	misunderstood	unheard
cheated	neglected	unseen
coerced	overworked	unsupported
co-opted	patronized	unwanted
cornered	pressured	used
diminished	provoked	

Building a Vocabulary for Feelings

In expressing our feelings, it helps to use words that refer to specific emotions, rather than words that are vague or general. For example, if we say, "I feel good about that," the word *good* could mean happy, excited, relieved, or a number of other emotions. Words such as *good* and *bad* prevent the listener from connecting easily with what we might actually be feeling.

The following lists have been compiled to help you increase your power to articulate feelings and clearly describe a whole range of emotional states.

表达想法而非感受的类似词语还有：

被抛弃	不受信任	被羞辱
受到虐待	被打断	被拒绝
受到攻击	受到恐吓	不受重视
受到背叛	被玩弄	受到要挟
被陷害	被操纵	不受赏识
受到霸凌	受到误解	不被理睬
受到欺骗	受到忽视	不被看见
受到胁迫	被挤压	不被支持
被差遣	被看不起	不被需要
被逼迫	被施压	被利用
被贬低	受到挑衅	

建立感受词汇表

使用具体而非模糊或笼统的情绪词汇，有助于我们表达感受。类似"好"与"坏"这样的词语很难让人明白我们的实际状态。例如，如果说"我感觉挺好"，"好"这个词相对宽泛，所表达的感受可能是高兴、兴奋，也可能是如释重负或别的。

以下列表有助于我们提升表达感受的能力，清晰描述各种情绪状态。

4 Identifying and Expressing Feelings

How we are likely to feel when our needs <u>are</u> being met

absorbed	engrossed	moved
adventurous	enlivened	optimistic
affectionate	enthusiastic	overjoyed
alert	excited	overwhelmed
alive	exhilarated	peaceful
amazed	expansive	perky
amused	expectant	pleasant
animated	exultant	pleased
appreciative	fascinated	proud
ardent	free	quiet
aroused	friendly	radiant
astonished	fulfilled	rapturous
blissful	glad	refreshed
breathless	gleeful	relaxed
buoyant	glorious	relieved
calm	glowing	satisfied
carefree	good-humored	secure
cheerful	grateful	sensitive
comfortable	gratified	serene
complacent	happy	spellbound
composed	helpful	splendid
concerned	hopeful	stimulated
confident	inquisitive	surprised
contented	inspired	tender
cool	intense	thankful
curious	interested	thrilled
dazzled	intrigued	touched
delighted	invigorated	tranquil
eager	involved	trusting
ebullient	joyous, joyful	upbeat
ecstatic	jubilant	warm
effervescent	keyed-up	wide-awake
elated	loving	wonderful
enchanted	mellow	zestful
encouraged	merry	
energetic	mirthful	

第四章　体会与表达感受

（1）当需要得到满足时，我们的感受可能是：

全神贯注 absorbed	聚精会神 engrossed	感动 moved
新奇 adventurous	活跃 enlivened	乐观 optimistic
深情 affectionate	热情 enthusiastic	大喜 over-joyed
机敏 alert	激动 excited	受宠若惊 overwhelmed
有活力 alive	兴奋 exhilarated	宁静 peaceful
惊奇 amazed	开朗 expansive	活泼 perky
开怀 amused	期盼 expectant	愉快 pleasant
生机勃勃 animated	兴高采烈 exultant	开心 pleased
感激 appreciative	着迷 fascinated	自豪 proud
热心 ardent	自在 free	安静 quiet
振作 aroused	友善 friendly	容光焕发 radiant
惊讶 astonished	满足 fulfilled	痴迷 rapturous
极为幸福 blissful	高兴 glad	神清气爽 refreshed
屏气敛息 breathless	欢呼雀跃 gleeful	放松 relaxed
快活 buoyant	明媚 glorious	如释重负 relieved
平静 calm	热情洋溢 glowing	满意 satisfied
无忧无虑 carefree	快乐 good-humored	安全 secure
开心 cheerful	感谢 grateful	敏感 sensitive
舒适 comfortable	心满意足 gratified	安详 serene
得意 complacent	幸福 happy	入迷 spellbound
镇静 composed	热心 helpful	心花怒放 splendid
关切 concerned	满怀希望 hopeful	激励 stimulated
自信 confident	感兴趣 inquisitive	惊喜 surprised

4 Identifying and Expressing Feelings

How we are likely to feel when our needs are **not** being met

afraid	disgusted	intense
aggravated	disheartened	irate
agitated	dismayed	irked
alarmed	displeased	irritated
aloof	disquieted	jealous
angry	distressed	jittery
anguished	disturbed	keyed-up
annoyed	downcast	lazy
anxious	downhearted	leery
apathetic	dull	lethargic
apprehensive	edgy	listless
aroused	embarrassed	lonely
ashamed	embittered	mad
beat	exasperated	mean
bewildered	exhausted	miserable
bitter	fatigued	mopey
blah	fearful	morose
blue	fidgety	mournful
bored	forlorn	nervous
brokenhearted	frightened	nettled
chagrined	frustrated	numb
cold	furious	overwhelmed
concerned	gloomy	panicky
confused	guilty	passive
cool	harried	perplexed
cross	heavy	pessimistic
dejected	helpless	puzzled
depressed	hesitant	rancorous
despairing	horrible	reluctant
despondent	horrified	repelled
detached	hostile	resentful
disaffected	hot	restless
disappointed	humdrum	sad
discouraged	hurt	scared
disenchanted	impatient	sensitive
disgruntled	indifferent	shaky

第四章　体会与表达感受

惬意 contented	受启发 inspired	柔软 tender
冷静 cool	热切 intense	欣慰 thankful
好奇 curious	趣味 interested	乐不可支 thrilled
倾倒 dazzled	迷住 intrigued	触动 touched
愉悦 delighted	精神焕发 invigorated	恬静 tranquil
热忱 eager	热衷 involved	满怀信任 trusting
奔放 ebullient	欢乐 joyous, joyful	乐观开朗 upbeat
欣喜若狂 ecstatic	欢腾 jubilant	温暖 warm
兴高采烈 effervescent	亢奋 keyed-up	清醒 wide-awake
欢欣鼓舞 elated	有爱心 loving	美妙 wonderful
陶醉 enchanted	甜美 mellow	热情高涨 zestful
受鼓舞 encouraged	轻快 merry	
精力充沛 energetic	欢喜 mirthful	

（2）当需要没有得到满足时，我们的感受可能是：

畏惧 afraid	烦躁 edgy	紧绷 overwhelmed
气恼 aggravated	惭愧 embarrassed	惊慌失措 panicky
焦躁 agitated	愤恨 embittered	被动 passive
惊慌 alarmed	恼火 exasperated	迷茫 perplexed
冷漠 aloof	耗尽 exhausted	悲观 pessimistic
愤怒 angry	精疲力竭 fatigued	苦思冥想 puzzled
痛苦 anguished	担忧 fearful	充满敌意 rancorous
烦扰 annoyed	坐立不安 fidgety	迟疑 reluctant
焦虑 anxious	愁苦 forlorn	排斥 repelled

4 Identifying and Expressing Feelings

shocked	terrified	upset
skeptical	tired	uptight
sleepy	troubled	vexed
sorrowful	uncomfortable	weary
sorry	unconcerned	wistful
spiritless	uneasy	withdrawn
startled	unglued	woeful
surprised	unhappy	worried
suspicious	unnerved	wretched
tepid	unsteady	

Summary

The second component necessary for expressing ourselves is feelings. By developing a vocabulary of feelings that allows us to clearly and specifically name or identify our emotions, we can connect more easily with one another. Allowing ourselves to be vulnerable by expressing our feelings can help resolve conflicts. NVC distinguishes the expression of actual feelings from words and statements that describe thoughts, assessments, and interpretations.

第四章 体会与表达感受

冷淡 apathetic	惊吓 frightened	仇恨 resentful
担心 apprehensive	懊恼 frustrated	躁动 restless
刺激 aroused	大怒 furious	难过 sad
羞愧 ashamed	低落 gloomy	害怕 scared
丧气 beat	内疚 guilty	敏感 sensitive
迷惑 bewildered	逼迫 harried	颤抖 shaky
苦涩 bitter	沉重 heavy	震惊 shocked
乏味 blah	无助 helpless	批判 skeptical
忧郁 blue	犹豫 hesitant	困乏 sleepy
无聊 bored	恐惧 horrified	哀痛 sorrowful
心碎 brokenhearted	敌对 hostile	歉意 sorry
屈辱 chagrined	灼热 hot	没有斗志 spiritless
寒冷 cold	单调 humdrum	失魂落魄 startled
忧虑 concerned	受伤 hurt	惊讶 surprised
困惑 confused	不耐烦 impatient	怀疑 suspicious
冷酷 cool	不在乎 indifferent	不冷不热 tepid
生气 cross	激烈 intense	惊恐 terrified
低落 dejected	怒气 irate	劳累 tired
抑郁 depressed	恼怒 irked	烦恼 troubled
绝望 despairing	激怒 irritated	不适 uncomfortable
沮丧 despondent	嫉妒 jealous	不感兴趣 unconcerned
抽离 detached	紧张不安 jittery	心神不宁 uneasy
不满 disaffected	激动不安 keyed-up	心烦意乱 unglued
失望 disappointed	懒散 lazy	不开心 unhappy

4 Identifying and Expressing Feelings

Exercise 2

EXPRESSING FEELINGS

If you would like to see whether we're in agreement about the verbal expression of feelings, circle the number in front of each of the following statements in which feelings are verbally expressed.

1. "I feel you don't love me."
2. "I'm sad that you're leaving."
3. "I feel scared when you say that."
4. "When you don't greet me, I feel neglected."
5. "I'm happy that you can come."
6. "You're disgusting."
7. "I feel like hitting you."
8. "I feel misunderstood."
9. "I feel good about what you did for me."
10. "I'm worthless."

Here are my responses for Exercise 2:

1. If you circled this number, we're not in agreement. I don't consider "you don't love me" to be a feeling. To me, it expresses what the speaker thinks the other person is feeling, rather than how the speaker is feeling. Whenever the words *I feel* are followed by the words *I, you, he, she, they, it, that, like,* or *as if,* what follows is generally not what I would consider to be a feeling. An expression of feeling in this case might be: "I'm sad," or "I'm feeling anguished."
2. If you circled this number, we're in agreement that a feeling was verbally expressed.

第四章 体会与表达感受

挫败 discouraged	疑虑 leery	气馁 unnerved
幻灭 disenchanted	倦怠 lethargic	不稳定 unsteady
不高兴 disgruntled	无精打采 listless	烦乱 upset
厌恶 disgusted	孤独 lonely	拘谨 uptight
灰心 disheartened	气愤 mad	棘手 vexed
惊愕 dismay	汗颜 mean	厌倦 weary
不快 displeased	郁闷 miserable	伤感 wistful
不安 disquieted	昏沉 mopey	退缩 withdrawn
苦恼 distressed	阴郁 morose	悲伤 woeful
麻烦 disturbed	哀悼 mournful	着急 worried
垂头丧气 downcast	紧张 nervous	糟糕 wretched
消沉 downhearted	心乱如麻 nettled	
沉闷 dull	麻木 numb	

小结

　　非暴力沟通的第二个要素是感受。通过建立表达感受的词汇表，我们可以更清晰明确地体会和表达感受，从而更好地与他人建立连结。允许自己表达感受、袒露脆弱，也会有助于化解冲突。此外，在非暴力沟通中，用来表达实际感受的语言和那些用来陈述想法、评论或诠释观点的语言是不同的。

4 Identifying and Expressing Feelings

3. If you circled this number, we're in agreement that a feeling was verbally expressed.
4. If you circled this number, we're not in agreement. I don't consider "neglected" to be a feeling. To me, it expresses what the speaker thinks the other person is doing to him or her. An expression of feeling might be: "When you don't greet me at the door, I feel lonely."
5. If you circled this number, we're in agreement that a feeling was verbally expressed.
6. If you circled this number, we're not in agreement. I don't consider "disgusting" to be a feeling. To me, it expresses how the speaker thinks about the other person, rather than how the speaker is feeling. An expression of feeling might be: "I feel disgusted."
7. If you circled this number, we're not in agreement. I don't consider "like hitting you" to be a feeling. To me, it expresses what the speaker imagines doing, rather than how the speaker is feeling. An expression of feeling might be: "I am furious at you."
8. If you circled this number, we're not in agreement. I don't consider "misunderstood" to be a feeling. To me, it expresses what the speaker thinks the other person is doing. An expression of feeling in this case might be: "I feel frustrated," or "I feel discouraged."
9. If you circled this number, we're in agreement that a feeling was verbally expressed. However, the word *good* is vague when used to convey a feeling. We can usually express our feelings more clearly by using other words, for example: *relieved, gratified,* or *encouraged.*
10. If you circled this number, we're not in agreement. I don't consider "worthless" to be a feeling. To me, it expresses how the speaker thinks about himself or herself, rather than how the speaker is feeling. An expression of feeling in this case might be: "I feel skeptical about my own talents," or "I feel wretched."

第四章　体会与表达感受

练习二：表达感受

下列的句子中,有哪些是在表达自己的感受呢?请标出这类句子,看看我们的意见是否一致。

1. "我觉得你不爱我。"
2. "你要离开了,我很伤心。"
3. "听你那么说,我感到害怕。"
4. "你没和我打招呼,我感到自己受到了冷落。"
5. "你能来,我真高兴。"
6. "你真令人厌恶。"
7. "我想要揍你。"
8. "我感到自己受到了误解。"
9. "你为我做那些事,我感觉很好。"
10. "我很没用。"

以下是我对练习二的回应:

1. 如果你认为这句话表达的是感受,我们的意见不一致。我认为"你不爱我"是对他人如何感受的判断,而不是感受。在"我感到"之后如果跟随的是我、你、他、她、他们、它、像、好似……通常都不是在表达感受。在这个例子中,我们可以这样来表达感受:"我很伤心"或"我感到很痛苦"。

2. 如果你认为这句话表达的是感受,我们的意见一致。

4 Identifying and Expressing Feelings

Use the words "I feel because I" to remind us that what we feel isn't because of what the other person did, but because of a choice I've made.

第四章 体会与表达感受

3. 如果你认为这句话表达的是感受，我们的意见一致。

4. 如果你认为这句话表达的是感受，我们的意见不一致。我认为"受到冷落"是对他人行为的判断，而非感受。我们可以这样来表达感受："我进来的时候，你没有和我打招呼，我感到孤单。"

5. 如果你认为这句话表达的是感受，我们的意见一致。

6. 如果你认为这句话表达的是感受，我们的意见不一致。我认为"令人厌恶"是对他人的想法，而非感受。我们可以这样来表达感受："我感到厌恶。"

7. 如果你认为这句话表达的是感受，我们的意见不一致。我认为"想要揍你"是说话人想要采取的行动，而非自己的感受。我们可以这样来表达感受："看到你刚才的行为，我很生气。"

8. 如果你认为这句话表达的是感受，我们的意见不一致。我认为"被误解"是对他人行为的判断，而非感受。我们可以这样来表达感受："我感到挫败"或"我很灰心"。

9. 如果你认为这句话表达的是感受，我们的意见不一致。"很好"这个词对于传递感受来说较为糢糊。我们可以借助其他的词语更清晰地表达感受，诸如欣慰、满足、鼓舞。

10. 如果你认为这句话表达的是感受，我们的意见不一致。我认为"没用"是对自己的评论，而非感受。我们可以这样来表达感受："想到我的能力，我感到怀疑"或"我觉得苦恼"。

4 Identifying and Expressing Feelings

The number one reason that we don't get our needs met, we don't express them. We express judgments. If we do express needs, the number two reasons we don't get our needs met, we don't make clear requests.

第五章

为自己的感受负责

人们之所以苦恼,并非因为事情本身,而是因为人们对事情的看法。
——爱比克泰德(Epictetus),古罗马哲学家

Taking Responsibility for Our Feelings

People are disturbed not by things, but by the view they take of them.

—Epictetus

Hearing a Negative Message: Four Options

The third component of NVC entails the acknowledgment of the root of our feelings. NVC heightens our awareness that what others say and do may be the *stimulus*, but never the *cause*, of our feelings. We see that our feelings result from how we *choose* to receive what others say and do, as well as from our particular needs and expectations in that moment. With this third component, we are led to accept responsibility for what we do to generate our own feelings.

> What others do may be the stimulus of our feelings, but not the cause.

When someone gives us a negative message, whether verbally or nonverbally, we have four options as to how to receive it. One option is to take it personally by hearing blame and criticism. For example, someone is angry and says, "You're the most self-centered person I've ever met!" If choosing to take it personally, we might react: "Oh, I should've been more sensitive!" We accept the other person's judgment and blame ourselves. We choose this option

> Four options for receiving negative messages:
>
> 1. blame ourselves.

105

第五章　为自己的感受负责

听到不中听的话有四种选择

非暴力沟通要我们意识到的是，他人的言行举止或许会激发我们的感受，但绝非产生这些感受的原因。感受源自我们如何看待他人的言行以及我们当时的需要和期待。

当他人通过语言或者非语言的方式向我们发出负面信息时，我们可以选择四种不同的方式来接收：

第一种选择是指责自己，将错误归咎到自己身上。例如，有人气愤地说："我从没见过像你这么自私的人！"如果选择认同对方的评判并且自我指责，我们也许就会表示："哦，我应该更体贴一点。"如此这般带给我们的感受是内疚、羞愧和压抑，我们的自尊心也会受到伤害。

第二种选择是指责对方，将错误归咎到对方身上。这时，我们也许会反驳对方说："你没有资格这么说！我总是考虑你的需要，你才自私呢！"此时我们通常会感到愤怒。

第三种选择是关注我们自己的感受和需要。我们会感到伤心，并发

5 Taking Responsibility for Our Feelings

at great cost to our self-esteem, for it inclines us toward feelings of guilt, shame, and depression.

A second option is to fault the speaker. For example, in response to "You're the most self-centered person I've ever met," we might protest: "You have no right to say that! I am always considering your needs. You're the one who is really self-centered." When we receive messages this way, and blame the speaker, we are likely to feel anger.

> 2. blame others.

When receiving negative messages, our third option would be to shine the light of consciousness on our own feelings and needs. Thus, we might reply, "When I hear you say that I am the most self-centered person you've ever met, I feel hurt, because I need some recognition of my efforts to be considerate of your preferences." By focusing attention on our own feelings and needs, we become conscious that our current feeling of hurt derives from a need for our efforts to be recognized.

> 3. sense our own feelings and needs.

Finally, a fourth option on receiving a negative message is to shine the light of consciousness on the *other* person's feelings and needs as they are currently expressed. We might for example ask, "Are you feeling hurt because you need more consideration for your preferences?"

> 4. sense others' feelings and needs.

We accept responsibility for our feelings, rather than blame other people, by acknowledging our own needs, desires, expectations, values, or thoughts. Note the difference between the following expressions of disappointment:

Example 1

A: "You disappointed me by not coming over last evening."

B: "I was disappointed when you didn't come over, because I wanted to talk over some things that were bothering me."

第五章 为自己的感受负责

现伤心的感受来自内在的需要——渴望自己的付出得到肯定。这时，我们也许会回应："听到你说'我从没见过像你这么自私的人'，我感到伤心，因为我渴望得到认可。我也在努力体贴你，希望这一点能得到你的认可。"

第四种选择是关注对方想要表达的感受和需要。这时，我们可能会问对方："你感到伤心，希望你的喜好能得到照顾，是吗？"

通过关注我们的需要、愿望、期待、价值观或想法，我们不再指责他人，而是为自身的感受负责。

在以下表达失望的例子中，请注意其中的差异：

例 1：
甲："昨晚你没来，让我很失望。"
乙："昨晚你没来，我很失望，因为我想要和你聊一些烦心事。"

在上面的例句中，甲把自己的失望完全归咎于对方的行为。而乙将他的失望归因于自己未被满足的需要。

例 2：
甲："他们撤销合同的做法让我很生气。"
乙："他们撤销了合同，我感到非常生气，因为我认为，这是极不负责的做法。"

在这个例子中，甲将自己的气恼归咎于他人的行为。而乙承认她的愤怒是由自己带有指责的想法所造成的，因此她为自己的感受承担了责任。非暴力沟通还会鼓励她进一步了解她想要什么：她有什么需要、渴望、期待、希望未能得到满足。我们越能将自己的感受和需要相连，他

5 Taking Responsibility for Our Feelings

Speaker A attributes responsibility for his disappointment solely to another person's action. Speaker B traces his feeling of disappointment to his own unfulfilled desire.

Example 2

A: "Their cancelling the contract really irritated me!"

B: "When they cancelled the contract, I felt really irritated because I was thinking to myself that it was an awfully irresponsible thing to do."

Speaker A attributes her irritation solely to the behavior of the other party, whereas Speaker B accepts responsibility for her feeling by acknowledging the thought behind it. She recognizes that her blaming way of thinking has generated her irritation. In NVC, however, we would urge this speaker to go a step further by identifying what she is wanting: what need, desire, expectation, hope, or value of hers has not been fulfilled? As we shall see, the more we are able to connect our feelings to our own needs, the easier it is for others to respond compassionately. To relate her feelings to what she is wanting, Speaker B might have said: "When they cancelled the contract, I felt really irritated because I was hoping for an opportunity to rehire the workers we laid off last year."

It is helpful to recognize a number of common speech patterns that tend to mask accountability for our own feelings:
1. Use of impersonal pronouns such as *it* and *that*:
   "It really infuriates me when spelling mistakes appear in our public brochures." "That bugs me a lot."
2. The use of the expression "I feel (an emotion) because . . . " followed by a person or personal pronoun other than *I*:
   "I feel hurt because you said you don't love me." "I feel angry because the supervisor broke her promise."
3. Statements that mention only the actions of others:
   "When you don't call me on my birthday, I feel hurt." "Mommy is disappointed when you don't finish your food."

第五章　为自己的感受负责

人就越容易对我们做出善意的回应。例如，乙可以这样表达："他们撤销了合同，我感到非常生气，因为我原本期盼着有机会能将去年辞退的工人们招回来。"

有些常见的语言模式容易掩盖我们对感受的责任，辨认出它们将有助于我们清晰表达。

1. 使用非人称代词，比如：这、它、那：
"我们公开发行的手册有拼写错误，这让我非常生气。"
"那太让我厌烦了。"
2. "我感到（某种情绪），因为（别人）……"：
"我感到伤心，因为你说你不爱我。"
"我感到愤怒，因为上司不守信用。"
3. 只提及他人的行为：
"你在我的生日那天没给我打电话，我感到伤心。"
"你没有把食物吃完，妈妈感到失望。"

为了让我们对自身所负的责任有更多的意识，我们可以替换成"我感到……因为我……"这样的句式来表达。例如：

1. "看到我们公开发行的手册有拼写错误，我感到非常生气，因为我希望公司呈现出专业的形象。"
2. "当上司违背了她的承诺，我感到愤怒，因为我原本希望用那个长假探望哥哥。"
3. "你没有把食物吃完，妈妈感到失望，因为我希望你身体强壮，

> Connect your feeling with your need: "I feel ... because I need ..."

In each of these instances, we can deepen our awareness of our own responsibility by substituting the phrase, "I feel ... because I ... " For example:

1. "*I feel* really infuriated when spelling mistakes like that appear in our public brochures, *because I* want our company to project a professional image."
2. "*I feel* angry that the supervisor broke her promise, *because I* was counting on getting that long weekend to visit my brother."
3. "*Mommy feels* disappointed when you don't finish your food, *because I* want you to grow up strong and healthy."

> Distinguish between giving from the heart and being motivated by guilt.

The basic mechanism of motivating by guilt is to attribute the responsibility for one's own feelings to others. When parents say, "It hurts Mommy and Daddy when you get poor grades at school," they are implying that the child's actions are the cause of the parents' happiness or unhappiness. On the surface, taking responsibility for the feelings of others can easily be mistaken for positive caring. It may appear that the child cares for the parent and feels bad because the parent is suffering. However, if children who assume this kind of responsibility change their behavior in accordance with parental wishes, they are not acting from the heart, but acting to avoid guilt.

The Needs at the Roots of Feelings

Judgments, criticisms, diagnoses, and interpretations of others are all alienated expressions of our needs. If someone says, "You never understand me," they are really telling us that their need to be understood is not being fulfilled. If a wife says, "You've been working late every night this week; you love your work more than you love

> Judgments of others are alienated expressions of our own unmet needs.

第五章　为自己的感受负责

健康成长。"

利用内疚感来推动他人的基本机制，是通过把自己的感受归咎于他人来实现的。家长也许会对孩子说："你成绩不好，让爸爸妈妈伤透了心！"言下之意，父母的幸福取决于孩子的行为。表面上看，让孩子为父母的感受负责似乎表现了孩子对父母的关心。孩子因为在意父母，而对父母的痛苦感到内疚。但是换一个角度想一下，孩子为了父母的感受而改变行为来迎合父母，那么改变也只是为了避免愧疚，而非出自真心。

需要：感受的根源

当我们评判、批评、分析或判断他人的言行时，实际上是在用疏离生命的方式表达自己的需要。如果有人说："你从不懂我。"他真正的心声是渴望得到理解。如果太太说："这星期你每天都工作到很晚，相比我，你更爱工作！"那她在诉说的是，亲密的需要未能得到满足。

当我们通过评判、判断和想象等方式间接地表达自己的需要时，他人很容易认为我们在批评他们，并随之启动自我辩护和反抗。我们越能直接说出感受以及相关联的需要，他人也越有可能对我们做出善意的回应。

不幸的是，大多数人从未学习过如何从"需要"的角度来思考。当需要未能得到满足时，我们习惯于认为是他人的错。例如，如果我们希望孩子把衣服收纳在衣橱里，而他们却丢在了沙发上，我们可能就

5 Taking Responsibility for Our Feelings

me," she is saying that her need for intimacy is not being met.

When we express our needs indirectly through the use of evaluations, interpretations, and images, others are likely to hear criticism. And when people hear anything that sounds like criticism, they tend to invest their energy in self-defense or counterattack. If we wish for a compassionate response from others, it is self-defeating to express our needs by interpreting or diagnosing their behavior. Instead, the more directly we can connect our feelings to our own needs, the easier it is for others to respond to us compassionately.

> If we express our needs, we have a better chance of getting them met.

Unfortunately, most of us have never been taught to think in terms of needs. We are accustomed to thinking about what's wrong with other people when our needs aren't being fulfilled. Thus, if we want coats to be hung up in the closet, we may characterize our children as lazy for leaving them on the couch. Or we may interpret our co-workers as irresponsible when they don't go about their tasks the way we would prefer them to.

I was once invited to Southern California to mediate between some landowners and migrant farm workers whose conflicts had grown increasingly hostile and violent. I began the meeting by asking these two questions: "What is it that you are each needing? And what would you like to request of the other in relation to these needs?"

"The problem is that these people are racist!" shouted a farm worker. "The problem is that these people don't respect law and order!" shouted a landowner even more loudly. As is often the case, these groups were more skilled in analyzing the perceived wrongness of others than in clearly expressing their own needs.

In a comparable situation, I once met with a group of Israelis and Palestinians who wanted to establish the mutual trust necessary to bring peace to their homelands. I opened the session with the same questions, "What is it you are needing and what would you like to request from one another in relation to those needs?" Instead of directly stating his needs, a Palestinian mukhtar (who is like a

第五章　为自己的感受负责

会说他们懒惰；如果我们不喜欢同事工作的方式，也许会指责他们不负责任。

有一次，我受邀到南加州调解一起农场主与外来工人间的冲突，双方的矛盾正愈演愈烈。会谈一开始，我向他们提出两个问题："你们各自的需要是什么？为了满足这些需要，你们想请求对方做什么？"

这时，一位外来工人喊道："他们就是一群种族歧视分子！"随即，一位农场主更大声地喊起来："他们这些人根本无视法律法规！"就像在大部分冲突事件中那样，人们更善于分析对方的错，而非清晰地表达自己的需要。

还有一次，我参与了一群以色列人和巴勒斯坦人的会面，他们希望能够建立互信，从而为家园带来和平。我在会议开始时问了同样的问题："你们各自的需要是什么？为了满足这些需要，你们想请求对方做什么？"一位巴勒斯坦村长直接说道："你们的所作所为和纳粹一样。"显然这样的话很难得到以色列人的配合。一位以色列妇女立即站起来反驳他："村长，这样的说法太不顾及我们的感受了。"

他们来这里原本是为了建立互信与和平，但会谈才刚开始，情况却变得更糟糕了。发生这样的情况，正是因为人们时常习惯于分析和指责他人，而非清晰地表达自己的需要。在这个例子中，如果这位妇女在回应村长时表达她的需要并向对方提出请求，她也许可以说："希望在对话中，我们能互相尊重。与其表达你对我们行为的看法，倒不如请你说一说，我们有哪些做法让你感到不舒服？"

根据我的经验，一旦人们开始谈论自己的需要而非相互指责，就更有可能找到满足大家需要的办法。以下是我们每个人共有的基本需要：

village mayor) answered, "You people are acting like a bunch of Nazis." A statement like that is not likely to get the cooperation of a group of Israelis! Almost immediately, an Israeli woman jumped up and countered, "Mukhtar, that was a totally insensitive thing for you to say!"

Here were people who had come together to build trust and harmony, but after only one interchange, matters were worse than before they began. This happens often when people are used to analyzing and blaming one another rather than clearly expressing what they need. In this case, the woman could have responded to the mukhtar in terms of her own needs and requests by saying, for example, "I am needing more respect in our dialogue. Instead of telling us how you think we are acting, would you tell us what it is we are doing that you find disturbing?"

It has been my experience over and over again that from the moment people begin talking about what they need rather than what's wrong with one another, the possibility of finding ways to meet everybody's needs is greatly increased. The following are some of the basic human needs we all share:

Autonomy
- to choose one's dreams, goals, values
- to choose one's plan for fulfilling one's dreams, goals, values

Celebration
- to celebrate the creation of life and dreams fulfilled
- to celebrate losses: loved ones, dreams, etc. (mourning)

Integrity
- authenticity
- creativity
- meaning
- self-worth

Interdependence
- acceptance
- appreciation
- closeness
- community
- consideration
- contribution to the enrichment of life (to exercise one's power by giving that which contributes to life)

第五章　为自己的感受负责

自主选择（Autonomy）

- 选择梦想、目标和价值
  To choose one's dreams, goals, values
- 选择实现梦想、目标和价值的方法
  To choose one's plan for fulfilling one's dreams, goals, values

内外一致（Integrity）

- 真实
  Authenticity
- 意义
  Meaning
- 创造力
  Creativity
- 自我价值
  Self-worth

庆祝/哀悼（Celebration）

- 庆祝人生的创造和梦想的实现
  To celebrate the creation of life and dreams fulfilled
- 哀悼失去：亲人离世、梦想破灭，等等
  To celebrate losses: loved ones, dreams, etc.(mourning)

相互依存（Interdependence）

- 接纳
  Acceptance
- 亲近
  Closeness
- 体谅
  Consideration
- 心理安全
  Emotional Safety
- 欣赏
  Appreciation
- 社群
  Community
- 服务生命
  Contribute to the enrichment of life
- 同理
  Empathy

Interdependence (continued)
- emotional safety
- empathy
- honesty (the empowering honesty that enables us to learn from our limitations)
- love
- reassurance
- respect
- support
- trust
- understanding
- warmth

Play
- fun
- laughter

Spiritual Communion
- beauty
- harmony
- inspiration
- order
- peace

Physical Nurturance
- air
- food
- movement, exercise
- protection from life-threatening forms of life: viruses, bacteria, insects, predatory animals
- rest
- sexual expression
- shelter
- touch
- water

The Pain of Expressing Our Needs versus the Pain of Not Expressing Our Needs

In a world where we're often judged harshly for identifying and revealing our needs, doing so can be very frightening. Women, in particular, are susceptible to criticism. For centuries, the image of the loving woman has been associated with sacrifice and the denial of one's own needs to take care of others. Because women are socialized to view the caretaking of others as their highest duty, they often learn to ignore their own needs.

At one workshop, we discussed what happens to women who internalize such beliefs. These women, if they ask for what they want, will often do so in a way that both reflects and reinforces the beliefs that they have no genuine right to their needs and that

- 诚实（有力量的诚实，可以让我们从自身的局限中得以学习）
  Honesty (the empowering honesty that enables us to learn from our limitations)
- 确认
  Reassurance
- 支持
  Support
- 理解
  Understanding

精神交融（Spiritual Communion）
- 美
  Beauty
- 启迪
  Inspiration
- 和平
  Peace

玩耍（Play）
- 乐趣
  Fun

滋养身体（Physical Nurturance）
- 空气
  Air

- 爱
  Love
- 尊重
  Respect
- 信任
  Trust
- 温暖
  Warmth

- 和谐
  Harmony
- 秩序
  Order

- 欢笑
  Laughter

- 食物
  Food

5 Taking Responsibility for Our Feelings

their needs are unimportant. For example, because she is fearful of asking for what she needs, a woman may fail to simply say that she's had a busy day, is feeling tired, and wants some time in the evening to herself; instead, her words come out sounding like a legal case: "You know I haven't had a moment to myself all day. I ironed all the shirts, did the whole week's laundry, took the dog to the vet, made dinner, packed the lunches, and called all the neighbors about the block meeting, so [imploringly] . . . so how about if you . . . ?"

"No!" comes the swift response. Her plaintive request elicits resistance rather than compassion from her listeners. They have difficulty hearing and valuing the needs behind her pleas, and furthermore react negatively to her weak attempt to argue from a position of what she "should" get or "deserves" to get from them. In the end the speaker is again persuaded that her needs don't matter, not realizing that they were expressed in a way unlikely to draw a positive response.

> If we don't value our needs, others may not either.

My mother was once at a workshop where other women were discussing how frightening it was to be expressing their needs. Suddenly she got up and left the room, and didn't return for a long time. She finally reappeared, looking very pale. In the presence of the group, I asked, "Mother, are you all right?"

"Yes," she answered, "but I just had a sudden realization that's very hard for me to take in."

"What's that?"

"I've just become aware that for thirty-six years, I was angry with your father for not meeting my needs, and now I realize that I never once clearly told him what I needed."

My mother's revelation was accurate. Not one time, that I can remember, did she clearly express her needs to my father. She'd hint around and go through all kinds of convolutions, but never would she ask directly for what she needed.

We tried to understand why it was so hard for her to have done so. My mother grew up in an economically impoverished family. She recalled asking for things as a child and being admonished by her brothers and sisters, "You shouldn't ask for that! You know

第五章　为自己的感受负责

- 运动，锻炼
  Movement, exercise

- 休息
  Rest
- 住所
  Shelter
- 水
  Water

- 保护（免受病毒、细菌、昆虫及食肉动物的威胁）
  Protection from life-threatening forms of life: Viruses, bacteria, insects, Predatory animals
- 性表达
  Sexual expression
- 触摸
  Touch

说出需要

在我们身处的世界中，我们时常会因为袒露自身需要而遭到强烈的评判，因而对表达需要感到害怕。对女性来说，尤其如此。长期以来，女性的形象就与照顾他人、自我牺牲和压抑需要相连。在社会文化的熏陶之下，女性也已经把照顾他人视为自己的最高职责，因而学会了无视自己的需要。

有一次我们在工作坊中展开讨论，女性若将这些社会教养固化成内在信念，对她们意味着什么？我们可以从许多妇女主张自己的方式中看到，她们并不相信自己有权满足自己的需要，甚至认为自己的需要无足

we're poor. Do you think you are the only person in the family?" Eventually she grew to fear that asking for what she needed would only lead to disapproval and judgment.

She related a childhood anecdote about one of her sisters who had had an appendix operation and afterwards had been given a beautiful little purse by another sister. My mother was fourteen at the time. Oh, how she yearned to have an exquisitely beaded purse like her sister's, but she dared not open her mouth. So guess what? She feigned a pain in her side and went the whole way with her story. Her family took her to several doctors. They were unable to produce a diagnosis and so opted for exploratory surgery. It had been a bold gamble on my mother's part, but it worked—she was given an identical little purse! When she received the coveted purse, my mother was elated despite being in physical agony from the surgery. Two nurses came in and one stuck a thermometer in her mouth. My mother said, "Ummm, ummm," to show the purse to the second nurse, who answered, "Oh, for me? Why, thank you!" and took the purse! My mother was at a loss, and never figured out how to say, "I didn't mean to give it to you. Please return it to me." Her story poignantly reveals how painful it can be when people don't openly acknowledge their needs.

From Emotional Slavery to Emotional Liberation

In our development toward a state of emotional liberation, most of us experience three stages in the way we relate to others.

Stage 1: In this stage, which I refer to as *emotional slavery*, we believe ourselves responsible for the feelings of others. We think we must constantly strive to keep everyone happy. If they don't appear happy, we feel responsible and compelled to do something about it. This can easily lead us to see the very people who are closest to us as burdens.

Taking responsibility for the feelings of others can be very detrimental to intimate relationships. I routinely hear variations on the following theme: "I'm really scared to be in a relationship.

第五章　为自己的感受负责

轻重。这样的信念还会不断被强化，例如，因为害怕表达自己的需要，一个女人可能不会直接说："我今天累坏了，想要晚上歇一会儿。"相反，她的话听起来也许就像辩护词，她会念叨："你知道我一整天都没歇过，我熨了所有的衬衣，把这周的脏衣服都洗了，带狗去看了宠物医生，准备了午餐便当，又做了晚餐，打电话给所有的邻居通知街区会议。所以（以一种近乎哀求的口吻）……你是否可以……？"

她这样哀怨地尝试证明自己"应当"获得某种权利，这非但不能引发听者的善意，反而使他们心生抗拒，于是对方立刻回应："不行！"对方既没有听到恳请背后的需要，还报以了负面的回应。最终，她们将再次说服自己：我的需要微不足道。实际上，如果直接说出自己的需要，她们则更有可能获得积极的回应。

我母亲曾参加过一次工作坊，期间一些女士谈到她们是如何害怕表达个人需要的，突然，她站起来走出房间，过了很久都没有回来。再次出现的时候，她看上去脸色苍白。我问她："妈妈，你还好吗？"

"没事，"她回答说，"刚才我意识到一件事情，心里极为难受。"

"什么事情？"

"36 年来，我一直生你父亲的气，我认为他不在乎我的需要。此刻我才意识到，我从没有清楚地告诉他我想要什么。"

是的。在我的记忆中，她从未直接向父亲说出过她的需要，而是以各种方式暗示或拐弯抹角地表达自己。

我们试着了解为什么这对她来说如此困难。母亲回忆起，她生长在一个贫穷的家庭，小时候想要什么东西时，哥哥和姐姐们就会责备她："你知道家里很穷，怎么还这么贪心！你以为家里就你一个人吗？"于是，长大后的她因为害怕遭到反对与评判，便不敢再说出她的需要。

5 Taking Responsibility for Our Feelings

> **First stage: Emotional slavery.** We see ourselves responsible for others' feelings.

Every time I see my partner in pain or needing something, I feel overwhelmed. I feel like I'm in prison, that I'm being smothered—and I just have to get out of the relationship as fast as possible." This response is common among those who experience love as denial of one's own needs in order to attend to the needs of the beloved. In the early days of a relationship, partners typically relate joyfully and compassionately to each other out of a sense of freedom. The relationship is exhilarating, spontaneous, wonderful. Eventually, however, as the relationship becomes "serious," partners may begin to assume responsibility for each other's feelings.

If I were a partner who is conscious of doing this, I might acknowledge the situation by explaining, "I can't bear it when I lose myself in relationships. When I see my partner's pain, I lose me, and then I just have to break free." However, if I have not reached this level of awareness, I am likely to blame my partner for the deterioration of the relationship. Thus I might say, "My partner is so needy and dependent it's really stressing out our relationship."

In such a case, my partner would do well to reject the notion that there is anything wrong with her needs. It would only make a bad situation worse to accept that blame. Instead, she could offer an empathic response to the pain of my emotional slavery: "So you find yourself in panic. It's very hard for you to hold on to the deep caring and love we've had without turning it into a responsibility, duty, obligation. . . . You sense your freedom closing down because you think you constantly have to take care of me." If, however, instead of an empathic response, she says, "Are you feeling tense because I have been making too many demands on you?" then both of us are likely to stay enmeshed in emotional slavery, making it that much more difficult for the relationship to survive.

Stage 2: In this stage, we become aware of the high costs of assuming responsibility for others' feelings and trying to accommodate them at our own expense. When we notice how much of our lives we've missed and how little we have responded

123

还有一次，她的妹妹在阑尾手术后得到了一个漂亮的小钱包。那年14岁的母亲也梦寐以求有那样一只绣着珠子的美丽钱包，却不敢开口。猜猜她接下来做了什么？她假装肚子痛。家人带她看了几个医生，都无法给出诊断，于是决定做开腹手术。这是一场多么大胆的赌博啊！最后她如愿以偿得到了一只一模一样的小钱包。尽管还带着手术的剧烈疼痛，母亲却欣喜若狂。此时两位护士走进病房，一位将体温计放进她的嘴里。我的母亲发出唔唔的声音想把钱包展示给另一位护士看。护士对她说："这是给我的吗？为什么？那谢谢了！"随即收下了钱包。我的母亲顿时陷入了茫然，又不知道如何说出心里话：我并没有要给你的意思，请把它还给我。这是个如此不幸的故事，一个人如果无法说出自己的需要，会造成何等痛苦的后果。

从情绪的奴隶到主人的自由之路

在通往情绪自由的成长过程中，我们通常会经历三个阶段。

第一阶段："情绪的奴隶"

在这个阶段，我们认为要为他人的感受负责，必须不断努力让所有人开心。如果别人不开心了，我们会感到不安，认为自己有责任要为此做些什么。因而，我们很可能会把亲近的人看作负担。

这对亲密关系非常有害。我常听人们说类似的话："我真的很害怕谈恋爱。每次看到伴侣处于痛苦之中，我就会受不了，感觉自己就像在坐牢，仿佛快要窒息了，只想尽快摆脱关系。"他们所认为的爱情，是

5 Taking Responsibility for Our Feelings

to the call of our own soul, we may get angry. I refer jokingly to this stage as the *obnoxious stage* because we tend toward obnoxious comments like, "That's *your* problem! *I'm* not responsible for your feelings!" when presented with another person's pain.

> Second stage: The obnoxious stage. We feel angry; we no longer want to be responsible for others' feelings.

We are clear what we are not responsible *for*, but have yet to learn how to be responsible *to* others in a way that is not emotionally enslaving.

As we emerge from the stage of emotional slavery, we may continue to carry remnants of fear and guilt around having our own needs. Thus it is not surprising that we end up expressing our needs in ways that sound rigid and unyielding to the ears of others. For example, during a break in one of my workshops, a young woman expressed appreciation for the insights she'd gained into her own state of emotional enslavement. When the workshop resumed, I suggested an activity to the group. The same young woman then declared assertively, "I'd rather do something else." I sensed she was exercising her newfound right to express her needs—even if they ran counter to those of others.

To encourage her to sort out what she wanted, I asked, "Do you want to do something else even if it conflicts with my needs?" She thought for a moment, and then stammered, "Yes. . . . er . . . I mean, no." Her confusion reflects how, in the obnoxious stage, we have yet to grasp that emotional liberation entails more than simply asserting our own needs.

I recall an incident during my daughter Marla's passage toward emotional liberation. She had always been the "perfect little girl" who denied her own needs to comply with the wishes of others. When I became aware of how frequently she suppressed her own desires in order to please others, I talked to her about how I'd enjoy hearing her express her needs more often. When we first broached the subject, Marla cried. "But, Daddy, I don't want to disappoint anybody!" she protested helplessly. I tried to show Marla how her honesty would be a gift more precious to others

放弃自己的需要来满足爱人的需要。刚谈恋爱时，伴侣通常能在自由的状态中欢喜友善地相处，这时的关系令人兴奋，融洽又美妙。然而，当关系变得"认真"起来，伴侣就开始为对方的喜怒哀乐承担起了责任。

如果我是亲密关系中的一方，当意识到这样的情况发生，我也许会承认："我无法忍受在关系中失去自己。当看到伴侣遭受痛苦，我就会丢掉自己，接着就想摆脱关系。"如果我意识不到自己正在承担对方的感受，便很有可能责怪对方破坏了关系，我可能会说："我的伴侣太黏人，这让我们的关系太紧张了。"

在这样的情形中，另一半大多要么抗拒指责，要么默默地收下了指责。后者更糟糕。其实，伴侣可以选择同理倾听我——一个正在经历痛苦的情绪奴隶："你想呵护我们的关系，又不想把它变为责任和义务，这巨大的挑战让你感到恐慌……你认为你必须要照顾好我，这让你感到失去了自由。"如果对方反过来指责我说："我的要求过分了吗？"那么，双方都很有可能沦为情绪的奴隶，让关系更加难以为继。

第二阶段："面目可憎"

在这个阶段，我们发现，为他人的感受负责并牺牲自己、成全对方，将会付出很大的代价。想到自己压抑了数不胜数的需要，鲜少按照内心的呼唤来行事，我们可能会感到愤怒。我把这个阶段戏称为"面目可憎"的阶段。因为此时的我们在面对他人的痛苦时，特别容易给出一些招人讨厌的回应，例如："这是你的问题！我不对你的感受负责！"我们已经清楚知道，自己并不为他人的感受负责，却还没有学会如何用一种不被情绪奴役的方式与他人互动。

虽然脱离了第一阶段，我们会意识到自己有需要，却可能还是会对

than accommodating them to prevent their upset. I also clarified ways she could empathize with people when they were upset without taking responsibility for their feelings.

A short time later, I saw evidence that my daughter was beginning to express her needs more openly. A call came from her school principal, apparently disturbed by a communication he'd had with Marla, who had arrived at school wearing overalls. "Marla," he'd said, "young women do not dress this way." To which Marla had responded, "Bug off!"

Hearing this was cause for celebration: Marla had graduated from emotional slavery to obnoxiousness! She was learning to express her needs and risk dealing with the displeasure of others. Surely she had yet to assert her needs comfortably and in a way that respected the needs of others, but I trusted this would occur in time.

Stage 3: At the third stage, *emotional liberation*, we respond to the needs of others out of compassion, never out of fear, guilt, or shame. Our actions are therefore fulfilling to us, as well as to those who receive our efforts. We accept full responsibility for our own intentions and actions, but not for the feelings of others. At this stage, we are aware that we can never meet our own needs at the expense of others. Emotional liberation involves stating clearly what we need in a way that communicates we are equally concerned that the needs of others be fulfilled. NVC is designed to support us in relating at this level.

> Third stage: Emotional liberation. We take responsibility for our intentions and actions.

Summary

The third component of NVC is the acknowledgment of the needs behind our feelings. What others say and do may be the stimulus for, but never the cause of, our feelings. When someone communicates negatively, we have four options as to how to receive the message: (1) blame ourselves, (2) blame others, (3) sense our own feelings and needs, (4) sense the feelings and needs hidden in the other person's negative message.

第五章　为自己的感受负责

怀有需要心存恐惧和羞愧。因而，会以一种听上去硬邦邦、不通人情的方式来表达自己的需要。有一次，一位年轻女士在工作坊休息期间向我表达感谢，说她很高兴认识到自己也曾是"情绪的奴隶"。工作坊重新开始后，我建议大家做一个练习，这位女士却斩钉截铁地说道："我宁可做点别的。"我意识到她正在行使新发现的权利——表达自己的需要，即使她采取的方式与他人的需要相冲突。

为了鼓励她理清自己想要什么，我问她："你想做点别的，即使那会与我的需要相冲突，是吗？"她想了片刻，接着有些结巴地说："是的……嗯……我的意思是……不是……"她的困惑正说明了，处于"面目可憎"阶段时，我们还未能意识到情绪自由不只是表达自己的需要。

这里，我想讲讲我的女儿玛拉在成长中的一段经历。一直以来，她是那个对他人的要求百依百顺的"完美小女孩"。意识到她时常为了讨好他人而压抑自己时，我想鼓励她更多地表达自己的需要。当我一开始谈到这个话题时，玛拉哭了，她无辜地申诉着："但是，爸爸，我不想让任何人失望。"我尝试让她明白，相比委曲求全，真诚待人是一份更加珍贵的礼物。同时我也向她展示了当他人生气时，她可以如何同理对方，而无须为他们的感受负责。

不久以后，我就发现玛拉开始有了变化。有一回，学校校长打电话给我，告诉我玛拉因为在学校的穿着与他发生了口角。校长对玛拉说："年轻女孩子不能这样穿衣服！"而玛拉却回答他："不关你什么事！"我可真想为之庆祝！玛拉正从"情绪的奴隶"成长为"面目可憎"！她开始敢于冒着得罪别人的危险表达自己的需要。当然她还要继续学习如何在表达自己需要的同时，尊重他人的需要。但我相信，这只是时间问题。

5 Taking Responsibility for Our Feelings

Judgments, criticisms, diagnoses, and interpretations of others are all alienated expressions of our own needs and values. When others hear criticism, they tend to invest their energy in self-defense or counterattack. The more directly we can connect our feelings to our needs, the easier it is for others to respond compassionately.

In a world where we are often harshly judged for identifying and revealing our needs, doing so can be very frightening, especially for women who are socialized to ignore their own needs while caring for others.

In the course of developing emotional responsibility, most of us experience three stages: (1) "emotional slavery"—believing ourselves responsible for the feelings of others, (2) "the obnoxious stage"—in which we refuse to admit to caring what anyone else feels or needs, and (3) "emotional liberation"—in which we accept full responsibility for our own feelings but not the feelings of others, while being aware that we can never meet our own needs at the expense of others.

NVC in Action

"Bring Back the Stigma of Illegitimacy!"

A student of Nonviolent Communication volunteering at a food bank was shocked when an elderly co-worker burst out from behind a newspaper, "What we need to do in this country is bring back the stigma of illegitimacy!"

The student's habitual reaction to this kind of statement would have been to say nothing, to judge the other severely but silently, and eventually to process her own feelings safely away from the scene. This time, she remembered she had the option of listening for the feelings and needs behind the words that had shocked her.

Student: *(first checking out her guess as to what the co-worker was observing)* Are you reading something about teenage pregnancies in the paper?

第三阶段："情绪的主人"

在这个阶段，我们不再出于恐惧、羞愧或内疚来回应他人的需要，而是因为发自内心的慈悲与爱而相互给予。我们既不再为他人的感受承担责任，又能全然地为自己的意愿、感受和行为负责。同时，我们也明白，若牺牲他人，我们也永远无法真正满足自己的需要。非暴力沟通帮助我们既清晰表达自己，又同样关心他人，从而实现我们的情绪自由并与他人建立连结。

小结

非暴力沟通的第三个要素，是看见感受背后的需要。他人的言行也许会刺激我们的感受，但并不是感受的根源。听到不中听的话时，我们可以有四种选择来接收：（1）指责自己；（2）指责他人；（3）体会自己的感受与需要；（4）体会他人在消极的话语下隐藏着什么感受与需要。

评判、批评、分析和论断他人，都使我们疏远了自己的需要和价值观。当人们听到批评，往往会以自我辩护或反击来回应。我们越能够直接说出自己的感受与需要，他人就越有可能对我们做出善意的回应。

在我们身处的世界中，我们时常会因为看见和袒露自身需要遭到强烈抨击，因而对表达需要感到害怕。对女性来说，尤其如此。长期以来，社会文化将她们塑造成了只懂照顾他人而无视自己需要的样子。

在通往情绪自由的成长路上，许多人都会经历三个阶段：（1）"情绪的奴隶"——我们认为自己要为他人的感受负责；（2）"面目可

5 Taking Responsibility for Our Feelings

Co-worker:	Yes, it's unbelievable how many of them are doing it!
Student:	*(now listening for the co-worker's feeling, and what unmet need might be giving rise to this feeling)* Are you feeling alarmed because you'd like kids to have stable families?
Co-worker:	Of course! Do you know, my father would have killed me if I had done anything like that!
Student:	So you're remembering how it was for the girls in your generation who got pregnant?
Co-worker:	Sure thing! We knew what would happen to us if we got pregnant. We were scared about it all the time, not like these girls nowadays.
Student:	Are you annoyed that there is no fear of punishment for the girls who get pregnant these days?
Co-worker:	Well, at least fear and punishment worked! It says here that there are girls sleeping around with different men just so they can get pregnant! That's right! They have babies and the rest of us in society pay for it!

The student of NVC heard two different feelings in this statement: astonishment that girls would deliberately get pregnant, and annoyance that taxpayers end up paying for children born in this way. She chose which feeling to empathize with.

Student:	Are you astonished to realize that people are getting pregnant these days without any consideration for reputation, consequences, financial stability . . . all the things you used to consider?
Co-worker:	Yeah, and guess who ends up paying for it?

第五章　为自己的感受负责

憎"——我们拒绝考虑他人的感受或需要；（3）"情绪的主人"——我们全然地为自己的感受负责，同时我们也意识到，牺牲他人的福祉也无法满足自己的需要。

非暴力沟通实例

　　一位非暴力沟通学员在一家食物银行作志愿者。有一天，一位年长同事在看报时突然气冲冲地说："我们需要让私生子女像以前那样见不得人！"听到这话时，她吃惊不已。

　　在过去，当听到不同意见时，她都默不作声，只是在心里责备对方，然后再到别处处理自己的感受。这一次，她想起可以有不一样的选择——去试着聆听这番令她震惊的话背后对方的感受和需要。

学员：（首先向同事确认观察）你正在阅读报上有关"少女妈妈"的报道吗？
同事：是的，有这么多少女未婚怀孕，真不可思议！
学员：（接着试着聆听同事的感受和需要）你感到担心，因为你希望孩子能生活在环境稳定的家庭中是吗？
同事：那当然！你知道吗，当年我要是敢这么做，不被我爸爸宰了

5 Taking Responsibility for Our Feelings

The co-worker, probably feeling heard around her astonishment, moved on to her other feeling: that of annoyance. As often happens when there is a mixture of feelings present, the speaker will return to those that have not received empathic attention. It is not necessary for the listener to reflect back a complex mixture of feelings all at once; the flow of compassion will continue as each feeling comes up again in its turn.

Student: Sounds like you're exasperated because you'd like your tax money to be used for other purposes. Is that so?

Co-worker: Certainly is! Do you know that my son and his wife want a second child and they can't have one—even though they have two jobs—because it costs so much?

Student: I guess you're sad about that? You'd probably love to have a second grandchild . . .

Co-worker: Yes, and it's not just for me that it would make a difference.

Student: . . . and for your son to have the family he wants . . . *(Even though the student guessed only partially correctly, she did not interrupt the flow of empathy, instead allowing the co-worker to continue and realize another concern.)*

Co-worker: Yes, I think it's sad to be a single child too.

Student: Oh, I see; you'd like for Katie to have a little brother?

Co-worker: That would be nice.

At this point, the student sensed a release in her co-worker. A moment of silence elapsed. She felt surprised to discover that, while she still wanted to express her own views, her urgency and tension had dissipated because she no longer felt "adversarial." She understood the feelings and needs

第五章　为自己的感受负责

才怪！

学员：所以你想到在你的那个年代，少女未婚先孕会遭遇什么！

同事：难道不是吗！我们都知道未婚怀孕会有什么下场。我们可不像如今的女孩子，那时我们整日都对意外怀孕担惊受怕。

学员：你很生气，因为这些女孩子根本不害怕怀孕会带来什么惩罚？

同事：怎么说呢，至少当年的女孩子因为害怕受到惩罚就不敢乱来吧！报纸上说有的女孩为了怀孕和不同的男人睡觉。她们倒好，生了孩子让我们来买单！

这位非暴力沟通学员从同事的话中听到了两种不同的感受：一方面，对一些女孩故意怀孕感到震惊；另一方面，对纳税人要为这些孩子买单感到气愤。她选择先同理其中一个感受。

学员：想到现在的女孩面对怀孕，不像你们从前那样顾及名誉、后果和经济条件，你有些吃惊，是吗？

同事：是的，你猜最后是谁为这些孩子买单？

同事的震惊之情多半已经被听到，便转而谈论她的愤怒。通常，当人们有许多感受时，会反复回到那些还未被听到的内容上。因此，聆听者无须一次把所有不同的感受都反映给对方，而是可以在每一个感受浮现时给予同理倾听，情感也会随之持续地流淌。

学员：听上去你感到气愤，因为你希望纳税人的钱能有更好的用途，对吗？

behind her co-worker's statements and no longer felt that the two of them were "worlds apart."

Student: *(expressing herself in NVC, and using all four parts of the process: observation [O], feeling [F], need [N], request [R])* You know, when you first said that we should bring back the stigma of illegitimacy (O), I got really scared (F), because it really matters to me that all of us here share a deep caring for people needing help (N). Some of the people coming here for food are teenage parents (O), and I want to make sure they feel welcome (N). Would you mind telling me how you feel when you see Dashal, or Amy and her boyfriend, walking in? (R)

The dialogue continued with several more exchanges until the woman got the reassurance she needed that her co-worker did indeed offer caring and respectful help to unmarried teen clients. Even more importantly, what the woman gained was a new experience in expressing disagreement in a way that met her needs for honesty and mutual respect.

In the meantime, the co-worker left satisfied that her concerns around teen pregnancy had been fully heard. Both parties felt understood, and their relationship benefited from their having shared their understanding and differences without hostility. In the absence of NVC, their relationship might have begun to deteriorate from this moment, and the work they both wanted to do in common—helping people—might have suffered.

第五章　为自己的感受负责

同事：那当然！我儿子和儿媳想要第二个孩子。可是，生养孩子太花钱了，虽然他们都有工作，但还是生不起！

学员：想到这事你感到难过，你很想再要一个孙子或孙女，是吗？

同事：是的，但不只是我想要……

学员：……你还希望儿子可以过上他想要的生活……（即使这位学员只是猜对了部分，她依然继续同理倾听同事。同事因此得以充分表达自己。）

同事：是啊，做独生子女也是挺凄惨的。

学员：我明白了，你希望凯蒂能有一个小弟弟？

同事：是啊，那该有多好呀！

　　就在那刻，这位同事似乎有些释然，她开始安静下来。学员惊讶地发现，尽管自己依然想要发表不同观点，内心的紧迫与紧张却已经消散了不少，因为她不再有"敌对"的感觉了。她理解了同事的想法背后有什么样的感受与需要，这时仿佛她们不再是两个世界的人了。接着，学员运用非暴力沟通的四个要素开启她的表达。

学员：你知道吗，当听到你说"让私生子女像以前那样见不得人"（观察），我感到非常害怕（感受），因为我希望我们都能从心底关心那些需要帮助的人（需要）。来我们这里领取食物的人，有些是未成年父母（观察），我想确保他们在这里是受欢迎的（需要）。你是否愿意告诉我，当你见到塔夏、艾米以及她们的男朋友来这里时，你是什么心情？（请求）

5 Taking Responsibility for Our Feelings

Exercise 3

ACKNOWLEDGING NEEDS

To practice identifying needs, please circle the number in front of each statement where the speaker is acknowledging responsibility for his or her feelings.

1. "You irritate me when you leave company documents on the conference room floor."
2. "I feel angry when you say that, because I am wanting respect and I hear your words as an insult."
3. "I feel frustrated when you come late."
4. "I'm sad that you won't be coming for dinner because I was hoping we could spend the evening together."
5. "I feel disappointed because you said you would do it and you didn't."
6. "I'm discouraged because I would have liked to have progressed further in my work by now."
7. "Little things people say sometimes hurt me."
8. "I feel happy that you received that award."
9. "I feel scared when you raise your voice."
10. "I am grateful that you offered me a ride because I was needing to get home before my children arrive."

Here are my responses for Exercise 3:

1. If you circled this number, we're not in agreement. To me, the statement implies that the other person's behavior is solely responsible for the speaker's feelings. It doesn't reveal the needs or thoughts that are contributing to the speaker's feelings. To do so, the speaker might have said, "I'm irritated when you leave company documents on the conference room floor, because I want our documents to be safely stored and accessible."

第五章　为自己的感受负责

她们持续交换了一些看法，直到女学员确信，她的同事从心底关爱与尊重那些未成年父母，并愿意帮助他们。更重要的是，她学习到了可以用诚实与相互尊重的态度来表达和对方不同的看法。

与此同时，同事也感到欣慰，因为她的担忧也得到了充分的聆听。通过不带敌意地交换不同意见，她们增进了相互理解，关系也变得更亲近了。如果没有使用非暴力沟通，她们的关系也许就会恶化。

练习三：体会需要

在以下例句中，说话的人是否对自己的感受负责。

1. "你把公司文件丢在办公室地上，这让我很生气。"
2. "听你这么说，我觉得很生气，因为我需要受到尊重，而我认为你那些话是在羞辱我。"
3. "你来晚了，让我很郁闷。"
4. "你没法来吃晚餐，我感到难过，我本来想和你共度这个夜晚。"
5. "我感到失望，因为你没有做你答应我的事情。"
6. "我感到挫败，因为我原本希望这件事情能够进展得更快些。"
7. "人们在背后议论我，这让我感到伤心。"
8. "我很高兴你获得了那个奖项。"
9. "你嗓门那么大，我很害怕。"
10. "感谢你让我搭顺风车回家，因为我想比孩子们先到家。"

5 Taking Responsibility for Our Feelings

2. If you circled this number, we're in agreement that the speaker is acknowledging responsibility for his or her feelings.
3. If you circled this number, we're not in agreement. To express the needs or thoughts underlying his or her feelings, the speaker might have said, "I feel frustrated when you come late because I was hoping we'd be able to get some front-row seats."
4. If you circled this number, we're in agreement that the speaker is acknowledging responsibility for his or her feelings.
5. If you circled this number, we're not in agreement. To express the needs and thoughts underlying his or her feelings, the speaker might have said, "When you said you'd do it and then didn't, I felt disappointed because I want to be able to rely upon your words."
6. If you circled this number, we're in agreement that the speaker is acknowledging responsibility for his or her feelings.
7. If you circled this number, we're not in agreement. To express the needs and thoughts underlying his or her feelings, the speaker might have said, "Sometimes when people say little things, I feel hurt because I want to be appreciated, not criticized."
8. If you circled this number, we're not in agreement. To express the needs and thoughts underlying his or her feelings, the speaker might have said, "When you received that award, I felt happy because I was hoping you'd be recognized for all the work you'd put into the project."
9. If you circled this number, we're not in agreement. To express the needs and thoughts underlying his or her feelings, the speaker might have said, "When you raise your voice, I feel scared because I'm telling myself someone might get hurt here, and I need to know that we're all safe."
10. If you circled this number, we're in agreement that the speaker is acknowledging responsibility for his or her feelings.

第五章　为自己的感受负责

以下是我对练习三的回应：

1. 如果你选择这一句，我们的看法不一致。在我看来，说这句话的人是在暗示，是对方的行为导致他／她的感受，而非他／她本身的需要或想法所致。若要为自己的感受负责，他／她可以说："当你把公司文件丢在办公室地上，我感到生气，因为我希望重要的文件能够得到妥善保管。"

2. 如果你选择这一句，我们的看法一致。

3. 如果你选择这一句，我们的看法不一致。说话者如果想要表达感受背后的需要或想法，可以说："你来晚了，我很郁闷，因为我本来希望我们可以坐在前排的位置。"

4. 如果你选择这一句，我们的看法一致。

5. 如果你选择这一句，我们的看法不一致。说话者如果想要表达感受背后的需要或想法，可以说："你没做你答应我的事情，我感到失望，因为我希望能信任你。"

6. 如果你选择这一句，我们的看法一致。

7. 如果你选择这一句，我们的看法不一致。说话者如果想要表达感受背后的需要或想法，可以说："人们在背后议论我，我感到伤心，因为我希望得到欣赏。"

8. 如果你选择这一句，我们的看法不一致。说话者如果想要表达感受背后的需要或想法，可以说："你获得了那个奖项我很高兴，因为我一直希望你的努力能得到认可。"

9. 如果你选择这一句，我们的看法不一致。说话者如果想要表达感受背后的需要或想法，可以说："你大声说话时我很害怕，我需要安全的环境。"

10. 如果你选择这一句，我们的看法一致。

5 Taking Responsibility for Our Feelings

Keep in mind that other people's actions can never "make" you feel any certain way. Feelings are your warning indicators.

第六章

提出请求，丰盈生命

Requesting That Which Would Enrich Life

We have now covered the first three components of NVC, which address what we are *observing, feeling,* and *needing.* We have learned to do this without criticizing, analyzing, blaming, or diagnosing others, and in a way likely to inspire compassion. The fourth and final component of this process addresses *what we would like to request of others* in order to enrich life for us. When our needs are not being fulfilled, we follow the expression of what we are observing, feeling, and needing with a specific request: we ask for actions that might fulfill our needs. How do we express our requests so that others are more willing to respond compassionately to our needs?

Using Positive Action Language

First of all, we express what we *are* requesting rather than what we *are not* requesting. "How do you do a *don't?*" goes a line of a children's song by my colleague Ruth Bebermeyer: "All I know is I feel *won't* when I'm told to do a *don't*." These lyrics reveal two problems commonly encountered when requests are worded in the negative. People are often confused as to what is actually being requested, and furthermore, negative requests are likely to provoke resistance.

A woman at a workshop, frustrated that her husband was spending so much time at work, described how her request had

> Use positive language when making requests.

第六章　提出请求，丰盈生命

我们已经介绍了非暴力沟通的三个要素：观察、感受和需要，学习了使用不带批评、分析、指责或诊断的沟通方式更有可能激发他人的善意与慈悲。非暴力沟通的第四个要素是——请求。提出请求是为了让我们的生命变得更加丰盈。在表达了观察、感受和需要之后，我们提出一个明确的请求来满足需要。那么，以什么样的方式提出请求，才能让别人更愿意对我们做出善意的回应呢？

使用正向、具体的语言

首先，清楚地告诉对方，我们请求他们去做什么，而非不要做什么。

我的同事鲁斯·贝本梅尔曾经写过一首儿歌。其中有两句歌词是："让我不要这么做，那我要怎么办？我只知道，让我不要这么做，我就偏不想答应你。"从中我们可以看到，用负向的语言提出请求通常会引发两个问题：1. 人们往往搞不清楚我们到底请求他们做什么；2. 负向的请求很容易使人产生抗拒的心理。

6 Requesting That Which Would Enrich Life

backfired: "I asked him not to spend so much time at work. Three weeks later, he responded by announcing that he'd signed up for a golf tournament!" She had successfully communicated to him what she did not want—his spending so much time at work—but had failed to request what she *did* want. Encouraged to reword her request, she thought a minute and said, "I wish I had told him that I would like him to spend at least one evening a week at home with the children and me."

During the Vietnam War, I was asked to debate the war issue on television with a man whose position differed from mine. The show was videotaped, so I was able to watch it at home that evening. When I saw myself on the screen communicating in ways I didn't want to be communicating, I felt very upset. "If I'm ever in another discussion," I told myself, "I am determined not to do what I did on that program! I'm not going to be defensive. I'm not going to let them make a fool of me." Notice how I spoke to myself in terms of what I *didn't* want to do rather than in terms of what I *did* want to do.

A chance to redeem myself came the very next week when I was invited to continue the debate on the same program. All the way to the studio, I repeated to myself all the things I didn't want to do. As soon as the program started, the man launched off in exactly the same way he had a week earlier. For about ten seconds after he'd finished talking, I managed not to communicate in the ways I had been reminding myself. In fact, I said nothing. I just sat there. As soon as I opened my mouth, however, I found words tumbling out in all the ways I had been so determined to avoid! It was a painful lesson about what can happen when I only identify what I *don't* want to do, without clarifying what I *do* want to do.

I was once invited to work with some high school students who suffered a long litany of grievances against their principal. They regarded the principal as racist, and searched for ways to get even with him. A minister who worked closely with the young people became deeply concerned over the prospect of violence. Out of respect for the minister, the students agreed to meet with me.

They began by describing what they saw as discrimination

第六章　提出请求，丰盈生命

一位女士在一次工作坊中谈到，她对先生在工作上投入许多时间十分苦恼，而她向先生提出的请求非但没有效果，甚至适得其反。"我请他不要花那么多时间在工作上。没想到3周后，他居然告诉我，他报名参加了一个高尔夫球比赛！"这位女士说出了她不想要什么——她不希望先生花太多时间在工作上，但却没有说清楚她想要什么。于是，当我鼓励她换一种方式提出请求时，她想了想说："我希望他每周至少有一个晚上在家陪我和孩子。要是一开始我这样和他说就好了。"

越战期间，我受邀参加一场电视辩论赛，就战争的议题和一位与我立场不同的男士展开辩论。当天晚上，当我在电视上看见自己的表现并不是我想要的那样时，我感到十分懊恼。于是我告诉自己："下一次辩论时，绝不能这么被动。我可不想让他把我当成傻瓜。"请注意，我只是告诉了自己不去做什么，而非我要的是什么。

一周后，我有了一次弥补的机会，这个节目邀请我继续上一次的辩论。在去演播室的路上，我反复告诫自己不要重蹈覆辙。节目一开始，对方就像上星期那样猛烈地攻击我。在他讲完的十秒内，我努力控制着不做自我辩护。实际上，我只是一言不发地坐在那里。而就在开口的瞬间，所有那些我不想讲的话都倾泻而出！我只知道自己不想要什么，却没有理清自己到底想要什么，这真是一次惨痛的教训。

还有一次我应邀前往一所学校和一群高中生交流。他们对校长满怀怨言，认为校长是一名种族歧视者，并且想办法要报复他。一位负责辅导他们的牧师十分担忧可能会发生暴力冲突，邀请我去协调矛盾。出于对这位牧师的尊重，学生们答应了与我见面。

会谈一开始，他们便向我描述校长有哪些歧视性行为。听完他们列举的控诉后，我建议他们明确一下希望校长具体怎么做。

on the part of the principal. After listening to several of their charges, I suggested that they proceed by clarifying what they wanted from the principal.

"What good would that do?" scoffed one student in disgust. "We already went to him to tell him what we wanted. His answer to us was, 'Get out of here! I don't need you people telling me what to do!'"

I asked the students what they had requested of the principal. They recalled saying to him that they didn't want him telling them how to wear their hair. I suggested that they might have received a more cooperative response if they had expressed what they *did*, rather than what they *did not*, want. They had then informed the principal that they wanted to be treated with fairness, at which he had become defensive, vociferously denying ever having been unfair. I ventured to guess that the principal would have responded more favorably if they had asked for specific actions rather than vague behavior like "fair treatment."

Working together, we found ways to express their requests in positive action language. At the end of the meeting, the students had clarified thirty-eight actions they wanted the principal to take, including "We'd like you to agree to black student representation on decisions made about dress code," and "We'd like you to refer to us as 'black students' and not 'you people.'" The following day, the students presented their requests to the principal using the positive action language we had practiced; that evening I received an elated phone call from them: their principal had agreed to all thirty-eight requests!

In addition to using positive language, we also want to word our requests in the form of concrete actions that others can undertake and to avoid vague, abstract, or ambiguous phrasing. A cartoon depicts a man who has fallen into a lake. As he struggles to swim, he shouts to his dog on shore, "Lassie, get help!" In the next frame, the dog is lying on a psychiatrist's couch. We all know how opinions vary as to what constitutes "help": some members of my family, when asked to help with the dishes, think "help" means supervision.

第六章　提出请求，丰盈生命

"那又有什么用？"一位学生不屑地说，"我们已经告诉过他我们的想法了，结果他对我们说'走开！我不需要你们这些人告诉我怎么做'。"

我问他们向校长提出了什么请求。他们说曾经告诉校长不要干涉他们的打扮。我向他们提议，如果他们能说出希望校长做的事，而非不希望他做的事，他们或许能得到比较积极的回应。

此外，他们还告诉校长，希望得到公正的对待。对此，校长则立马大声否认说，他没有不公正地对待他们。我告诉学生们，如果你们请求他采取一些特定的行动，而不是抽象模糊的"公正对待"，校长可能会做出比较正面的回应。

接着，我和他们一起讨论如何用正向的语言提出具体的请求来满足需要。会议最后，学生罗列了希望校长做到的38件事，包括"让黑人学生代表参与有关服饰穿着的决策小组""请称呼我们为'黑人学生'，而不是'你们这些人'"。第二天，学生们向校长提交了书面请求。当晚，他们在电话里兴奋地告诉我，校长同意了所有38项请求！

除了使用正向语言，我们提出的请求越具体越好。如果我们的表达含糊不清或过分抽象、模棱两可，他人很难知道如何去行动。有一则漫画描绘了一个男人跌到了水里，他一边挣扎着往岸边游，一边冲着岸上的狗喊道："拉西，快去找人帮助！"在第二幅画中，他的狗躺在了心理医生的沙发上。这是因为"帮助"这个词对不同的人有着不同的含义。

一对关系紧张的夫妻参加了一个工作坊，他们再一次让我们看到，模糊的语言如何引发误会和沟通上的障碍。

"我希望你让我做自己！"妻子大声向先生宣告。

6 Requesting That Which Would Enrich Life

A couple in distress attending a workshop provides an additional illustration of how nonspecific language can hamper understanding and communication. "I want you to let me be me," the woman declared to her husband. "I do!" he retorted. "No, you don't!" she insisted. Asked to express herself in positive action language, the woman replied, "I want you to give me the freedom to grow and be myself." Such a statement, however, is just as vague and likely to provoke a defensive response. She struggled to formulate her request clearly, and then admitted, "It's kind of awkward, but if I were to be precise, I guess what I want is for you to smile and say that anything I do is okay." Often, the use of vague and abstract language can mask oppressive interpersonal games.

> Making requests in clear, positive, concrete action language reveals what we really want.

A similar lack of clarity occurred between a father and his fifteen-year-old son when they came in for counseling. "All I want is for you to start showing a little responsibility," claimed the father. "Is that asking too much?" I suggested that he specify what it would take for his son to demonstrate the responsibility he was seeking. After a discussion on how to clarify his request, the father responded sheepishly, "Well, it doesn't sound so good, but when I say that I want responsibility, what I really mean is that I want him to do what I ask, without question—to jump when I say jump, and to smile while doing it." He then agreed with me that if his son were to actually behave this way, it would demonstrate obedience rather than responsibility.

Like this father, we often use vague and abstract language to indicate how we want other people to feel or be without naming a concrete action they could take to reach that state. For example, an employer makes a genuine effort to invite feedback, telling the employees, "I want you to feel free to express yourself around me." The statement communicates the employer's desire for the employees to "feel free," but not what they could do in order to feel this way. Instead, the

> Vague language contributes to internal confusion.

149

第六章 提出请求，丰盈生命

"我没有吗？"先生反驳道。

"不，你没有！"妻子坚持着。

当我请她以正向的具体语言来表达时，她说："我希望你给我自由，让我成长并且做自己。"然而，如此模糊的语句只会引发对方的防卫。她继续艰难地尝试提出一个清晰明确的请求，最后却不得不承认："这听上去有些令人不好意思……我希望不论我做什么，你都能微笑着点头称是。"人们往往使用模糊、抽象的语言来掩盖操控对方的意图。

还有一次，一位父亲带着他 15 岁的儿子来找我咨询。父亲向孩子提出的请求同样含糊不清，他说："我只是希望你能对自己多一些责任感。这个要求难道过分吗？"我建议他具体说明，儿子需要怎样做才算是有责任感。经过一番讨论，父亲有些不好意思地回答道："嗯，这听上去有些不对，当我说希望他能有点责任感时，我真正的意思是，希望他能听我的话，我让他跳他就要跳，并且做的时候还要面带微笑。"我表示，如果儿子真的表现出了这样的"责任感"，那不过是顺从罢了。他同意了我的看法。

就像这位父亲，人们习惯于使用含糊、抽象的语言将自己的愿望暗示给他人，却不提及希望对方采取哪些具体的行动。例如，这位雇主希望员工们能给他一些反馈，于是他说："我希望你们和我在一起时，可以畅所欲言。"雇主向员工们传递了自己的愿望，希望他们能"畅所欲言"，却并未说明他们要如何做到。为了让请求更具有建设性，这位雇主可以使用正向的具体语言来提出请求："请你们告诉我，我怎么做才能让你们在和我谈话时更敢于表达意见。"

最后，我想再举例说明含糊的语言如何妨碍了对自我的清晰认识。

我在担任临床心理医生期间，接待过许多受到抑郁困扰的来访者。

employer could use positive action language to make a request: "I'd like you to *tell* me what I might *do* to make it easier for you to feel free to express yourselves around me."

As a final illustration of how the use of vague language contributes to internal confusion, I would like to present the conversation that I would invariably have during my practice as a clinical psychologist with the many clients who came to me with complaints of depression. After I empathized with the depth of feeling that a client had just expressed, our exchanges would typically proceed in the following manner:

> **Depression is the reward we get for being "good."**

MBR: What are you wanting that you are not receiving?
Client: I don't know what I want.
MBR: I guessed that you would say that.
Client: Why?
MBR: My theory is that we get depressed because we're not getting what we want, and we're not getting what we want because we have never been taught to get what we want. Instead, we've been taught to be good little boys and girls and good mothers and fathers. If we're going to be one of those good things, better get used to being depressed. Depression is the reward we get for being "good." But, if you want to feel better, I'd like you to clarify what you would like people to do to make life more wonderful for you.
Client: I just want someone to love me. That's hardly unreasonable, is it?
MBR: It's a good start. Now I'd like you to clarify what you would like people to do that would fulfill your need to be loved. For example, what could I do right now?
Client: Oh, you know . . .
MBR: I'm not sure I do. I'd like you to tell me what you would like me, or others, to do to give you the love you're looking for.
Client: That's hard.

第六章 提出请求，丰盈生命

在我深度同理了他们后，我们的交流通常会这样继续：

马歇尔：有什么是你想要却没有得到的？
来访者：我不知道我想要什么。
马歇尔：我猜到你会这样说。
来访者：为什么？
马歇尔：我认为，我们之所以会抑郁是因为未能实现自己的愿望；之所以如此，是因为从来没有人教导过我们去实现愿望。相反，我们被教育成乖孩子、好妈妈、好爸爸。如果我们要成为那样的好人，就得习惯压抑自己。抑郁，是我们做一个"好人"的"代价"。如果你想要让自己好起来，我希望你能清楚地说出，为了让你的生活变得美好，你希望他人做些什么。
来访者：我只是希望有人能爱我。这并非完全不现实，不是吗？
马歇尔：这是个好的开始。现在我想请你清晰地说出，他人怎么做才能满足你爱的需要？例如，我此刻可以做些什么？
来访者：哦，你知道的……
马歇尔：我不确定我知道。我想请你告诉我，为了让你得到你想要的爱，你希望我或者他人怎样做？
来访者：这很难说清楚。
马歇尔：是的，提出清晰的请求是困难的。但是请想一想，如果我们讲不清楚自己想要什么，别人要回应我们的请求该会有多困难！
来访者：我开始明白，我希望别人做什么来爱我了。不过，我不太好意思说出来。
马歇尔：是的，这经常是令人尴尬的。那么，你希望我或者他人怎

6 Requesting That Which Would Enrich Life

MBR: Yes, it can be difficult to make clear requests. But think how hard it will be for others to respond to our request if we're not even clear what it is!

Client: I'm starting to get clear what I want from others to fulfill my need for love, but it's embarrassing.

MBR: Yes, very often it is embarrassing. So what would you like for me or others to do?

Client: If I really reflect upon what I'm requesting when I ask to be loved, I suppose I want you to guess what I want before I'm even aware of it. And then I want you to always do it.

MBR: I'm grateful for your clarity. I hope you can see how you are not likely to find someone who can fulfill your need for love if that's what it takes.

Very often, my clients were able to see how the lack of awareness of what they wanted from others had contributed significantly to their frustrations and depression.

Making Requests Consciously

Sometimes we may be able to communicate a clear request without putting it in words. Suppose you're in the kitchen and your sister, who is watching television in the living room, calls out, "I'm thirsty." In this case, it may be obvious that she is requesting you to bring her a glass of water from the kitchen.

However, in other instances, we may express our discomfort and incorrectly assume that the listener has understood the underlying request. For example, a woman might say to her husband, "I'm annoyed you forgot the butter and onions I asked you to pick up for dinner." While it may be obvious to her that she is asking him to go back to the store, the husband may think that her words were uttered solely to make him feel guilty.

> When we simply express our feelings, it may not be clear to the listener what we want them to do.

第六章 提出请求，丰盈生命

么做？

来访者：我认真思考了，当我说希望得到爱时，我实际想要的是，即使我还不知道我的需要，你也能猜到我想要什么，并且我希望你一直都这样。

马歇尔：我很感激你做了澄清，我也希望你已经明白了，找到这样一个人用这样的方式来爱你是不可能的。

经过这样的对话，许多来访者才发现，他们之所以感到沮丧和压抑，很大程度上是因为他们不清楚自己希望他人如何来满足自己的需要。

有意识地提出请求

有的时候，表达清晰的请求也许无需过多的言语。例如，你正在厨房里，在客厅看电视的妹妹喊道："我口渴。"在这种情况下，多半她在请求你给她从厨房倒一杯水。

但有时，我们在表达自己的不快时，却误以为对方能明白我们想要什么。例如，一位妻子对丈夫说："我不是让你在路上带一些黄油和洋葱回来吗？！你怎么忘记了？！真气人！"也许，妻子的意思是希望丈夫再去一趟商店买东西，但丈夫却很有可能将太太的话视作对他的指责。如果我们只是表达自己的感受，别人可能并不清楚我们想要他们做什么。

更为常见的是，我们对提出什么样的请求缺乏意识。我们和他人说

6 Requesting That Which Would Enrich Life

Even more often, we are simply not conscious of what we are requesting when we speak. We talk *to* others or *at* them without knowing how to engage in a dialogue *with* them. We toss out words,

> We are often not conscious of what we are requesting.

using the presence of others as a wastebasket. In such situations, the listener, unable to discern a clear request in the speaker's words, may experience the kind of distress illustrated in the following anecdote.

I was seated directly across the aisle from a couple on a mini-train that carries passengers to their respective terminals at the Dallas/Fort Worth International Airport. For passengers in a hurry to catch a plane, the snail's pace of the train may well be irritating. The man turned to his wife and said with intensity, "I have never seen a train go so slow in all my life." She said nothing, appearing tense and uneasy as to what response he might be expecting from her. He then did what many of us do when we're not getting the response we want: he repeated himself. In a markedly stronger voice, he exclaimed, "I have never seen a train go so slow in all my life!"

The wife, at a loss for response, looked even more distressed. In desperation, she turned to him and said, "They're electronically timed." I didn't think this piece of information would satisfy him, and indeed it did not, for he repeated himself a third time—even more loudly, "*I HAVE NEVER SEEN A TRAIN GO SO SLOW IN ALL MY LIFE!*" The wife's patience was clearly exhausted as she snapped back angrily, "Well, what do you want me to do about it? Get out and push?" Now there were two people in pain!

What response was the man wanting? I believe he wanted to hear that his pain was understood. If his wife had known this, she might have responded, "It sounds like you're scared we might miss our plane, and disgusted because you'd like a faster train running between these terminals."

> Requests may sound like demands when unaccompanied by the speaker's feelings and needs.

第六章 提出请求,丰盈生命

话或者谈论事情,却并不知道如何开展一场对话。我们只是把自己想说的话丢给他人,将他人当作垃圾桶。如果他人无法分辨出讲话的人想要什么,则会苦不堪言。

有一次,在达拉斯国际机场航站楼间的小火车上,我坐在一对夫妻对面。由于小火车开得很慢,赶飞机的旅客们可能会感到心烦。只见对面的那位先生气冲冲地转向妻子说:"我这辈子都没见过开这么慢的火车!"妻子看起来有点不知所措,什么话也没有说。就像许多人在没有得到期待的回应时所做的那样,先生重复了一遍刚才的话,并且带着更为强烈的语气高喊:"我这辈子都没有见过开这么慢的火车!"

妻子看起来更加茫然不知所措。无可奈何之下,她转向先生,对他说:"这辆火车的速度是电脑控制的。"我不认为这样的回答会让那位先生满意。果不其然,他更大声地重复了第三遍:"我这辈子都没见过开这么慢的火车!"妻子的耐心显然已经殆尽,她恼怒地厉声回应:"那你想让我怎么做?下去推车吗?"这时,他们双双陷入了痛苦中!

这个男人希望得到怎样的回应呢?我猜他希望自己的痛苦得到理解。如果他的妻子能明白这一点,可以这样回应:"你似乎很担心误机,并且对火车的速度感到不满,希望它能开快一些吧?"而在之前的对话中,妻子感受到丈夫的不安,却不明白他想要什么。

同样地,如果一个人只提出请求,却没有首先表达感受与需要,也有可能导致交流的困难,尤其是在人们以问话的形式提出请求时。例如,如果父母问孩子:"你为什么不去理发呢?"这样的请求很容易被孩子听成要求或指责。对此,父母可以先说出感受和需要:"我们担心你的头发太长会遮住视线,特别是在骑自行车的时候,你要不要去理个头发呢?"

6 Requesting That Which Would Enrich Life

In the above exchange, the wife heard the husband's frustration but was clueless as to what he was asking for. Equally problematic is the reverse situation—when people state their requests without first communicating the feelings and needs behind them. This is especially true when the request takes the form of a question. "Why don't you go and get a haircut?" can easily be heard by youngsters as a demand or an attack unless parents remember to first reveal their own feelings and needs: "We're worried that your hair is getting so long it might keep you from seeing things, especially when you're on your bike. How about a haircut?"

It is more common, however, for people to talk without being conscious of what they are asking for. "I'm not requesting anything," they might remark. "I just felt like saying what I said." My belief is that, whenever we say something to another person, we are requesting something in return. It may simply be an empathic connection—a verbal or nonverbal acknowledgment, as with the man on the train, that our words have been understood. Or we may be requesting honesty: we wish to know the listener's honest reaction to our words. Or we may be requesting an action that we hope would fulfill our needs. The clearer we are on what we want back from the other person, the more likely it is that our needs will be met.

> The clearer we are about what we want, the more likely it is that we'll get it.

Asking for a Reflection

As we know, the message we send is not always the message that's received. We generally rely on verbal cues to determine whether our message has been understood to our satisfaction. If, however, we're uncertain that it has been received as intended, we need to be able to clearly request a response that tells us how the message was heard so as to be able to correct any misunderstanding. On some occasions, a simple question

> To make sure the message we sent is the message that's received, ask the listener to reflect it back.

第六章　提出请求，丰盈生命

更常见的是，人们在说话时并不知道自己到底想要什么。他们可能会说："我没有什么请求。""我只是把我想说的说出来。"但在我看来，不论我们在对另一个人说什么，都希望他人有所回应。也许，（1）我们期待对方的理解——就像那位乘火车去机场的丈夫，希望对方能同理我们，与我们连结。（2）我们也可以请求对方给予我们一些坦诚的回应，来了解对方对我们的话有什么样的反应。（3）我们还有可能请求他人采取某种行动来满足需要。我们越是清楚自己想要什么，就越是能够实现所想。

请求对方重述你的话

我们的本意和他人的理解有时可能是两回事。通常我们会在对话中捕捉线索，来确定他人是否理解了我们的意思。但如果不确定，我们就需要提出明确的请求，请对方告诉我们他们听到了什么，以便在有误解的时候做出修正。有时，简单地问一句"这样清楚吗"就够了。但有些时候，即便对方说"是的，我明白了"，我们还是无法确保他们是否真正理解了我们的意思。这时，我们可以请对方再多回应一些，这样，一旦对方的理解与我们的意思有所不同或者有所遗漏，我们就有机会做出补充。

例如，一位老师对她的学生说："皮特，我昨天批改作业时没有看到你的作业本。我想和你确认这件事。请你在课后来我办公室一下，好吗？"皮特咕哝着说："好，我知道了。"便转过身准备离开。这位老师不确定皮特是否准确理解了她的意思，便立即请他重述一次："可否告

6 Requesting That Which Would Enrich Life

like, "Is that clear?" will suffice. At other times, we need more than "Yes, I understood you," to feel confident that we've been truly understood. At such times, we might ask others to reflect back in their own words what they heard us say. We then have the opportunity to restate parts of our message to address any discrepancy or omission we might have noticed in their reflection.

For example, a teacher approaches a student and says, "Peter, I got concerned when I checked my record book yesterday. I want to make sure you're aware of the homework I'm missing from you. Will you drop by my office after school?" Peter mumbles, "Okay, I know," and then turns away, leaving the teacher uneasy as to whether her message had been accurately received. She asks for a reflection—"Could you tell me what you just heard me say?"—to which Peter replies, "You said I gotta miss soccer to stay after school because you didn't like my homework." Confirmed in her suspicion that Peter had not heard her intended message, the teacher tries to restate it, but first she is careful of her next remark.

An assertion like "You didn't hear me," "That's not what I said," or "You're misunderstanding me," may easily lead Peter to think that he is being chastised. Since the teacher perceives Peter as having sincerely responded to her request for a reflection, she might say, "I'm grateful to you for telling me what you heard. I can see that I didn't make myself as clear as I'd have liked, so let me try again."

> **Express appreciation when your listener tries to meet your request for a reflection.**

When we first begin asking others to reflect back what they hear us say, it may feel awkward and strange because such requests are rarely made. When I emphasize the importance of our ability to ask for reflections, people often express reservations. They are worried about reactions like, "What do you think I am—deaf?" or, "Quit playing your psychological games." To prevent such responses, we can explain to people ahead of time why we may sometimes ask them to reflect back our words. We make clear that we're not testing their listening

> **Empathize with the listener who doesn't want to reflect back.**

诉我你听到的,我请你做的事情是什么?"皮特回答说:"你让我在课后留下来,不能去踢足球,因为你对我的作业不满意。"皮特果然没有听见她要传达的信息,于是她决定重新尝试,并在这一次更加注意自己的表达方式。

诸如"你没有听明白我的话""这不是我的意思""你误会了"这样的判断,很容易被他人视为指责。因为皮特很坦率地回应了她,这位老师先向他表达了谢意。她说:"谢谢你告诉我你听到我说了什么,我想我说得不够清楚,所以请允许我再试一次。"

刚开始尝试请他人重述我们的话时,可能会觉得有点不自然。因为在日常交流中,我们很少会提出这样的请求。当我强调请他人重述我们的话是一种重要的能力时,人们通常担心有人会这样反应:"你觉得我是聋子吗?""别跟我玩心理学的那一套!"为了避免这样的反应发生,我们可以先向他人解释这样做的原因,清楚表明这不是在测试他们的聆听能力,而是核实我们是否已经清晰地表达了自己的意思。然而,如果对方说"我听到你说什么了!我又不是傻瓜!"我们依然可以继续体会对方的感受和需要,并选择用言语来询问:"你有些生气吗?因为你希望我相信你理解了我说的话,对吗?"

请求诚实表达

在诚实表达了自己并确认对方已经明白后,我们多半会很想了解对方的反应。请求他人给予诚实表达大致可以分为三个方面:

skills, but checking out whether we've expressed ourselves clearly. However, should the listener retort, "I heard what you said; I'm not stupid!" we have the option to focus on the listener's feelings and needs and ask—either aloud or silently—"Are you saying you're feeling annoyed because you want respect for your ability to understand things?"

Requesting Honesty

After we've openly expressed ourselves and received the understanding we want, we're often eager to know the other person's reaction to what we've said. Usually the honesty we would like to receive takes one of three directions:

> After we express ourselves vulnerably, we often want to know (1) what the listener is feeling;

- Sometimes we'd like to know the feelings that are stimulated by what we said, and the reasons for those feelings. We might request this by asking, "I would like you to tell me how you feel about what I just said, and your reasons for feeling as you do."

- Sometimes we'd like to know something about our listener's thoughts in response to what they just heard us say. At these times, it's important to specify which thoughts we'd like them to share. For example, we might say, "I'd like you to tell me if you predict that my proposal would be successful, and if not, what you believe would prevent its success," rather than simply saying, "I'd like you to tell me what you think about what I've said." When we don't specify which thoughts we would like to receive, the other person may respond at great length with thoughts that aren't the ones we are seeking.

> (2) what the listener is thinking; or

- Sometimes we'd like to know whether the person is willing to take certain actions that we've recommended. Such a request

- 对方的感受和感受的原因

有时我们想要了解对方听到我们的话有什么感受以及产生这些感受的原因。一种可能的请求方式是："听到我说这些，你的感受是什么？"然后，我们可以进一步问："为什么有这种感受呢？"

- 对方的想法

有时，我们想了解对方在听了我们的话之后有什么想法。这时，重要的是说清楚我们想听的是哪方面的想法。例如，可以问对方："我想请你谈谈我的提案是否可行。如果不太可行，你认为有哪些阻碍因素？"如果我们只是宽泛简单地问："你对这个提案的想法是什么？"而不是具体说明想要哪方面的回答，对方也许会长篇大论，说的却不是我们想要了解的内容。

- 对方是否有意愿采取特定行动

还有些时候，我们想要知道对方是否愿意采纳我们的提议。我们可以问："我想知道，你是否同意将我们的会议推迟一周？"

在使用非暴力沟通时，我们需要清楚自己希望对方给予什么样的回应，并且清晰地提出相应的请求。

在团体中提出请求

在团体中发言时，更要说清楚我们希望得到什么样的回应，否则对话很可能不着边际、徒劳无功，也无法满足任何人的需要。

我经常受邀与关心种族歧视问题的团体一起工作。这些群体时常面

may sound like this: "I'd like you to tell me if you would be willing to postpone our meeting for one week."

> (3) whether the listener would be willing to take a particular action.

The use of NVC requires that we be conscious of the specific form of honesty we would like to receive, and to make that request for honesty in concrete language.

Making Requests of a Group

It is especially important when we are addressing a group to be clear about the kind of understanding or honesty we want back after we've expressed ourselves. When we are not clear about the response we'd like, we may initiate unproductive conversations that end up satisfying no one's needs.

I've been invited from time to time to work with groups of citizens concerned about racism in their communities. One issue that frequently arises among these groups is that their meetings are tedious and fruitless. This lack of productivity is very costly for group members, who often expend limited resources to arrange for transportation and child care in order to attend meetings. Frustrated by prolonged discussions that yield little direction, many members quit the groups, declaring meetings a waste of time. Furthermore, the institutional changes they are striving to make are not usually ones that occur quickly or easily. For all these reasons, when such groups do meet, it's important that they make good use of their time together.

I knew members of one such group that had been organized to effect change in the local school system. It was their belief that various elements in the school system discriminated against students on the basis of race. Because their meetings were unproductive and the group was losing members, they invited me to observe their discussions. I suggested that they conduct their meeting as usual, and that I would let them know if I saw any ways NVC might help.

One man began the meeting by calling the group's attention to a recent newspaper article in which a minority mother had raised

第六章 提出请求，丰盈生命

临会议冗长又毫无成效的问题。为了参加会议，参与者们时常要将有限的精力用来安排行程、托人照顾孩子，没有成效的会议对他们来说代价高昂。许多人因为会议太浪费时间而退出了团体。此外，他们所追寻的机构变革也不如想象中快速和顺利。因而，使会议变得富有成效对他们来说显得十分重要。

有一个团体致力于推动当地的学校改革，他们认为学生们遭受来自学校的多方面的种族歧视。由于他们的集体会议缺乏效率，成员相继离开。我受邀前去旁听他们的会议。我提议他们按照往常的方式开会，而我会适时告诉他们何时使用非暴力沟通来获得帮助。

会议一开始，一位男士请大家关注一则最近的新闻，其中报道了一位少数族裔的妇女抱怨女儿在学校受到来自校方的不公正待遇。一位女士随即分享了当年她在同一所学校就读时的个人经历。紧接着，其他人开始分享类似的经历。20分钟后，我询问与会人员，目前的讨论是否能满足他们的需要。没有一个人的回答是肯定的。一位男士甚至气冲冲地说："每次开会都是这样！与其坐在这里听这些老生常谈，真不如去干点别的！"

于是我询问发起讨论的那位男士，"你提到那篇文章，是希望得到什么样的回应呢？"

他回答："我认为这篇文章很有意思。"我向他解释：我想知道的并非他对这篇文章的看法，而是他想从其他人那里获得怎样的回应。他想了一会儿，然后承认："我不确定我想要的是什么。"

我想，这就是他们浪费了会议前20分钟的原因。如果我们在集体讨论时漫无目的地发言，这样的会议很可能毫无成效。然而，只要有一个人意识到这一点，就可以提醒其他成员有效地展开讨论。例如，在那

complaints and concerns regarding the principal's treatment of her daughter. A woman responded by sharing a situation that had occurred to her when she was a student at the same school. One by one, each member then related a similar personal experience. After twenty minutes I asked the group if their needs were being met by the current discussion. Not one person said yes. "This is what happens all the time in these meetings!" huffed one man, "I have better things to do with my time than sit around listening to the same old bullshit."

I then addressed the man who had initiated the discussion: "Can you tell me, when you brought up the newspaper article, what response you were wanting from the group?"

"I thought it was interesting," he replied. I explained that I was asking what response he wanted from the group, rather than what he thought about the article. He pondered awhile and then conceded, "I'm not sure what I wanted."

And that's why, I believe, twenty minutes of the group's valuable time had been squandered on fruitless discourse. When we address a group without being clear what we are wanting back, unproductive discussions will often follow. However, if even one member of a group is conscious of the importance of clearly requesting the response that is desired, he or she can extend this consciousness to the group. For example, when this particular speaker didn't define what response he wanted, a member of the group might have said, "I'm confused about how you'd like us to respond to your story. Would you be willing to say what response you'd like from us?" Such interventions can prevent the waste of precious group time.

> In a group, much time is wasted when speakers aren't certain what response they're wanting.

Conversations often drag on and on, fulfilling no one's needs, because it is unclear whether the initiator of the conversation has gotten what she or he wanted. In India, when people have received the response they want in conversations they have initiated, they say "*bas*" (pronounced "bus"). This means, "You need not say more. I feel satisfied and am now ready to move on to something else."

第六章 提出请求，丰盈生命

位男士没有说明他希望得到怎样的回应时，只要有人说："我不清楚你希望我们给你什么样的回应，可以请你告诉我们吗？"这样的提醒也许就可以避免继续浪费人们的宝贵时间。

团体会议时，如果话题的发起人不清楚自己想要什么，讨论就会漫无目的地拖延下去，却又无法满足任何人的需要。在印度，当某个话题的发起人获得了想要的回应，他们会说"bas"（发音同"巴斯"），意思是"谢谢你的回应，我很满意，我准备好了谈论下一个话题"。尽管我们的语言中没有这样的词，但我们可以在交流中培养和鼓励这种意识。

区分请求与要求

如果人们因为没答应我们的请求而受到责罚，他们就会将我们的"请求"视为"要求"。在听见要求时，一个人通常只能看到两种选择：屈服或者反抗。无论如何，只要人们认为我们在强迫他们，就很难友善地回应我们的请求。

让我们看看一种情况的两个版本。杰克对他的朋友珍妮说："我感到很孤单，你今晚能来陪我吗？"这是"请求"还是"要求"呢？现在还不好说。只有看到杰克在珍妮没有同意后的反应，我们才能做出判断。假如她回答说："杰克，我今天很累，如果你想今晚有人陪你，可以找其他人吗？"如果杰克的回应是："你就是这样自私！"那么，他提出的其实是一个"要求"而非"请求"。他没有同理倾听珍妮想要休息的需要，而是指责她。

6 Requesting That Which Would Enrich Life

Though we lack such a word in our own language, we can benefit from developing and promoting "bas-consciousness" in all our interactions.

Requests versus Demands

Our requests are received as demands when others believe they will be blamed or punished if they do not comply. When people hear a demand, they see only two options: submission or rebellion. Either way, the person requesting is perceived as coercive, and the listener's capacity to respond compassionately to the request is diminished.

> When the other person hears a demand from us, they see two options: to submit or to rebel.

The more we have in the past blamed, punished, or "laid guilt trips" on others when they haven't responded to our requests, the higher the likelihood that our requests will now be heard as demands. We also pay for others' use of such tactics. To the degree that people in our lives have been blamed, punished, or urged to feel guilty for not doing what others have requested, the more likely they are to carry this baggage to every subsequent relationship and hear a demand in any request.

> To tell if it's a demand or a request, observe what the speaker does if the request is not complied with.

Let's look at two variations of a situation. Jack says to his friend Jane, "I'm lonely and would like you to spend the evening with me." Is that a request or a demand? The answer is that we don't know until we observe how Jack treats Jane if she doesn't comply. Suppose she replies, "Jack, I'm really tired. If you'd like some company, how about finding someone else to be with you this evening?"

> It's a demand if the speaker then criticizes or judges.

If Jack then remarks, "How typical of you to be so selfish!" his request was in fact a demand. Instead of empathizing with her need to rest, he has blamed her.

第六章 提出请求，丰盈生命

让我们再来看另外一个版本：

杰克：我感到很孤单，希望今晚你能来陪陪我。
珍妮：杰克，我今天很累，如果你想今晚有人陪你，可以找其他人吗？
杰克一声不吭地走开了。
珍妮感受到杰克的难过，就问他：你是不是有些难过？
杰克：没有。
珍妮：我感到你有些不对劲，怎么了？
杰克：你知道我有多么孤单吗？！你要是真的爱我，晚上就会留下来陪我。

同样地，杰克没有体会珍妮的需要，而是认为珍妮不爱他、拒绝了他。我们越是将对方的不应允诠释为拒绝，他人就越有可能将我们的"请求"视为"要求"。人们听见的要求越多，就越不喜欢与我们相处，我们的判断最终成了真。

反之，如果杰克理解并且尊重珍妮的感受和需要，对她说："珍妮，你的意思是你已经很累了，今晚需要休息？"那么他表达的就是真正的"请求"，而非"要求"。

如果希望他人相信我们所提出的是"请求"而非"要求"，我们可以向他人表明希望他们出于自愿来回应请求。例如，我们可以说："你是否愿意铺一下桌子？"而不是："我想要你铺一下桌子。"总之，要让他人明白我们提出的是真正的请求，最重要的沟通方式是即便在他人拒绝时我们也能同理他们的感受和需要。

同时，我们选择"请求"而非"要求"，并不意味着在他人说"不"

6 Requesting That Which Would Enrich Life

Consider a second scenario:

Jack: I'm lonely and would like you to spend the evening with me.

Jane: Jack, I'm really tired. If you'd like some company, how about finding someone else to be with you tonight?

Jack: *(turns away wordlessly)*

Jane: *(sensing he is upset)* Is something bothering you?

Jack: No.

Jane: Come on, Jack, I can sense something's going on. What's the matter?

Jack: You know how lonely I'm feeling. If you really loved me, you'd spend the evening with me.

Again, instead of empathizing, Jack now interprets Jane's response to mean that she doesn't love him and that she has rejected him. The more we interpret noncompliance as rejection, the more likely our requests will be heard as demands. This leads to a self-fulfilling prophecy, for the more people hear demands, the less they enjoy being around us.

> It's a demand if the speaker then lays a guilt trip.

On the other hand, we would know that Jack's request had been a genuine request, not a demand, if his response to Jane had expressed a respectful recognition of her feelings and needs. For example: "So, Jane, you're feeling worn out and needing some rest this evening?"

We can help others trust that we are requesting, not demanding, by indicating that we would only want them to comply if they can do so willingly. Thus we might ask, "Would you be willing to set the table?" rather than "I would like you to set the table." However, the most powerful way to communicate that we are making a genuine request is to empathize with people when they don't agree to the request.

> It's a request if the speaker then shows empathy toward the other person's needs.

We demonstrate that we are making a request rather than a demand by how we respond when others don't comply. If we are prepared to show an empathic understanding

第六章　提出请求，丰盈生命

时，我们就只能放弃自己的诉求。选择请求意味着，我们首先同理他人为什么没有说"是"，而不是要说服他们必须答应我们。

阐明提出请求的目的

要表达真正的请求，我们还需要知道请求的目的是什么。如果只是为了改变他人来寻求自己的利益，那么，非暴力沟通并不是一个适当的工具。使用非暴力沟通时，我们希望他人的改变和回应是出于自愿和善意。非暴力沟通的意图是，建立一种基于坦诚与同理心的关系。只有当他人相信我们将彼此的关系放在首位并致力于满足彼此的需要时，人们才能够相信我们所提出的是真正的"请求"，而非伪装的"要求"。

然而，在沟通中对意图保持觉知是不容易的，尤其是父母、教师、管理人员，还有那些在工作中以影响和改变他人为目标的人们。有位母亲在一次工作坊的午间休息时对我说："马歇尔，我回家后试用了非暴力沟通，但没什么用。"于是，我请她描述一下她做了什么。

她说："就像我们上午练习的那样，回家后我向儿子表达了我的感受和需要，既没有责备也没有评判他。我只是说：'你看，当我看到你没有做你答应要做的家务活，我很失望。我希望回家后看到家里是整洁的。'接着我提出了一个请求，希望他立刻去打扫。"

"听上去你很清晰地表达了非暴力沟通的四个要素。"我回答说，"然后呢？"

"他什么都没做。"

"再然后呢？"我继续问她。

6 Requesting That Which Would Enrich Life

of what prevents someone from doing as we asked, then by my definition, we have made a request, not a demand. Choosing to request rather than demand does not mean we give up when someone says no to our request. It does mean that we don't engage in persuasion until we have empathized with what's preventing the other person from saying yes.

Defining Our Objective When Making Requests

Expressing genuine requests also requires an awareness of our objective. If our objective is only to change people and their behavior or to get our way, then NVC is not an appropriate tool. The process is designed for those of us who would like others to change and respond, but only if they choose to do so willingly and compassionately. The objective of NVC is to establish a relationship based on honesty and empathy. When others trust that our primary commitment is to the quality of the relationship, and

> Our objective is a relationship based on honesty and empathy.

that we expect this process to fulfill everyone's needs, then they can trust that our requests are true requests and not camouflaged demands.

A consciousness of this objective is difficult to maintain, especially for parents, teachers, managers, and others whose work centers around influencing people and obtaining behavioral results. A mother who once returned to a workshop after a lunch break announced, "Marshall, I went home and tried it. It didn't work." I asked her to describe what she'd done.

"I went home and expressed my feelings and needs, just as we'd practiced. I made no criticism, no judgments of my son. I simply said, 'Look, when I see that you haven't done the work you said you were going to do, I feel very disappointed. I wanted to be able to come home and find the house in order and your chores completed.' Then I made a request: I told him I wanted him to clean it up immediately."

"It sounds like you clearly expressed all the components," I commented. "What happened?"

第六章　提出请求，丰盈生命

"我对他说，他不能一辈子都这样懒惰和不负责任！"

我注意到，这位女士还无法区分"请求"和"要求"的不同。在她看来，使用非暴力沟通是否成功，取决于她的"请求"是否能得到满足。我们在刚开始学习非暴力沟通时，或许会发现自己只是在机械地使用它的要素，却没有意识到它真正的意图是什么。

有些时候，即使我们带着非暴力沟通的意图和关爱提出请求，有些人仍然会把它看成要求，特别是当我们处于权力上强势的一方，而对方恰恰曾受过来自权威的威逼压迫时。

一次，一所高中的管理团队邀请我向教师们示范，如何运用非暴力沟通与那些不配合的学生沟通。在校方的安排下，我和40来位被视为"社交与情绪不良"的学生会面。令我印象深刻的是，这些学生被贴上了这样的标签后，果然就表现出了"社交与情绪不良"行为。试想，如果你被贴上了如此标签，那岂不是说不遵守学校规矩是正常的吗？！我们给他人贴上标签反而造就了那些让我们烦恼的行为，而这些行为又进一步确认着我们对他们的判断。所以，当我走进教室，看到大部分的学生围在窗边对着楼下的同学大声骂脏话时，我并不感到意外。

我首先向他们提出了一个请求："请你们回到教室里坐好，好让我能介绍我自己和我们今天要做的事情。"大概有一半的学生回到了教室里。我不确定是否所有人都听清了我的请求，于是我又重复了一遍。这时，其他的学生都回到了座位，除了两位男生还靠在窗边，他们是这个班上块头最大的学生。

"请问，"我对他们说，"你们两位有谁可以告诉我，听到我说了什么呢？"其中一位转过身，不耐烦地说道："你说我们必须回来坐下。"这让我明白了，他把我的请求听成了要求。

6 Requesting That Which Would Enrich Life

"He didn't do it."

"Then what happened?" I asked.

"I told him he couldn't go through life being lazy and irresponsible."

I could see that this woman was not yet able to distinguish between expressing requests and making demands. She was still defining the process as successful only if she got compliance for her "requests." During the initial phases of learning this process, we may find ourselves applying the components of NVC mechanically without awareness of the underlying purpose.

Sometimes, however, even when we're conscious of our intent and express our request with care, people may still hear a demand. This is particularly true when we occupy positions of authority and are speaking with those who have had past experiences with coercive authority figures.

Once, the administrator of a high school invited me to demonstrate to teachers how NVC might help them communicate with students who weren't cooperating as the teachers would have liked.

I was asked to meet with forty students who had been deemed "socially and emotionally maladjusted." I was struck by the way such labels serve as self-fulfilling prophecies. If you were a student who had been thus labeled, wouldn't it just give you permission to have some fun at school by resisting whatever was asked of you? When we give people labels, we tend to act in a way that contributes to the very behavior that concerns us, which we then view as further confirmation of our diagnosis. Since these students knew they had been classified as "socially and emotionally maladjusted," I wasn't surprised that when I walked in, most of them were hanging out the window hollering obscenities at their friends in the courtyard below.

I began by making a request: "I'd like you all to come over and sit down so I can tell you who I am and what I'd like us to do today." About half the students came over. Uncertain that they had all heard me, I repeated my request. With that, the remainder

第六章 提出请求，丰盈生命

我接着说："先生！"我已经学会了管那些强壮魁梧的人叫"先生"，特别是其中一位身上还刺着文身的时候更要这样。"你是否愿意告诉我，我怎样表达能让你明白这是我的愿望，而不是在对你发号施令呢？"

"什么？"他显然早已习惯将权威人物的话当成命令，我这样不同的表达，对他是不寻常的。于是我重复了我的话："怎样才能让你知道我希望你做什么，而不会让你认为我在发号施令呢？"他想了想，然后耸了耸肩说："我不知道。"

"现在我们两人之间的对话，正是我今天想和你们讨论的话题。我相信，人们如果可以说出自己的愿望，但又不对他人发号施令，人与人之间可以相处得更加愉快。我说出我的愿望，并不是要求你非做不可；也不是如果你不做，就要让你的日子难过。我不知道，如何表达才能让你信任这一点。"这番话似乎触动了这位年轻男子，他与伙伴慢慢走回了座位，我也感到松了口气。在类似的情况下，有的时候我们需要花一些时间让人们了解我们提出的是"请求"而不是"要求"。

在提出请求时，我们不妨仔细观察一下自己是否带着这样一些不假思索的想法。如果有，那么我所提出的"请求"就会变成"要求"：

- 他**应该**自己把房间打扫干净。
- 她**应当**按照我说的做。
- 老板**理应**给我加薪。
- 我有**理由**让他们留得更晚。
- 我**有权**多休几天假。

6 Requesting That Which Would Enrich Life

of the students sat down, with the exception of two young men who remained draped over the windowsill. Unfortunately for me, these two were the biggest students in the class.

"Excuse me," I addressed them, "would one of you two gentlemen tell me what you heard me say?" One of them turned toward me and snorted, "Yeah, you said we had to go over there and sit down." I thought to myself, "Uh, oh, he's heard my request as a demand."

Out loud I said, "Sir"—I've learned always to say "sir" to people with biceps like his, especially when one of them sports a tattoo—"would you be willing to tell me how I could have let you know what I was wanting so that it wouldn't sound like I was bossing you around?"

"Huh?" Having been conditioned to expect demands from authorities, he was not used to my different approach. "How can I let you know what I'm wanting from you so it doesn't sound like I don't care about what you'd like?" I repeated. He hesitated for a moment and shrugged, "I don't know."

"What's going on between you and me right now is a good example of what I was wanting us to talk about today. I believe people can enjoy each other a lot better if they can say what they would like without bossing others around. When I tell you what I'd like, I'm not saying that you have to do it or I'll try to make your life miserable. I don't know how to say that in a way that you can trust." To my relief, this seemed to make sense to the young man who, together with his friend, sauntered over to join the group. In certain situations, such as this one, it may take awhile for our requests to be clearly seen for what they are.

When making a request, it is also helpful to scan our minds for the sort of thoughts that automatically transform requests into demands:

- He *should* be cleaning up after himself.
- She's *supposed* to do what I ask.
- I *deserve* to get a raise.
- I'm *justified* in having them stay later.
- I have a *right* to more time off.

第六章　提出请求，丰盈生命

　　如果以这样的想法来表达需要，一旦别人没有满足我们的请求，我们势必会指责他们。有一次，我的小儿子布拉特没有倒垃圾，我就有了类似自以为是的想法。之前我们在讨论家务分工时，他认领了清理垃圾的工作，但后来我们还是每天为此产生口角。为了让他去倒垃圾，我一再地提醒他："这是你的活儿。"或是"我们每个人都有自己的任务。"

　　后来有一天晚上，我和他又针对这件事做了一番交流，这一次，我仔细聆听，终于听到了他不愿倒垃圾行为背后的心声。于是，我写下了这首《布拉特之歌》。

　　　　如果我知道你并不是在要求我，
　　　　当你召唤我时，我会乐意回应你。
　　　　如果你高高在上，像个盛气凌人的老板，
　　　　你将会发现，你一头撞在了墙上。
　　　　当你假惺惺地提醒我，你为我做的各种事情，
　　　　你最好准备再次碰壁！
　　　　就算你大喊、大怒、抱怨、叹息，甚至要揍我，
　　　　我依然不会去倒垃圾。
　　　　而现在，即使你改变方式，
　　　　我也需要花一些时间来原谅你。
　　　　因为，在我看来，当我不符合你的期待，
　　　　你似乎就不会把我当人看待。

　　当布拉特感受到了我已经理解并尊重他的立场后，他开始主动倒垃圾，那之后我再也没有为此提醒过他。

6 Requesting That Which Would Enrich Life

When we frame our needs with these thoughts, we are bound to judge others when they don't do as we request. I had these self-righteous thoughts in my mind once when my younger son was not taking out the garbage. When we were dividing the household chores, he had agreed to this task, but every day we would have another struggle about getting the garbage out. Every day I would remind him, "This is your job," and "We all have jobs"—with the sole objective of getting him to take out the garbage.

Finally, one night I listened more closely to what he'd been telling me all along about why the garbage wasn't going out. I wrote the following song after that evening's discussion. After my son felt my empathy for his position, he began taking out the garbage without any further reminder from me.

> *If I clearly understand*
> *you intend no demand,*
> *I'll usually respond when you call.*
> *But if you come across*
> *like a high and mighty boss,*
> *you'll feel like you ran into a wall.*
> *And when you remind me*
> *so piously*
> *about all those things you've done for me,*
> *you'd better get ready:*
> *Here comes another bout!*
> *Then you can shout,*
> *you can spit,*
> *moan, groan, and throw a fit;*
> *I still won't take the garbage out.*
> *Now even if you should change your style,*
> *It's going to take me a little while*
> *before I can forgive and forget.*
> *Because it seems to me that you*
> *didn't see me as human too*
> *until all your standards were met.*
>
> —"Song from Brett" by Marshall B. Rosenberg

第六章　提出请求，丰盈生命

小结

非暴力沟通的第四个要素是提出请求，以便让我们的生命更加丰盈。在提出请求时，我们要尽力避免模糊、抽象或模棱两可的语言，说明我们要什么，而不是不要什么。

在开口时，我们越是把想要得到的回应表达清楚，就越有可能得到这样的回应。由于我们所表达的信息与别人的理解有可能不一致，我们需要学习去发现对方是否已经准确无误地接收到了我们的信息。特别是在团体讨论中，更需要清楚知道和说明我们想要的回应。否则，讨论可能只是在浪费大家的时间。

一旦人们认为不答应我们的请求就会受到责罚，"请求"就成了"要求"。为了让人们信任我们所提出的是"请求"而非"要求"，可以清楚地表明我们希望人们出于自愿来满足请求。非暴力沟通的意图不是为了改变他人来满足自己，而是帮助双方建立坦诚和有同理心的关系，最终每个人的需要都能得到满足。

非暴力沟通实例

与好友谈论戒烟

阿尔与博尔特是30多年的好朋友。博尔特每天要抽两包烟，多年

6 Requesting That Which Would Enrich Life

Summary

The fourth component of NVC addresses the question of *what we would like to request of each other to enrich each of our lives*. We try to avoid vague, abstract, or ambiguous phrasing, and remember to use positive action language by stating what we *are* requesting rather than what we are *not*.

Each time we speak, the clearer we are about what we want back, the more likely we are to get it. Since the message we send is not always the message that's received, we need to learn how to find out if our message has been accurately heard. Especially when we are expressing ourselves in a group, we need to be clear about the nature of the response we are wanting. Otherwise we may be initiating unproductive conversations that waste considerable group time.

Requests are received as demands when listeners believe that they will be blamed or punished if they do not comply. We can help others trust that we are requesting, not demanding, by indicating our desire for them to comply only if they can do so willingly. The objective of NVC is not to change people and their behavior in order to get our way; it is to establish relationships based on honesty and empathy that will eventually fulfill everyone's needs.

NVC in Action

Sharing Fears About a Best Friend's Smoking

Al and Burt have been best friends for over thirty years. Al, a nonsmoker, has done everything he can over the years to persuade Burt to give up his two-pack-a-day habit. In the past, when Al had tried to get him to quit, Burt had often accused Al of judging him.

Aware during the past year of the increasing severity of his friend's hacking cough, Al finds himself bursting out one day with all the energy and life that had been buried in his unexpressed anger and fear.

第六章　提出请求，丰盈生命

来，不抽烟的阿尔想尽一切办法劝说博尔特戒烟。而每当阿尔尝试这么做时，博尔特多半会认为阿尔在批评他。

过去一年来，眼见博尔特咳嗽得越来越厉害，有一天，阿尔终于忍不住将所有埋在心里的怒气和忧虑告诉了博尔特。

阿　　尔：博尔特，我知道这件事情我们已经说过无数次了。可是我还是想告诉你，我害怕那该死的香烟会送了你的性命！你是我最好的朋友，我希望你能与我一起活着，越久越好。请不要认为我又在指责你，我真的没有。我只是很担心你。

博尔特：我知道你在担心我。我们是那么多年的朋友了……

阿　　尔：（提出请求）你愿意戒烟吗？

博尔特：我也希望我做得到。

阿　　尔：（聆听博尔特做不到背后的感受与需要）想到戒烟，你害怕自己做不到是吗？

博尔特：是的……你知道我已经尝试了好多次，但都没有成功……大家都看不起我。

阿　　尔：（猜测博尔特想要提出的请求）我没有瞧不起你，即使你再次戒烟失败，我也不会看不起你。我只是希望你再试一下。

博尔特：谢谢。但只有你没有看不起我……我能从其他人的眼里看出，他们都认为我是个没用的人。

阿　　尔：（试着同理倾听博尔特的感受）是不是戒烟已经够难了，还要担心其他人会怎么看你，这对你来说压力很大？

博尔特：我真的很憎恨自己被香烟摆布……

阿　　尔：（阿尔看着博尔特的双眼，点了点头沉默了片刻，他的眼神流露出他对博尔特深深的关心。）

6 Requesting That Which Would Enrich Life

Al: Burt, I know we've talked about this a dozen times, but listen. I'm scared your damned cigarettes are going to kill you! You're my best friend, and I want you around for as long as I can have you. Please don't think I'm judging you. I'm not—I'm just really worried.

Burt: No, I hear your concern. We've been friends for a long time . . .

Al: *(making a request)* Would you be willing to quit?

Burt: I wish I could.

Al: *(listening for the feelings and needs preventing Burt from agreeing to the request)* Are you scared to try because you don't want to fail?

Burt: Yeah . . . you know how many times I've tried before . . . I know people think less of me for not being able to quit.

Al: *(guessing at what Burt might want to request)* I don't think less of you. And if you tried and failed again, I still wouldn't. I just wish you'd try.

Burt: Thanks. But you're not the only one. . . . It's everyone: you can see it in their eyes—they think you're a failure.

Al: *(empathizing with Burt's feeling)* Is it kind of overwhelming to worry about what others might think, when just quitting is hard enough?

Burt: I really hate the idea that I might be addicted, that I have something that I just can't control . . .

Al: *(Al's eyes connect with Burt's; he nods his head. Al's interest and attention to Burt's deep feelings and needs are revealed through his eyes and the silence that follows.)*

Burt: I mean, I don't even like smoking any more. It's like you're a pariah if you do it in public. It's embarrassing.

Al: *(continuing to empathize)* It sounds like you'd really like to quit, but are scared you might fail—and how that would be for your self-image and confidence.

第六章　提出请求，丰盈生命

博尔特：其实我已经不再喜欢抽烟了。特别是在公众场合，抽烟就会被别人厌恶，我觉得很尴尬。

阿　尔：（继续体会博尔特的感受和需要）听起来你真的很想戒烟，可又担心失败，让你因此看不起自己并失去信心。

博尔特：嗯，我想是吧……你知道吗？我从来没有和你说过，以前要是有人要是劝我戒烟，我就会让他们滚蛋。我想要戒烟，但我不希望别人给我压力。

阿　尔：我不想给你包袱，我也不知道能否让你打消顾虑，但只要你愿意，我一定会尽力支持你。

博尔特：我愿意。你那么关心和支持我，我真的很感动。但是……如果我现在还没有准备好，你会介意吗？

阿　尔：当然不会，博尔特。我依然爱着你，我只是希望我能爱你更久一些。

　　因为阿尔提出的是真正的请求而不是要求，因此，不论博尔特如何回应，他都始终专注在双方的连结上。通过"我依然爱你"这句话，他向博尔特表达了他的心意和对博尔特的尊重。同时，在说"希望能爱你更久一些"时，阿尔也表达了自己的需要。

博尔特：好，我会再试一次……但不要告诉别人好吗？

阿　尔：当然，由你决定什么时候准备好了，我不会告诉任何人。

练习四：表达请求

　　根据你的理解，下列哪些句子是一个清晰、具体、可行的请求？

> **Burt:** Yeah, I guess that's it. . . . You know, I don't think I've ever talked about it before. Usually when people tell me to quit, I just tell them to get lost. I'd like to quit, but I don't want all that pressure from people.
>
> **Al:** I wouldn't want to pressure you. I don't know if I could reassure you about your fears around not succeeding, but I sure would like to support you in any way I can. That is . . . if you want me to. . . .
>
> **Burt:** Yes, I do. I'm really touched by your concern and willingness. But . . . suppose I'm not ready to try yet, is that okay with you too?
>
> **Al:** Of course, Burt, I'll still like you as much. It's just that I want to like you for longer!

Because Al's request was a genuine request, not a demand, he maintained awareness of his commitment to the quality of the relationship, regardless of Burt's response. He expressed this awareness and his respect for Burt's need for autonomy through his words, "I'll still like you," while simultaneously expressing his own need "to like you for longer."

> **Burt:** Well, then, maybe I will try again . . . but don't tell anyone else, okay?
>
> **Al:** Sure, you decide when you're ready; I won't be mentioning it to anybody.

第六章　提出请求，丰盈生命

1. "我希望你理解我。"
2. "请告诉我，你欣赏我做的哪一件事情。"
3. "我希望你能更加自信。"
4. "我希望你不要再喝酒了。"
5. "请你让我做自己吧。"
6. "关于昨天的会议，我希望你能和我说实话。"
7. "我希望你在规定的时速内驾驶。"
8. "我想更好地了解你。"
9. "我希望你尊重我的隐私。"
10. "我希望你能经常做晚饭。"

以下是我对练习四的回应：

1. 如果你选择这一句，我们意见不一致。在我看来，"你理解我"并不是一个具体明确的行动。一个具体明确的请求可以是："你是否可以告诉我，在你听来，我刚才说的是什么意思。"

2. 如果你选择这一句，我们的意见一致。

3. 如果你选择这一句，我们意见不一致。如果改为"我希望你能参加一个关于提升主动性的培训，这会让你更有自信"，那么，我认为这是一个明确的请求。

4. 如果你选择这一句，我们意见不一致。在我看来，"不要再喝酒"并没有表达出说话的人想要什么，而是不想要什么。一个具体明确的请求可以是："你是否可以告诉我，喝酒可以满足你什么需要？是否还有别的方式能满足这些需要。"

5. 如果你选择这一句，我们意见不一致。"让我做自己"并不是一

6 Requesting That Which Would Enrich Life

Exercise 4

EXPRESSING REQUESTS

To see whether we're in agreement about the clear expression of requests, circle the number in front of each of the following statements in which the speaker is clearly requesting that a specific action be taken.

1. "I want you to understand me."
2. "I'd like you to tell me one thing that I did that you appreciate."
3. "I'd like you to feel more confidence in yourself."
4. "I want you to stop drinking."
5. "I'd like you to let me be me."
6. "I'd like you to be honest with me about yesterday's meeting."
7. "I would like you to drive at or below the speed limit."
8. "I'd like to get to know you better."
9. "I would like you to show respect for my privacy."
10. "I'd like you to prepare supper more often."

Here are my responses for Exercise 4:

1. If you circled this number, we're not in agreement. To me, the word *understand* does not clearly express a request for a specific action. A request for a specific action might be: "I want you to tell me what you heard me say."
2. If you circled this number, we're in agreement that the speaker is clearly requesting a specific action.
3. If you circled this number, we're not in agreement. To me, the words *feel more confidence* do not clearly express a request for a specific action. A request for a specific action might be: "I'd like you to take a course in assertiveness training, which I believe would increase your self-confidence."

个具体明确的行动。一个具体明确的请求可以是："我希望你告诉我，即使我做了让你不喜欢的事情，你仍然会和我在一起。"

6. 如果你选择这一句，我们意见不一致。"和我说实话"不是一个具体明确的行动。一个具体明确的请求可以是："请告诉我，你对我做的事情有什么感受，你希望我能有什么样的改变？"

7. 如果你选择这一句，我们的意见一致。

8. 如果你选择这一句，我们意见不一致。如果改为"请告诉我，你是否愿意每周和我吃一次午餐"，那么，在我看来，这是一个具体明确的请求。

9. 如果你选择这一句，我们意见不一致。"尊重隐私"并不是一个具体明确的行动。一个具体明确的请求可以是："请答应我，进我的房间前先敲门。"

10. 如果你选择这一句，我们意见不一致。在我看来，"经常"的意思并不明确。一个具体明确的请求可以是："我想请你在每周一准备晚餐。"

6 Requesting That Which Would Enrich Life

4. If you circled this number, we're not in agreement. To me, the words *stop drinking* do not express what the speaker wants, but rather what he or she doesn't want. A request for a specific action might be: "I want you to tell me what needs of yours are met by drinking, and to discuss with me other ways of meeting those needs."

5. If you circled this number, we're not in agreement. To me, the words *let me be me* do not clearly express a request for a specific action. A request for a specific action might be: "I want you to tell me you won't leave our relationship—even if I do some things that you don't like."

6. If you circled this number, we're not in agreement. To me, the words *be honest with me* do not clearly express a request for a specific action. A request for a specific action might be: "I want you to tell me how you feel about what I did and what you'd like me to do differently."

7. If you circled this number, we're in agreement that the speaker is clearly requesting a specific action.

8. If you circled this number, we're not in agreement. To me, the words *get to know you better* do not clearly express a request for a specific action. A request for a specific action might be: "I'd like you to tell me if you would be willing to meet for lunch once a week."

9. If you circled this number, we're not in agreement. To me, the words *show respect for my privacy* do not clearly express a request for a specific action. A request for a specific action might be: "I'd like you to agree to knock before you enter my office."

10. If you circled this number, we're not in agreement. To me, the words *more often* do not clearly express a request for a specific action. A request for a specific action might be: "I'd like you to prepare supper every Monday night."

第七章

以同理心倾听

Receiving Empathically

The last four chapters described the four components of NVC: what we are observing, feeling, and needing, and what we would like to request to enrich our lives. Now we turn from self-expression to apply these same four components to hearing what others are observing, feeling, needing, and requesting. We refer to this part of the communication process as *receiving empathically*.

> The two parts of NVC:
> 1. expressing honestly
> 2. receiving empathically

Presence: Don't Just Do Something, Stand There

Empathy is a respectful understanding of what others are experiencing. The Chinese philosopher Chuang-Tzu stated that true empathy requires listening with the whole being: "The hearing that is only in the ears is one thing. The hearing of the understanding is another. But the hearing of the spirit is not limited to any one faculty, to the ear, or to the mind. Hence it demands the emptiness of all the faculties. And when the faculties are empty, then the whole being listens. There is then a direct grasp of what is right there before you that can never be heard with the ear or understood with the mind."

> Empathy: emptying our mind and listening with our whole being

Empathy with others occurs only when we have successfully shed all preconceived ideas and judgments about them. The Austrian-born Israeli philosopher Martin Buber describes this quality of presence that life demands of us: "In spite of all similarities, every

第七章　以同理心倾听

前四章介绍了如何通过非暴力沟通的四个要素诚实地表达自己：我们观察到什么，有什么感受和需要，提出什么请求来丰盈自己的生命。本章我们将这四个要素运用于沟通过程的另一部分——同理倾听他人的观察、感受、需要和请求。

不去做什么，只是在那里

同理意味着，以尊重的态度来了解他人的体验。中国先哲庄子称，真正的同理需要全身心地倾听："只用耳朵来听是一回事，用理解去听是另一回事。而听其神则并不受限于我们的任何器官，不受限于耳朵或者头脑。因而这样的听需要我们全然地放空感官。当感官空灵，你的生命就作为整体的存在开始倾听。如此，便能直接感知在你面前的人、事、物，这是永远无法用耳朵听见或用头脑理解的。"

要同理他人，必须完全卸下对他人先入为主的成见和评判，这就是与他人"同在"的状态。出生于奥地利的以色列哲学家马丁·布伯（Martin Buber）形容这是我们面对生命时所需具备的态度："生命中的

7 Receiving Empathically

living situation has, like a newborn child, a new face, that has never been before and will never come again. It demands of you a reaction that cannot be prepared beforehand. It demands nothing of what is past. It demands presence, responsibility; it demands you."

The presence that empathy requires is not easy to maintain. "The capacity to give one's attention to a sufferer is a very rare and diffi-cult thing; it is almost a miracle; it is a miracle," asserts French philosopher Simone Weil. "Nearly all those who think they have the capacity do not possess it." Instead of offering empathy, we tend instead to give advice or reassurance and to explain our own position or feeling. Empathy, on the other hand, requires us to focus full attention on the other person's message. We give to others the time and space they need to express themselves fully and to feel understood. There is a Buddhist saying that aptly describes this ability: "Don't just do something, stand there."

> Ask before offering advice or reassurance.

It is often frustrating for someone needing empathy to have us assume that they want reassurance or "fix-it" advice. I received a lesson from my daughter that taught me to check whether advice or reassurance is wanted before offering any. She was looking in the mirror one day and said, "I'm as ugly as a pig."

"You're the most gorgeous creature God ever put on the face of the earth," I declared. She shot me a look of exasperation, exclaimed, "Oh, Daddy!" and slammed the door as she left the room. I later found out that she had wanted some empathy. Instead of my ill-timed reassurance, I could have asked, "Are you feeling disappointed with your appearance today?"

My friend Holley Humphrey identified some common behaviors that prevent us from being sufficiently present to connect empathically with others. The following are examples:

- Advising: "I think you should . . . " "How come you didn't . . . ?"
- One-upping: "That's nothing; wait'll you hear what happened to me."
- Educating: "This could turn into a very positive experience for you if you just . . . "

第七章 以同理心倾听

情境虽有诸多相似之处，但每时每刻却如新生儿般，带着崭新的面孔，从未有过也永不再现。你无法提前准备如何回应，也无法停留在过去。生命呼唤着你与它同在当下，负起责任而又全心投入。"

然而，保持临在绝非易事。法国哲学家西蒙娜·薇依（Simone Weil）写道："将注意力给予受苦之人，是极其稀缺的能力，也是困难的事情。这近乎奇迹。可以说这就是奇迹。几乎所有认为自己可以做到的人，实际上并不具备这种能力。"我们常常给予他人建议或宽慰，或者解释自己的立场或感受，而非同理。同理心需要我们将注意力全然地聚焦在他人想传达的信息上，给予他人足够的时间与空间充分地表达。用佛家的一句话"不去做什么，只是在那里"来描述同理这个能力再恰当不过了。

如果一个人需要同理，我们却试图通过安慰或建议来"搞定"对方的问题，他人往往会感到沮丧。对此，我的女儿给我上了一课。她教会我在给予建议或安慰前，先核实那是不是对方想要的。

有一天，女儿看着镜子中的自己说："我丑得像头猪。"

"你是上帝带到这个地球上最美丽的礼物。"我立马信誓旦旦地对她说。没想到，女儿生气地对我喊了声"爸爸，你真是的！"，随即砰地一声甩门离去。后来我才意识到，她想要的只是我能同理她的心情，我的宽慰是那么地不合时宜。其实我只须对她说："你对你今天的样子感到失望是吗？"

我的朋友霍莉·汉弗里（Holley Humphrey）做了一些归纳，来说明哪些行为会妨碍我们以同理心与他人连结。

给建议："我认为你应该……""为什么你没有这样……"

- Consoling: "It wasn't your fault; you did the best you could."
- Story-telling: "That reminds me of the time . . . "
- Shutting down: "Cheer up. Don't feel so bad."
- Sympathizing: "Oh, you poor thing . . . "
- Interrogating: "When did this begin?"
- Explaining: "I would have called but . . . "
- Correcting: "That's not how it happened."

In his book *When Bad Things Happen to Good People*, Rabbi Harold Kushner describes how painful it was for him, when his son was dying, to hear the words people offered that were intended to make him feel better. Even more painful was his recognition that for twenty years he had been saying the same things to other people in similar situations!

Believing we have to "fix" situations and make others feel better prevents us from being present. Those of us in the role of counselor or psychotherapist are particularly susceptible to this belief. Once, when I was working with twenty-three mental health professionals, I asked them to write, word for word, how they would respond to a client who says, "I'm feeling very depressed. I just don't see any reason to go on." I collected the answers they had written down and announced, "I am now going to read out loud what each of you wrote. Imagine yourself in the role of the person who expressed the feeling of depression, and raise your hand after each statement you hear that gives you a sense that you've been understood." Hands were raised to only three of the twenty-three responses. Questions such as, "When did this begin?" constituted the most frequent response; they give the appearance that the professional is obtaining the information necessary to diagnose and then treat the problem. In fact, such intellectual understanding of a problem

> Intellectual understanding blocks empathy.

blocks the kind of presence that empathy requires. When we are thinking about people's words and listening to how they connect to our theories, we are looking at people—we are not with them.

第七章 以同理心倾听

比惨:"这算不了什么。你听听我曾经经历过的。"
说教:"如果你这样做……这就会转变成一个非常积极的体验。"
安慰:"这不是你的错,你尽力了。"
讲故事:"这让我想到曾经……"
摆脱感受:"高兴一点儿,不要这么难过。"
同情:"哦,你真是可怜……"
询问:"这种情况是什么时候开始的?"
解释:"我本来想打电话给你,可是……"
纠正:"事情不是这样的。"

在《当你遇到创伤时》[①]一书中,犹太教拉比哈罗德·库什纳(Harold Kushner)讲述,经历了丧子之痛,他听到人们的安慰极为痛苦。然而更令他难过的是,他发现过去20多年来,自己在别人遭遇不幸时也说着同样的话。

我们常常认为要想办法解决问题或让他人好受些,但这些却恰恰阻碍了与他人同在。对于咨询师或心理治疗师来说,更容易如此。一次,我与一群精神健康专家工作。我问他们,当来访者表达"我感到非常压抑,找不到任何活下去的理由"时,他们会如何回应,同时我请他们将回应逐字逐句写下。收集好他们的回答,我说:"我念出你们每个人写下的回应。想象一下,你是那位求助者,如果你认为某个回答表达了对你的理解,就请你举手。"在23个回答中,只有3个有人举手。最频

---

① 《当你遇到创伤时》(*When Bad Things Happen to Good People*)中文简体版由华夏出版社出版。

The key ingredient of empathy is presence: we are wholly present with the other party and what they are experiencing. This quality of presence distinguishes empathy from either mental understanding or sympathy. While we may choose at times to sympathize with others by feeling their feelings, it's helpful to be aware that during the moment we are offering sympathy, we are not empathizing.

Listening for Feelings and Needs

In NVC, no matter what words people use to express themselves, we listen for their observations, feelings, needs, and requests. Imagine you've loaned your car to a new neighbor who had a personal emergency, and when your family finds out, they react with intensity: "You are a fool for having trusted a total stranger!" You can use the components of NVC to tune in to the feelings and needs of those family members in contrast to either (1) blaming yourself by taking the message personally, or (2) blaming and judging them.

> No matter what others say, we only hear what they are (1) observing, (2) feeling, (3) needing, and (4) requesting.

In this situation, it's obvious what the family is observing and reacting to: the lending of the car to a relative stranger. In other situations, it may not be so clear. If a colleague tells us, "You're not a good team player," we may not know what he or she is observing, although we can usually guess at the behavior that might have triggered such a statement.

The following exchange, from a workshop, demonstrates the difficulty of focusing on other people's feelings and needs when we are accustomed to assuming responsibility for their feelings and taking messages personally. The woman in this dialogue wanted to learn to hear the feelings and needs behind certain of her husband's statements. I suggested that she guess at his feelings and needs and then check it out with him.

第七章 以同理心倾听

繁的回应是"这是什么时候开始的",乍看之下,这类提问是专业人士为诊断以及治疗收集信息,事实上,试图分析问题无法让我们与他人同在。如果我们只是关心别人的话是否符合我们的理论,我们是在审视他们,而没有与他们同在。同理的核心是"临在"——全然地与他人以及他们当下的体验同在。因此,"同理心"不同于头脑上的理解,也并非"同情"。有时我们会因为体会到他人的感受而心生同情,这时我们需要格外警惕,当我们对他人表达同情时,就不是在同理他们。

倾听他人的感受和需要

不论人们以什么样的方式来表达自己,我们都可以用心聆听他们的观察、感受、需要和请求。想像一下,你将自己的轿车借给了有急事的新邻居,你的家人知道后反应强烈:"你这样信任一个陌生人实在太傻了!"此时,你就可以借助非暴力沟通的要素来聆听他们的感受和需要,而非自责或反驳他们。

在这个例子中,你显然可以看出家人观察到的事实是:你将轿车借给一个陌生人。而有些时候,我们并不清晰别人的话是基于怎样的观察。例如,一位同事对你说:"你没有团队精神。"你可能一头雾水,不知道同事指的究竟是哪件事,但我们可以通过询问来猜测是什么事情引发了这句话。

此外,如果我们习惯为他人的感受承担责任并因此而自责,那么关注他人的感受与需要则会变得非常困难。在一次工作坊上,有位女士想要学习聆听先生的感受和需要。我建议她在表达自己之前,先来猜测先

7 Receiving Empathically

Husband's statement: What good does talking to you do? You never listen.

Woman: Are you feeling unhappy with me?

MBR: When you say "with me," you imply that his feelings are the result of what you did. I would prefer for you to say, "Are you unhappy because you were needing . . . ?" and not "Are you unhappy with me?" It would put your attention on what's going on within him and decrease the likelihood of your taking the message personally.

Woman: But what would I say? "Are you unhappy because you . . . ? Because you what?"

MBR: Get your clue from the content of your husband's message, "What good does talking to you do? You never listen." What is he needing that he's not getting when he says that?

Woman: *(trying to empathize with the needs expressed through her husband's message)* Are you feeling unhappy because you feel like I don't understand you?

MBR: Notice that you are focusing on what he's thinking, and not on what he's needing. I think you'll find people to be less threatening if you hear what they're needing rather than what they're thinking about you. Instead of hearing that he's unhappy because he thinks you don't listen, focus on what he's needing by saying, "Are you unhappy because you are needing . . ."

> Listen to what people are needing rather than what they are thinking.

Woman: *(trying again)* Are you feeling unhappy because you are needing to be heard?

MBR: That's what I had in mind. Does it make a difference for you to hear him this way?

Woman: Definitely—a big difference. I see what's going on for him without hearing that I had done anything wrong.

第七章 以同理心倾听

生的感受和需要,再与他核实。

(先生的表达:"和你讲话有什么用?你从来都不听!")

太　　太:你是在生我的气吗?

马歇尔:你这么说,暗含着是你的行为导致了他的感受。我建议你说:"你不高兴,是因为你需要……?"这有助于你将注意力放在对方身上,了解他此刻的内心,而避免认为对方会怪罪自己。

太　　太:那我要怎么说呢?"你不高兴,因为你需要……?需要什么呢?"

马歇尔:从你先生的话中去寻找线索——"和你讲话有什么用?你从来都不听"。当他那样说的时候,是因为有什么需要没有得到满足?

太　　太:(尝试着透过丈夫的表达,同理他的需要)你感到不高兴,是因为你觉得我不理解你吗?

马歇尔:你现在关注的是他的想法而非他的需要。我认为,如果我们选择关注对方的需要,而不是他们对我们的看法,就比较不会认为他们在攻击。不把注意力放在"他不高兴是因为你没听",而是专注在他想满足的需要上,用"你感到不高兴,是因为你需要……"

太　　太:(再次尝试)你感到不高兴,是因为你需要被听见吗?

马歇尔:这正是我的意思。用这样的方式聆听他,对你来说有什么不同吗?

太　　太:确实太不同了。我听到的是他的心声,而不是我的过错。

Paraphrasing

After we focus our attention and hear what others are observing, feeling, and needing and what they are requesting to enrich their lives, we may wish to reflect back by paraphrasing what we have understood. In our previous discussion on requests (Chapter 6), we discussed how to ask for a reflection; now we will look at how to offer it to others.

If we have accurately received the other party's message, our paraphrasing will confirm this for them. If, on the other hand, our paraphrase is incorrect, we give the speaker an opportunity to correct us. Another advantage of choosing to reflect a message back to the other party is that it offers them time to reflect on what they've said and an opportunity to delve deeper into themselves.

NVC suggests that our paraphrasing take the form of questions that reveal our understanding while eliciting any necessary corrections from the speaker. Questions may focus on these components:

1. what others are observing: "Are you reacting to how many evenings I was gone last week?"
2. how others are feeling and the needs generating their feelings: "Are you feeling hurt because you would have liked more appreciation of your efforts than you received?"
3. what others are requesting: "Are you wanting me to tell you my reasons for saying what I did?"

These questions require us to sense what's going on within other people, while inviting their corrections should we have sensed incorrectly. Notice the difference between these questions and the ones below:

1. "What did I do that you are referring to?"
2. "How are you feeling?" "Why are you feeling that way?"
3. "What are you wanting me to do about it?"

第七章　以同理心倾听

复述

在谈到"请求"的第六章中，我们学习了如何邀请他人来重述我们所说的话。现在，我们将学习在聆听他人的观察、感受、需要和请求后，通过复述对方的话，将我们的理解反馈给对方。

复述对方的话可以让对方知道我们是否已经准确地领会了他们的意思；如果我们的复述还不到位，他人就有机会加以更正。此外，这样做还有一个好处是，给了对方一些时间来思考自己所说的话，从而有机会深入了解自己。

非暴力沟通建议我们用提问的形式来复述我们的理解，便于对方做出必要的更正。我们的提问可以专注于以下几个方面：

1. 对方所观察到的事实："上周我有几个晚上不在家，你说的是这件事吗？"

2. 对方的感受以及引发感受的需要："你很伤心，因为你希望自己的努力得到肯定，是吗？"

3. 对方提出的请求："你是不是希望我告诉你，为什么我会说这些话？"

要提出这些问题，我们要能感知他人的内在状态（感受和需要），同时邀请他人更正我们没有理解到位的地方。请注意上述问题与以下问题的区别：

7 Receiving Empathically

This second set of questions asks for information without first sensing the speaker's reality. Though they may appear to be the most direct way to connect with what's going on within the other person, I've found that questions like these are not the safest route to obtain the information we seek. Many such ques-tions may give speakers the impression that we're a schoolteacher examining them or a psychotherapist working on a case. If we do decide to ask for information in this way, however, I've found that people feel safer if we first reveal the feelings and needs within ourselves that are generating the question. Thus, instead of asking someone, "What did I do?" we might say, "I'm frustrated because I'd like to be clearer about what you are referring to. Would you be willing to tell me what I've done that leads you to see me in this way?" While this step may not be necessary—or even helpful—in situations where our feelings and needs are clearly conveyed by the context or tone of voice, I would recommend it particularly during moments when the questions we ask are accompanied by strong emotions.

> When asking for information, first express our own feelings and needs.

How do we determine if an occasion calls for us to reflect people's messages back to them? Certainly if we are unsure that we have accurately understood the message, we might use paraphrasing to elicit a correction to our guess. But even if we are confident that we've understood them, we may sense the other party wanting confirmation that their message has been accurately received. They may even express this desire overtly by asking, "Is that clear?" or "Do you understand what I mean?" At such moments, hearing a clear paraphrase will often be more reassuring to the speaker than hearing simply, "Yes, I understand."

For example, shortly after participating in an NVC training, a volunteer at a hospital was requested by some nurses to talk to an elderly patient: "We've told this woman she isn't that sick and that she'd get better if she took her medicine, but all she does is sit in her room all day long repeating, 'I want to die. I want to die.'" The volunteer approached the elderly woman, and as the nurses

第七章 以同理心倾听

1. "你指的是我做的哪件事情？"
2. "你现在心情怎么样？" "为什么你会有那样的感受？"
3. "你希望我怎么做？"

第二组问题并不需要我们感知他人的内在。尽管这些问题看起来很直接，但我却发现，它们并不是获取讯息的最佳途径。这样的提问方式，就像老师在考学生，或是心理咨询师在问诊。如果我们实在要这么问，根据我的经验，最好先披露自己的感受和需要，让对方明白我们为什么这样问。这样，人们会感到更安全些。例如，与其问别人："你指的是哪件事？"不如说："我有些困惑，我想知道你指的是哪件事。你愿意告诉我吗？"如果我们已经通过互动或说话的语气表明了我们的感受和需要，这一步也许并不是必要的。但若我们在提问时带有强烈的情绪，我建议最好清晰表达我们的感受和需要。

如何决定什么时候需要复述他人的话呢？显然，当我们不确定自己是否理解了对方的意思，就可以通过复述让对方有机会做出说明或更正。即便我们确信已经理解了对方，可能还会发现对方也想对此做出确认。有时，他们会直接问："这样说清楚吗？"或"你明白我的意思吗？"这时，如果你能把听到的话清楚地复述出来，往往会比一句"我明白了"更能让对方安心。

一位医院志愿者参加了非暴力沟通工作坊，不久后，护士们请她和一位上了年纪的病人沟通。护士们告诉她，老太太的病情并不严重，只要服药就能好转。但她整天一个人坐在房间里反复地念着"我不想活了，我不想活了"。这位志愿者见到老太太时，发现她就像护士们说的，一个人坐在那里，一遍遍地喃喃自语："我不想活了……"

had predicted, found her sitting alone, whispering over and over, "I want to die."

"So you would like to die," the volunteer empathized. Surprised, the woman broke off her chant and appeared relieved. She began to talk about how no one understood how terrible she was feeling. The volunteer continued to reflect back the woman's feelings; before long, such warmth had entered their dialogue that they were sitting with their arms locked around each other. Later that day, the nurses questioned the volunteer about her magic formula: the elderly woman had started to eat and take her medicine, and was apparently in better spirits. Although the nurses had tried to help her with advice and reassurance, it wasn't until her interaction with the volunteer that this woman received what she was truly needing: connection with another human being who could hear her profound despair.

There are no infallible guidelines regarding when to paraphrase, but as a rule of thumb, it is safe to assume that speakers expressing intensely emotional messages would appreciate our reflecting these back to them. When we ourselves are talking, we can make it easier for the listener if we clearly signify when we want or don't want our words to be reflected back to us.

> Reflect back messages that are emotionally charged.

There are occasions when we may choose not to verbally reflect someone's statements out of respect for certain cultural norms. For example, a Chinese man once attended a workshop to learn how to hear the feelings and needs behind his father's remarks. Because he could not bear the criticism and attack he continually heard in his father's words, this man dreaded visiting his father and avoided him for months at a time. He came to me ten years later and reported that his ability to hear feelings and needs had radically transformed his relationship with his father to the point where they now enjoy a close and loving connection. Although he listens for his father's feelings and needs, however, he does not paraphrase

> Paraphrase only when it contributes to greater compassion and understanding.

第七章　以同理心倾听

"你的意思是你不愿意活下去了？"这位志愿者同理了老人。老人很惊讶，她停了下来，仿佛松了口气。接着，她开始诉说从没有人明白她是多么痛苦。这位志愿者持续地反馈着老人的意思，说着说着，两人就愈来愈亲热，手挽手地坐在了一起。后来，护士们问这位志愿者用了什么妙招，因为老人开始吃饭、服药，连精神状态也明显好转。护士们并不知道，尽管她们一直尝试帮助老人，安慰她、劝解她，但直到和这位志愿者谈话时，老人才获得她真正需要的——有人能够听见她内心深处的苦痛。

究竟何时进行复述，并没有严格的规定。一般来说，如果说话者带有强烈情绪，反馈他们的情绪会让他们感到欣慰。如果我们是说话者，不妨清楚地表明是否希望对方把我们的话复述出来，这样对方会更清晰。

还有些时候，出于对不同文化习俗的尊重，我们可以选择不用语言反馈他人。一位华人男子为了学习如何同理父亲参加了非暴力沟通工作坊。他过去常常在父亲的话中听到批评与攻击。为此，他极度害怕探望父亲，每隔几个月才硬着头皮去一次。此后又过去10年，我们再次见面，他告诉我，聆听感受和需要的能力，彻底改变了他与父亲的关系，他们的连结变得亲密且充满爱。但尽管如此，在聆听父亲的感受和需要时，他并不会用语言复述出来。"我从不说出来，"他解释说，"在我们的文化中，直接谈论一个人的感受是很少见的。但重要的是，我不再将父亲的话视为对我的攻击，而是体会他说那些话背后的感受和需要，我们的关系便日益好转了。"

"你的意思是，你永远不会直接和父亲说他的感受，只要能够听出他的感受就能帮到你们的关系？"我问他。

what he hears. "I never say it out loud," he explained. "In our culture, to direct-talk to a person about their feelings is something they're not used to. But thanks to the fact that I no longer hear what he says as an attack, but as his own feelings and needs, our relationship has become enormously wonderful."

"So you're never going to talk directly to him about feelings, but it helps to be able to hear them?" I asked.

"No, now I think I'm probably ready," he answered. "Now that we have such a solid relationship, if I were to say to him, 'Dad, I'd like to be able to talk directly to you about what we are feeling,' I think he just might be ready to do it."

When we paraphrase, the tone of voice we use is highly important. When hearing themselves reflected back, people are likely to be sensitive to the slightest hint of criticism or sarcasm. They are likewise negatively affected by a declarative tone that implies that we are telling them what is going on inside of them. If we are consciously listening for other people's feelings and needs, however, our tone communicates that we're asking whether we have understood—not claiming that we have understood.

We also need to be prepared for the possibility that the intention behind our paraphrasing will be misinterpreted. "Don't pull any of that psychology crap on me!" we may be told. Should this occur, we continue our effort to sense the speaker's feelings and needs; perhaps we see in this case that the speaker doesn't trust our motives and needs more understanding of our intentions before he can appreciate hearing our paraphrases. As we've seen, all criticism, attack, insults, and judgments vanish when we focus attention on hearing the feelings and needs behind a message. The more we practice in this way, the more we realize a simple truth: behind all those messages we've allowed ourselves to be intimidated by are just individuals with unmet needs appealing to us to contribute to their well-being. When we receive messages with this awareness, we never feel dehumanized by what others have to say to us. We

> Behind intimidating messages are merely people appealing to us to meet their needs.

第七章 以同理心倾听

"不。我想现在已经准备好了。如今,我们的感情已经足够深厚了,如果我对他说'爸爸,我想和你谈谈感受',我想他也不会觉得意外了。"他回答说。

在复述时,要特别注意语气。一个人在听别人反馈自己的话时,哪怕听到一点点批评或嘲讽,都会格外敏感。如果我们的语气像是在下判断,仿佛认定对方心里在想什么,这通常会让他人感到不舒服。因而,带着觉知聆听他人的感受和需要时,我们的语气是探询式的,是为了确认我们的理解是否到位,而不是在下结论。

有时,人们可能会错误地理解复述的意图。如果对方回应我们:"少跟我玩这套心理学的把戏了!"我们可以继续感知对方的感受和需要。我们也许会发现,对方并不信任我们的动机,需要更进一步了解我们的用意,才有可能欣然接受我们的表达方式。正如先前提到的,当我们专注于话语背后的感受和需要时,就再也听不到任何批评、攻击、辱骂和评判了。我们越是这样做,就越能够领悟到一个简单的真谛:我们以为自己受到了指责,实际上,人们之所以会说那些话,其实是在诉说他们有一些需要没有得到满足,希望得到我们的帮助。如果意识到这点,我们就永远不会因他人的话而认为自己受到了屈辱。而我们之所以认为自己尊严受损没有被当人看,正是因为我们陷入对他人的负面评判中,或沉浸在认为自己犯了错而自责的想法中。

作家、神话学家约瑟夫·坎贝尔说过:"腾出'他人如何看待我'这个想法的空间给天赐之福。"一旦我们将那些原本听起来像批评或指责的话看作来自他人的礼物——为身处痛苦中的人们提供服务的机会,我们就会感受到这份极致的幸福。

如果人们常常怀疑我们在复述时的动机和诚意,那么,我们就需要

only feel dehumanized when we get trapped in derogatory images of other people or thoughts of wrongness about ourselves. As author and mythologist Joseph Campbell suggested, "'What will they think of me?' must be put aside for bliss." We begin to feel this bliss when messages previously experienced as critical or blaming begin to be seen for the gifts they are: opportunities to give to people who are in pain.

> A difficult message becomes an opportunity to enrich someone's life.

If it happens regularly that people distrust our motives and sincerity when we paraphrase their words, we may need to examine our own intentions more closely. Perhaps we are paraphrasing and engaging the components of NVC in a mechanistic way without maintaining clear consciousness of purpose. We might ask ourselves, for example, whether we are more intent on applying the process "correctly" than on connecting with the human being in front of us. Or perhaps, even though we are using the form of NVC, our only interest is in changing the other person's behavior.

Some people resist paraphrasing as a waste of time. One city administrator explained during a practice session, "I'm paid to give facts and solutions, not to sit around doing psychotherapy with everyone who comes into my office." This same administrator, however, was being confronted by angry citizens who would come to him with their passionate concerns and leave dissatisfied for not having been heard. Some of these citizens later confided to me, "When you go to his office, he gives you a bunch of facts, but you never know whether he's heard you first. When that happens, you start to distrust his facts." Paraphrasing tends to save, rather than waste, time. Studies in labor-management negotiations demonstrate that the time required to reach conflict resolution is cut in half when each negotiator agrees, before responding, to accurately repeat what the previous speaker had said.

> Paraphrasing saves time.

I recall a man who was initially skeptical about the value of paraphrasing. He and his wife were attending an NVC workshop

第七章　以同理心倾听

好好审视自己的意图。也许，我们只是在机械地复述和运用非暴力沟通的要素，而不清晰这样做目的何在。如果是这样，我们可以问自己，是否更多地将关注放在了"正确"运用流程上，而没有用心和眼前的人连结。又或许，我们虽然使用非暴力沟通的形式，但真正想要的却是改变他人的行为。

还有的人认为在沟通中进行复述是浪费时间。一位市政府行政管理人员在一次练习中表示："我的职责是给出事实和解决方案，不是干坐在这里，为每个来找我的人做心理咨询。"然而，许多市民带着热切关注的议题而来，却因为没有被听到而带着愤怒离开，公众因而对他心怀不满。有些市民私下向我吐露："每次去他的办公室，他就给你讲一堆事实，你却从来不知道你的话他有没有听进去。在这种情况下，你自然会开始怀疑他讲的事情。"

事实上，复述往往能够节省时间而非浪费时间。一项有关劳资管理谈判的研究显示，在谈判中，如果一方在回应前先准确复述对方说过的话，那么，达成和解的时间则会缩短一半。

我记得，曾经有一位男子因为婚姻出现了严重问题，便和妻子一起参加了我的工作坊。最初他也不相信复述会有什么效果。在课堂上，太太对他说："你从不好好听我说话。"

"我怎么没听。"他答道。

"不，你没听。"太太反驳道。

这时，我对这位先生说："恐怕你刚刚已经证实了她的观点。你回应她的方式并没有让她知道你在听她说话。"

对于我的观点，他有些困惑。于是，我问他是否可以让我来扮演他的角色，与他的妻子对话。由于一直以来在这方面不甚成功，他欣然答

during a time when their marriage was beset by serious problems. During the workshop, his wife said to him, "You never listen to me."

"I do too," he replied.

"No, you don't," she countered.

I addressed the husband: "I'm afraid you just proved her point. You didn't respond in a way that lets her know that you were listening to her."

He was puzzled by the point I was making, so I asked for permission to play his role—which he gladly gave since he wasn't having too much success with it. His wife and I then had the following exchange:

Wife: "You never listen to me."

MBR in role of husband: "It sounds like you're terribly frustrated because you would like to feel more connection when we speak."

The wife was moved to tears when she finally received this confirmation that she had been understood. I turned to the husband and explained, "I believe this is what she is telling you she needs—a reflection of her feelings and needs as a confirmation that she'd been heard." The husband seemed dumbfounded. "Is that all she wanted?" he asked, incredulous that such a simple act could have had such a strong impact on his wife.

A short time later, he enjoyed the satisfaction firsthand when his wife reflected back to him a statement that he had made with great emotional intensity. Savoring her paraphrase, he looked at me and declared, "It's valid." It is a poignant experience to receive concrete evidence that someone is empathically connected to us.

Sustaining Empathy

I recommend allowing others the opportunity to fully express themselves before turning our attention to solutions or requests for relief. When we proceed too quickly to what people might be requesting, we may not convey our genuine interest in their feelings and needs; instead, they may get the impression that we're in a hurry to either be free of them or to fix their problem. Furthermore, an initial message is often like the tip of an iceberg;

应了。接着,我和他的太太便展开了以下这段对话:

太太:"你从不好好听我说话。"

我(扮演她的丈夫):"听起来,你很失望,你希望在我们的沟通中感受到更多的连结。"

听到这些话时,太太的眼里泛起了泪水,她终于体验到了被人理解是怎样的感觉。我转向她的先生,向他解释:"我相信这就是她一直以来渴望的,从复述她的感受和需要中得到确认,你真的在听她说话。"这位先生十分惊讶:"她想要的就是这样吗?"他难以置信如此简单的行为,居然能对太太产生如此大的影响。

接下来,这位先生也就某件事表达了对太太的不满。当太太将他的话复述给他时,先生也亲身体验到了那种满足感。他看着我说:"这样做有价值!"一个人能够明确地感受来自他人的同理心,是一种多么深刻的体验。

持续同理他人

我建议,在关注解决方案或提出请求前,让他人有机会充分表达自己。如果急于提及他人的请求,人们或许会以为我们对他们的感受和需要并不真的感兴趣,只是急着要摆脱或解决他们的问题。此外,人们在谈话开始所透露的信息往往只是冰山一角,有许多相关且更为强烈的感受尚未表达。当我们持续关注他人的内心世界时,便让他人有了机会充分探索和表达自己。

假如一位母亲诉苦说:"我的孩子简直难以理喻。不管我要他做什

it may be followed by as yet unexpressed, but related—and often more powerful—feelings. By maintaining our attention on what's going on within others, we offer them a chance to fully explore and express their interior selves. We would stem this flow if we were to shift attention too quickly either to their request or to our own desire to express ourselves.

> When we stay with empathy, we allow speakers to touch deeper levels of themselves.

Suppose a mother comes to us, saying, "My child is impossible. No matter what I tell him to do, he doesn't listen." We might reflect her feelings and needs by saying, "It sounds like you're feeling desperate and would like to find some way of connecting with your son." Such a paraphrase often encourages a person to look within. If we have accurately reflected her statement, the mother might touch upon other feelings: "Maybe it's my fault. I'm always yelling at him." As the listener, we would continue to stay with the feelings and needs being expressed and say, for example, "Are you feeling guilty because you would have liked to have been more understanding of him than you have been at times?" If the mother continues to sense understanding in our reflection, she might move further into her feelings and declare, "I'm just a failure as a mother." We continue to remain with the feelings and needs being expressed: "So you're feeling discouraged and want to relate differently to him?" We persist in this manner until the person has exhausted all her feelings surrounding this issue.

What evidence is there that we've adequately empathized with the other person? First, when an individual realizes that everything going on within has received full empathic understanding, they will experience a sense of relief. We can become aware of this phenomenon by noticing a corresponding release of tension in our own body. A second, even more obvious sign is that the person will

> We know a speaker has received adequate empathy when (1) we sense a release of tension, or (2) the flow of words comes to a halt.

第七章　以同理心倾听

么，他都不听。"这时，我们可以反馈她的感受和需要："听起来，你很伤心，你希望找到办法和儿子连结。"这样的回应往往会促使对方审视自己的内心。如果我们准确地反映了她想表达的意思，她也许还会触碰到其他感受："也许这是我的问题，我总是冲他大喊大叫。"作为聆听者，我们可以继续关注她所表达的感受和需要，并表达同理："你是否有些内疚，你希望能更多理解孩子？"如果这位母亲能持续地感受到我们的理解，也许会说出她内心深处的感受或想法："我是个失败的母亲。"我们同样继续聆听她的感受和需要："你有些气馁，你想加深与儿子的情感联系，是吗？"我们持续这般地同理她，直到她充分表达了相关的所有感受。

　　如何知道我们已经充分同理了他人呢？首先，如果一个人体验到当下的内心世界被他人充分理解了，就会感到轻松。这时，我们也会相应地在自己身上感受到不再那么紧绷。还有一个更明显的迹象是，对方会安静下来停止说话。如果我们无法确定对方是否充分地表达了自己，不妨问一句："还有什么是你想要说的吗？"

当我们痛苦得无法同理

　　我们无法把自己没有的东西给予他人。有时，我们会发现，即使做出了努力，也无法或不想同理他人，这通常表明我们自己并没有得到足够的同理。有时，如果我们能够坦然地承认，自己正处于痛苦中，以致无法同理对方，他人很可能会反过来同理我们。

　　有时我们也需要给予自己一些同理"急救"，关注和聆听自己的内

stop talking. If we are uncertain as to whether we have stayed long enough in the process, we can always ask, "Is there more that you wanted to say?"

When Pain Blocks Our Ability to Empathize

It is impossible for us to give something to another if we don't have it ourselves. Likewise, if we find ourselves unable or unwilling to empathize despite our efforts, it is usually a sign that we are too starved for empathy to be able to offer

> We need empathy to give empathy.

it to others. Sometimes, if we openly acknowledge that our own distress is preventing us from responding empathically, the other person may come through with the empathy we need.

At other times, it may be necessary to provide ourselves with some "emergency first aid" empathy by listening to what's going on in ourselves with the same quality of presence and attention that we offer to others. Former United Nations Secretary-General Dag Hammarskjold once said, "The more faithfully you listen to the voice within you, the better you will hear what is happening outside." If we become skilled at giving ourselves empathy, we often experience in just a few seconds a natural release of energy that then enables us to be present with the other person. If this fails to happen, however, we have a couple of other choices.

We can scream—nonviolently. I recall spending three days mediating between two gangs that had been killing each other off. One gang called themselves Black Egyptians; the other, the East St. Louis Police Department. The score was two to one—a total of three dead within a month. After three tense days trying to bring these groups together to hear each other and resolve their differences, I was driving home and thinking how I never wanted to be in the middle of a conflict again for the rest of my life.

The first thing I saw when I walked through the back door was my children entangled in a fight. I had no energy to empathize with them so I screamed nonviolently: "Hey, I'm in a lot of pain! Right now I really do *not* want to deal with your fighting! I just

第七章　以同理心倾听

心世界。联合国前秘书长达格·哈马舍尔德（Dag Hammarskjöld）曾说："你越是忠实地聆听自己内心的声音，就越能听到外面的世界。"如果我们善于同理自己，就有能力迅速地调整好状态，得以与他人同在。

如果做不到，我们还有另外一些选择。

一种选择是以非暴力的方式呐喊——"非暴力呐喊"。有一次，我花了3天时间调停两派人马之间的冲突。其中一派称自己为"埃及黑人"，另一派来自东圣路易斯警察局。一个月内，一方死了2人，另一方死了1人。那3天中，我努力帮助双方相互听见并化解分歧。我记得最后一天开车回家的路上，我和自己说："这辈子再也不想身处这样的冲突中了。"

没想到一进家门，我就看到孩子们正在打架。那时，我已经没有力气去同理他们了，便用非暴力沟通的方式大声地呐喊道："我现在很难受！真的不想来管你们打架的事情，我只想要安静一会儿！"听到这番话，我年仅9岁的大儿子停了下来，看着我问道："你愿意和我们说说吗？"

我发现，如果我们能坦诚并且不带指责地谈论自己的痛苦，即使对方也处于苦痛之中，有时也能够听见我们的需要。在前述的例子中，我不想冲着孩子大喊："这怎么回事？你们就不能乖一点吗？我在外面辛苦了一整天才回到家啊！"我也不想用任何其他方式来暗示对方错了。"非暴力呐喊"就是提醒他人注意我在当下的痛苦和迫切的需要。

不过，如果对方也处于强烈的情绪中，无法听见我们，也不肯放过我们，而同时，同理"急救"和"非暴力呐喊"都无法帮助我们的话，我们的另一种选择就是：暂时离开现场，得到自己所需的同理心，等到心境调整好了之后再回去。

want some peace and quiet!" My older son, then nine, stopped short, looked at me, and asked, "Do you want to talk about it?"

If we are able to speak our pain nakedly without blame, I find that even people in distress are sometimes able to hear our need. Of course I wouldn't want to scream, "What's the matter with you? Don't you know how to behave any better? I just got home after a rough day!" or insinuate in any way that their behavior was at fault. I scream nonviolently by calling attention to my own desperate needs and pain in the moment.

If, however, the other party is also experiencing such intensity of feelings that they can neither hear us nor leave us alone, and neither emergency empathy nor nonviolent screaming has served us well, our third recourse is to physically remove ourselves from the situation. We give ourselves time out and the opportunity to acquire the empathy we need to return in a different frame of mind.

Summary

Empathy is a respectful understanding of what others are experiencing. We often have a strong urge to give advice or reassurance and to explain our own position or feeling. Empathy, however, calls upon us to empty our mind and listen to others with our whole being.

In NVC, no matter what words others may use to express themselves, we simply listen for their observations, feelings, needs, and requests. Then we may wish to reflect back, paraphrasing what we have understood. We stay with empathy and allow others the opportunity to fully express themselves before we turn our attention to solutions or requests for relief.

We need empathy to give empathy. When we sense ourselves being defensive or unable to empathize, we need to (1) stop, breathe, give ourselves empathy; (2) scream nonviolently; or (3) take time out.

第七章　以同理心倾听

小结

　　所谓"同理"就是带着尊重来理解他人的经历。我们常常有强烈的冲动想给他人建议或安慰，或是解释自己的立场和感受。同理则邀请我们清空先入为主的想法，全身心地聆听他人。

　　活在非暴力沟通中意味着，不论他人用什么样的言辞来表达自己，我们都只是聆听他们的观察、感受、需要和请求。接着，我们可以选择反馈他们的意思、复述我们的理解。此外，持续地同理让他人有机会充分表达自己，当他人感到被充分理解后，我们再来关注解决方案或提出请求。

　　我们自己也需要获得同理才能更好地同理他人。当意识到自己处于辩解防卫的状态或痛苦得无法同理他人时，我们可以选择（1）停顿，深呼吸，同理自己；（2）"非暴力呐喊"；（3）离开现场。

7 Receiving Empathically

> ### NVC in Action
>
> **A Wife Connects With Her Dying Husband**
>
> A patient had just been diagnosed with an advanced stage of lung cancer. The following scene at his home, involving the patient, his wife, and a visiting nurse, represents a last opportunity for him to connect emotionally with his wife and discuss his dying before being admitted to the hospital. The wife began the conversation with the nurse by complaining about the physical therapist who was part of the home health care team assigned to her husband's care.
>
> **Wife:** She's a bad therapist.
>
> **Nurse:** *(listening empathically to what the wife is feeling and wanting)* Are you feeling annoyed and wanting to see a different quality of care?
>
> **Wife:** She doesn't do anything. She made him stop walking when his pulse got high.
>
> **Nurse:** *(continuing to hear the wife's feelings and wants)* Is it because you want your husband to get better that you're scared if the physical therapist doesn't push him, he won't get stronger?
>
> **Wife:** *(starting to cry)* Yes, I'm so scared!
>
> **Nurse:** Are you scared of losing him?
>
> **Wife:** Yes, we've been together so long.
>
> **Nurse:** *(listening for other feelings behind the fear)* Are you worrying about how you would feel if he dies?
>
> **Wife:** I just can't imagine how I am going to live without him. He's always been there for me. Always.
>
> **Nurse:** So you're sad when you think of living without him?
>
> **Wife:** There is no one else besides him. He's all I have, you know. My daughter won't even talk to me.

第七章　以同理心倾听

非暴力沟通实例

一位丈夫在临死前与太太的对话

　　一位病人被诊断为肺癌晚期。在他被送往医院前,这是他最后一次有机会和妻子建立情感上的连结,并且谈论他的死亡。现场还有协助他的护士。谈话一开始,妻子就向护士抱怨护理先生的一位理疗师。

妻子：这位治疗师很差劲。
护士：(同理太太的感受和渴望) 你是不是有些生气,希望先生得到更好的照料?
妻子：她什么都不做。只要发现他的脉搏稍微快一些,就不让他走路了。
护士：(继续聆听她的感受和需要) 是不是你害怕,如果治疗师不鼓励他多活动,他就没有办法好起来呢?
妻子：(哭了起来) 是的,我真的很害怕!
护士：你害怕会失去他是吗?
妻子：是的,我们一起生活了这么久。
护士：(聆听她害怕背后的其他感受) 你担心如果他走了,你不知道怎么办是吗?
妻子：我完全无法想象,没有他,我怎么活下去。一直以来他都在我身边,从来都是啊。

Nurse:	It sounds like when you think of your daughter, you feel frustrated because you wish you had a different relationship with her.
Wife:	I wish I did, but she is such a selfish person. I don't know why I even bothered having kids. A lot of good it does me now!
Nurse:	Sounds to me like you might be somewhat angry and disappointed because you want more support from the family during your husband's illness.
Wife:	Yes, he's so sick; I don't know how I am going to get through this alone. I haven't anyone . . . not even to talk to, except with you here . . . now. Even he won't talk about it. . . . Look at him! *(Husband remains silent and impassive.)* He doesn't say anything!
Nurse:	Are you sad, wishing the two of you could support each other and feel more connected?
Wife:	Yes. *(She pauses, then makes a request.)* Talk to him the way you talk to me.
Nurse:	*(wishing to clearly understand the need that is being addressed behind the wife's request)* Are you wanting him to be listened to in a way that helps him express what he's feeling inside?
Wife:	Yes, yes, that's exactly it! I want him to feel comfortable talking and I want to know what he is feeling.

Using the nurse's guess, the wife was able to first become aware of what she wanted and then find the words to articulate it. This was a key moment: often it is difficult for people to identify what they want in a situation, even though they may know what they don't want. We see how a clear request—"Talk to him the way you talk to me"—is a gift that empowers the other person. The nurse was then able to act in a way she knew to be in harmony with the

第七章　以同理心倾听

护士：想到将失去他，你很悲伤，是吗？

妻子：除了他，我身边没有其他人了。他是我的全部。我女儿甚至都不和我说话。

护士：想到你女儿，你感到灰心，希望与她的关系能好些，是吗？

妻子：是的。但她很自私。我甚至不明白为什么要生孩子！如果没有孩子，我现在会过得更好。

护士：听起来，你有些愤怒和失望，在先生生病的时候，你希望家里人能给你更多支持。

妻子：是的，他病得这么重，我不知道我一个人怎么撑过去。除了有你在……现在……我身边连个说话的人也没有。他也不愿和我说这些……你看看，他一句话也不说！"（先生面无表情地保持着沉默。）

护士：你是不是很难过，希望你们能相互扶持，有更亲密的连结？

妻子：是的。（她停了一下，然后，提出了一个请求。）我想请你用和我说话的方式与我先生谈谈。

护士：（想了解太太请求背后的需要）你是不是希望他能得到同理，这能帮助他说出内心的感受？

妻子：是的，是的，就是这样！我希望他能把心里的话说出来，我想了解他现在的心情。

借助护士的猜测，这位太太意识到自己的愿望并清楚地表达了请求。这是一个关键性的时刻，身处某个情景之中，人们知道自己不想要什么，却往往很难看到自己想要什么。在这个例子中，我们可以看到，一个清晰的请求——"请你用这样的方式和我先生谈谈"是如何赋予了

7 Receiving Empathically

wife's wishes. This altered the atmosphere in the room, as the nurse and the wife could now "work together," both in a compassionate mode.

Nurse: *(turning to the husband)* How do you feel when you hear what your wife has shared?
Husband: I really love her.
Nurse: Are you glad to have an opportunity to talk about this with her?
Husband: Yes, we need to talk about it.
Nurse: Would you be willing to say how you are feeling about the cancer?
Husband: *(after a brief silence)* Not very good.

The words *good* and *bad* are often used to describe feelings when people have yet to identify the specific emotion they are experiencing. Expressing his feelings more precisely would help this patient with the emotional connection he was seeking with his wife.

Nurse: *(encouraging him to move toward more precision)* Are you scared about dying?
Husband: No, not scared. *(Notice the nurse's incorrect guess does not hamper the continued flow of dialogue.)*
Nurse: *(Because this patient isn't able to verbalize his internal experience easily, the nurse continues to support him in the process.)* Do you feel angry about dying?
Husband: No, not angry.
Nurse: *(At this point, after two incorrect guesses, the nurse decides to express her own feelings.)* Well, now I'm puzzled about what you may be feeling, and wonder if you can tell me.
Husband: I reckon, I'm thinking how she'll do without me.

第七章 以同理心倾听

他人某种力量。因为知道了这位太太的心愿,护士现在就可以采取行动来满足她。这意味着她们将带着爱"一起工作",屋内的气氛也因而变得不同。

护士:(转向那位先生)听了太太的分享,你现在感觉怎么样呀?
丈夫:我真的很爱她。
护士:你愿意现在和她谈谈吗?
丈夫:是的,我们需要谈一谈。
护士:你得了重病,你愿意告诉她你的感受吗?
丈夫:(他沉默了一会儿)感觉不太好。

人们常常在不清楚自己具体有些什么感受时,用"好"与"坏"来描述。如果先生能够更准确地表达感受,将会帮助他和妻子建立他所渴望的情感连结。

护士:(鼓励他更准确地表达自己)你是不是害怕即将走向生命终点?
先生:不,我不害怕这个。(请注意,护士虽然猜得不准确,但这并没有阻碍交流继续下去。)
护士:(由于这位先生很难说出他的内心世界,护士便继续协助他。)想到死亡,你感到愤怒吗?
先生:不,我并不愤怒。
护士:(猜错了两次后,护士决定说出她的感受。)我有些迷茫,不知道你现在的感受是怎样的。你愿意和我说说吗?
丈夫:我在想,我走了以后她怎么办。

7 Receiving Empathically

Nurse: Oh, are you worried she may not be able to handle her life without you?

Husband: Yes, worried she'll miss me.

Nurse: *(She is aware that dying patients often hang on due to worry over those they are leaving behind, and sometimes need reassurance that loved ones can accept their death before they can let themselves go.)* Do you want to hear how your wife feels when you say that?

Husband: Yes.

Here the wife joined the conversation; in the continued presence of the nurse, the couple began to express themselves openly to each other.

In this dialogue, the wife began with a complaint about the physical therapist. However, after a series of exchanges during which she felt empathically received, she was able to determine that what she really sought was a deeper connection with her husband during this critical stage of their lives.

第七章 以同理心倾听

护士：你担心，没有你在身边，她无法照顾好自己的生活吗？

丈夫：是的，担心她会想我。

护士：（她知道弥留之际的病人常常放心不下心爱的人。有时他们需要得到确认，心爱的人准备好了接受他们的死亡，他们才能放心地离去。）你想要听听太太现在的心情吗？

丈夫：想。

这时，太太加入了对话。因为护士始终带着同理心陪伴着这对夫妻，他们开始向彼此敞开心扉，表达自己。

在这段对话中，太太一开始是在抱怨理疗师。但在对话过程中，护士不断地同理妻子，她终于意识到自己真正渴望的是在生命中的这个关键时刻，和先生有更深的连结。

练习五：以同理或非同理的方式回应他人

让我们练习用语言来表达对他人的同理。在以下十组 A 和 B 的对话中，请问，在哪些对话中，B 同理回应了 A。

1. A: 我怎么会做这么愚蠢的事？
   B: 没有人是完美的。你对自己太苛刻了。
2. A: 在我看来，所有这些移民，从哪儿来就该送回哪儿去。
   B: 你认为这样就真的解决所有问题了？
3. A: 你以为你是上帝吗？！

Exercise 5

RECEIVING EMPATHICALLY VERSUS NON-EMPATHICALLY

To see whether we are in agreement about the verbal expression of empathy, please circle the number in front of each statement in which person B is responding empathically to what is going on within Person A.

1. Person A: How could I do something so stupid?
   Person B: Nobody is perfect; you're too hard on yourself.

2. Person A: If you ask me, we ought to ship all these immigrants back to where they came from.
   Person B: Do you really think that would solve anything?

3. Person A: You aren't God!
   Person B: Are you feeling frustrated because you would like me to admit that there can be other ways of interpreting this matter?

4. Person A: I think that you take me for granted. I wonder how you would manage without me.
   Person B: That's not true! I don't take you for granted.

5. Person A: How could you say a thing like that to me?
   Person B: Are you feeling hurt because I said that?

6. Person A: I'm furious with my husband. He's never around when I need him.
   Person B: You think he should be around more than he is?

7. Person A: I'm disgusted with how heavy I'm getting.
   Person B: Perhaps jogging would help.

8. Person A: I've been a nervous wreck planning for my daughter's wedding. Her fiancé's family is not helping. About every day they change their minds about the kind of wedding they would like.

第七章 以同理心倾听

    B：听起来你有些生气，是不是因为你希望我能看到，一件事情可以从不同的角度来看待？

4. A：你从不把我当回儿事。没有我的话，天晓得你能怎么办。

    B：不是这样的！我没有不把你当回事儿。

5. A：你怎么可以这样和我说话？

    B：我那样说话，你是不是很伤心？

6. A：想到我先生，我就很生气。我需要他的时候，他从来都不在。

    B：你认为他应该多陪陪你？

7. A：我讨厌自己变得越来越胖。

    B：慢跑也许能帮助你。

8. A：为了准备女儿的婚礼，我紧张得要命。可是，她的婆家什么忙都不帮，还几乎每天都要改变想法。

    B：听起来，为了安排这场婚礼，你很紧张。你希望亲家在做决定时能体谅你吗？

9. A：当亲戚们不请自来时，我感到被侵犯。这让我想起，我的父母在过去经常无视我的需要，替我做安排。

    B：我明白你的感受，曾经我也是这样。

10. A：你的表现让我很失望，我本来指望你们部门上个月的产量会翻番。

    B：我知道你很失望，但上个月我们部门有很多人请了病假。

以下是我对练习五的回应：

1. 如果你选择这个对话，我们的意见不一致。我认为B是在安慰A，而非同理回应A。

7 Receiving Empathically

Person B: So you're feeling nervous about how to make arrangements and would appreciate it if your future in-laws could be more aware of the complications their indecision creates for you?

9. Person A: When my relatives come without letting me know ahead of time, I feel invaded. It reminds me of how my parents used to disregard my needs and would plan things for me.

   Person B: I know how you feel. I used to feel that way too.

10. Person A: I'm disappointed with your performance. I would have liked your department to double your production last month.

    Person B: I understand that you are disappointed, but we have had many absences due to illness.

Here are my responses for Exercise 5:

1. I didn't circle this one because I see Person B giving reassurance to Person A rather than empathically receiving what Person A is expressing.

2. I see Person B attempting to educate Person A rather than empathically receiving what Person A is expressing.

3. If you circled this we are in agreement. I see Person B empathically receiving what Person A is expressing.

4. I didn't circle this one because I see Person B disagreeing and defending rather than empathically receiving what is going on in Person A.

5. I see Person B taking responsibility for Person A's feelings rather than empathically receiving what is going on in Person A. An example of an empathic response might be: "Are you feeling hurt because you would have liked me to agree to do what you requested?"

第七章 以同理心倾听

2. 如果你选择这个对话，我们的意见不一致。我认为 B 在试图教育 A，而非同理回应 A。

3. 如果你选择这个对话，我们的意见一致。

4. 如果你选择这个对话，我们的意见不一致。我认为 B 在否认和辩解，而非同理 A 的内心世界。

5. 如果你选择这个对话，我们的意见不一致。我认为 B 在为 A 的感受承担责任，而非同理 A 的内心世界。如果用同理的方式来回应 A，B 可以说："你是不是有些伤心，你希望我能同意你的请求？"

6. 如果你选择这个对话，我们的意见不完全一致。我认为 B 回应了 A 的想法。然而，我相信，同理感受和需要而不只是回应想法，更能够促进人与人的连结。如果用同理的方式来回应 A，B 可以说："听起来，你很生气，因为你希望他能多陪陪你？"

7. 如果你选择这个对话，我们的意见不一致。我认为 B 是在提建议，而非同理回应 A 的体验。

8. 如果你选择这个对话，我们的意见一致。

9. 如果你选择这个对话，我们的意见不一致。我认为，B 认为自己理解了 A，并且谈论起自己的感受，而非同理回应 A 的体验。

10. 如果你选择这个对话，我们的意见不一致。我认为，虽然一开始 B 关注了 A 的感受，但之后就开始解释自己的情况。

6. If you circled this we are in partial agreement. I see Person B receiving Person A's thoughts. However, I believe we connect more deeply when we receive the feelings and needs being expressed rather than the thoughts. Therefore, I would have preferred it if Person B had said, "So you're feeling furious because you would like him to be around more than he is?"

7. I didn't circle this one because I see Person B giving advice rather than empathically receiving what is going on in Person A.

8. If you circled this we are in agreement. I see Person B empathically receiving what is going on in Person A.

9. I didn't circle this one because I see Person B assuming they understand and talking about their own feelings rather than empathically receiving what is going on in Person A.

10. I didn't circle this one because I see Person B starting by focusing on Person A's feelings but then shifting to explaining.

第八章

同理心的力量

The Power of Empathy

Empathy That Heals

Carl Rogers described the impact of empathy on its recipients: "When ... someone really hears you without passing judgment on you, without trying to take responsibility for you, without trying to mold you, it feels damn good! ... When I have been listened to and when I have been heard, I am able to reperceive my world in a new way and to go on. It is astonishing how elements that seem insoluble become soluble when someone listens, how confusions that seem irremediable turn into relatively clear flowing streams when one is heard."

> Empathy allows us "to reperceive [our] world in a new way and to go on."

One of my favorite stories about empathy comes from the principal of an innovative school. She had returned after lunch one day to find Milly, an elementary school student, sitting dejectedly in her office waiting to see her. She sat down next to Milly, who began, "Mrs. Anderson, have you ever had a week when everything you did hurt somebody else, and you never intended to hurt anyone at all?"

"Yes," the principal replied, "I think I understand," whereupon Milly proceeded to describe her week. "By now," the principal related, "I was quite late for a very important meeting—still had my coat on—and anxious not to keep a room full of people waiting, and so I asked, 'Milly, what can I do for you?' Milly reached over, took both my shoulders in her hands, looked me straight in the

> "Don't just do something...."

第八章　同理心的力量

同理心的疗愈作用

卡尔·罗杰斯（Carl Rogers）曾经这样描述同理心对人的影响："如果有人真的听到了你的心声，不对你评头论足，不试图为你承担责任，也不想改变你，这多么美好啊！……当得到人们的倾听和理解，我就能以一种全新的眼光看世界，并继续前进。令人难以置信的是，原本看似无解的问题因此有了解决办法，千头万绪的思路也会变得清楚分明。"

安德森女士是一所实验小学的校长，我很喜欢她和我分享的这个同理心小故事。有一天，她午饭后回到办公室，发现有位叫米莉的女生正垂头丧气地坐着等她。她走到米莉身边坐下，米莉随即问她："安德森女士，你有没有这样的经历，仿佛做任何事都会让别人受伤，可你原本不想伤害任何人。""有啊！"安德森回答说，"我想我明白你的意思。"米莉随即开始讲述她这个星期以来的遭遇。

那位校长回忆着当时的情景说："那时，我快要赶不上一个很重要的会议了，而我连外套还没来得及脱下。我很着急，不想让整个会议室的人等我一个人。于是我问她：'米莉，我能为你做什么吗？'没想到，

eyes, and said very firmly, 'Mrs. Anderson, I don't want you to *do* anything; I just want you to listen.'

"This was one of the most significant moments of learning in my life—taught to me by a child—so I thought, 'Never mind the roomful of adults waiting for me!' Milly and I moved over to a bench that afforded us more privacy and sat, my arm around her shoulders, her head on my chest, and her arm around my waist, while she talked until she was done. And you know, it didn't take that long."

One of the most satisfying aspects of my work is to hear how individuals have used NVC to strengthen their ability to connect empathically with others. My friend Laurence, who lives in Switzerland, described how upset she felt when her six-year-old son had stormed away angrily while she was still talking to him. Isabelle, her ten-year-old daughter, who had accompanied her to a recent NVC workshop, remarked, "So you're really angry, Mom. You'd like for him to talk when he's angry and not run off." Laurence marveled at how, upon hearing Isabelle's words, she felt an immediate diminishing of tension, and was subsequently able to be more understanding with her son when he returned.

A college instructor described how relationships between students and faculty had been affected when several members of the faculty learned to listen empathically and to express themselves more vulnerably and honestly. "The students opened up more and more and told us about the various personal problems that were interfering with their studies. The more they talked about it, the more work they were able to complete. Even though this kind of listening took a lot of our time, we were glad to spend it in this way. Unfortunately, the dean got upset; he said we were not counselors and should spend more time teaching and less time talking with the students."

When I asked how the faculty had dealt with this, the instructor replied, "We empathized with the dean's concern. We heard that he felt worried and wanted to know that we weren't getting involved in things we couldn't handle. We also heard that he needed reassurance that the time spent on talking wasn't cutting into our

第八章　同理心的力量

米莉伸手按住我的肩膀，看着我的眼睛，语气坚定地说：'安德森太太，我不要你做任何事，我只要你听我说话。'那一刻，我收获了生命中极其重要的一课，是一个孩子教会我的。当时我想：不管那一屋子的大人了，就让他们等一会儿吧！于是，我带着米莉找到一个不大会被人打扰的角落，在一张长椅上坐下，我搂住她的肩膀，她依偎着我，搂着我的腰。我们就这样坐着，直到米莉说完了她的心事。其实，这样做并没有花费太多时间。"

在我的工作中，最令我满足的一件事，就是听到人们告诉我，他们如何通过非暴力沟通增强了同理的能力，与他人建立了心与心的连结。我有位朋友劳伦斯来自瑞士，她也和我分享了一段经历。有一次，她和6岁的儿子谈话，话还没说完，儿子就气冲冲地夺门而去。她生气极了。这时，10岁的女儿伊莎贝尔（不久前她陪着劳伦斯参加了一场非暴力沟通工作坊）对她说："妈妈，你看起来很生气，你希望他在生气时能把话说出来，而不是像这样一走了之？"劳伦斯惊讶地发现，听到女儿的话后，她的气就消了。当儿子回来后，劳伦斯也更能体谅他了。

一位大学老师曾经告诉我，系里的一些老师学习了非暴力沟通后，师生关系得到了明显改善。他说："学生们越来越愿意对我们敞开心扉，分享他们的困难。他们越是愿意谈论那些影响学习的困难，就越能更好地完成学业。因此，尽管用了许多时间来聆听他们，我们还是很乐意这样做。可惜系主任却不太高兴。他认为我们不是心理咨询师，不需要花那么多时间和学生谈心，应该把那些时间用来教书才对。"

当我问他老师们如何回应时，他答道："我们同理了系主任的顾虑。告诉他，我们听到了他的担心，他希望我们不会牵扯进一些处理不了的事中。他还希望我们与学生谈心不会影响教学任务。听到这些，他似乎

teaching responsibilities. He seemed relieved by the way we listened to him. We continued to talk with the students because we could see that the more we listened to them, the better they did in their studies."

When we work in a hierarchically structured institution, there is a tendency to hear commands and judgments from those higher up in the hierarchy. While we may easily empathize with our peers and with those in less powerful positions, we may find ourselves being defensive or apologetic, instead of empathic, in the presence of those we identify as our "superiors." This is why I was particularly pleased that these faculty members had remembered to empathize with their dean as well as with their students.

> It's harder to empathize with those who appear to possess more power, status, or resources.

Empathy and the Ability to Be Vulnerable

Because we are called to reveal our deepest feelings and needs, we may sometimes find it challenging to express ourselves in NVC. Self-expression becomes easier, however, after we empathize with others, because we will then have touched their humanness and realized the common qualities we share. The more we connect with the feelings and needs behind their words, the less frightening it is to open up to other people. The situations where we are the most reluctant to express vulnerability are often those where we want to maintain a "tough image" for fear of losing authority or control.

> The more we empathize with the other party, the safer we feel.

Once I showed my vulnerability to some members of a street gang in Cleveland by acknowledging the hurt I was feeling and my desire to be treated with more respect. "Oh, look," one of them remarked, "he's feeling hurt; isn't that too bad!" at which point all his friends chimed in laughing. Here again, I could interpret them as taking advantage of my vulnerability (Option 2: Blame others), or I could empathize with the feelings and needs behind their behavior (Option 4: Sense others' feelings and needs).

第八章　同理心的力量

松了口气。后来，我们仍然继续和学生们谈心。因为我们发现，越是聆听他们的心声，他们的学业表现就越好。"

在一个有着阶层制度的组织机构中工作，我们往往会把上司的话视为命令与评判。比起那些让我们视为"上司"的人，同理自己的同事或下级要容易得多。在"上司"面前，我们时常急着为自己辩护或向对方道歉，以致无法安静下来同理他们。因此，听到这些老师不但能同理学生，也能同理系主任，我感到特别欣慰。

同理心与袒露内心脆弱的能力

非暴力沟通鼓励我们连结内心最深处的感受和需要，有时表达它们并不容易。然而，同理心让我们能触碰彼此共通的人性，我们的自我表达也会变得容易些。我们越是能够与他人的感受和需要相连，就越不害怕袒露自己。很多时候，我们之所以不愿意展现内心的脆弱，往往是因为我们想要显得"强悍"，害怕失去权威感和掌控感。

有一次，我在和克里夫兰市的一群街头帮派成员谈话时，向他们袒露了内心的脆弱。我告诉他们我感到难过，希望得到更多的尊重。接着，其中一个人说："嘿，你们看！他说他感到难过，这可太糟糕了！"其他成员随即哄堂大笑。听到这样的话，我可以认为他们在利用我的脆弱（第二个选择：指责他人），也可以同理他们的行为（第四个选择：感知他人的感受和需要）。

如果认为他们在羞辱或利用我，我很可能会感到受伤、气愤或害怕，也因此无法同理他们。这时，我也许就需要先离开现场，以便给自

If, however, I have an image that I'm being humiliated and taken advantage of, I may feel too wounded, angry, or scared to be able to empathize. At such a moment, I would need to withdraw physically in order to offer myself some empathy or to request it from a reliable source. After discovering the needs that had been so powerfully triggered in me and receiving adequate empathy for them, I would then be ready to return and empathize with the other party. In situations of pain, I recommend first getting the empathy necessary to go beyond the thoughts occupying our heads and recognize our deeper needs.

As I listened closely to the gang member's remark, "Oh look, he's feeling hurt; isn't that too bad?" and the laughter that followed, I sensed that he and his friends were annoyed and not wanting to be subjected to guilt trips and manipulation. They may have been reacting to people in their pasts who used phrases like *that hurts me* to imply disapproval. Since I didn't verify it with them out loud, I have no way of knowing if my guess was in fact accurate. Just focusing my attention there, however, kept me from either taking it personally or getting angry. Instead of judging them for ridiculing me or treating me disrespectfully, I concentrated on hearing the pain and the needs behind such behavior.

"Hey," one of them burst out, "this is a bunch of crap you're offering us! Suppose there are members of another gang here and they have guns and you don't. And you say just stand there and *talk* to them? Crap!"

Then everybody was laughing again, and again I directed my attention to their feelings and needs: "So it sounds like you're really fed up with learning something that has no relevance in those situations?"

"Yeah, and if you lived in this neighborhood, you'd *know* this is a bunch of crap."

"So you need to trust that someone teaching you something has some knowledge of your neighborhood?"

"Damn right. Some of these dudes would blast you away before you got two words out of your mouth!"

第八章 同理心的力量

己一些同理或请求信赖的人来支持我。当我发现情绪背后的需要,并获得了足够的同理后,便准备好了再回去同理他人。因而,在痛苦的情境中,我们要先让自己得到足够的同理,才能不被自己的各种想法所束缚,并且找到内在更深层的需要。

当我用心体会那位年轻人的话以及后来的笑声时,我意识到他们有些不高兴,因为他们可能会认为我在利用内疚感给他们下圈套或操纵他们。我猜他们之所以有这样的反应,或许是因为过去有人用"这让我难过"之类的表达来暗示对他们的不满。尽管我并未向他们求证,无从知道这种猜测是否准确,然而,当我将注意力放在这里时,我就不会再认为他们在针对我,也不会生气了,而是能做到用心地听取他们的感受和需要。

"喂!"有个人突然大声说道:"你说的都是一些废话!如果在你面前是另一伙人,他们有枪而你没有,你还认为站在这里和他们说话就可以了吗?真是胡扯!"

所有人闻言又笑了起来,而我也再次关注他们的感受和需要:"所以听起来,你们受够了,不想学一些你们认为在这里派不上用场的事情,对吗?"

"是的。如果你住在这个街区,就会知道这些都是胡扯!"

"所以你需要确定,来教你们的人对你们的街区有所了解?"

"那当然!在我们这儿,有些人二话不说就会拿枪把你毙了!"

"所以,你很希望来教你们的人能了解这里的危险?"我继续以这样的方式同理他们,有时用语言表达我所听到的,有时只是静默地体会。就这样持续了 45 分钟后,我感到气氛发生了明显的变化,他们开

"And you need to trust that someone trying to teach you something understands the dangers around here?" I continued to listen in this manner, sometimes verbalizing what I heard and sometimes not. This continued for forty-five minutes, and then I sensed a shift: they felt that I was truly understanding them. A counselor in the program noticed the shift, and asked them out loud, "What do you think of this man?" The gentleman who had been giving me the roughest time replied, "He's the best speaker we've ever had."

Astonished, the counselor turned to me and whispered, "But you haven't said anything!" In fact, I had said a lot by demon-strating that there was nothing they could throw at me that couldn't be translated into universal human feelings and needs.

> We "say a lot" by listening for other people's feelings and needs.

Using Empathy to Defuse Danger

The ability to offer empathy to people in stressful situations can defuse potential violence.

A teacher in the inner city of St. Louis related an incident where she had conscientiously stayed after school to help a student, even though teachers were warned, for their own safety, to leave the building after classes were dismissed. A stranger entered her classroom, where the following exchange took place:

Young man: Take off your clothes.
  Teacher: *(noticing that the young man was shaking)* I'm sensing this is very scary for you.
Young man: Did you hear me? God damn it, take off your clothes!
  Teacher: I'm sensing you're really pissed off right now and you want me to do what you're telling me.
Young man: You're damned right, and you're going to get hurt if you don't.
  Teacher: I'd like you to tell me if there's some other way of meeting your needs that wouldn't hurt me.
Young man: I said take them off.

第八章　同理心的力量

始认为我真的能够理解他们。参与这项计划的一名辅导员也注意到了转变，便大声问道："你们觉得这个男人怎么样？"结果之前一直挑战我的那位男士回应道："他是我们遇到过的最好的讲师！"

辅导员听了以后非常惊讶，他凑近我的耳朵小声说道："可是你什么也没说啊！"实际上，我说了很多。我向他们示范的是，无论他们对我说什么，我都可以翻译成人类共通的语言——感受和需要。

以同理心化解危险

在紧张的情态下，如果能够同理他人，或许可以避免潜在的暴力。

一位在圣路易斯中心任教的老师和我分享了她的一段亲身经历。由于学校位于市中心的贫民区，出于安全的考虑，校方告诫老师们必须在放学后立即离校。然而有一天，为了给一位学生补课，这位老师主动在放学后留了下来。不久，一位陌生的年轻男子闯进了她的教室。

年轻男子：把你的衣服脱掉。
老　　师：（注意到这位男子正浑身颤抖着）我感受到你非常害怕。
年轻男子：妈的，你没听见我的话吗？快脱了你的衣服！
老　　师：我感受到你现在非常生气，你想让我按照你的话去做。
年轻男子：没错！你如果不想受伤，就马上照着我的话做。
老　　师：我想请你告诉我，除了伤害我，是否还有其他的方式来满足你的需要。
年轻男子：我说了，把衣服脱了。

8 The Power of Empathy

Teacher: I can hear how much you want this. At the same time, I want you to know how scared and horrible I feel, and how grateful I'd be if you'd leave without hurting me.

Young man: Give me your purse.

The teacher handed the stranger her purse, relieved not to be raped. She later described how, each time she empathized with the young man, she could sense him becoming less adamant in his intention to follow through with the rape.

A metropolitan police officer attending a follow-up training in NVC once greeted me with this account:

> I'm sure glad you had us practicing empathy with angry people that last time. Just a few days after our session, I went to arrest someone in a public housing project. When I brought him out, my car was surrounded by about sixty people screaming things at me like, 'Let him go! He didn't do anything! You police are a bunch of racist pigs!' Although I was skeptical that empathy would help, I didn't have many other options. So I reflected back the feelings that were coming at me; I said things like, 'So you don't trust my reasons for arresting this man? You think it has to do with race?' After several minutes of my continuing to reflect their feelings, the group became less hostile. In the end they opened a path so I could get to my car.

Finally, I'd like to illustrate how a young woman used empathy to bypass violence during her night shift at a drug detoxification center in Toronto. The young woman recounted this story during the second NVC workshop she attended. At eleven o'clock one night, a few weeks after her first NVC training, a man who'd obviously been taking drugs walked in off the street and demanded a room. The young woman started to explain to him

第八章　同理心的力量

老　　　师：我听得出来你很想要我这样做。同时，我希望你知道我有多
　　　　　　么害怕、多么难受，如果你愿意离开这里而不伤害我，我会
　　　　　　非常感激你。
年轻男子：把你的钱包给我。

　　这位教师立刻把钱包递给年轻男子。因为躲过了强暴，她大大地松了口气。后来，她回忆道，当她每次同理这个男人时，都能感受到对方不再那么坚定地想用强暴的方式来达到他的目的。

　　还有一次，一位纽约市警官在非暴力沟通工作坊开始前和我分享了他的经历：

　　我真的很开心，在上一次的工作坊中，你让我们练习了如何同理愤怒中的人们。过了几天后，我被派去逮捕一个住在公共房屋项目中的人。当我将他带出来时，有60来人围着我的车并向我喊叫："放开他！他什么都没做！你们这些警察都是种族主义分子，是一群猪！"虽然怀疑同理心能否在那时发挥作用，但我没有别的选择。于是，我试着把他们话中所隐含的感受说出来："你们不相信逮捕这位先生是合理的？你们认为这与种族有关？"这样持续了几分钟后，这群人不再像刚开始那样针锋相对了。最后，他们让开了一条路，让我上了车。

　　我想再举一个例子来说明怎样借助同理心来避免暴力。这是一个年轻的女学员在第二次参加非暴力沟通工作坊时讲述的亲身经历。这位女学员在多伦多一个戒毒中心上班。她参加完第一次非暴力沟通工作坊几周后，一天正轮到她值夜班。晚上11点左右，一个看起来服用了毒品的男人从街上走进中心，要求给他一个房间。女学员向他解释说，

that all the rooms had been filled for the night. She was about to hand the man the address of another detox center when he hurled her to the ground. "The next thing I knew, he was sitting across my chest holding a knife to my throat and shouting, 'You bitch, don't lie to me! You do too have a room!'"

She then proceeded to apply her training by listening for his feelings and needs.

"You remembered to do that under those conditions?" I asked, impressed.

"What choice did I have? Desperation sometimes makes good communicators of us all! You know, Marshall," she added, "that joke you told in the workshop really helped me. In fact, I think it saved my life."

"What joke?"

"Remember when you said never to put your 'but' in the face of an angry person? I was all ready to start arguing with him; I was about to say, '*But* I don't have a room!' when I remembered your joke. It had really stayed with me because only the week before, I was arguing with my mother and she'd said to me, 'I could kill you when you answer "but" to everything I say!' Imagine, if my own mother was angry enough to kill me for using that word, what would this man have done? If I'd said, 'But I don't have a room!' when he was screaming at me, I have no doubt he would have slit my throat.

> Rather than put your "but" in the face of an angry person, empathize.

"So instead, I took a deep breath and said, 'It sounds like you're really angry and you want to be given a room.' He yelled back, 'I may be an addict, but by God, I deserve respect. I'm tired of nobody giving me respect. My parents don't give me respect. I'm gonna get respect!' I just focused on his feelings and needs and said, 'Are you fed up, not getting the respect that you want?'"

"How long did this go on?" I asked.

"Oh, about another thirty-five minutes," she replied.

"That must have been terrifying."

第八章　同理心的力量

当晚已经没有空房了。正当她将另一个戒毒中心的地址递给他时，男子将她推倒在地。"当我回过神来，他已经坐在我的胸膛上，拿着一把刀抵着我的喉咙，大声说：'你这个婊子，别骗我！你们肯定腾得出一间房！'"

接着，这位女学员开始运用她所学到的非暴力沟通方法，同理起男子的感受和需要。

"在那样的情况下，你竟然记得运用非暴力沟通？"我十分钦佩地问她。

"要不然我还能怎么办呢？绝望有时会激发出潜在的沟通能力！你知道吗，马歇尔，"她补充说，"上回，你在工作坊里讲的一个笑话真的帮助了我。事实上，那个笑话救了我的命。"

"什么笑话？"

"你记得你说过，在一个愤怒的人面前，绝不要说'可是''但是'吗？当时我差点要和这个男人理论，我想告诉他'可是，我们真的一间房都没有了'，但在那时，我突然想起了你说的那个笑话。之所以会记得那么清楚，是因为在一周前，我在和妈妈吵架时，她对我说：'每次我说了什么，你都用"但是"来回答我，我真想杀了你！'你想，如果连我自己的妈妈都会因为这个词气得想要杀我，更何况这个男人呢？如果我在他愤怒时对他说：'可是，我们真的没有房间了！'我想我早就没命了。

"于是，我深吸了一口气，对他说：'听起来你真的很生气，你想有一个房间可以休息。'他大声回应：'也许我是一个瘾君子，但在上帝面前，我也配得到尊重！我受够了没有人尊重我，连我的父母也看不起我，我需要得到尊重！！'我全然地关注着他的感受和需要，并对他

"No, not after the first couple of interchanges, because then something else we'd learned here became apparent. When I concentrated on listening for his feelings and needs, I stopped seeing him as a monster. I could see, just as you'd said, how people who seem like monsters are simply human beings whose language and behavior sometimes keep us from seeing their humanness. The more I was able to focus my attention on his feelings and needs, the more I saw him as a person full of despair whose needs weren't being met. I became confident that if I held my attention there, I wouldn't be hurt. After he'd received the empathy he needed, he got off me, put the knife away, and I helped him find a room at another center."

> When we listen for feelings and needs, we no longer see people as monsters.

Delighted that she'd learned to respond empathically in such an extreme situation, I asked curiously, "What are you doing back here? It sounds like you've mastered NVC and should be out teaching others what you've learned."

"Now I need you to help me with a hard one," she said.

"I'm almost afraid to ask. What could be harder than that?"

"Now I need you to help me with my mother. Despite all the insight I got into that 'but' phenomenon, you know what happened? At supper the next evening when I told my mother what had happened, she said, 'You're going to cause your father and me to have a heart attack if you keep that job. You simply have to find different work!' So guess what I said to her? 'But, mother, it's my life!'"

> It may be difficult to empathize with those who are closest to us.

I couldn't have asked for a more compelling example of how difficult it can be to respond empathically to one's own family members!

Empathy in Hearing Someone's "No!"

Because of our tendency to read rejection into someone else's "no" and "I don't want to . . . ," these are important messages for

第八章　同理心的力量

说：'你是不是已经受够了得不到你想要的尊重？'"

"你们的对话持续了多长时间？"我问女学员。

"大概有 35 分钟。"她答道。

"这个过程一定很吓人吧。"

"不，我们说了几句话后，我就不害怕了。因为当我专心聆听他的感受和需要时，我就不再把他当成恶魔了。就像你说的，那些被我们看作恶魔的人，也是人。只不过有时他们的言语和行为，阻碍了我们看见他们的人性。我越是关注他的感受和需要，就越能够看见他只是一个因为需要没有得到满足而感到绝望的人。我开始相信，只要继续这么做，他就不会伤害我。当获得了同理后，他放开了我，收起了刀。接着，我帮他在另一个中心找到了一个房间。"

听到她在如此险境中仍能记得以同理心做出回应，我十分欣喜，并且好奇地问她："那你怎么还回来上课呢？看起来，你已经熟练掌握了非暴力沟通，应该到外面去把你所学到的东西教给别人呀。"

"我遇到了更大的困难，需要你的帮助。"她说。

"还有什么事会比你刚才描述的情况更棘手呢？"

"关于我和我妈妈的沟通。虽然我已经领悟到要谨慎使用'但是'这类词语，可你知道吗，在事发之后的晚餐上，我告诉了她事情的经过，她对我说：'如果你继续做这份工作，我和你爸迟早会因此心脏病发作。你得立即换一份工作！'你猜我怎么回答她？'但是，妈妈，这是我的生活啊！'"

带着同理心回应我们的家人多难啊，对此，我实在找不出更贴切的例子来说明了。

us to be able to empathize with. If we take them personally, we may feel hurt without understanding what's actually going on within the other person. When we shine the light of consciousness on

> Empathizing with someone's "no" protects us from taking it personally.

the feelings and needs behind someone else's "no," however, we become cognizant of what they are wanting that prevents them from responding as we would like.

One time I asked a woman during a workshop break to join me and other participants for some ice cream nearby. "No!" she replied brusquely. The tone of her voice led me to interpret her answer as a rejection, until I reminded myself to tune in to the feelings and needs she might be expressing through her "no." "I sense that you are angry," I said. "Is that so?"

"No," she replied, "it's just that I don't want to be corrected every time I open my mouth."

Now I sensed that she was fearful rather than angry. I checked this out by asking, "So you're feeling fearful and want to protect yourself from being in a situation where you might be judged for how you communicate?"

"Yes," she affirmed, "I can imagine sitting in the ice cream shop with you and having you notice everything I say."

I then discovered that the way I'd been providing feedback in the workshop had been frightening to her. My empathy for her message had taken the sting out of her "no" for me: I heard her desire to avoid receiving similar feedback in public. Assuring her that I wouldn't evaluate her communication in public, I then conferred with her on ways to give feedback that would leave her feeling safe. And yes, she joined the group for ice cream.

Empathy to Revive a Lifeless Conversation

We have all found ourselves in the midst of a lifeless conversation. Perhaps we're at a social event, hearing words without feeling any connection to the speaker. Or we're listening to someone my friend Kelly Bryson would call a "Babble-on-ian"—someone who

第八章　同理心的力量

当对方说"不"

当别人对我们的请求说"不要""我不想……"时,我们常常会将这类话解读为对我们的拒绝,或是认为自己有什么问题,因此无法了解对方实际上是怎么想的而感到受伤。如果能够体会对方在说"不"背后的感受和需要,我们就能明白是什么使他们无法答应我们的请求。

有一次,在工作坊休息期间,我邀请大家一起去附近吃冰激凌。有位女学员猛然回应道:"我不去!"因为这番语气,我立刻将她的回答解读为对我的拒绝。后来我提醒自己去体会她想要通过"不"表达什么样的感受和需要,于是我问她:"你好像有些生气,是吗?"

"不,我没生气。"她说,"我只是不想每次一张嘴说话都被你纠正。"

此时,我意识到她并没有生气,而是有些不安。为了核实我的猜测,我询问她:"你担心,我在场的话,有可能会评论你的沟通方式,是吗?"

"没错!我可以想象,和你一起坐在冰激凌店里,而你会关注我说的每句话……"

这时我发现,对于我在课堂上给予学员反馈的方式,她感到不自在,不想在公共场合出现那样的情境。因为体会到了她的感受和需要,我也拔除了听见"不"时扎进我心中的那根刺。于是,我向她保证,在公共场合不会评论她的沟通方式。同时,我们还讨论了什么样的反馈能够让她感到安心。最后,她和我们一起享用了冰激凌。

8 The Power of Empathy

elicits in their listeners the fear of interminable conversation. Vitality drains out of conversations when we lose connection with the feelings and needs generating the speaker's words, and with the requests associated with those needs. This effect is common when people talk without consciousness of what they are feeling, needing, or requesting. Instead of being engaged in an exchange of life energy with other human beings, we see ourselves becoming wastebaskets for their words.

How and when do we interrupt a dead conversation to bring it back to life? I'd suggest the best time to interrupt is when we've heard one word more than we want to hear. The longer we wait, the harder it is to be civil when we do step in. Our intention in interrupting is not to claim the floor for ourselves, but to help the speaker connect to the life energy behind the words being spoken.

We do this by tuning in to possible feelings and needs. Thus, if an aunt is repeating the story about how twenty years ago her husband deserted her and her two small children, we might interrupt by saying, "So, Auntie, it sounds like you are still feeling hurt, wishing you'd been treated more fairly." People are not aware that empathy is often what they are needing. Neither do they realize that they are more likely to receive that empathy by expressing the feelings and needs that are alive in them than by recounting tales of past injustice and hardship.

> To bring a conversation back to life: interrupt with empathy.

Another way to bring a conversation to life is to openly express our desire to be more connected, and to request information that would help us establish that connection. Once, at a cocktail party, I was in the midst of an abundant flow of words that to me seemed lifeless. "Excuse me," I broke in, addressing the group of nine other people I'd found myself with, "I'm feeling impatient because I'd like to be more connected with you, but our conversation isn't creating the kind of connection I'm wanting. I'd like to know if the conversation we've been having is meeting your needs, and if so, what needs of yours are being met through it."

第八章　同理心的力量

使乏味的对话变有趣

我们都经历过乏味的谈话，也许是在某个社交场合中：我们无法从说话的内容中感受到和讲述者的连结；还有些人一旦开始讲话便喋喋不休，让听的人害怕对话会没完没了。当我们无法与讲述者的感受、需要、请求建立连结时，对话便会失去生机。当讲述者不清楚自己的感受、需要和请求时，说出来的话就会乏味。这时，我们非但无法与对方建立连结，反而成了承接对方讲话的垃圾桶。

那么，我们要怎么做以及在何时打破死气沉沉的对话呢？我建议，当我们连一个字都听不下去时，就是打断的最好时机。我们等得越久，就越难在这样做时保持礼貌。而打断的目的并非在于让自己发言，而是帮助讲述者与表达背后的生命能量建立连结。

做法便是去体会对方心中可能会有的感受和需要。例如，如果你的阿姨再度讲起20年前她的丈夫如何抛弃了她和两个孩子，你可以试着打断她，对她说："阿姨，听起来，你现在依然感到愤愤不平，希望当年得到公平的对待。"人们往往没有意识到他们要的其实是别人的同理。他们也不知道，与讲述过去所遭遇到的不公和困难相比，直接表达自己的感受和需要，更有可能得到来自他人的同理。

使谈话变得生动有趣的另一种方法是，直接告诉对方我们想和他们建立更多连结，并请求对方的支持。有一次，在一个酒会上，听着周围人说的话，我感觉颇为无趣。于是，我打断了他们的谈话，对着其他9个人说："打扰了，我有点不耐烦，因为我想与你们加深联系，但我们的对话无法带给我想要的连结。我想知道，刚才我们的谈话能否满足你

8 The Power of Empathy

All nine people stared at me as if I had thrown a rat in the punch bowl. Fortunately, I remembered to tune in to the feelings and needs being expressed through their silence. "Are you annoyed with my interrupting because you would have liked to continue the conversation?" I asked.

After another silence, one of the men replied, "No, I'm not annoyed. I was thinking about what you were asking. And no, I wasn't enjoying the conversation; in fact, I was totally bored with it."

At the time, I was surprised to hear his response because he had been the one doing most of the talking! Now I am no longer surprised: I have since discovered that conversations that are lifeless for the listener are equally so for the speaker.

> **What bores the listener bores the speaker too.**

You may wonder how we can muster the courage to flatly interrupt someone in the middle of a sentence. I once conducted an informal survey, posing the following question: "If you are using more words than somebody wants to hear, do you want that person to pretend to listen or to stop you?" Of the scores of people I approached, all but one expressed a preference to be stopped. Their answers gave me courage by convincing me that it is more considerate to interrupt people than to pretend to listen. All of us want our words to enrich others, not to burden them.

> **Speakers prefer that listeners interrupt rather than pretend to listen.**

Empathy for Silence

One of the hardest messages for many of us to empathize with is silence. This is especially true when we've expressed ourselves vulnerably and need to know how others are reacting to our words. At such times, it's easy to project our worst fears onto the lack of response and forget to connect with the feelings and needs being expressed through the silence.

第八章　同理心的力量

们的需要？如果能，你们的哪些需要得到了满足呢？"

刹时，那9个人都看向了我，仿佛我向鸡尾酒桶里扔了一只老鼠。幸好，当时我还记得去体会他们透过沉默所传递的感受和需要。于是，我同理他们说："对于我的打断，你们是否有些不高兴，因为你们想继续聊下去？"

又是一番沉默后，有个人回答道："不，我没有不高兴。我刚才是在思考你的问题。其实，我并不喜欢刚才的谈话，觉得无聊透了。"

听他这么说，我吃了一惊，因为他可是刚才话讲得最多的那个人！不过如今，我已不会为此感到惊讶，因为我发现：如果听的人觉得很无聊，说的人也一样感到无趣。

你可能想知道，如何鼓起勇气打断别人说了一半的话。有一次我做了一项非正式调查。我的问题是："如果你说的话别人不想听，你是希望对方假装听下去，还是希望对方直接打断你的话呢？"我问了许多人，结果只有一个人不希望被打断。因此，我更坚信，与其假装听别人说话，打断他们才是更体贴的做法。因为，所有人都希望自己的话对人有益，而非成为他人的负担。

当他人保持沉默

对许多人来说，在面对他人的沉默时做到同理是极为困难的。尤其当我们已经表达了内心深处的脆弱，很想知道他人的回应，对方却沉默不语时，我们会感到格外不安，容易把事情往坏处想，因而很难去体会对方透过沉默表达的感受和需要。

8 The Power of Empathy

One time when I was working with the staff of a business organization, I was talking about something deeply emotional and began to cry. When I looked up, I received a response from the organization's director that was not easy for me to receive: silence. He turned his face from me with what I interpreted to be an expression of disgust. Fortunately, I remembered to put my attention on what might be going on within him, and said, "I'm sensing from your response to my crying that you're feeling disgusted, and you'd prefer to have someone more in control of his feelings consulting with your staff."

> Empathize with silence by listening for the feelings and needs behind it.

If he had answered yes, I would have been able to accept that we had different values around expressing emotions, without somehow thinking that I was wrong for having expressed my emotions as I did. But instead of "yes," the director replied, "No, not at all. I was just thinking of how my wife wishes I could cry." He went on to reveal that his wife, who was divorcing him, had been complaining that living with him was like living with a rock.

During my practice as a psychotherapist, I was contacted by the parents of a twenty-year-old woman under psychiatric care. She had been undergoing medication, hospitalization, and shock treatments for several months, and had become mute three months before her parents contacted me. When they brought her to my office, she had to be assisted because, left to herself, she didn't move.

In my office, she crouched in her chair, shaking, her eyes on the floor. Trying to connect empathically with the feelings and needs being expressed through her nonverbal message, I said, "I'm sensing that you are frightened and would like to be sure that it's safe to talk. Is that accurate?"

She showed no reaction, so I expressed my own feeling by saying, "I'm very concerned about you, and I'd like you to tell me if there's something I could say or do to make you feel safer." Still no response. For the next forty minutes, I continued to either

第八章　同理心的力量

有一次，在为一家公司的员工上课时，我谈起一件对我深有触动的事，说着说着，我流泪了。当我抬起头时，看到公司的董事长转开了脸，默不作声。面对沉默，我有些不知所措，甚至将他的动作理解为对我的嫌弃。好在，我记得让自己将注意力关注在他的内心世界。于是，我问他："看到我流泪，你似乎有些厌恶，是不是你希望请来的顾问能控制好自己的情绪？"

如果他当时回答"是"，那意味着我们对表达情感有不同的理解，我也不会因此认为自己的情感表达方式有什么不对。然而，他却回答我说："不，不是这样。我只是在想我的太太多么希望我会流泪啊。"接着他告诉我，他的太太正要和他离婚。很长时间以来，她一直抱怨与他生活就像和一块石头在一起。

记得我还在担任心理医生时，有一对父母联系了我。他们有一个20岁的女儿，正在接受精神疾病治疗，经历了长达数月的服药、住院、休克疗法。3个月前，她停止了讲话。她的父母搀扶着她来到我的办公室，因为她已经无法靠自己行走了。

到了我的办公室后，她蜷缩在椅子上，全身不停地发抖，眼睛呆呆地看着地板。我尝试着同理她通过肢体语言表达的感受和需要，对她说："你很害怕，希望确定你在这里能够安心地说话，对吗？"

眼见她没有反应，我便表达了自己的感受："我很关心你。希望你能告诉我，我要怎么说或怎么做，能让你觉得安全些呢？"依然没有回应。在接下来的40分钟里，我继续揣摩着她的感受和需要，或是把我的感受和需要说出来。她一直都没有任何明显的反应，仿佛根本没有意识到我正试着和她沟通。最后，我告诉她我累了，并希望她第二天再来。

接下来的几天，情况和第一天没有什么不同。而我依然全然地关注

reflect her feelings and needs or express my own. There was no visible response, nor even the slightest recognition that I was trying to communicate with her. Finally I expressed that I was tired, and that I wanted her to return the following day.

The next few days were like the first. I continued focusing my attention on her feelings and needs, sometimes verbally reflecting what I understood and sometimes doing so silently. From time to time I would express what was going on in myself. She sat shaking in her chair, saying nothing.

On the fourth day, when she still didn't respond, I reached over and held her hand. Not knowing whether my words were communicating my concern, I hoped the physical contact might do so more effectively. At first contact, her muscles tensed and she shrank further back into her chair. I was about to release her hand when I sensed a slight yielding, so I kept my hold; after a few moments I noticed a progressive relaxation on her part. I held her hand for several minutes while I talked to her as I had the first few days. Still she said nothing.

When she arrived the next day, she appeared even more tense than before, but there was one difference: she extended a clenched fist toward me while turning her face away from me. I was at first confused by the gesture, but then sensed she had something in her hand she wanted me to have. Taking her fist in my hand, I pried open her fingers. In her palm was a crumpled note with the following message: "Please help me say what's inside."

I was elated to receive this sign of her desire to communicate. After another hour of encouragement, she finally expressed a first sentence, slowly and fearfully. When I reflected back what I had heard her saying, she appeared relieved and then continued, slowly and fearfully, to talk. A year later, she sent me a copy of the following entries from her journal:

> I came out of the hospital, away from shock treatments and strong medicine. That was about April. The three months before that are completely

第八章　同理心的力量

她的感受和需要，有时说出我的理解，有时则默默体会。我也时不时会表达自己的感受和需要。而她依然坐在椅子上，全身不停地颤抖，不说任何话。

到了第 4 天，她还是没有反应。由于不知道语言是否可以传递我对她的关心，我寄希望于身体接触能更为有效。于是，我向她伸出手，想要握住她的手。我的手一碰到她，她的肌肉立刻紧绷起来，人也越发缩进椅子里。我正要松开手时，突然感到她稍微放松了些，于是我继续握着她的手。在接下来的几分钟内，我一边握着她的手，一边像前几天那样和她说话。我发现她越来越放松。但她依然什么也没有说。

第 5 天，她再来的时候，整个人看起来甚至更紧绷了，然而不同的是：她一边将脸转开，一边向我伸出一只握紧的拳头。一开始，我有些困惑，后来我意识到她的手中似乎有个东西要给我。我将她的拳头放在我的手中，打开她的手指，在她的手掌中有一张皱巴巴的纸条，上面写着："请帮我把心里话说出来。"

她终于向我发出了沟通的信号，我真是高兴极了！经过了 1 小时的鼓励，她终于慢慢地、胆怯地说出了第一句话。当我复述她的意思时，她看上去松了一口气，然后继续慢慢地、胆怯地说下去。一年后，她把她写的几篇日记抄录下来寄给我：

我出院了，不用再接受休克疗法，也不用再服用强效的药物。那时大概是四月。前 3 个月发生了什么，我头脑里一片空白；四月之前的 3 年半，我也记不得了。

他们告诉我，我出院后有段时间呆在家里，什么也不吃，一句话也不说，一直躺在床上。后来，他们把我送到了卢森堡博士那里。之后那两三个月发生的事情，我都不太记得了，只记得我在他的办公室和他说话。

8 The Power of Empathy

blank in my mind, as well as the three and a half years before April.

They say that, after getting out of the hospital, I went through a time at home of not eating, not talking, and wanting to stay in bed all the time. Then I was referred to Dr. Rosenberg for counseling. I don't remember much of those next two or three months other than being in Dr. Rosenberg's office and talking with him.

I'd begun 'waking up' since that first session with him. I'd begun sharing with him things that bothered me—things that I would never have dreamed of telling anyone about. And I remember how much that meant to me. It was so hard to talk. But Dr. Rosenberg cared about me and showed it, and I wanted to talk with him. I was always glad afterwards that I had let something out. I remember counting the days, even the hours, until my next appointment with him.

I've also learned that facing reality is not all bad. I am realizing more and more of the things that I need to stand up to, things that I need to get out and do on my own.

This is scary. And it's very hard. And it's so discouraging that when I am trying really a lot, I can still fail so terribly. But the good part of reality is that I've been seeing that it includes wonderful things, too.

I've learned in the past year about how wonderful it can be to share myself with other people. I think it was mostly just one part that I learned, about the thrill of my talking to other people and having them actually listen—even really understand at times.

I continue to be amazed by the healing power of empathy. Time and again I have witnessed people transcend the paralyzing effects of psychological pain when they have sufficient contact with

第八章 同理心的力量

第一次与他会面后,我就开始"醒"了过来。之后我开始告诉他我的烦恼,一些我从来没有想过会告诉别人的事。我记得这对我来说是多么重要。那时,说话对我来说是困难的。但卢森堡博士关心我,我也感受到他的关心,所以我愿意说给他听。当我把心事说出来后,总是觉得很快乐。我记得每次见完他之后,就开始计算离下次见面还有多少天,甚至多少个小时。

我认识到,面对现实并没有那么糟糕。我还越来越意识到,我需要直面一些事情、放下一些事情,并且由我自己来承担一些事情。

这令人害怕,也很困难。有时我竭尽全力,却仍然惨遭失败,我会感到气馁。但我发现,现实也有美好之处,因为事情总有好的一面。

过去一年来,我发现,和别人谈心,得到他人的聆听,有时甚至是他人的理解,是多么美好!

同理心的疗愈力量总是让我感到惊喜。一次又一次,我见证了,同理心是如何帮助人们从伤痛和打击中走出来。作为一个倾听者,我们并不需要懂得心理学理论或接受精神疗法的训练。关键是,我们能够与他人那一刻的独特感受和需要同在。

小结

同理他人使得我们敢于呈现自己的脆弱,平息潜在的暴力,让乏味的对话变得有趣,并了解"不"和沉默所传达的感受和需要。一次又一次,我见证了同理倾听帮助人们疗愈心灵的伤痛。

someone who can hear them empathically. As listeners, we don't need insights into psychological dynamics or training in psychotherapy. What is essential is our

> **Empathy lies in our ability to be present.**

ability to be present to what's really going on within—to the unique feelings and needs a person is experiencing in that very moment.

Summary

Our ability to offer empathy can allow us to stay vulnerable, defuse potential violence, hear the word *no* without taking it as a rejection, revive a lifeless conversation, and even hear the feelings and needs expressed through silence. Time and again, people transcend the paralyzing effects of psychological pain when they have sufficient contact with someone who can hear them empathically.

第九章

爱自己

若要寻求这个世界的改变,就让自己成为改变。

——甘地

Connecting Compassionately With Ourselves

Let us become the change we seek in the world.

—Mahatma Gandhi

We have seen how NVC contributes to relationships with friends and family, at work and in the political arena. Its most crucial application, however, may be in the way we treat ourselves. When we are internally violent toward ourselves, it is difficult to be genuinely compassionate toward others.

> NVC's most important use may be in developing self-compassion.

Remembering the Specialness of What We Are

In the play *A Thousand Clowns* by Herb Gardner, the protagonist refuses to release his twelve-year-old nephew to child-welfare authorities, declaring, "I want him to get to know exactly the special thing he is or else he won't notice it when it starts to go. I want him to stay awake . . . I want to be sure he sees all the wild possibilities. I want him to know it's worth all the trouble just to give the world a little goosing when you get the chance. And I want him to know the subtle, sneaky, important reason why he was born a human being and not a chair."

I am gravely concerned that many of us have lost awareness of "the special thing" we are; we have forgotten the "subtle, sneaky,

第九章　爱自己

我们已经看到非暴力沟通如何改善与朋友、亲人、同事乃至政治对手之间的关系。然而，它最关键的应用或许在于改变我们对待自己的方式。我们若用暴力的方式对待自己，就很难真正做到善待他人。

每个人都是独一无二的

在赫布·加德纳（Herb Gardner）创作的戏剧《一千个小丑》中，主人公拒绝将他 12 岁的外甥交给儿童福利院，他郑重地说道："我希望他明明白白地知道自己是独一无二的。不然，这份独特会在不经意间离他而去。我希望他对此保持清醒……希望他能尽情地拥抱各种奇妙的可能。我想让他知道，一旦有机会，排除万难为这个世界做点什么是值得的。我还希望他明白，生而为人，而不是一把椅子，有着多么深刻又无以言表的原因。"

我非常担忧，许多人已经意识不到自己是"独一无二"的了，遗忘了生而为人背后"深刻又无以言表的原因"。当看不见自身的美好，我们就和生命的源头、那神圣的能量失去了连结。一旦我们将自己视为充

important reason" the uncle so passionately wanted his nephew to know. When critical self-concepts prevent us from seeing the beauty in ourselves, we lose connection with the divine energy that is our source. Conditioned to view ourselves as objects—objects full of shortcomings—is it any wonder that many of us end up relating violently to ourselves?

An important area where this violence can be replaced with compassion is in our moment-to-moment evaluation of ourselves. Since we want whatever we do to lead to the enrichment of life, it is critical to know how to evaluate events and conditions in ways that help us learn and make ongoing choices that serve us. Unfortunately, the way we've been trained to evaluate ourselves often promotes more self-hatred than learning.

> We use NVC to evaluate ourselves in ways that engender growth rather than self-hatred.

Evaluating Ourselves When We've Been Less Than Perfect

In a routine workshop activity, I ask participants to recall a recent occasion when they did something they wish they hadn't. We then look at how they spoke to themselves immediately after having made what is referred in common language as a "mistake" or "error." Typical statements were: "That was dumb!" "How could you do such a stupid thing?" "What's wrong with you?" "You're always messing up!" "That's selfish!"

These speakers had been taught to judge themselves in ways that imply that what they did was wrong or bad; their self-admonishment implicitly assumes that they deserve to suffer for what they've done. It is tragic that so many of us get enmeshed in self-hatred rather than benefit from our mistakes, which show us our limitations and guide us towards growth.

Even when we sometimes do "learn a lesson" from mistakes for which we judge ourselves harshly, I worry about the nature of the energy behind that kind of change and learning. I'd like change

第九章　爱自己

满瑕疵的丑陋物件，那么以暴力的方式来对待自己还奇怪吗？

我们如何能以善意和友爱对待自己，而非以暴力相向呢？一个重要的因素是转变每时每刻的自我评价。既然希望自己所做的每件事对生命有益，那么，我们就要知道如何做出有助于生命成长的自我评价，进而做出符合生命需要的选择。然而，不幸的是，我们长期以来所习得的评价方式往往导致自我憎恨，而无助于成长。

面对自己的不完美

在一次工作坊中，我请学员回忆一件最近让他们感到后悔的事情。接着，我请他们留意，当认为自己"犯了错""失误了"之后，他们会对自己说什么。比较有代表性的说法是："笨蛋！""这种蠢事你也干得出！""你有毛病吗？""你总是把事情搞砸！""真自私！"

人们被教导的方式充满着好坏对错，也因此用这样的方式指责自己，认为自己所做的事情是错的或不好的，活该受到惩罚。可悲的是，这样的方式只会让我们陷入自我憎恨，而无法从失误中学习——而失误恰恰能让我们看见局限，并引导成长。

即使我们有时能从错误中"得到教训"并做出改变，但在我看来，那背后的驱动力也不是正向的。我希望，我们的改变是出于想为自己和他人创造更美好的生活，而并不是因为羞愧、内疚这样一些具有破坏性的驱动力。

假如自我评价的方式让我们感到羞愧，并因而改变行为，即我们的学习和成长便会被"自我憎恨"主导。羞愧是自我憎恨的一种形式，出

to be stimulated by a clear desire to enrich life for ourselves or for others rather than by destructive energies such as shame or guilt.

If the way we evaluate ourselves leads us to feel shame, and we consequently change our behavior, we are allowing our growing and learning to be guided by self-hatred. Shame is a form of self-hatred, and actions taken in reaction to shame are not free and joyful acts. Even if our intention is to behave with more kindness and sensitivity, if people sense shame or guilt behind our actions, they are less likely to appreciate what we do than if we are motivated purely by the human desire to contribute to life.

In our language there is a word with enormous power to create shame and guilt. This violent word, which we commonly use to evaluate ourselves, is so deeply ingrained in our consciousness that many of us would have trouble imagining how to live without it. It is the word *should*, as in "I should have known better" or "I shouldn't have done that." Most of the time when we use this word with ourselves, we resist learning, because *should* implies that there is no choice. Human beings, when hearing any kind of demand, tend to resist because it threatens our autonomy—our strong need for choice. We have this reaction to tyranny even when it's internal tyranny in the form of a *should*.

> Avoid shoulding yourself!

A similar expression of internal demand occurs in the following self-evaluation: "What I'm doing is just terrible. I really must do something about it!" Think for a moment of all the people you've heard say, "I really should give up smoking," or, "I really have to do something about exercising more." They keep saying what they "must" do and they keep resisting doing it, because human beings were not meant to be slaves. We were not meant to succumb to the dictates of *should* and *have to*, whether they come from outside or inside of ourselves. And if we do yield and submit to these demands, our actions arise from an energy that is devoid of life-giving joy.

第九章　爱自己

于羞愧的行为不是自由和喜悦的行为。一旦人们意识到我们的行为是出于羞愧或内疚，而非让生活更加美好，就算我们试图更加友善和体贴，他人也很难欣赏我们的行为。

在我们的语言中，有一个词拥有强大的威力激发人们的羞愧感和罪恶感，并经常被我们用来评价自己。它充满暴力，并且根深蒂固地烙印在我们的意识中，以致于许多人无法想象如果没有它要怎么生活。这个词便是"应该"，例如，"我早应该知道的"或"我不应该那么做"。通常，当我们对自己说这个词时，我们会心生抗拒，因为"应该"暗示别无选择。人类在听到任何形式的要求时，都会不由自主地抗拒，因为要求威胁着我们作为人的自主性——我们有强烈的需要为自己做选择。不管是外在的强权还是内在的暴君对我们说"应该"，我们都会心生抵抗。

我们还会用一些别的说法来要求自己，例如："我表现得太糟糕了，必须改改了！"想一下，你是否常常会听到人们对自己说："我真的应该戒烟了。"或"我真的应该要多健身了。"虽然不断地对自己说"必须"做这做那，却又始终抗拒着行动。那是因为，人天生就不想成为奴隶，不愿意服从于"应该"和"不得不"的支配——不论来自外部世界还是我们自身。即使对要求屈服或让步，但我们的行动却无法为生命带来喜悦。

转化自我评判和自我要求

如果我们经常以评判、指责、命令的方式与自己沟通，我们看待自

Translating Self-Judgments and Inner Demands

When we communicate with ourselves on a regular basis through inner judgment, blame, and demand, it's not surprising that our self-concept gives in to feeling more like a chair than a human being. A basic premise of NVC is that whenever we imply that someone is wrong or bad, what we are really saying is that he or she is not acting in harmony with our needs. If the person we are judging happens to be ourselves, what we are saying is, "I myself am not behaving in harmony with my own needs." I am convinced that if we learn to evaluate ourselves in terms of whether and how well our needs are being fulfilled, we are much more likely to learn from the evaluation.

> Self-judgments, like all judgments, are tragic expressions of unmet needs.

Our challenge then, when we are doing something that is not enriching life, is to evaluate ourselves moment by moment in a way that inspires change both (1) in the direction of where we would like to go, and (2) out of respect and compassion for ourselves, rather than out of self-hatred, guilt or shame.

NVC Mourning

After a lifetime of schooling and socialization, it is probably too late for most of us to train our minds to think purely in terms of what we need and value from moment to moment. However, just as we have learned to translate judgments when conversing with others, we can train ourselves to recognize judgmental self-talk and to immediately focus our attention on the underlying needs.

For example, if we find ourselves reacting reproachfully to something we did ("Look, you just messed up again!"), we can quickly stop and ask ourselves, "What unmet need of mine is being expressed through this moralistic judgment?" When we do connect to the need—and there may be several layers of needs—we will notice a remarkable shift in our bodies. Instead of the shame, guilt, or depression we likely feel when criticizing ourselves for having "messed up again," we will experience any number of

第九章　爱自己

己便仿佛更像一个物件而不是一个人。非暴力沟通认为，每当我们认为他人是错的或是不好的，我们真正的心声是——他人的行为与我们的需要有冲突；如果我们指责的人恰好是自己，我们真正的心声是——我的所作所为没有满足我的需要。因而我坚信，如果我们以需要是否得到满足来评价自己，就更有可能从自我评价的过程中获益。

因此，当我们意识到正在做的事情无法滋养生命时，我们的挑战是，在当下要如何来评价自己——是否对自己怀有尊重与慈悲，而不是心怀怨恨或愧疚。

非暴力沟通的哀悼

大多数人在经过长期的学校教育和社会教化后，已经很难时时刻刻从"自己需要什么"的角度来思考了。然而，就像我们已经学习了用需要来转化他人的评判那样，我们也可以培养对自我评判的觉察，并随即将注意力放在这些评判背后隐藏的需要上。

例如，如果意识到自己正为了某件事情谴责自己："你看你，又把事情搞砸了！"这时可以停下来问自己："我这样指责自己，是因为什么需要没有得到满足？"当我们和自己的需要（可能是多个层面的需要）连结时，我们会在自己的身体上体会到明显的变化。这时，我们因自我批评而产生的羞愧、内疚或压抑，便会被其他的感受取代。不论是难过、挫败、失望、恐惧、悲伤或别的，这些都是我们与生俱来的感受，其目的是推动我们去满足和追寻自己的价值观和需要；而内疚、羞愧和压抑则会切断我们与自己的连结。这两类感受对我们的身心影响可谓大不

other feelings. Whether it's sadness, frustration, disappointment, fear, grief, or some other feeling, we have been endowed by nature with these feelings for a purpose: they mobilize us to pursue and fulfill what we need or value. The impact of these feelings on our spirit and bodies is substantially different from the disconnection that is brought on by guilt, shame, and depression.

Mourning in NVC is the process of fully connecting with the unmet needs and the feelings that are generated when we have been less than perfect. It is an experience of regret, but regret that helps us learn from what we have done without blaming or hating ourselves. We see how our behavior ran counter to our own needs and values, and we open ourselves to feelings that arise out of that awareness. When our consciousness is focused on what we need, we are naturally stimulated toward creative possibilities for how to get that need met. In contrast, the moralistic judgments we use when blaming ourselves tend to obscure such possibilities and to perpetuate a state of self-punishment.

> NVC mourning: connecting with the feelings and unmet needs stimulated by past actions we now regret.

Self-Forgiveness

We follow up on the process of mourning with self-forgiveness. Turning our attention to the part of the self which chose to act in the way that led to the present situation, we ask ourselves, "When I behaved in the way which I now regret, what need of mine was I trying to meet?" I believe that human beings are always acting in the service of needs and values. This is true whether the action does or does not meet the need, or whether it's one we end up celebrating or regretting.

When we listen empathically to ourselves, we will be able to hear the underlying need. Self-forgiveness occurs the moment this empathic connection is made. Then we are able to recognize how our choice was an attempt to serve life, even as the mourning process teaches us how it fell short of fulfilling our needs.

第九章　爱自己

相同。

在非暴力沟通中，所谓"哀悼"（mourning）是充分连结未被满足的需要以及因为自认为做得不够完美而引发的感受。哀悼，让我们不再以指责或怨恨自己的方式陷入后悔，而是帮助我们从中学习。我们会看见自己的行为如何与我们的需要和价值观产生冲突，并且接纳在这个过程中浮现的感受。当我们将注意力放在需要上，自然就能激发出充满创造力的可能性来满足需要。相反，如果以道德评判来谴责自己，我们不仅难以看到这些可能性，而且容易陷入自我惩罚的状态。

自我宽恕

哀悼过后，我们可以尝试"自我宽恕"这一过程。想一想自己为何要采取那个行动，问自己："我当时那样做，是要满足什么需要呢？"我相信，人的行为都是为了满足需要所做的尝试，不论它是否能够实现目的，也不论我们事后感到庆幸还是遗憾。

以同理心倾听自己，我们就能听见行为背后那内心深处的需要。一旦和自己建立了充满同理心的连结，我们就能宽恕自己。我们发现，尽管过去的选择并不理想，需要为之哀悼，但那也是想让自己的生命更加美好。

要善意地对待自己，关键在于带着同理心拥抱两个"自己"：对过去的行为感到懊恼的自己以及当初做了那件事的自己。通过"哀悼"和"自我宽恕"，我们不再谴责自己，进而从中有所收获和成长，并因而获得自由。如果能时时和自己的需要相连，我们就能采取更富有创造力的行动来满足需要。

> **NVC self-forgiveness: connecting with the need we were trying to meet when we took the action that we now regret.**

An important aspect of self-compassion is to be able to empathically hold both parts of ourselves—the self that regrets a past action and the self that took the action in the first place. The process of mourning and self-forgiveness frees us in the direction of learning and growing. In connecting moment by moment to our needs, we increase our creative capacity to act in harmony with them.

The Lesson of the Polka-Dotted Suit

I would like to illustrate the process of mourning and self-forgiveness by recalling a personal event. The day before an important workshop, I had bought a light gray summer suit to wear. At the end of the well-attended workshop, I was swarmed by participants asking for my signature, address, and other information. With time closing in on another appointment, I hastened to attend to the requests of the participants, signing and scribbling on the many bits of paper thrust in front of me. As I rushed out the door, I stuck my pen—uncapped—in the pocket of my new suit. Once outside, I discovered to my horror that instead of the nice light gray suit, I now had a polka-dotted suit!

For twenty minutes I was brutal with myself: "How could you be so careless? What a stupid thing to do!" I had just ruined a brand-new suit: if ever I needed compassion and understanding, this was the time, yet there I was responding to myself in a way that left me feeling worse than ever.

Fortunately—after only twenty minutes—I noticed what I was doing. I stopped, looked for the need of mine that was unmet by having left the pen uncapped, and asked myself, "What need lies behind my judging myself as 'careless' and 'stupid?'"

Immediately I saw that it was to take better care of myself: to have given more attention to my own needs while I was rushing

第九章　爱自己

圆点外衣带给我的教训

　　我想通过一个我的亲身经历来说明非暴力沟通的"哀悼"和"自我宽恕"。有一回，我穿着一套新买的淡灰色夏季外衣去主持一个很重要的工作坊。当天的学员很多，课程结束时，许多人围着我索取签名、询问地址和其他资料。为了能赶上下一场会晤，我便加快速度回应参与者的请求，仓促地在我面前的纸上签名、留言。当我飞快地走出门时，我将钢笔插在了新衣口袋中，居然忘了盖上笔套！走到外面后，我赫然发现那件好看的淡灰色上衣已经变成了一件圆点花纹衫了！

　　在足足20分钟内，我不停地斥责自己："你怎么可以这么粗心大意？看看你干了什么蠢事！"我刚毁了一件崭新的外衣，这可能是我最需要得到体谅的时刻，但我却不断地谴责自己，让自己愈发难受。

　　幸好，20分钟后，我开始意识到自己正在做什么。于是，我停下来去体会，在这件事上，我有哪些需要没有得到满足。我问自己："我指责自己'粗心大意'和'愚蠢'，是出于什么样的需要呢？"这时，我立刻意识到我的需要是：好好地照顾自己——在匆忙回应他人需要的同时，也能更多地关注自己的需要。当我听见内心深处的渴望（更多地觉察自己和关心自己的需要），我的感受也立刻发生了转变。随着愤怒、羞愧和内疚感逐渐消散，我的身体也不再那么紧绷了。我充分地哀悼着那件毁掉的外衣和没有盖上笔套的行为，并且当我看到自己渴望更好地照顾自己时，我全然地允许和体会着从中升起的难过之情。

　　接着，我开始思索，我将那支没套上笔盖的钢笔插在新衣口袋中是为了满足什么需要。我发现，关心和体贴别人的需要，对我是多么重

to address everyone else's needs. As soon as I touched that part of myself and connected to the deep longing to be more aware and caring of my own needs, my feelings shifted. There was a release of tension in my body as the anger, shame, and guilt I was harboring toward myself dissipated. I fully mourned the ruined suit and uncapped pen as I opened to feelings of sadness arising along with the yearning to take better care of myself.

Next I shifted my attention to the need I was meeting when I slipped the uncapped pen into my pocket. I recognized how much I valued care and consideration for other people's needs. Of course, in taking such good care of other people's needs, I had not taken the time to do the same for myself. But instead of blame, I felt a wave of compassion for myself as I realized that even my rushing and putting the pen away unthinkingly had come out of serving my own need to respond to others in a caring way!

In that compassionate place, I am able to hold both needs: in one hand, to respond in a caring way to others' needs, and in the other, to be aware of and take better care of my own needs. On becoming conscious of both needs, I can imagine ways of behaving differently in similar situations and arriving at solutions more resourcefully than if I lose that consciousness in a sea of self-judgment.

> We are compassionate with ourselves when we are able to embrace all parts of ourselves and recognize the needs and values expressed by each part.

Don't Do Anything That Isn't Play!

In addition to the process of mourning and self-forgiveness, another aspect of self-compassion I emphasize is in the energy that's behind whatever action we take. When I advise, "Don't do anything that isn't play!" some take me to be radical, even insane. I earnestly believe, however, that an important form of self-compassion is to make choices motivated purely by our desire to contribute to life rather than out of fear, guilt, shame, duty, or obligation. When we are conscious of the life-enriching purpose

第九章　爱自己

要。我意识到，尽管我没有花时间好好照顾自己，但匆忙之中心不在焉地把笔塞进口袋，也是为了满足服务他人的需要。想到这里，我便不再责备自己，反而升起了对自己的疼爱之情。

带着对自己的善意，我拥抱自己的两方面需要：一方面，服务他人；另一方面，照顾好自己。我也因而能想象自己在类似的情境中做出不一样的选择，并且更有可能找到解决方法，而没有在一味自责中失去觉察。

不做任何没有乐趣的事！

非暴力沟通的"哀悼"和"自我宽恕"是爱自己的重要方面。此外，还有一点也很重要，那就是：觉察自己每个行为举动背后的能量。当我建议人们"不做任何没有乐趣的事"，有的人认为我太极端，甚至有些疯狂。然而，我深信，出于对生命纯粹的爱，而不是出于恐惧、内疚、羞愧、义务或者职责来做出选择，是我们爱自己的重要体现。当我们清楚地知道自己的行动是为了滋养生命，当我们做事的动机纯粹只是为了让自己和他人的生命变得更加美好，即使工作辛苦，我们也会乐在其中。反之，如果我们的行动是出于义务、职责、恐惧、内疚或羞愧，那么，即使有意思的事情也会失去它的乐趣，最终让人心生抗拒。

在第二章，我们探讨了人们如何在语言表达中暗示自己缺乏选择，并重新学会用语言认清我们是有选择的。许多年以前，有个练习给我带来了极大的喜悦和幸福感，并减少了我的压抑、内疚和羞愧感。这个练习让我时刻清晰地觉知每个行动背后滋养生命的需要。我将在下文中介绍这个练习，希望它能帮助我们善待自己，出于喜悦和乐趣来生活。

9 Connecting Compassionately With Ourselves

> We want to take action out of the desire to contribute to life rather than out of fear, guilt, shame, or obligation.

behind an action we take, when the sole energy that motivates us is simply to make life wonderful for others and ourselves, then even hard work has an element of play in it. Correspondingly, an otherwise joyful activity performed out of obligation, duty, fear, guilt, or shame will lose its joy and eventually engender resistance.

In Chapter 2, we considered replacing language that implies lack of choice with language that acknowledges choice. Many years ago I began to engage in an activity which significantly enlarged the pool of joy and happiness available to my life, while diminishing depression, guilt, and shame. I offer it here as a possible way to deepen our compassion for ourselves, to help us live our lives out of joyous play by staying grounded in a clear awareness of the life-enriching need behind everything we do.

Translating "Have to" to "Choose to"

Step 1
What do you do in your life that you don't experience as playful? List on a piece of paper all those things that you tell yourself you have to do. List any activity you dread but do anyway because you perceive yourself to have no choice.

When I first reviewed my own list, just seeing how long it was gave me insight as to why so much of my time was spent not enjoying life. I noticed how many ordinary, daily things I was doing by tricking myself into believing that I had to do them.

The first item on my list was "write clinical reports." I hated writing these reports, yet I was spending at least an hour of agony over them every day. My second item was "drive the children's car pool to school."

Step 2
After completing your list, clearly acknowledge to yourself that you are doing these things because you choose to do them, not

第九章　爱自己

"不得不"转化为"我选择"

第一步：

在你的生活中，哪些事情让你觉得无趣，却又不得不去做？你不想做它们，但还是去做了，因为你认为自己没有选择。请将这些事情列在一张纸上。

当我第一次审视我的清单时，发现上面的事情可真不少，我恍然大悟自己为何常常无法享受生活。有许多事情，我之所以日复一日地去做，是因为我糊弄自己去相信那是不得不做的。

清单上的第一项是：写临床报告。我痛恨撰写这些报告，但却每天至少要花一个小时在上面，这让我苦不堪言。清单的第二项是：开车送孩子们上学。

第二步：

写完清单后，清楚地告诉自己：你之所以做这些事情，是因为你选择了它们，而非你不得不做。在你所列出的每一件事情前加上"我选择做……"。

我记得当时我对这一步有些抗拒。我一直信誓旦旦地认为："写临床报告不是我选择要做的事情，而是我不得不做的事。我是一名临床心理医生，当然必须要写这些报告。"

because you have to. Insert the words "*I choose to . . .* " in front of each item you listed.

I recall my own resistance to this step. "Writing clinical reports," I insisted to myself, "is not something I choose to do! I have to do it. I'm a clinical psychologist. I have to write these reports."

Step 3

After having acknowledged that you choose to do a particular activity, get in touch with the intention behind your choice by completing the statement, I choose to . . . because I want . . . .

At first I fumbled to identify what I wanted from writing clinical reports. I had already determined, several months earlier, that the reports did not serve my clients enough to justify the time they were taking, so why was I continuing to invest so much energy in their preparation? Finally I realized that I was choosing to write the reports solely because I wanted the income they provided. As soon as I recognized this, I never wrote another clinical report. I can't tell you how joyful I feel just thinking of how many clinical reports I haven't written since that moment thirty-five years ago! When I realized that money was my primary motivation, I immediately saw that I could find other ways to take care of myself financially, and that in fact, I'd rather scavenge in garbage cans for food than write another clinical report.

The next item on my list of unjoyful tasks was driving the children to school. When I examined the reason behind that chore, however, I felt appreciation for the benefits my children received from attending their school. They could easily walk to the neighborhood school, but their own school was far more in harmony with my educational values. I continued to drive, but with a different energy; instead of "Oh, darn, I have to drive the car pool today," I was conscious of my purpose, which was for my children to have a quality of education that was very dear to me. Of course I sometimes needed to remind myself two or three times during the drive to refocus my mind on what purpose my action was serving.

> With every choice you make, be conscious of what need it serves.

第九章　爱自己

第三步：

一旦你认同了之所以做某件事是出于自己的选择，请试着体会选择背后的意图是什么，然后以"我选择做……因为我想要……"来表述。

起初，我怎么也想不清楚到底为什么要写临床报告。几个月前，我已经认定这些报告对我的咨询病人来说用处不大，不值得花那么多时间。既然如此，为什么我还投入那么多精力在这上面呢？最终我发现，我选择写这些报告，仅仅是因为想要获得这份工作带来的收入。意识到这点，我再也没有写过任何临床报告了。想到这35年来，自己少写了无数的报告，我就开心得不得了！当意识到金钱是我的首要驱动力时，我立刻就想到可以用别的方式来获得收入。事实上，我宁愿在垃圾桶里觅食，也不愿再多写一份临床报告！

我列出的第二项不情愿做的事：开车送孩子们上学。当我仔细思索为什么要这么做时，我发现，对于孩子们从学校收获的好处，我心怀感恩。虽然他们可以步行到附近的学校上学，但现在的这所学校更符合我的教育理念。于是，我还是继续开车送孩子们上学，不过心态已经不一样了。我不再对自己说："讨厌，今天我又必须做车夫了。"因为我已经清楚地知道，这是为了让孩子们受到良好的教育，因为我很重视教育的品质。当然，有时候我需要在开车时提醒自己好多次，重新关注这样做的目的。

培养觉察力，理解行为背后的动机

当你在思考"我选择做……是因为我想要……"这样的陈述时，也

Cultivating Awareness of the Energy Behind Our Actions

As you explore the statement, "I choose to . . . because I want . . . ," you may discover—as I did with the children's car pool—the important values behind the choices you've made. I am convinced that after we gain clarity regarding the need being served by our actions, we can experience those actions as play even when they involve hard work, challenge, or frustration.

For some items on your list, however, you might uncover one or several of the following motivations:

(1) FOR MONEY

Money is a major form of extrinsic reward in our society. Choices prompted by a desire for reward are costly: they deprive us of the joy in life that comes with actions grounded in the clear intention to contribute to a human need. Money is not a "need" as we define it in NVC; it is one of countless strategies that may be selected to address a need.

(2) FOR APPROVAL

Like money, approval from others is a form of extrinsic reward. Our culture has educated us to hunger for reward. We attended schools that used extrinsic means to motivate us to study; we grew up in homes where we were rewarded for being good little boys and girls, and were punished when our caretakers judged us to be otherwise. Thus, as adults, we easily trick ourselves into believing that life consists of doing things for reward; we are addicted to getting a smile, a pat on the back, and people's verbal judgments that we are a "good person," "good parent," "good citizen," "good worker," "good friend," and so forth. We do things to get people to like us and avoid things that may lead people to dislike or punish us.

I find it tragic that we work so hard to buy love and assume that we must deny ourselves and do for others in order to be liked. In fact, when we do things solely in the spirit of enhancing life, we will find others appreciating us. Their appreciation, however, is only a feedback mechanism confirming that our efforts had the

第九章　爱自己

许会发现自己是基于一些重要的理念才会做出那样的决定，就像我问自己为何要开车送孩子们上学。我相信，一旦意识到行为所服务的需要，即使工作很艰苦、富有挑战，甚至举步维艰，我们仍然能乐在其中。

不过，你也许会在清单上发现，有的行为是出于以下动机。

1. 为了钱

金钱是我们社会中最主要的一种外在奖励形式。只是为了获得金钱奖励而做的选择代价高昂，我们会因而失去生活的乐趣。而当我们清楚地知道自己的行为是为了满足人的需要时，喜悦就会伴随着我们。"金钱"并不是非暴力沟通所指的"需要"，而是可以用来满足某个需要的无数策略之一。

2. 为了得到他人的认可

他人的认可和金钱一样，也是一种外在奖励形式。受社会文化的影响，我们如饥似渴般追求奖励。学校会以外在手段来激励我们学习；在家里，如果我们当一个乖小孩，就会得到奖励，如果不乖，就会受到惩罚。于是，长大以后，我们很容易误以为做事的目的就是为了获得奖赏。我们渴望得到他人对我们的微笑、拍拍我们的背，夸我们是"好人、好父母、好公民、好员工、好朋友"等等，好像上了瘾一般。我们会去做讨他人喜欢的事，而避开做那些让他人不喜欢或可能会使自己受到惩罚的事情。

我们如此努力地讨喜，并认为必须用牺牲自己的方式来做贡献才能博得他人欢心，真让人感到悲哀啊。事实上，如果我们的行动只是为了让生命更加美好，人们自然会来欣赏我们。不过，他人的赏识也只是一

intended effect. The recognition that we have chosen to use our power to serve life and have done so successfully brings us the genuine joy of celebrating ourselves in a way that approval from others can never offer.

(3) TO ESCAPE PUNISHMENT

Some of us pay income tax primarily to avoid punishment. As a consequence, we are likely to approach that yearly ritual with a degree of resentment. I recall, however, from my childhood how differently my father and grandfather felt about paying taxes. They had immigrated to the United States from Russia and were desirous of supporting a government they believed was protecting people in a way that the czar had not. Imagining the many people whose welfare was being served by their tax money, they felt earnest pleasure as they sent their checks to the U.S. government.

(4) TO AVOID SHAME

There may be some tasks we choose to do just to avoid shame. We know that if we don't do them, we'll end up suffering severe self-judgment, hearing our own voice telling us there is something wrong or stupid about us. If we do something stimulated solely by the urge to avoid shame, we will generally end up detesting it.

(5) TO AVOID GUILT

In other instances, we may think, "If I don't do this, people will be disappointed in me." We are afraid we'll end up feeling guilty for failing to fulfill other people's expectations of us. There is a world of difference between doing something for others in order to avoid guilt and doing it out of a clear awareness of our own need to contribute to the happiness of other human beings. The first is a world filled with misery; the second is a world filled with play.

> Be conscious of actions motivated by the desire for money or approval, and by fear, shame, or guilt. Know the price you pay for them.

(6) TO SATISFY A SENSE OF DUTY

When we use language which denies choice (for example, words such as *should, have to, ought, must, can't, supposed to,* etc.), our behaviors arise out of a vague sense of guilt, duty, or obligation.

第九章 爱自己

项反馈机制,让我们知道自己的努力达到了预期的效果。当我们认识到靠自身的力量让生命更加美好,由此而产生的喜悦是他人的肯定永远无法比拟的。

3. 为了免受惩罚

有些人之所以缴纳个人所得税,主要是为了免受惩罚。这使他们对每年度例行的纳税心怀抵触情绪。但我却记得小时候父亲和祖父对于纳税则有着全然不同的态度。他们从俄罗斯移民到美国,经历了沙皇的统治后,真心渴望能支持一个在他们心中有能力保护人民的政府。想到许多人会因为他们的税金获得福利,他们会满怀真挚的喜悦将支票寄给政府。

4. 为了避免羞愧

有时,我们会选择做某些事情,只是为了免于让自己感到羞愧。我们知道如果不这样做,我们会严厉地抨击自己。然而,如果我们仅仅因为不想让自己感到羞愧而做某件事,通常会以厌恶此事而告终。

5. 为了免于内疚

还有些时候,我们也许会认为"如果我不做这件事,别人会对我失望",这时我们往往会产生内疚感。同样做一件事情,不同的目的会给我们带来截然不同的感受。如果仅仅是为了避免内疚,整个人会感到苦不堪言;然而,如果是为了对他人的幸福做出贡献,整件事情也会充满乐趣。

9 Connecting Compassionately With Ourselves

I consider this to be the most socially dangerous and personally unfortunate of all the ways we act when we're cut off from our needs.

In Chapter 2 we saw how the concept of *Amtssprache* allowed Adolf Eichmann and his colleagues to send tens of thousands of people to their deaths without feeling emotionally affected or personally responsible. When we speak a language that denies choice, we forfeit the life in ourselves for a robotlike mentality that disconnects us from our own core.

> The most dangerous of all behaviors may consist of doing things "because we're supposed to."

After examining the list of items you have generated, you may decide to stop doing certain things in the same spirit that I chose to forego writing clinical reports. As radical as it may seem, it is possible to do things only out of play. I believe that to the degree that we engage moment by moment in the playfulness of enriching life—motivated solely by the desire for enriching life—to that degree are we being compassionate with ourselves.

Summary

The most crucial application of NVC may be in the way we treat ourselves. When we make mistakes, instead of getting caught up in moralistic self-judgments, we can use the process of NVC mourning and self-forgiveness to show us where we can grow. By assessing our behaviors in terms of our own unmet needs, the impetus for change comes not out of shame, guilt, anger, or depression, but out of the genuine desire to contribute to our own and others' well-being.

We also cultivate self-compassion by consciously choosing in daily life to act only in service to our own needs and values rather than out of duty, for extrinsic rewards, or to avoid guilt, shame, and punishment. If we review the joyless acts to which we currently subject ourselves and make the translation from "have to" to "choose to," we will discover more play and integrity in our lives.

第九章 爱自己

6. 为了履行职责

当我们以"应该""不得不""应当""必须""不能""理应"这些暗示着别无他选的语言来描述我们所采取的行动时，则意味着驱动我们的是某种无可奈何的职责或义务感，而没有与我们的需要连结。在我看来，若我们的行动与生命的需要切断了连结，这对社会来说极其危险，对个人来说也是极为不幸的。

在第二章，我们看到了在"军官语言"思维的影响下，阿道夫·艾希曼和他的部下使数以万计的人丧命，却毫不为之所动，也不认为个人对此负有责任。当我们的语言否认了个人选择，我们就与自己失去了连结而沦为机器，我们的内在便丧失了生命的价值。

在仔细审视清单上所列出的各项事情后，你也许会决定从此不再继续做某些事，就像我决定不再写临床报告那样。即使这听起来有些激进，然而只做有乐趣的事情还是有可能的。我相信，我们能时时刻刻地感受到滋养生命所带来的乐趣，并选择只为滋养生命而行动，我们就是在真正地爱自己、善待自己。

小结

非暴力沟通最关键的应用或许就是让我们学会善待自己。犯了错误，我们可以运用非暴力沟通的"哀悼"与"自我宽恕"来看清个人可以成长的方向，而不会陷入对自己的道德评判。评价自己的行为时，若着眼于"有哪些未被满足的需要"，我们的改变就能不受羞愧、内疚、愤怒或

9 Connecting Compassionately With Ourselves

If the other person's behavior is not in harmony with my own needs, the more I empathize with them and their needs, the more likely I am to get my own needs met.

第九章　爱自己

压抑所驱动，而是由衷地想要对自己和他人的幸福做出贡献。

同时，在日常生活中，有觉知地根据需要和价值观来选择行动，而不是为了履行职责、获得外在的奖励，或是逃避内疚、羞愧和惩罚，我们便是在培养对自己的爱。当我们重新检视那些无法带着乐趣来做的事情，并将"我不得不做"的想法化为"我选择这么做"，我们将会在生活中发现更多的乐趣，并且成为一个更完整的人。

9 Connecting Compassionately With Ourselves

To practice NVC, it's critical for me to be able to slow down, take my time, to come from an energy I choose, the one I believe that we were meant to come from, not the one I was programmed into. I start the day with a remembering of where I want to be.

第十章

充分表达愤怒

Expressing Anger Fully

The subject of anger gives us a unique opportunity to dive more deeply into NVC. Because it brings many aspects of this process into sharp focus, the expression of anger clearly demonstrates the difference between NVC and other forms of communication.

I would like to suggest that hitting, blaming, hurting others—whether physically or emotionally—are all superficial expressions of what is going on within us when we are angry. If we are truly angry, we would want a much more powerful way to fully express ourselves.

> Hurting people is too superficial.

This understanding comes as a relief to many groups I work with that experience oppression and discrimination and want to increase their power to effect change. Such groups are uneasy when they hear the terms *nonviolent* or *compassionate* communication because they have so often been urged to stifle their anger, calm down, and accept the status quo. They worry about approaches that view their anger as an undesirable quality needing to be purged. The process we are describing, however, does not encourage us to ignore, squash, or swallow anger, but rather to express the core of our anger fully and wholeheartedly.

Distinguishing Stimulus From Cause

The first step to fully expressing anger in NVC is to divorce the other person from any responsibility for our anger. We rid ourselves of thoughts such as, "He (or she or they) made me angry

第十章　充分表达愤怒

探索"愤怒"是我们深入学习非暴力沟通的独特机会。这个过程聚焦了非暴力沟通的许多方面,让我们清楚地了解非暴力沟通与其他沟通形式的关键区别。

在我看来,通过打骂、指责或伤害他人的方式(无论是在身体或情感上)来宣泄愤怒,只是肤浅地表达心声。如果真的很生气,我们需要找到更强有力的方式充分表达自己。

我与许多遭到过压迫与歧视的团体一起工作,听到这样的观点,他们都会松口气。这些团体都希望提升能力、更有效地推动改变,但却时常遭遇人们的劝说——要他们克制愤怒、保持冷静并接受现状。因而,在初次听到"非暴力沟通"时,他们会感到不安,担心自己的愤怒被视为负面情绪,需要被洗涤和净化。幸运的是,非暴力沟通并不鼓励我们忽视、否定或压抑愤怒,而是通过了解让我们愤怒的核心本质来充分且诚挚地表达自己。

区分刺激与原因

要充分表达愤怒,第一步是不再将愤怒的责任归咎于他人。带着类

10 Expressing Anger Fully

> We are never angry because of what others say or do.

when they did that." Such thinking leads us to express our anger superficially by blaming or punishing the other person. Earlier we saw that the behavior of others may be a stimulus for our feelings, but not the cause. We are never angry because of what someone else did. We can identify the other person's behavior as the stimulus, but it is important to establish a clear separation between stimulus and cause.

I'd like to illustrate this distinction with an example from my work at a Swedish prison. My job was to show prisoners who had behaved in violent ways how to fully express their anger rather than to kill, beat, or rape other people. During an exercise calling on participants to identify the stimulus of their anger, one prisoner wrote: "Three weeks ago I made a request to the prison officials and they still haven't responded to it." His statement was a clear observation of a stimulus, describing what other people had done.

I then asked him to state the cause of his anger: "When this happened, you felt angry because *what*?"

"I just told you," he exclaimed. "I felt angry because they didn't respond to my request!" By equating stimulus and cause, he had tricked himself into thinking that it was the behavior of the prison officials that was making him angry. This is an easy habit to acquire in a culture that uses guilt as a means of controlling people. In such cultures, it becomes important to trick people into thinking that we can *make* others feel a certain way.

Where guilt is a tactic of manipulation and coercion, it is useful to confuse stimulus and cause. As mentioned earlier, children who hear, "It hurts Mommy and Daddy when you get poor grades," are led to believe that their behavior is the cause of their parents' pain. The same dynamic is observed among intimate partners: "It really disappoints me when you're not here for my birthday." The English language facilitates the use of this guilt-inducing tactic.

> To motivate by guilt, mix up stimulus and cause.

We say: "You make me angry." "You hurt me by doing that."

第十章　充分表达愤怒

似"我很生气，是因为他人做了什么"的想法，我们便会指责或惩罚他人，而无法深入地表达让我们愤怒的核心。在前文中，我们已经探讨了，别人的言行会引发我们的感受，却并非产生感受的根本原因。实际上，我们之所以生气，绝非因为他人的言行，而是他人的行为刺激了我们的情绪反应。

我想举个例子来说明"刺激"与"原因"之间的区别。在瑞典的一座监狱，我曾经向那里的囚犯讲解如何不以杀人、打人或强奸的方式来表达愤怒。在一次练习中，我让学员寻找是什么刺激了他们的愤怒。一名囚犯写道："3周前，我向监狱长官提出了一个请求，他们到现在还没有给我回复。"他清楚地写下了他所观察到的刺激——他人做了什么。

接着，我请他说明愤怒的原因："当事情发生时，因为什么原因你会生气呢？"

"我刚才已经和你说了，"他提高了嗓门说道，"我生气是因为他们没有回应我的请求！"由于将"刺激"等同于"原因"，他误以为让自己生气的是监狱长官的作为。我们很容易有这样的习惯思维，因为我们的文化常以内疚感作为控制人的手段。对这样的文化来说，重要的是驱使人们相信，一个人能操纵他人的感受。将刺激与原因混为一谈，成功地让内疚成为操控和强迫的一种手段。

正如前文提到的，当孩子听到"你成绩不好让爸爸妈妈伤透了心"，他们就会认为是自己的行为造成了父母的痛苦。许多伴侣也会相互制造内疚感，例如说："我生日你不在，让我好失望。"

语言助长着这种使人内疚的手段。我们会说"你让我生气""你这样做伤害了我""你那样做让我很难过"。这些方式都让我们误认为是他人的言行导致了我们的感受。而要学习如何充分表达愤怒，第一步就是

10 Expressing Anger Fully

"I feel sad because you did that." We use our language in many different ways to trick ourselves into believing that our feelings result from what others do. The first step in the process of fully expressing our anger is to realize that what other people do is never the cause of how we feel.

So what is the cause of anger? In Chapter 5, we discussed the four options we have when confronted with a message or behavior that we don't like. Anger is generated when we choose the second option: whenever we are angry, we are finding fault—we are choosing to play God by judging or blaming the other person for being wrong or deserving punishment. I would like to suggest that this is the cause of anger. Even if we are not initially conscious of it, the cause of anger is located in our own thinking.

> The cause of anger lies in our thinking—in thoughts of blame and judgment.

The third option described in Chapter 5 is to shine the light of consciousness on our own feelings and needs. Rather than going up to our head to make a mental analysis of wrongness regarding somebody, we choose to connect to the life that is within us. This life energy is most palpable and accessible when we focus on what we need in each moment.

For example, if someone arrives late for an appointment and we need reassurance that she cares about us, we may feel hurt. If, instead, our need is to spend time purposefully and constructively, we may feel frustrated. But if our need is for thirty minutes of quiet solitude, we may be grateful for her tardiness and feel pleased. Thus, it is not the behavior of the other person but our own need that causes our feeling. When we are connected to our need, whether it is for reassurance, purposefulness, or solitude, we are in touch with our life energy. We may have strong feelings, but we are never angry. Anger is a result of life-alienating thinking that is disconnected from needs. It indicates that we have moved up to our head to analyze and judge somebody rather than focus on which of our needs are not getting met.

In addition to the third option of focusing on our own needs and feelings, the choice is ours at any moment to shine the light

第十章　充分表达愤怒

要认清：不论他人做了什么，都绝非自身感受的原因。

那么，到底是什么让我们生气呢？我们在第五章中曾经讨论过，当面对不喜欢的言语或行为时，我们有四种回应选择：1. 指责自己；2. 指责他人；3. 同理自己；4. 同理他人。当我们选择第 2 种方式时，愤怒便产生了。每当我们在生气时将错误归咎于他人，我们就在选择扮演上帝的角色，去评断或指责他人犯了过错或要受到惩罚。我认为，这才是我们生气的原因，只是我们起初对此是无意识的。

当选择第 3 种反应时，我们觉察自己的感受与需要。这并非用脑袋去分析别人的是非对错，而是与我们的内在生命连结。我们越是能聚焦于每个当下的需要，就越是能触及和体会这股生命能量。

例如，我们约了个人，时间到了，对方却没来。若我们的需要是确认对方是否在意自己，可能就会感到伤心。如果我们看重有意义和有效地使用时间，也许就感到恼火。但如果此刻我们正好希望有一些安静独处的时间，可能反而会庆幸对方来晚了。可见，产生感受的原因在于我们自身的需要，而非他人的言行。一旦意识到自己的需要——不论是确定、意义或独处，我们就能触碰到自己的生命能量。此时，我们可能会有强烈的感受，但绝不会生气。而导致我们愤怒的是那些指责的想法，它们切断了我们和需要的连结。愤怒提醒我们正在用头脑分析和评断他人，而没有关注自己有哪些需要没有得到满足。

除了关注自己的感受和需要，我们还可以选择在任何时刻去觉察和体会对方的感受和需要，也就是第 4 种选择。这时，我们也不会感到生气。这并非在压抑愤怒，而是当我们全然地与他人的感受和需要同在时，心中自然不会生出怒气。

of consciousness on the other person's feelings and needs. When we choose this fourth option, we also never feel anger. We are not repressing the anger; we see how anger is simply absent in each moment that we are fully present with the other person's feelings and needs.

All Anger Has a Life-Serving Core

"But," I am asked, "aren't there circumstances in which anger is justified? Isn't 'righteous indignation' called for in the face of careless, thoughtless pollution of the environment, for example?" My answer is that I strongly believe that to whatever degree I support the consciousness that there *is* such a thing as a "careless action" or a "conscientious action," a "greedy person" or a "moral person," I am contributing to violence on this planet. Rather than agreeing or disagreeing about what people *are* for murdering, raping, or polluting the environment, I believe we serve life better by focusing attention on what we are needing.

> When we judge others, we contribute to violence.

I see all anger as a result of life-alienating, violence-provoking thinking. At the core of all anger is a need that is not being fulfilled. Thus anger can be valuable if we use it as an alarm clock to wake us up—to realize we have a need that isn't being met and that we are thinking in a way that makes it unlikely to be met.

To fully express anger requires full consciousness of our need. In addition, energy is required to get the need met. Anger, however, co-opts our energy by directing it toward punishing people rather than meeting our needs. Instead of engaging in "righteous indignation," I recommend connecting empathically with our own needs or those of others. This may take extensive practice, whereby over and over again, we consciously replace the phrase "I am angry because they . . . " with "I am angry *because I am needing . . .* "

> Use anger as a wake-up call.

I once was taught a remarkable lesson while working with students in a correctional school for children in Wisconsin. On two

第十章　充分表达愤怒

愤怒的核心：服务生命

"但是，"有人问我，"在有些情况下，愤怒不是理所当然的吗？例如，看到有人随意破坏环境，'义愤填膺'不正是有良知的表现吗？"我的回答是：我坚信，不论在什么情况下，只要我有意识地将有的行为看作"不负责的"或"有良知的"，将有的人看作"贪婪的"或"道德的"，便是在助长这个地球上的暴力。如果我们想让生命更美好，与其去论断那些杀害、强暴他人或污染环境者们是什么样的人，不如将注意力放在我们的需要上。

在我看来，愤怒是疏离生命、引发暴力的思维方式造成的。所有的怒气背后，都有一个没有被满足的需要。如果我们能善用愤怒，视之为唤醒自己的报警器，意识到自己有一个需要没有得到满足，而导致我们生气的思维方式并无法使我们的需要得到满足，那愤怒就是有价值的。为了充分表达愤怒，我们要明了自己的需要，并且花费力气来满足需要。愤怒往往驱使着我们把能量用于惩罚他人，而非满足需要。因此，我建议，与其沉浸在"义愤填膺"中，不如带着同理心与自己和他人的需要连结。这也许需要一些时间，但通过反复的练习，我们的思维将会有意识地以"我生气，因为我需要……"来取代"我生气，是因为他们……"。

我在威斯康辛州一所儿童矫正学校辅导孩童时，收获了一个宝贵的教训。接连两天，我的鼻子都被学生打到。第一天，为阻止两个学生打架，我的鼻子被其中一个孩子的肘部击中。我生气极了，竭尽全力让自己不还击。在我长大的底特律街头，要挑起我的愤怒，可用不着这一

successive days I was hit on the nose in remarkably similar ways. The first time, I received a sharp blow across the nose from an elbow while interceding in a fight between two students. I was

> Anger co-opts our energy by diverting it toward punitive actions.

so enraged it was all I could do to keep myself from hitting back. (On the streets of Detroit where I grew up, it took far less than an elbow in the nose to provoke me to rage.) The second day: similar situation, same nose—and thus more physical pain—but not a bit of anger!

Reflecting deeply that evening on this experience, I recognized how I had labeled the first child in my mind as a "spoiled brat." That image was in my head before his elbow ever caught my nose, and when it did, it was no longer simply an elbow hitting my nose. It was: "That obnoxious brat has no right to do this!" I had another judgment about the second child; I saw him as a "pathetic creature." Since I had a tendency to worry about this child, even though my nose was hurting and bleeding much more severely, the second day I felt no rage at all. I could not have received a more powerful lesson to help me see that it's not what the other person does, but the images and interpretations in my own head that produce my anger.

Stimulus versus Cause: Practical Implications

I emphasize the distinction between cause and stimulus on practical and tactical as well as on philosophical grounds. I'd like to illustrate this point by returning to my dialogue with John, the Swedish prisoner:

John: Three weeks ago I made a request to the prison officials and they still haven't responded to my request.
MBR: So when this happened, you felt angry because *what*?
John: I just told you. They didn't respond to my request!
MBR: Hold it. Instead of saying, "I felt angry because *they* . . . ," stop and become conscious of what you're telling yourself that's making you so angry.

第十章　充分表达愤怒

肘！第二天，类似的事情又发生了，我的鼻子因为再次被击中痛得更厉害。然而，我却丝毫没有生气！

当我回想起那两天的经历，我发现，我一开始就把第一个孩子看作是"被宠坏的小鬼"。他的手肘还没碰到我的鼻子之前，这个标签就已经烙在了我的脑海中。因此，当一切发生时，对我来说便不仅仅是被他的手肘打到了鼻子，而是想着："这讨厌的小鬼太猖狂了！"相较之下，我对第二个孩子的看法则不同，我认为他是个"可怜的孩子"，更关心这个孩子。因此，尽管我的鼻子被他打伤，感觉远比前一天更痛，流了更多血，我却丝毫没有怒气。这段经历对我而言真是一个宝贵的教训，它让我认清，让我愤怒的并非他人的行为，而是我在头脑中对他人及其行为的看法和解读。

"刺激"与"原因"：实践的启示

无论从实践、技巧还是理论角度，感受的"刺激"和"根源"都不相同。我将继续以和那位瑞典囚犯约翰的对话为例，来加以说明。

约　翰：3个星期前，我向监狱长官提出了一个请求，但他们到现在都没有给我回复。

马歇尔：这件事情发生时，使你生气的原因是什么呢？

约　翰：我刚刚不是告诉你了吗，他们一直都没有回应我的请求！

马歇尔：等一下。在你说"我生气是因为他们……"时，请停下来想一想，觉察你对自己说了什么话，让你如此生气。

10 Expressing Anger Fully

John: I'm not telling myself anything.

MBR: Stop, slow down, just listen to what's going on inside.

John: *(after silently reflecting)* I'm telling myself that they have no respect for human beings; they are a bunch of cold, faceless bureaucrats who don't give a damn about anybody but themselves! They're a real bunch of . . .

MBR: Thanks, that's enough. Now you know why you're angry—it's that kind of thinking.

John: But what's wrong with thinking that way?

MBR: I'm not saying there is anything wrong with thinking that way. Notice if I say there is something wrong with you for thinking that way, I'd be thinking the same way about *you*. I don't say it's *wrong* to judge people, to call them faceless bureaucrats or to label their actions inconsiderate or selfish. However, it's that kind of thinking on your part that makes you feel very angry. Focus your attention on your needs: what are your needs in this situation?

John: *(after a long silence)* Marshall, I need the training I was requesting. If I don't get that training, as sure as I'm sitting here, I'm gonna end up back in this prison when I get out.

MBR: Now that your attention is on your needs, how do you feel?

John: Scared.

MBR: Now put yourself in the shoes of a prison official. If I'm an inmate, am I more likely to get my needs met if I come to you saying, "Hey, I really need that training and I'm scared of what's going to happen if I don't get it," or if I approach while seeing you as a faceless bureaucrat? Even if I don't say those words out loud, my eyes will reveal that kind of thinking. Which way am I more likely to get my needs met? *(John stares at the floor and remains silent.)*

MBR: Hey, buddy, what's going on?

John: Can't talk about it.

> When we become aware of our needs, anger gives way to life-serving feelings.

第十章　充分表达愤怒

约　翰：我没和自己说什么。

马歇尔：等一下，慢下来，你要聆听的是内心的声音。

约　翰：（默默地沉思了一会儿后）我告诉自己：他们一点都不尊重人！他们是一群冷血的官僚，一点人味儿也没有，只在乎自己，对其他人都不屑一顾！他们就是一群……

马歇尔：谢谢，这足够了。现在你知道你为什么会生气了吗？是因为你的这些想法。

约　翰：但是，这样想有什么不对吗？

马歇尔：我不是说这样想有什么不对。请注意，如果我告诉你这样想是不对的，那我看待你的方式，和你看待狱方是一样的。我不是说评判他人、称他们为"冷血的官僚"或认为他们"只在乎自己"等是错的。然而，让你生气的正是这些想法。现在，请你把注意力放在自己的需要上：在这个事件中，你的需要是什么？

约　翰：（沉默了很久后）马歇尔，我希望他们能让我参加我需要的培训。否则，出狱后，我迟早还是会像现在这样回到这里。

马歇尔：现在你已经把注意力放在你的需要上了，你的心情如何？

约　翰：我很害怕。

马歇尔：现在，假定你是监狱官，而我是犯人。我走到你跟前对你说："我真的很需要那个培训。如果不能参加，我很害怕，不知道未来会发生什么。"这样说的话，是不是我的需要更有可能得到满足呢？如果我把你看作冷血的官僚，即使没有这样说出来，我的眼睛也会有所流露。你认为，哪种方式更有可能使我的愿望得到满足呢？

10 Expressing Anger Fully

Three hours later, John approached me and said, "Marshall, I wish you had taught me two years ago what you taught me this morning. I wouldn't have had to kill my best friend."

All violence is the result of people tricking themselves, as did this young man, into believing that their pain derives from other people and that consequently those people deserve to be punished.

> Violence comes from the belief that other people cause our pain and therefore deserve punishment.

One time I saw my younger son take a fifty-cent piece from his sister's room. I said, "Brett, did you ask your sister whether you could have that?" "I didn't take it from her," he answered. Now I faced my four options. I could have called him a liar, which would, however, have worked against my getting my needs met since any judgment of another person diminishes the likelihood of our needs being met. Where I focused my attention at that moment was critical. If I were to judge him a liar, it would point me in one direction. If I were to think that he didn't respect me enough to tell me the truth, I would be pointed in another direction. If, however, I were either to empathize with him at that moment, or express nakedly what I was feeling and needing, I would greatly increase the possibility of getting my needs met.

> We recall four options when hearing a difficult message:
> 1. Blame ourselves
> 2. Blame others
> 3. Sense our own feelings and needs
> 4. Sense others' feelings and needs

The way I expressed my choice—which in this situation turned out to be helpful—was not so much through what I said, but through what I did. Instead of judging him as lying, I tried to hear his feeling: he was scared, and his need was to protect himself from being punished. By empathizing with him, I had a chance of making an emotional connection out of which we could both get our needs met. However, if I had approached him with the view that he was lying—even if I hadn't expressed it out loud—he would have been less likely to feel safe expressing truthfully what had

第十章　充分表达愤怒

（约翰的眼睛盯着地板，沉默不语。）

马歇尔：嘿，兄弟，你怎么啦？

约　　翰：一言难尽。

　　3个小时后，约翰过来和我说："马歇尔，我真希望，两年前就学到你今天上午所教会我的。那样，我就不会杀了我最好的朋友。"

　　暴力之所以产生，都是因为人们误以为自己的痛苦是由他人造成的，他人应当受到惩罚，就像这位年轻男子所做的。

　　一次，我看到小儿子从她姐姐的房间拿了一枚50美分硬币。我问他："布莱特，你问过姐姐可以拿她的硬币吗？"他回答："我不是从她那里拿的。"这时，我便面临之前提到的4种选择。关键在于，我在这个当下把注意力放在哪里。如果评断他在撒谎，我会有某种反应；如果认为他不尊重我，所以没有告诉我实话，我则会有另外一种反应。可是，指责他人往往使我们的愿望更难得到满足。但如果我选择同理他或诚实表达我的感受和需要，我的需要就更有可能得到满足。

　　于是我决定同理他。事实证明，这个决定是对的。而发挥作用的并非在于我说了什么，而是同理的做法。我试着聆听他的感受：他很害怕，他的需要是保护自己免于惩罚。通过同理他的感受和需要，让我有机会和他建立情感上的连结。这样，双方的需要都得到了满足。然而，如果我在心里认定他在撒谎，就算我没有说出来，他也很难感到足够安全来真实表达自己。我对于他不诚实的预言很可能就会成真——他真的不得不用说谎来逃避惩罚。试想，人们要是知道自己会因为说真话而受到评判和惩罚，为什么还要说真话呢？

　　如果我们满脑子的是非对错、评判和分析，认为别人不好、贪婪、

happened. I would have then become part of the process: by the very act of judging another person as a liar, I would contribute to a self-fulfilling prophecy. Why would people want to tell the truth, knowing they will be judged and punished for doing so?

> Judgments of others contribute to self-fulfilling prophecies.

I would like to suggest that when our heads are filled with judgments and analyses that others are bad, greedy, irresponsible, lying, cheating, polluting the environment, valuing profit more than life, or behaving in other ways they shouldn't, very few of them will be interested in our needs. If we want to protect the environment, and we go to a corporate executive with the attitude, "You know, you are really a killer of the planet, you have no right to abuse the land in this way," we have severely impaired our chances of getting our needs met. It is a rare human being who can maintain focus on our needs when we are expressing them through images of their wrongness. Of course, we may be successful in using such judgments to intimidate people into meeting our needs. If they feel so frightened, guilty, or ashamed that they change their behavior, we may come to believe that it is possible to "win" by telling people what's wrong with them.

With a broader perspective, however, we realize that each time our needs are met in this way, we not only lose, but we have contributed very tangibly to violence on the planet. We may have solved an immediate problem, but we will have created another one. The more people hear blame and judgment, the more defensive and aggressive they become and the less they will care about our needs in the future. So even if our present need is met in the sense that people do what we want, we will pay for it later.

Four Steps to Expressing Anger

Let's look at what the process of fully expressing our anger actually requires in concrete form. The first step is to stop and do nothing except to breathe. We refrain from making any move to blame or punish the other person. We simply stay quiet. Then we

第十章　充分表达愤怒

不负责任、说谎、作弊、污染环境、要钱不要命或做了不对的事……他人就不太可能对我们的需要有兴趣。例如，为了保护环境，我们和一家企业的高管对话，说："你知道吗？你们真是地球的刽子手，你们无权糟蹋我们的土地。"很明显，这样的沟通很难让我们的需要得到满足。在受到指责时，很少有人还能把注意力放在对方的需要上。当然，也许这样的评判可以成功地胁迫他人满足我们的需要，他人会出于害怕、内疚或羞愧而改变行为，我们会就此以为指责他人能让自己"取得胜利"。

然而，以更长远的眼光来看，我们就会发现，若每一次都以这样的方式来满足需要，我们不仅无法胜利，还会助长地球上的暴力。为了解决眼前的问题，我们制造了新的问题。指责和评判使人倾向于自我保护并变得更有攻击性，日后也不可能关心我们的需要。因此，即便他人照着我们的意思满足了我们眼下的需要，之后我们也会为此付出代价。

表达愤怒的四个步骤

1. 停下来，深呼吸。
2. 看看我们有哪些评判性的想法。
3. 与我们的需要连结。
4. 表达我们的感受和未被满足的需要。

来看看充分表达愤怒的具体步骤。首先，停下来，除了深呼吸，什么都别做；不去指责或惩罚他人，只是保持安静。接着，看一看是什么想法让我们生气。例如，无意中听到某人说了一些话，使我们相信自己

identify the thoughts that are making us angry. For example, we overhear a statement that leads us to believe that we've been excluded from a conversation because of race. We sense anger, stop, and recognize the thoughts stirring in our head: "It's unfair to act like that. She's being racist." We know that all judgments like these are tragic expressions of unmet needs, so we take the next step and connect to the needs behind those thoughts. If we judge someone to be racist, the need may be for inclusion, equality, respect, or connection.

> Steps to expressing anger:
> 1. Stop. Breathe.
> 2. Identify our judgmental thoughts.
> 3. Connect with our needs.
> 4. Express our feelings and unmet needs.

To fully express ourselves, we now open our mouth and speak the anger—but the anger has been transformed into needs and need-connected feelings. To articulate these feelings may require a lot of courage. For me it's easy to get angry and tell people, "That was a racist thing to do!" In fact, I may even enjoy saying such things, but to get down to the deeper feelings and needs behind such a statement may be very frightening. To fully express our anger, we may say to the other person, "When you entered the room and started talking to the others and didn't say anything to me, and then made the comment about white people, I felt really sick to my stomach, and got so scared; it triggered off all kinds of needs on my part to be treated equally. I'd like you to tell me how you feel when I tell you this."

Offering Empathy First

In most cases, however, another step needs to take place before we can expect the other party to connect with what is going on in us. Because it will often be difficult for others to receive our feelings and needs in such situations, if we want them to hear us we would need first to empathize with them. The more we empathize with what leads them to behave in the ways that are not meeting our needs, the more likely it is that they will be able to reciprocate afterwards.

第十章　充分表达愤怒

由于种族的缘故遭到了排斥。感知到自己的怒气时，如果停下来，便会看到头脑中盘旋的想法："这太不公平了！她这是种族歧视！"我们知道，所有的评判都在用可悲的方式表达未满足的需要。于是，接下来的第3步是：与这些想法背后的需要连结。如果指责某人是种族主义者，我们的需要也许是融合、平等、尊重或者与人连结。

为了充分表达自己，我们要采取的第4步是开口表达愤怒——怒火此时已被转化为感受和需要。然而，表达此时的感受也许要很大的勇气。对我来说，生气并冲着人们嚷"你这样做是种族歧视"是很容易的，甚至还会感到很畅快。然而，要说出内心深处的感受和需要，却可能令人却步。为了充分表达愤怒，我们也许可以试着和对方说："你走进房间后，开始与其他人聊天，却没有和我说话。接着，你开始议论有关白人的种种。当注意到这些时，我的胃非常不舒服，我也很害怕。这使我意识到，我非常希望受到平等的对待。我想请你告诉我，听到这些话，你的感受是怎么样的？"

先同理他人

在大多数情况下，如果希望他人听见我们的心声，与我们的内心产生连结，我们需要先同理对方。如果对方还处于某种情绪中，他们就很难平静下来体会我们的感受和需要。我们越能用心同理对方，理解对方为何做出那些不符合我们需要的行为，对方就越有可能同理我们。

过去30年来，我以非暴力沟通的方式与许许多多持有强烈种族偏见的人展开交流。有一天清早，我从机场搭乘了一辆出租车进城。突

10 Expressing Anger Fully

> The more we hear them, the more they'll hear us.

Over the last thirty years I've had a wealth of experience speaking NVC with people who harbor strong beliefs about specific races and ethnic groups. Early one morning I was picked up by a cab at an airport to take me into town. A message from the dispatcher came over the loudspeaker for the cabbie: "Pick up Mr. Fishman at the synagogue on Main Street." The man next to me in the cab muttered, "These kikes get up early in the morning so they can screw everybody out of their money."

For twenty seconds, there was smoke coming out of my ears. In earlier years, my first reaction would have been to want to physically hurt such a person. Instead I took a few deep breaths and then gave myself some empathy for the hurt, fear, and rage that were stirring inside me. I attended to my feelings. I stayed conscious that my anger wasn't coming from my fellow passenger nor the statement he had just made. His comment had triggered off a volcano inside of me, but I knew that my anger and profound fear came from a far deeper source than those words he had just uttered. I sat back and simply allowed the violent thoughts to play themselves out. I even enjoyed the image of actually grabbing his head and smashing it.

Giving myself this empathy enabled me to then focus my attention on the humanness behind his message, after which the first words out of my mouth were, "Are you feeling . . . ?" I tried to empathize with him, to hear his pain. Why? Because I wanted to see the beauty in him, and I wanted for him to fully apprehend what I had experienced when he made his remark. I knew I wouldn't receive that kind of understanding if there were a storm brewing inside of him. My intention was to connect with him and show a respectful empathy for the life energy in him that was behind the comment. My experience told me that if I were able to empathize, then he would be able to hear me in return. It would not be easy, but he would be able to.

> Stay conscious of the violent thoughts that arise in our minds, without judging them.

第十章　充分表达愤怒

然，车上的喇叭传来车辆调度员发给司机的消息："请到主大街的犹太教堂接费希曼先生。"接着，坐在我旁边的一位先生开始嘀咕："这些犹太佬起那么早，还不是为了要把所有人的钱都榨干。"

整整有20秒钟的时间，我气得仿佛耳朵冒烟。若是在年轻时，听到这样的话，我的第一反应可能就是揍他一顿。而当时，我选择了做几次深呼吸，并且开始同理自己心中涌现的痛苦、恐惧和愤怒。我一边觉察着自己的感受，一边提醒自己：让我生气的并不是身旁的那位乘客，也不是他说的话。尽管他的言论点燃了我内在的火山，但我知道，我的愤怒和恐惧来自一个更深的地方。于是，我靠后坐了坐，让自己在脑海中把所有的暴力想法倾泻而出。看到自己揪着他的头痛揍他的画面，我甚至还挺乐的。

在得到了我需要的同理后，我开始能够试着去体会他的内心。于是，我对他说的第一句话是："你是感到……？"我尝试去同理这个男人，聆听他的痛苦。为什么？因为我想要看见他的美好，也希望让他充分体会我对他那番话的感受。但我知道，如果他的内心正狂风大作，那么，这样的理解就不会发生。因而，我的意图是与他连结，带着尊重和同理心，聆听他在说那番话背后的心声。过去的经历告诉我，如果我能够同理他，最终他也能够听见我。虽然这并不容易，但相信他会做到这一点。

"你是感到恼怒吗？"我问他，"听起来，似乎你在和犹太人打交道时，有过一些不愉快的经历。"

他打量了我一番，说："是的！这些人令人作呕。为了钱，他们什么事情都做得出来。"

"所以，你在和他们有金钱往来时很难相信他们，想要保护好自己，

10 Expressing Anger Fully

"Are you feeling frustrated?" I asked. "It appears that you might have had some bad experiences with Jewish people."

He eyed me for a moment. "Yeah! These people are disgusting. They'll do anything for money."

"You feel distrust and the need to protect yourself when you're involved in financial affairs with them?"

"That's right!" he exclaimed, continuing to release more judgments, as I listened for the feeling and need behind each one. When we settle our attention on other people's feelings and needs, we experience our common humanity. When I hear that he's scared and wants to protect himself, I recognize how I also have a need to protect myself and I too know what it's like to be scared. When my consciousness is focused on another human being's feelings and needs, I see the universality of our experience. I had a major conflict with what went on in his head, but I've learned that I enjoy human beings more if I don't hear what they think. Especially with folks who have his kind of thoughts. I've learned to savor life much more by only hearing what's going on in their hearts and not getting caught up with the stuff in their heads.

> When we hear another person's feelings and needs, we recognize our common humanity.

This man kept on pouring out his sadness and frustration. Before I knew it, he'd finished with Jews and moved on to blacks. He was charged with pain around a number of subjects. After nearly ten minutes of my just listening, he stopped: he had felt understood.

Then I let him know what was going on in me:

MBR: You know, when you first started to talk, I felt a lot of anger, a lot of frustration, sadness, and discouragement, because I've had very different experiences with Jews than you've had, and I was wanting you to have much more the kind of experiences I've had. Can you tell me what you heard me say?

Man: Oh, I'm not saying they're all . . .

MBR: Excuse me, hold on, hold it. Can you tell me what you heard me say?

第十章　充分表达愤怒

对吗？"

"没错！"他大声说道，接着继续发表他对犹太人的看法。我则试着体会在每一个评判背后他的感受和需要。若将注意力放在他人的感受和需要上，我们就能体会彼此生而为人的共同点。听到他说感到害怕、想要保护自己，我意识到我也有保护自己的需要，也明白害怕的感受。当专注在他的感受和需要时，我们的体验是相通的。虽然我极不认同他的观点，但我已经学会了，如果不去听别人的想法，我会更乐于和他们相处。特别是在遇到有着像这个男人那样想法的人时，只要专心关注对方的心声，而非受困于他们的想法，我的生活就会变得愉快得多。

这个男人一直诉说着他的悲哀与恼怒。不经意间，话题已经从犹太人转移到了黑人身上。他的内心装满了许多苦痛。我静静地聆听着他，大概10分钟后，他停了下来——他感觉得到了理解。

然后，我开始告诉他我的心声：

马歇尔：你知道吗？最初听到你说犹太人的那些话时，我很生气，也很难过和沮丧，因为我和犹太人相处的经验和你很不一样。而我多么希望，你能有更多不同的体验。你能告诉我，你听见我说了什么吗？

男　子：喔，我并没有说他们都是……

马歇尔：抱歉，等一下，你可以告诉我，你刚才听到我在说什么吗？

男　子：你在说什么？

马歇尔：让我再说一次吧。我真的希望你能了解，当我听到你之前讲的那些话，心里有多么难受。你听到我的痛苦对我很重要。我很难过，因为我和犹太人相处的经验和你大不相同。我很希望，

10 Expressing Anger Fully

Man: What are you talking about?

MBR: Let me repeat what I'm trying to say. I really want you to just hear the pain I felt when I heard your words. It's really important to me that you hear that. I was saying I felt a real sense of sadness because my experiences with Jewish people have been very different. I was just wishing that you had had some experiences that were different from the ones you were describing. Can you tell me what you heard me say?

Man: You're saying I have no right to talk the way I did.

MBR: No, I would like you to hear me differently. I really don't want to blame you. I have no desire to blame you.

> Our need is for the other person to truly hear our pain.

I intended to slow down the conversation, because in my experience, to whatever degree people hear blame, they have failed to hear our pain. If this man said, "Those were terrible things for me to say; those were racist remarks I made," he would not have heard my pain. As soon as people think that they have done something wrong, they will not be fully apprehending our pain.

> People do not hear our pain when they believe they are at fault.

I didn't want him to hear blame, because I wanted him to know what had gone on in my heart when he uttered his remark. Blaming is easy. People are used to hearing blame; sometimes they agree with it and hate themselves—which doesn't stop them from behaving the same way—and sometimes they hate us for calling them racists or whatever—which also doesn't stop their behavior. If we sense blame entering their mind, as I did in the cab, we may need to slow down, go back, and hear their pain for a while more.

Taking Our Time

Probably the most important part of learning how to live the process we have been discussing is to take our time. We may feel awkward deviating from the habitual behaviors that our conditioning has

你能有一些不一样的经验。你可以告诉我,你听到我说了什么吗?

男　子:你的意思是,我刚才没有权利说那些话。

马歇尔:不,我希望你对我的话有不同的理解。我真的不想指责你,我无意指责你。

于是,我试着放慢对话的节奏。根据我的经验,只要人们在我们的话中听到指责,哪怕只有一点点,便很难转向体会我们的痛苦。如果这位先生的回应是"我那样说真的很糟糕,我真不该说那些种族歧视的话",那就表示他并没有听见我。人们一旦认为自己做错了事,便无法全然领会他人心中的痛苦。

我不希望他听到的是指责,我希望他听见我的心声。指责别人是很容易的,人们也习惯了听见指责。有时,他们会认同这些指责,因而自责。有时,他们会痛恨我们批评他们——但这样都无法令他们做出改变。一旦我们注意到他们认为自己受到了指责,就像出租车里的那位先生一样,我们也许就需要慢下来,再花点时间去聆听他们的痛苦。

给自己时间

学习在日常生活中运用非暴力沟通,最重要的也许是——慢下来。在社会的制约下,我们养成了许多习惯性反应。要从中跳脱出来,或许会让人感到别扭。然而,如果想要清醒地活出自己的价值观,我们就要给自己充足的时间。

10 Expressing Anger Fully

rendered automatic, but if our intention is to consciously live life in harmony with our values, then we'll want to take our time.

A friend of mine, Sam Williams, jotted down the basic components of the NVC process on a three-by-five card, which he would use as a cheat sheet at work. When his boss would confront him, Sam would stop, refer to the card in his hand, and take time to remember how to respond. When I asked whether his colleagues were finding him a little strange, constantly staring into his hand and taking so much time to form his sentences, Sam replied, "It doesn't actually take that much more time, but even if it did, it's still worth it to me. It's important for me to know that I am responding to people the way I really want to." At home he was more overt, explaining to his wife and children why he was taking the time and trouble to consult the card. Whenever there was an argument in the family, he would pull out the card and take his time. After about a month, he felt comfortable enough to put it away. Then one evening, he and Scottie, age four, were having a conflict over television and it wasn't going well. "Daddy," Scottie said urgently, "get the card!"

For those of you wishing to apply NVC, especially in challenging situations of anger, I would suggest the following exercise. As we have seen, our anger comes from judgments, labels, and thoughts of blame, of what people "should" do and what they "deserve." List the judgments that float most frequently in your head by using the cue, "I don't like people who are . . . " Collect all such negative judgments in your head and then ask yourself, "When I make that judgment of a person, what am I needing and not getting?" In this way, you train yourself to frame your thinking in terms of unmet needs rather than in terms of judgments of other people.

> **Practice translating each judgment into an unmet need.**

> **Take your time.**

Practice is essential, because most of us were raised, if not on the streets of Detroit, then somewhere only slightly less violent. Judging and blaming have become second nature to us. To practice NVC, we need to proceed slowly, think carefully before

第十章　充分表达愤怒

我的一位朋友山姆曾将非暴力沟通的基本要素写在了一张 3 英寸 x5 英寸的卡片上,当成他在上班时使用的"小妙招"。每当老板批评他时,山姆就会停下来,看看手中的卡片,并且花点时间想一下如何回应。我问他,这样时不时盯着自己的手心,慢慢组织语句,同事们会不会觉得奇怪。山姆回答说:"其实也没花太多时间,就算时间长了点,我认为也是值得的。因为,对我来说,重要的是,用我真正想要的方式回应他人。"在家里,他会更加开诚布公地使用卡片,并向太太和孩子们解释为什么要不嫌麻烦地花时间这样做。每当和家人发生争执,他就拿出卡片,认真考虑如何做出回应。1 个月之后,他就不需要再用卡片来提醒自己了。有天晚上,为了看电视的事情他和 4 岁的儿子斯科特发生了争执,眼看争吵要升级了,孩子着急地说道:"爸爸,快拿卡片!"

如果你希望自己在诸如生气这样的艰难时刻也能运用非暴力沟通,不妨来做以下练习。诚如我们已经探讨过的,愤怒来自我们对他人持有的评判、标签、指责——认为他人"应该"怎样做、"活该"遭受什么等等。将你头脑中时常浮现的评判列出来,你可以参考"我不喜欢……的人"这样的句子。收集所有的负面评判,接着问自己:"当我对他人有这番评判时,我有什么样的需要没有得到满足?"通过这样的方式,我们可以训练自己从"我有什么需要没有得到满足"的角度来思考,而非评判和责怪他人。

练习是关键。大多数人的成长环境和我小时候生活的底特律街头相比,也许会少一些暴力,但也相差不远。评判和指责已成为我们的第二天性。因此,要运用非暴力沟通,需要慢慢推进,先想清楚再开口。有时,甚至只要深吸一口气,什么都不说就足够了。学习以及运用这个过程,并非一蹴而就,都需要花一些时间。

we speak, and often just take a deep breath and not speak at all. Learning the process and applying it both take time.

Summary

Blaming and punishing others are superficial expressions of anger. If we wish to fully express anger, the first step is to divorce the other person from any responsibility for our anger. Instead we shine the light of consciousness on our own feelings and needs. By expressing our needs, we are far more likely to get them met than by judging, blaming, or punishing others.

The four steps to expressing anger are (1) stop and breathe, (2) identify our judgmental thoughts, (3) connect with our needs, and (4) express our feelings and unmet needs. Sometimes, in between steps 3 and 4, we may choose to empathize with the other person so that he or she will be better able to hear us when we express ourselves in step 4.

We need to take our time both in learning and in applying the process of NVC.

NVC in Action

Parent and Teen Dialogue: A Life-Threatening Issue

In this situation, fifteen-year-old Bill took a car, without permission, from Jorge, a family friend. He went on a joy ride with two friends and returned the car undamaged to the garage, where its absence had not been detected. Since then, however, Jorge's fourteen-year-old daughter, Eva, who had gone along for the ride, told her father what had happened. Jorge informed Bill's father, who is now approaching his son. The father has just recently been practicing NVC.

Father: So I hear you, Eva, and Dave took Jorge's car without asking.

Bill: No, we didn't!

第十章　充分表达愤怒

小结

生气时，指责和惩罚他人都无法真正传达我们的心声。如果想充分表达愤怒，首先要认识到他人并不需要对我们的愤怒负责。取而代之的是，把注意力放在自己的感受和需要上。相较于评判、指责或惩罚他人，我们若能把自己的需要表达出来，将更有可能让这些需要得到满足。

表达愤怒的4个步骤是：（1）停下来，深吸一口气；（2）辨识脑海中评判性的想法；（3）与自己的需要连结；（4）表达自己的感受和未满足的需要。有时，在第3和第4步之间，我们也许需要先同理对方。这样，当我们在第4步表达自己时，对方才能更好地听见我们。

我们需要给自己充足的时间来学习和实践非暴力沟通。

10 Expressing Anger Fully

Father: *(in a loud voice)* Don't lie to me; it'll only make it worse!

Then he remembered to first connect to his own feelings and needs in order to stay in connection with his son.

Father: You just sit there for a moment; I need to think.

Going inside himself, he saw how angry and scared he was. Angry when telling himself, "Bill should have known better!" and "What a liar he's become!" Scared when he thinks of all the potential consequences of not only Bill's action, but his own misjudgment of what his son might do.

Father: *(silently to himself)* That was stupid of me to assume he knows better. Someone could have gotten killed in this! (then catching himself) Oops, I need to translate the labels "stupid" and "liar" into feelings and needs. For "stupid," I guess the feeling is disappointment in myself: I would have liked to think that I knew him better. And as for "liar," I'm feeling pretty scared because I want to be able to count on getting accurate information to deal with this situation.

Father: *(out loud, after silence while he mulls over how to begin talking)* Bill, are you worried that you'd be punished if you gave me accurate information?

Bill: Yeah, you're always so mean whenever I do anything you don't like.

Father: Are you saying you'd like more understanding and fairer treatment for what you do?

Bill: Oh, sure, like I'm really gonna get fair treatment and understanding from you!

第十章　充分表达愤怒

非暴力沟通实例

父子间的对话：一个生死攸关的事件

15岁的比尔悄悄开走了父亲的朋友乔治的车，他载着两个朋友（其中一位是乔治14岁的女儿伊娃）兜完风，将车完好无损地放回了车库。对此，乔治也毫无察觉。但后来，伊娃将此事告知了父亲。接着，乔治又告诉了比尔的父亲。这位父亲刚刚学习了非暴力沟通，以下是他和儿子比尔之间的对话。

父亲：我听说你、伊娃和戴维，没有和乔治打招呼，就开走了他的车。
比尔：没有这回事！
父亲：（提高了嗓门）不要骗我！这样只会把事情弄得更糟！
　　突然，他意识到，为了和儿子连结，他需要先和自己的感受连结。
父亲：你坐一下，我需要想一想。

他检视着自己的内心，发现自己又气又怕。他生气，是因为他对自己说："比尔应该懂事点！""他怎么变得会说谎了！"他害怕，是因为想到比尔的行为以及他对儿子的误判可能造成的后果。

父亲：（默默地想）我真是个笨蛋，居然以为他很懂事！他这样做可能

10 Expressing Anger Fully

Father:	*(silently to himself)* Boy, do I get angry when he says that! Can't he see how hard I'm trying? I really need a little respect for how hard this is, and I guess also a little caring for how scared I'm feeling.
Father:	*(out loud to Bill)* Sounds to me like you're worried that no matter what you say, you won't be treated fairly?
Bill:	What do you care about treating me fairly? When something happens, you just want someone to punish. Besides, what's the big deal? Even if we did take the car, no one got hurt and it's back where it was. I mean, this is no major crime wave.
Father:	Are you scared there'll be harsh consequences if you admit to taking the car, and you want to trust that you'll be treated justly?
Bill:	Yeah.
Father:	*(allowing time for silence and the connection to go deeper)* What could I do to give you that reassurance?
Bill:	Promise to never punish me again.
Father:	*(Aware that punishment will not help Bill develop consciousness around potential consequences of his behavior, but will only contribute to greater disconnection and resistance, Bill's father expresses willingness to agree to Bill's request.)* I'd be open to that agreement if you agree to stay in dialogue with me. That is, we talk until I'm satisfied you're aware of all the possible consequences of your having taken that car. However, in the future, if it happens that I'm not confident that you see the potential danger of what you're in for, I might still use force—but only in order to protect you.
Bill:	Wow, great! It really feels good knowing I'm so stupid you have to use force to protect me from myself!

第十章　充分表达愤怒

会闹出人命啊！（立刻又意识到自己在评判）哎呀，我要把"笨蛋"和"说谎"这样的标签转换为感受和需要。我猜我之所以会说自己是"笨蛋"，是因为我对自己感到失望，我希望自己能更了解儿子。至于"说谎"，是因为我很害怕，我希望能够准确地了解这件事再来处理它。

父亲：（安静地想了一会儿后开口）比尔，你是不是担心你如果说实话会受到处罚？

比尔：是的，每次我做了你不喜欢的事，你就凶得很。

父亲：你的意思是，希望我能更多地理解你，对你更公平一点？

比尔：有可能吗？说得跟真的一样！

父亲：（在心里念叨着）天哪，他这样说话，简直太气人了！他难道看不出来我多么努力地在和他沟通吗？我也需要得到一点尊重。而且我为他这么担惊受怕，也需要得到一些关怀。

父亲：（开口对比尔说）听起来，你似乎担心，不管你说什么，都不会受到公平的对待？

比尔：你会在乎这个吗？一有什么事，你就只是想处罚人。另外，发生什么大不了的事了吗？就算我们开了车，但没有人受伤，车也还回去了。我们又没有杀人放火！

父亲：你是不是担心，如果承认自己开走了车，你的下场会很惨？你希望得到公正的对待？

儿子：是的。

父亲：（给自己一些时间，安静地做更深的连结）我怎么做，你才会放心？

比尔：你要和我保证，以后绝不再处罚我。

10 Expressing Anger Fully

Father:	*(losing touch with his own needs, but silently)* Man, there are times when I could just kill the little . . . I'm so furious when he says things like that! It really doesn't seem like he cares. . . . Damn, what am I needing here? I'm needing to know, when I'm working this hard, that at least he cares.)
Father:	*(out loud, angrily)* You know, Bill, when you say things like that, I get really pissed off. I'm trying so hard to stay with you on this, and when I hear things like that . . . Look, I need to know if you even want to keep talking with me.
Bill:	I don't care.
Father:	Bill, I really want to listen to you rather than fall into my old habits of blaming and threatening you whenever something comes up that I'm upset about. But when I hear you say things like, "It feels good to know I'm so stupid," in the tone of voice you just used, I find it hard to control myself. I could use your help on this. That is, if you would rather me listen to you than blame or threaten. Or if not, then, I suppose my other option is to just handle this the way I'm used to handling things.
Bill:	And what would that be?
Father:	Well, by now, I'd probably be saying, "Hey, you're grounded for two years: no TV, no car, no money, no dates, no nothing!"
Bill:	Well, I guess I'd want you to do it the new way then.
Father:	*(with humor)* I'm glad to see that your sense of self-preservation is still intact. Now I need you to tell me whether you're willing to share some honesty and vulnerability.
Bill:	What do you mean by "vulnerability"?

第十章 充分表达愤怒

父亲：（意识到惩罚并不能让比尔明白自己的行为可能造成的后果，反而会让父子关系更加隔阂和疏远，他表示愿意答应比尔的请求。）如果你同意和我好好谈一谈，我愿意答应你的请求。我的意思是，我们要好好地聊一聊，直到我确定你明白，把车子开出去这件事可能会造成的后果。如果我不确定你知道自己做的事可能会有什么危险，我也许还是会对你采取强制性手段，但目的只是为了保护你。

比尔：哇，这可真是太有意思了！我竟然蠢到要你用强制的手段来保护我，真是好极了！

父亲：（一时和自己的需要失去了连结，默默地对自己说）天哪，有时我真恨不得宰了这小子……听到他这么说，我真是一肚子火！看上去他根本什么都不在乎……该死，我现在的需要是什么？我需要知道的是，我已经如此努力了，对于我说的话，他多少会有些在意吧。

父亲：（生气地大声说）你知道吗，比尔，你这么和我说话，我真的非常生气。我非常努力地尝试理解你，而你……好，我需要知道你还想和我谈下去吗？

比尔：我无所谓。

父亲：比尔，我真的很想听你的心里话。我不想像过去那样，在发生让我生气的事情时就来指责你、威胁你。可是刚才听到你说"我竟然蠢到要你用强制的手段来保护我……"，还有你说这话时的语气，我真的很难再控制自己的脾气。我希望你能帮助我。我的意思是，如果你希望我听你说话，而不是指责你或威胁你，那就请帮助我了解你的想法。如果你不愿意，我只好用老办法来

Father: It means that you tell me what you are really feeling about the things we're talking about, and I tell you the same from my end. *(in a firm voice)* Are you willing?

Bill: Okay, I'll try.

Father: *(with sigh of relief)* Thank you. I'm grateful for your willingness to try. Did I tell you—Jorge grounded Eva for three months—she won't be allowed to do anything. How do you feel about that?

Bill: Oh man, what a bummer; that's so unfair!

Father: I'd like to hear how you really feel about it.

Bill: I told you—it's totally unfair!

Father: *(realizing Bill isn't in touch with what he's feeling, decides to guess)* Are you sad that she's having to pay so much for her mistake?

Bill: No, it's not that. I mean, it wasn't her mistake really.

Father: Oh, so are you upset she's paying for something that was your idea to start with?

Bill: Well, yeah, she just went along with what I told her to do.

Father: Sounds to me like you're kind of hurting inside seeing the kind of effect your decision had on Eva.

Bill: Sorta.

Father: Billy, I really need to know that you are able to see how your actions have consequences.

Bill: Well, I wasn't thinking about what could've gone wrong. Yeah, I guess I did really screw up bad.

Father: I'd rather you see it as something you did that didn't turn out the way you wanted. And I still need reassurance about your being aware of the consequences. Would you tell me what you're feeling right now about what you did?

Bill: I feel really stupid, Dad. . . . I didn't mean to hurt anyone.

第十章　充分表达愤怒

处理这件事情。

比尔：什么老办法？

父亲：用老办法，我到这时多半已经会告诉你："在接下来的两年里，不准看电视，不准开车，没有零花钱，不准外出约会，什么都不能做！"

比尔：呃，那我还是希望你用新办法。

父亲：（带点幽默地说）很高兴你的自我保护意识完好无损。现在，我想知道，你是否愿意和我坦诚地交流，包括分享你的脆弱。

比尔：你说的"脆弱"是什么意思？

父亲：就是请你告诉我，对于我们谈论的这件事，你的感受是什么？同样地，我也会告诉你我的感受。（语气坚定地）你愿意吗？

比尔：好吧，我试试。

父亲：（有点宽慰，舒了口气）谢谢。你愿意试一试，我真的很感激。我告诉你，伊娃被乔治禁足3个月，不允许她做任何事。听到这个消息，你有什么感受？

比尔：天哪，这太不公平了！

父亲：我想知道你的感受。

比尔：我刚才说了，这完全不公平！

父亲：（意识到比尔并没有真正触碰自己的感受，他决定来猜一下）听到伊娃要为她的错误付出那么大的代价，你感到难过，是吗？

比尔：不，不是这样。我的意思是，那根本不是她的错。

父亲：哦，所以你很难过，因为那是你的主意，但她却为此付出代价？

比尔：是的，她只是跟着我，做了我让她做的事罢了。

父亲：看到你的决定对伊娃的影响，你似乎有些心疼？

10 Expressing Anger Fully

Father: *(translating Bill's self-judgments into feelings and needs)* So you're sad, and regret what you did because you'd like to be trusted not to do harm?

Bill: Yeah, I didn't mean to cause so much trouble. I just didn't think about it.

Father: Are you saying you wish you had thought about it more and gotten clearer before you acted?

Bill: *(reflecting)* Yeah . . .

Father: Well, it's reassuring for me to hear that, and for there to be some real healing with Jorge, I would like you to go to him and tell him what you just told me. Would you be willing to do that?

Bill: Oh man, that's so scary; he'll be really mad!

Father: Yeah, it's likely he will be. That's one of the consequences. Are you willing to be responsible for your actions? I like Jorge and I want to keep him for a friend, and I'm guessing that you would like to keep your connection with Eva. Is that the case?

Bill: She's one of my best friends.

Father: So shall we go see them?

Bill: *(fearfully and reluctantly)* Well . . . okay. Yeah, I guess so.

Father: Are you scared and needing to know that you will be safe if you go there?

Bill: Yeah.

Father: We'll go together: I'll be there for you and with you. I'm really proud that you are willing.

第十章　充分表达愤怒

比尔：也许是吧。

父亲：比尔，我真的希望你能明白，你的行为是有后果的。

比尔：好吧，我没有想过兜风会出什么差错。嗯，我想这次我确实把事情给搞砸了。

父亲：不要这么想。我希望你看到的是，在这件事情上，你没有料到会有这样的后果。所以，我希望确保你能够意识到行为会带来的后果。你能告诉我，对于你做的事，现在的感受是什么吗？

比尔：我觉得自己很蠢，爸……我没有想要伤害任何人。

父亲：（尝试将比尔的自我批评转换为感受和需要）所以你对于自己做的事情感到伤心和悔恨，因为你希望我们相信你无意伤害任何人？

比尔：是的，我没有想到会惹这么大的麻烦。我只是没有把事情想清楚。

父亲：你是不是想说，希望自己当时能够三思而后行？

比尔：（沉思着）是的……

父亲：听到你这么说，我就放心了。为了修复和乔治家的关系，我希望你去找他，并且告诉他你刚才的那些话，你愿意这样做吗？

比尔：天啊，那太可怕了。他一定会很生气！

父亲：是的，他很有可能会生气。不过，这就是你要面对的一个后果，你愿意为你的行为负责吗？我喜欢乔治，不想失去这个朋友。而且，我猜你也想继续和伊娃做朋友，对吗？

比尔：她是我的好朋友。

父亲：那我们去见他们好吗？

比尔：（害怕且犹豫着）好吧……好。我想可以吧。

10 Expressing Anger Fully

Anger can be a wonderful wake up call to help you understand what you need and what you value.

第十章 充分表达愤怒

父亲：你是不是有点害怕去见他们，你希望能有安全感？
比尔：嗯！
父亲：那我们一起去吧！我会陪你、支持你。你愿意这么做，我真的以你为荣。

10 Expressing Anger Fully

When we sense ourselves being defensive or unable to empathize, we need to (a) stop, breathe, give ourselves empathy, (b) express nonviolently, or (c) take time out.

第十一章

化解冲突，调和纷争

11

Conflict Resolution and Mediation

Now that you are familiar with the steps involved in Nonviolent Communication, I want to address how to apply them in resolving conflicts. These could be conflicts between yourself and someone else, or you may be asked to—or choose to—involve yourself in a conflict between others: family members, partners, co-workers, or even strangers in conflict. Whatever the situation may be, resolving conflicts involves all the principles I outlined previously in this book: observing, identifying and expressing feelings, connecting feelings with needs, and making doable requests of another person using clear, concrete, positive action language.

Over the course of several decades, I've used Nonviolent Communication to resolve conflicts around the world. I've met with unhappy couples, families, workers and their employers, and ethnic groups at war with each other. My experience has taught me that it's possible to resolve just about any conflict to everybody's satisfaction. All it takes is a lot of patience, the willingness to establish a human connection, the intention to follow NVC principles until you reach a resolution, and trust that the process will work.

Human Connection

In NVC-style conflict resolution, creating a connection between the people who are in conflict is the most important thing. This

> Creating a connection between people is the most important thing.

第十一章　化解冲突，调和纷争

你已经熟悉了非暴力沟通的步骤，接着我将介绍如何用它来化解冲突和纠纷。这些冲突可能是你与他人间的，也可能是他人之间（可能涉及家人、伴侣、同事乃至陌生人）的。无论何种情况，化解冲突须用到之前提及的所有原则：观察，识别和表达感受，将感受和需要相连，并且用清晰、具体、正向的行动语言向另一方提出可行的请求。

数十年来，我用非暴力沟通在世界各地开展化解冲突的工作：从争吵的情侣、家人，到劳资双方和相互交战的族群。我的经验教会我：化解任何形式的冲突直至皆大欢喜，是完全有可能的。我们只需要有耐心，愿意建立人与人之间的连结，跟随非暴力沟通的原则直至达成和解，并且信任这个过程会行得通。

人与人的连结

用非暴力沟通化解冲突时，最重要的是建立冲突双方之间的连结。人与人之间只有建立了连结，才会发自内心地想要了解彼此的感受和需要。唯有如此，非暴力沟通的步骤才能发挥效用。此外，你从一开始就

is what enables all the other steps of NVC to work, because it's not until you have forged that connection that each side will seek to know exactly what the other side is feeling and needing. The parties also need to know from the start that the objective is *not* to get the other side to do what they want them to do. And once the two sides understand that, it becomes possible—sometimes even easy—to have a conversation about how to meet their needs.

With NVC, we're trying to live a different value system while we are asking for things to change. What's most important is that every connection along the line mirrors the kind of world we're trying to create. Each step needs to reflect energetically what we're after, which is a holographic image of the quality of relationships we're trying to create. In short, how we ask for change reflects the value system we're trying to support. When we see the difference between these two objectives, we consciously refrain from trying to get a person to do what we want. Instead we work to create that quality of mutual concern and respect where each party thinks their own needs matter and they are conscious that their needs and the other person's well-being are interdependent. When that happens, it's amazing how conflicts that otherwise seem irresolvable are easily resolved.

When I'm asked to resolve a conflict, I work to lead the two sides to this caring and respectful connection. This is often the tough part. Once that is accomplished, I help both sides create strategies that will resolve the conflict to both sides' satisfaction.

Notice that I use the word *satisfaction* instead of *compromise*! Most attempts at resolution search for compromise, which means everybody gives something up and neither side is satisfied. NVC is different; our objective is to meet everyone's needs fully.

NVC Conflict Resolution versus Traditional Mediation

Let's consider the human connection aspect of NVC again, this time looking at third-party mediation—a person stepping in to resolve a conflict between two other parties. When I'm working with two people, or two groups, that have a conflict they haven't

第十一章　化解冲突，调和纷争

要让双方明白，冲突调解的目标并非让一方服从于另一方。只有当双方都能理解这点，才有可能（甚至很容易）就如何满足大家的需要开展对话。

以非暴力沟通的方式寻求改变时，我们也在努力实践一种不同的价值观：我们建立的每一段关系都反映着我们想要创造什么样的世界，我们迈出的每一步都折射着我们追求什么样的关系。简而言之，我们寻求改变的方式反映着我们所认同的价值观。我们了解了非暴力沟通的不同之处在于，不去要求他人按照我们的意愿行事，而是学习有意识地克制自己，努力创造人与人之间的关爱与尊重，使冲突的双方在重视自己需要的同时，也意识到自己的需要和对方的福祉是相互依存的。如果能这样，你将会惊讶地发现，那些原本看似无解的冲突竟能轻而易举地被化解。

因此，受邀化解冲突时，我的工作核心就是带领双方创造充满关爱与尊重的关系，在这个基础上相互连结，而这往往是最困难的部分。一旦关系建立了，我只需支持双方找到解决冲突的策略，直到大家都心满意足。

请注意，我说的是满意，而非妥协。大部分的冲突解决工作致力于妥协。这意味着大家都得让步，没有一方是全然满意的，而非暴力沟通的目标是——让各方的需要都得到充分的满足。

非暴力沟通冲突解决与传统冲突解决的不同

非暴力沟通鼓励我们建立人与人之间的连结，这意味着，当我作为

11 Conflict Resolution and Mediation

been able to resolve, I approach this very differently from the way professional mediators often approach a conflict.

For example, once I was in Austria meeting with a group of professional mediators who work on many kinds of international conflicts, including those between unions and management. I described several conflicts I had mediated, such as one in California between landowners and migrant workers where there had been considerable physical violence. And I talked about mediating between two African tribes (which I discuss fully in my book *Speak Peace in a World of Conflict*) and a few other extremely entrenched, dangerous conflicts.

I was asked how much time I give myself to study a situation I was to mediate. He was referring to the process most mediators use: educating themselves about the issues involved in the conflict and then mediating with *those issues* as the focus instead of focusing on creating a human connection. In fact, in typical third-party mediation, the conflicting parties may not even be in the same room. Once, as a participant in mediation, our party was in one room and the other party was in another room, with the mediator traveling back and forth between rooms. He'd ask us, "What do you want them to do?" and he'd take that back to the other side and see if they were willing to do it. Then he would come back and say, "They're unwilling to do that, but how about this?"

Many mediators define their role as a "third head" trying to think of a way to get everybody to come to an agreement. They are not at all concerned with creating a quality of connection, thus overlooking the only conflict resolution tool I have ever known to work. When I described the NVC method and the role of human connection, one of the participants at the Austria meeting raised the objection that I was talking about psychotherapy, and that mediators were not psychotherapists.

In my experience, connecting people at this level isn't psychotherapy; it's actually the core of mediation because when you make the connection, the problem solves itself most of the time.

> When you make the connection, the problem usually solves itself.

第十一章　化解冲突，调和纷争

第三方调解人（即有一位第三方人员介入冲突的两方进行调和工作）和冲突中的双方（个人或者团体）开展工作时，我的工作方法和职业调解人常采用的方法大不相同。

有一次我在奥地利和一群职业调解人开会，他们在处理国际冲突方面经验丰富，包括工会与资方间的冲突。在会上，我讲述了由我调停过的几起冲突，例如，加州土地所有人与外来劳工间的暴力冲突，也谈到我如何化解两个非洲部落间的纠纷（这部分在《用非暴力沟通化解冲突》一书中有详尽说明）以及其他一些极其困难又危险的冲突。

会上有人问我会花多少时间来研究冲突的情势。这是大部分职业调解人开展工作的流程：先对导致冲突的问题做一番研究，然后开展实际的调停工作。他们关注的重点放在那些问题而非建立人的连结上。事实上，在传统的"第三方调解"方法中，冲突双方甚至不一定同时在场。有一次，我作为接受调解的一方，与我方成员坐在一个房间里，对方则坐在另一个房间，调解人就在两个房间之间来回穿梭。他问我们："你们希望他们怎么做？"然后将我们的话带给另一方，并询问他们的意愿。接着他又回到我们这里，告诉我们："他们不愿意那样做，但如果……，你们觉得怎么样？"

许多调解人认为，自己所扮演的角色是所谓的"第三个脑袋"，努力想出办法让所有人达成共识。他们毫不关心要在这个过程中创造人与人的连结。当我描述非暴力沟通的方法以及人与人建立连结的重要性时，一位参会者提出了质疑，他认为我谈论的属于心理治疗范畴，而调解人并不是心理治疗师。

然而，根据我的经验，连结人非但不是心理治疗，还是化解冲突的关键，是唯一能够有效化解冲突的方式。一旦你成功地建立了人与人之

Instead of a third head asking, "What can we agree to here?," if we had a clear statement of each person's needs—what those parties need *right now* from each other—we will then discover what can be done to get everybody's needs met. These become the strategies the parties agree to implement after the mediation session concludes and the parties leave the room.

NVC Conflict Resolution Steps—A Quick Overview

Before we get deeper into a discussion of some of the other key elements of conflict resolution, let me give you a thumbnail sketch of the steps involved in resolving a conflict between ourselves and somebody else. There are five steps in this process. Either side may express their needs first, but for the sake of simplicity in this overview, let's assume we begin with our needs.

- First, we express our own needs.
- Second, we search for the real needs of the other person, no matter how they are expressing themselves. If they are not expressing a need, but instead an opinion, judgment, or analysis, we recognize that, and continue to seek the need behind their words, the need underneath what they are saying.
- Third, we verify that we both accurately recognize the other person's needs, and if not, continue to seek the need behind their words.
- Fourth, we provide as much empathy as is required for us to mutually hear each other's needs accurately.
- And fifth, having clarified both parties' needs in the situation, we propose strategies for resolving the conflict, framing them in positive action language.

> Avoid the use of language that implies wrongness.

Throughout, we're listening to each other with utmost care, avoiding the use of language that implies wrongness on either side.

第十一章　化解冲突，调和纷争

间的连结，问题多半会自行解决。与其由这"第三个脑袋"来问"我们可以达成什么样的共识"，不如让每个人清楚表明自己的需要，此刻希望对方做什么。在双方都明白对方的需要后，自然就能找出方法来满足彼此的需要，也就是双方都能认同在调解工作结束后所实施的策略。

非暴力沟通化解冲突的步骤

在详细讨论化解冲突的核心要素之前，我先大致介绍一下在化解自己和他人的冲突过程中所涉及的5个步骤。任何一方都可以先表达自己的需要，简便起见，假设先由我方表达。

- 首先，我们要表达自己的需要。
- 其次，不论对方说什么，设法找出他们真正的需要。如果发现他们表达的是想法、评判或分析，而不是需要，我们可以继续寻找话语背后的需要。
- 第三，确认我们都准确理解了彼此的需要，否则，继续寻找话语背后所隐含的需要。
- 第四，尽可能地同理对方，以便让双方都能确切地了解彼此的需要。
- 第五，当双方都澄清了事件中的需要后，我们就可以用正向的描述行动的语言提出化解冲突的策略。

在整个过程中，我们要仔细聆听彼此的心声，避免在言语中影射对方有错。

11 Conflict Resolution and Mediation

On Needs, Strategies, and Analysis

Since the understanding and expression of needs are essential to resolving conflicts through NVC, let us review this vital concept which has been emphasized throughout this book, and particularly in Chapter 5.

Fundamentally, needs are the resources life requires to sustain itself. We all have physical needs: air, water, food, rest. And we have psychological needs such as understanding, support, honesty, and meaning. I believe that all people basically have the same needs regardless of nationality, religion, gender, income, education, etc.

Next, let's consider the difference between a person's needs and his or her strategy for fulfilling them. It is important, when resolving conflicts, that we can clearly recognize the difference between needs and strategies.

Many of us have great difficulty expressing our needs: we have been taught by society to criticize, insult, and otherwise (mis)communicate in ways that keep us apart. In a conflict, both parties usually spend too much time intent on proving themselves right, and the other party wrong, rather than paying attention to their own and the other's needs. And such verbal conflicts can far too easily escalate into violence—and even war.

In order not to confuse needs and strategies, it is important to recall that *needs contain no reference to anybody taking any particular action.* On the other hand, strategies, which may appear in the form of requests, desires, wants, and "solutions," refer to *specific actions that specific people may take.*

For example, I once met with a couple who had just about given up on their marriage. I asked the husband what needs of his weren't being fulfilled in the marriage. He said, "I need to get out of this marriage." What he was describing was a specific person (himself) taking a specific action (leaving the marriage). He wasn't expressing a need; he was identifying a strategy.

I pointed this out to the husband and suggested that he first clarify his and his wife's needs before undertaking the strategy of

第十一章　化解冲突，调和纷争

需要、策略以及分析

理解与表达需要是非暴力沟通冲突解决的核心，让我们来回顾这一贯穿本书（尤其在第五章中）的核心概念。

本质上，需要是我们用以维系生命的资源。人人都有身体上的需要，如空气、水、食物、休息；也有心理上的需要，如理解、支持、诚实和意义。我相信，无论国籍、宗教、性别、收入、教育程度等如何，每个人的需要都是相通的。

我们还要明了"需要"和满足需要的"策略"是不同的。在化解冲突时，清晰分辨"需要"和"策略"的不同是非常重要的。

许多人很难表达自己的需要。社会教会了我们评判和侮辱性的语言，这些沟通方式让我们彼此疏离。在冲突中，双方通常会花大量时间证明自己是对的、对方是错的，而不会关注自己和对方的需要。语言上的冲突一不小心便升级为肢体暴力，甚至是战争。

为了避免将"需要"和"策略"混为一谈，我们一定要记得，"需要"并不涉及某个人所采取的特定行动；相反，"策略"则涉及某个人可能采取的某个行动，它的形式可以是请求、诉求、愿望以及"解决方案"等。

举例来说，有一次，我遇到一对正准备离婚的夫妻。我问那位先生：在婚姻中，他有哪些需要没有得到满足。他说："我需要结束这段婚姻。"他所表述的是某个人（他自己）采取的某个行动（结束婚姻），因而，他表达的并非一个"需要"，而是"策略"。

我向那位先生指出了这一点，并建议他先来厘清自己和太太的需

11 Conflict Resolution and Mediation

"getting out of this marriage." After both of them had connected with their own and each other's needs, they discovered that these needs could be met with strategies other than ending the marriage. The husband acknowledged his needs for appreciation and understanding for the stress generated by his rather demanding job; the wife recognized her needs for closeness and connection in a situation where she experienced her husband's job occupying much of his time.

Once they truly understood their mutual needs, this husband and wife were able to arrive at a set of agreements that satisfied both their needs while working around the demands of the husband's job.

In the case of another couple, the lack of "needs literacy" took the form of confusion between the expression of needs and the expression of analysis, and ultimately led to their inflicting physical violence on each other. I was invited to mediate in this situation at the end of a workplace training when a man tearfully described his situation and asked if he and his wife could speak with me in private.

I agreed to meet them at their home, and opened the evening by saying: "I'm aware that you're both in a lot of pain. Let's begin with each of you expressing whatever needs of yours aren't being fulfilled in your relationship. Once you understand each other's needs, I'm confident we can work on strategies to meet those needs."

Not being "needs literate," the husband started off by telling his wife, "The problem with you is that you're totally insensitive to my needs."

She answered in the same manner, "That's typical of you to say unfair things like that!"

Instead of expressing needs, they were doing analysis, which is easily heard as criticism by a listener. As mentioned earlier in this book, analyses that imply wrongness are essentially tragic expressions of unmet needs. In the case of this couple, the husband had a need for support and understanding but expressed it in terms of the wife's "insensitivity." The wife also had a need

第十一章 化解冲突，调和纷争

要，然后再看看要不要采取"结束婚姻"的策略。当他们连结了各自和对方的需要后，便发现，除了离婚，他们还可以通过其他的策略来满足这些需要。那位先生承认，因为工作辛苦、压力很大，他的需要是得到欣赏和理解。他的太太则意识到，她的需要是亲密和连结，但丈夫的工作却占据了他太多时间。当他们真正理解了彼此的需要，就能够达成一些约定，在顾及先生工作的情况下，满足双方的需要。

还有一对夫妻，因为不了解何谓"需要"，以为"表达需要"就是"分析对方的问题"，两人甚至走到拳脚相向的境地。那位先生在工作坊结束后找到我，含着泪描述了他的境况，并问我是否愿意私下为他和妻子做调解。

我答应了去他家与夫妻俩见面。那天晚上，我开门见山地对他们说："我知道你们两人都很痛苦。首先，我想请你们各自表达你们在这段婚姻关系中没有被满足的需要。我相信，一旦你们明白了彼此的需要，就能找到策略来满足这些需要。"

由于不知道什么是需要，那位先生劈头盖脸地对着太太说："你的问题就在于对我的需要无动于衷。"

他的妻子也用同样的方式回答道："你每次都这么说，这对我太不公平了！"

他们两人都没有表达自己的需要，而是在分析对方的问题，人们又往往很容易将分析听成批评。诚如我在先前所提到的，分析对方的问题或暗示对方有错，实质是在表达自己未被满足的需要，但这种表达方式却会带来糟糕的影响。以这对夫妻为例，先生的需要是得到支持与理解，但他所表达出来的却是妻子"无动于衷"；妻子也希望得到真正的理解，但她说出来的却是先生对她"不公平"。他们花了好些时间才终

for being accurately understood, but she expressed it in terms of the husband's "unfairness." It took a while to move through the layers of needs on the part of both husband and wife, but only through truly acknowledging and appreciating each other's needs were they finally able to begin the process of exploring strategies to address their long-standing conflicts.

I once worked with a company where both morale and productivity took a dive due to a very disturbing conflict. Two factions in the same department were fighting over which software to use, generating strong emotions on both sides. One faction had worked especially hard to develop the software that was presently in use, and wanted to see its continued use. The other faction had strong emotions tied up in creating new software.

I started by asking each side to tell me what needs of theirs would be better fulfilled by the software they advocated. Their response was to offer an intellectual analysis that the other side received as criticism. A member on the side that favored new software said: "We can continue to be overly conservative, but if we do that, I think we could be out of work in the future. Progress means that we take some risks, and dare to show that we are beyond old-fashioned ways of doing things." A member of the opposing faction responded, "But I think that impulsively grabbing for every new thing that comes along is not in our best interest." They acknowledged that they had been repeating these same analyses for months and were getting nowhere other than increasing tension for themselves.

> Intellectual analysis is often received as criticism.

When we don't know how to directly and clearly express what we need, but can only make analyses of others that sound like criticism to them, wars are never far away—whether verbal, psychological, or physical.

第十一章　化解冲突，调和纷争

于找到了彼此的需要，但一直等到真正认可和理解了对方的需要后，他们才得以寻求策略，来化解长久以来的矛盾。

还有一次，我为一家公司做顾问。由于严重的内部派系纷争，公司员工的士气和产量都一落千丈。纷争的起因是，同一部门内的两个团队因为使用哪个软件而各执己见、争执不休。其中一个团队曾花了很多心血研发出公司当时正在使用的软件，因此希望能继续使用下去；另一个团队则坚决主张开发一款新软件。

首先我请双方告诉我，他们各自坚持使用的那个软件，能满足自己什么样的需要。但他们习惯以理性分析的方式回答，这往往会被另一方视为对自己的批评。主张开发新软件的一位团队成员表示："我们当然可以继续维持这种过分保守的作风，但这样下去，我想未来等待我们的就是失业。要进步就得冒一些险，敢于突破固有的做法。"反对派的一位成员则回应道："盲目冲动地追逐新事物并不符合我们的最佳利益。"他们承认，几个月来双方都在重复类似的分析，非但没有解决问题，反而加剧了关系的紧张。

若不知道如何清楚直接地表达自己的需要，而只是分析对方的问题，就会让对方认为遭受到了批评，我们就把自己一步步推向了战争（无论是语言、心理或是肢体上的）。

超越语言，感知需要

要用非暴力沟通来化解冲突，我们需要训练自己——无论他人用什么方式来表达，都听见那背后的需要。如果我们真的想支持他人，就要

Sensing Others' Needs, No Matter What They're Saying

To resolve conflicts using NVC, we need to train ourselves to hear people expressing needs regardless of how they do the expressing. If we really want to be of assistance to others, the first thing to learn is to translate *any* message into an expression of a need. The message might take the form of silence, denial, a judgmental remark, a gesture—or, hopefully, a request. We hone our skills to hear the need within every message, even if at first we have to rely on guesses.

For example, in the middle of a conversation, if I ask the other person something about what they've just said, and I am met with "That's a stupid question," I hear them expressing a need in the form of a judgment of me. I proceed to guess what that need might be—maybe the question I asked did not fulfill their need to be understood. Or if I ask my partner to talk about the stress in our relationship and they answer, "I don't want to talk about it," I may sense that their need is for protection from what they imagine could happen if we were to communicate about our relationship. So this is our work: learning to recognize the need in statements that don't overtly express any need. It takes practice, and it always involves some guessing. Once we sense what the other person needs, we can check in with them, and then help them put their need into words. If we are able to truly hear their need, a new level of connection is forged—a critical piece that moves the conflict toward successful resolution.

> Learn to hear needs regardless of how people express them.

In workshops for married couples, I often look for the couple with the longest unresolved conflict to demonstrate my prediction that, once each side can state the other side's needs, it would take no more than twenty minutes for the conflict to come to a resolution. Once there was a couple whose marriage suffered thirty-nine years of conflict about money. Six months into the marriage, the wife had twice overdrawn their checking account

第十一章　化解冲突，调和纷争

先学习将任何信息翻译为需要。沉默、否定、评判、肢体语言或请求等都是"信息"的不同呈现形式。我们要磨练的技巧是聆听每个信息中所隐含的需要，即使一开始是通过猜测。

例如，在和别人交谈时，如果我问对方刚才说的话是什么意思，对方回应我的是："你这个问题真傻！"这时我就知道，那人只不过是以评判的方式来表达某个自己的需要。于是，我接着来猜测那是什么样的需要——也许我的提问无法满足他被理解的需要。再例如，当我请伴侣谈谈我们在关系中所面临的压力时，对方回答："我不想谈。"我猜，也许她的需要是保护自己，她担心谈了之后会有什么别的问题。因此，我们的功课是去学习在别人不明说的情况下，识别话语中隐含的需要，通常这要靠猜测。一旦感知到对方的需要，就可以向他们求证，再支持他们说出自己的需要。如果我们能够真正听见他人的需要，就能建立更深层的连结，这是成功化解冲突的关键。

我认为，冲突中的人们一旦可以说出对方的需要，最多只要 20 分钟，冲突就可以得到解决。在伴侣工作坊中，我通常会让吵得最久的夫妻参与现场的演示，借以证明我的预测。有对夫妻在他们 39 年的婚姻中为了金钱问题争吵不断。婚后 6 个月中，太太两度透支了账户里的钱，于是先生便掌管了家里的经济大权，不许太太再开支票。从此，两人一直为此争吵不休。

一开始，那位太太质疑我的预测。她认为，即使他们的婚姻关系不错、沟通良好，但这么快化解经年累月的冲突是不可能的。

随即，我先邀请她告诉我，是否知道在和金钱有关的冲突中丈夫的需要是什么。

她回答："很明显，他就是一分钱都不想让我花。"

11 Conflict Resolution and Mediation

whereupon the husband took control of the finances and would no longer let her write checks. The two of them had never stopped arguing about it since.

The wife challenged my prediction, saying that even though they had a good marriage and can communicate well, it wouldn't be possible for their historically entrenched conflict to resolve so quickly.

I invited her to begin by telling me if she knew what her husband's needs were in this conflict.

She replied, "He obviously doesn't want me to spend any money."

To which her husband exclaimed: "That's ridiculous!"

In stating that her husband didn't want her to spend any money, the wife was identifying what I call a strategy. Even if she had been accurate in guessing her husband's *strategy*, she had nowhere identified his *need*. Here again is the key distinction. By my definition, a need doesn't refer to a specific action, such as spending or not spending money. I told the wife that all people share the same needs, and if she could only understand her husband's needs, the issue would be resolved. When encouraged again to state her husband's needs, she replied, "He is just like his father," describing how his father had been reluctant to spend money. At this point, she was making an analysis.

I stopped her to ask again, "What was his need?"

It became clear that, even after thirty-nine years of "communicating well," she still had no idea what his needs were.

I then turned to the husband. "Since your wife isn't in touch with what your needs are, why don't you tell her? What needs are you meeting by keeping the checkbook from her?"

> **Criticism and diagnosis get in the way of peaceful resolution of conflicts.**

To which he responded, "Marshall, she's a wonderful wife, a wonderful mother. But when it comes to money, she's totally irresponsible." His use of *diagnosis* ("She is irresponsible.") is reflective of language that gets in the way of peaceful resolution of conflicts. When either side hears itself criticized, diagnosed, or interpreted, the energy of the situation will likely turn

第十一章 化解冲突，调和纷争

丈夫闻言大声叫出："这太荒谬了！"

当太太说丈夫"一分钱都不想让我花"时，她所表达的是我所谓的"策略"，而不是"需要"。即使她猜对了丈夫的策略，却并没有看见他的"需要"。因为，"需要"指的并不是任何特定的行为，例如"花钱"或"不花钱"。我告诉这位太太，所有人都有着共通的需要，只要她能理解丈夫的需要，问题就可以得到解决。我再次鼓励她说出丈夫的需要，她回答："他和他爸一个样子。"接着开始诉说他的父亲是如何不舍得花钱。这时，她开始"分析"起丈夫的问题。

我打断她的话，再次问道："那他的需要是什么呢？"

显然，即使39年来她和丈夫"沟通良好"，她还是不知道对方的需要是什么。

我转向那位先生，询问他："既然你太太不知道你的需要，不如你来告诉她，你不让她开支票是为了满足你的什么需要呢？"

他答道："马歇尔，她是个很棒的太太和妈妈。但在花钱这件事上，她完全没有责任感。"这类"诊断"式的语言（"没有责任感"）根本无助于解决冲突，当一方听到对方的批评、诊断或分析，沟通就会演变为自我辩护或相互指责。

于是，我试着聆听他在说太太"完全没有责任感"背后有着什么样的感受和需要："你是不是感到害怕，因为你需要在经济上保护你们的家庭？"他表示确实如此。诚然，我的猜测是正确的，但就算我第一次猜错也没有关系，因为我还是会把注意力放在他的需要上——这才是问题的核心。事实上，就算猜得不对，我们也可以支持对方关注自己真正的需要，从而跳脱出分析，与自己的内在生命建立更多连结。

toward self-defense and counter-accusations rather than toward resolution.

I tried to hear the feeling and need behind him stating that his wife was irresponsible: "Are you feeling *scared* because you have a need to protect your family economically?" He agreed that this was indeed the case. Admittedly, I had merely guessed correctly, but I didn't have to get it right the first time because even if I had guessed wrong, I would still have been focusing on his needs—and that's the heart of the matter. In fact, when we reflect back incorrect guesses to others, it may help them get in touch with their true needs. It takes them out of analysis toward greater connection to life.

Have the Needs Been Heard?

The husband had finally acknowledged his need: to keep his family safe. The next step is to ascertain that the wife heard that need. This is a crucial stage in conflict resolution. We must not assume that when one party expresses a need clearly, that the other party hears it accurately. I asked the wife, "Can you tell me back what you heard to be your husband's needs in this situation?"

"Well, just because I overdrew the bank account a couple of times, it doesn't mean I'm going to continue doing it."

Her response was not unusual. When we have pain built up over many years, it can get in the way of our ability to hear clearly, even when what is being expressed is clear to others. To continue, I said to the wife: "I'd like to tell you what I heard your husband say, and I'd like you to repeat it back. I heard that your husband says he has a need to protect the family, and he's scared because he wants to be sure that the family is protected."

Empathy to Ease the Pain That Prevents Hearing

But she was still in too much pain to hear me. This brings up another skill that is needed if we are to effectively engage the NVC process of conflict resolution. When people are upset, they often need empathy before they can hear what is being said to

第十一章　化解冲突，调和纷争

需要被听到了吗？

　　那位先生终于承认了他的需要是保护家庭的安全。下一步就是确认他的太太听见他的需要。这是化解冲突的关键步骤。我们不能假定当一方清楚地表达了自己的需要，另一方就一定准确地听到了。我问那位太太："你可不可以告诉我，你听到你的丈夫在这件事中的需要是什么了吗？"

　　"喔，我只不过是让账户透支了几次，但这也不代表我会一直这么做吧。"

　　她的反应并不令人意外。就算对方的表达在他人看来已经足够清晰，但当事者却会因为心中的积怨而无法听见对方。于是，我接着对太太说："我想告诉你，我刚才听到你丈夫说了什么，也请你把这些内容复述给他。我听到你丈夫说，他希望保护家庭，确保家里的经济无恙，但他担心他做不到，所以他很害怕。"

痛苦阻碍聆听，同理舒解痛苦

　　然而，这位太太依然深陷痛苦而无法听见我的表达。这就涉及另一个可以有效化解冲突的技巧。当人们心烦意乱时，往往需要先得到同理才有可能听进去别人的话。因此，我不再让她复述先生的话，而是试着理解她的痛苦。面对处于痛苦中的人们，尤其是经受了长年累月的苦痛，重要的是给予他们足够的同理，让他们感受到自己的痛苦被看见、被理解了。

them. In this instance, I changed course: instead of trying to have her repeat what her husband had said, I tried to understand the pain she was in—the pain that kept her from hearing him. Especially if there is a long history of pain, it is important to offer enough empathy so that the parties feel reassured that their pain is being recognized and understood.

> People often need empathy before they are able to hear what is being said.

When I addressed the wife with empathy, "I sense that you're feeling really hurt and you need to be trusted that you can learn from past experience," the expression in her eyes showed me how much she needed that understanding. "Yes, exactly," she replied, but when asked to repeat back what her husband had said, she answered, "He thinks I spend too much money."

Just as we are not trained to express our own needs, most of us have not been trained in hearing the needs of others. All this wife could hear was criticism or diagnosis on part of her husband. I encouraged her to try to simply hear his needs. After I repeated his need—for safety for his family—two more times, she finally was able to hear it. Then, after a few more rounds, they were both able to hear each other's needs. And just as I had predicted, once they understood—for the first time in thirty-nine years—each other's needs concerning the checkbook, it took less than twenty minutes to find practical ways to meet both their needs.

The more experience I have gained in mediating conflicts over the years and the more I've seen what leads families to argue and nations to go to war, the more convinced I am that most schoolchildren could solve these conflicts. If we could just say, "Here are the needs of both sides. Here are the resources. What can be done to meet these needs?," conflicts would be easily resolved. But instead, our thinking is focused on dehumanizing one another with labels and judgments until even the simplest of conflicts becomes very difficult to solve. NVC helps us avoid that trap, thereby enhancing the chances of reaching a satisfying resolution.

第十一章　化解冲突，调和纷争

于是，我便开始同理那位太太："我体会到你很伤心，你希望丈夫信任你能从过去的经验中学习。"她的眼神告诉我，她是多么渴望得到这样的理解："是的，一点没错！"然而，当我再次请她复述丈夫刚才说的话时，她还是回答："他认为我花钱太大手大脚了。"

大部分人从来没有被教导过如何表达自己的需要，也没有学习过如何听见他人的需要。这位太太所听到的都是先生对她的批评或诊断。我继续鼓励她尝试听一下先生的需要。在我重复了两遍他的需要是"家庭安全"后，她终于能够听见了。这样来来回回几次，他们终于听到了彼此的需要。这是 39 年来他们第一次了解彼此在银行账户这件事情上的需要。正如我先前所预料的，他们果然用了不到 20 分钟的时间便找到了可行的解决方法，双方的需要都得到了满足。

这些年来，我在化解冲突上持续累积的经验让我了解到了家庭失和、两国交战的真正原因，使我越发相信，化解这些冲突是连孩子都能做到的事。只要我们能表明这是双方的需要，这是现有的资源，我们可以做什么来满足这些需要，冲突就可以轻而易举地得到化解。然而，我们的思想却更多地聚焦在用标签和评判来彼此伤害，以至于原本微不足道的冲突变得不可收拾。非暴力沟通能帮助我们免于掉入这样的圈套，从而达成令人满意的共识。

用此刻可回应的、正向的行动语言化解冲突

在第六章中，我提到了要使用**此刻可回应的**、正向的行动语言提出请求。在这里，我想再举几个例子来说明这对化解冲突很重要。一旦冲

Using Present and Positive Action Language to Resolve Conflict

Although I addressed the use of present, positive action language in Chapter 6, I'd like to present a few more examples to demonstrate its importance in resolving conflicts. Once both parties have connected with each other's needs, the next step is to arrive at strategies that meet those needs. It's important to avoid moving hastily into strategies, as this may result in a compromise that lacks the deep quality of authentic resolution that is possible. By fully hearing each other's needs before addressing solutions, parties in conflict are much more likely to adhere to the agreements they make to each other. The process of resolving conflict has to end with actions that meet everybody's needs. It is the presentation of strategies in clear, present, positive action language that moves conflicts toward resolution.

A *present language* statement refers to what is wanted *at this moment*. For example, one party might say, "I'd like you to tell me if you would be willing to—" and describe the action they'd like the other party to take. The use of a present language request that begins with "Would you be willing to . . ." helps foster a respectful discussion. If the other side answers that they are not willing, it invites the next step of understanding what prevents their willingness.

On the other hand, in the absence of present language, a request such as "I'd like you to go to the show with me Saturday night" fails to convey what's being asked of the listener *at that moment*. The use of present language to hone such a request, for example, "Would you be willing to tell me whether you will go to the show with me Saturday night?," supports clarity and ongoing connection in the exchange. We can further clarify the request by indicating what we may want from the other person in the present moment, "Would you be willing to tell me how you feel about going to the show with me Saturday night?" The clearer we are regarding the response we want right now from the other party, the more effectively we move the conflict toward resolution.

突双方理解了彼此的需要，下一步就是寻找满足需要的策略。此时，一定要避免仓促行事，否则就可能会导致妥协和让步。而彼此若有可能真诚地达成和解，便能体验到这个过程的深度。双方在谈论解决方案前越能充分聆听彼此的需要，日后就越有可能更好地遵守彼此的约定。找到了满足所有需要的行动策略，化解冲突的过程才真正结束。用清晰的、**此刻可回应的**、正向行动的语言来表述策略，冲突才能走向和解。

"此刻可回应的语言"指的是当下的诉求，比如可以这样说："我想请你告诉我，你是否愿意……（描述想要对方采取的行动）？"用**此刻可回应的**语言表达请求（"你是否愿意……"），有利于双方在讨论时保持相互尊重的态度。如果对方表示不愿意，我们可以进一步了解是什么原因让他们不愿意。

相反，如果在提出请求时不使用**此刻可回应的**语言，诸如"我希望你周六晚陪我一起去看戏"，对方便无从知晓当下可以怎么做。若用**此刻可回应的**语言来修改，让请求变得清晰并有利于保持两人的连结，则可以问："你能告诉我，你愿意周六晚上和我一起去看戏吗？"若要进一步向对方澄清我们在此刻希望得到的回应，我们可以问："你是否愿意告诉我，对于周六晚上跟我一起看戏这件事，你有什么想法？"我们把此刻所希望得到的回应说得越清楚，就越能够有效地化解冲突。

使用行动语言

在第六章中，我们还提到了在提出请求时"行动语言"所扮演的角色。在冲突化解中，我们更要把焦点放在自己真正"想要"的，而非

Using Action Verbs

In Chapter 6, we touched upon the role of action language in forming NVC requests. In situations of conflict, it is especially important to focus on what we *do* want rather than what we *do not* want. Talking about what one *doesn't* want can easily create confusion and resistance among conflicting parties.

Action language requires the use of action verbs, while also avoiding language that obscures, or language that can readily be inferred as an attack. I'd like to illustrate this with a situation where a woman expressed a need for understanding that wasn't being met in her primary relationship. After her partner was able to accurately hear and reflect back the need for understanding, I turned to the woman and said, "Okay, let's get down to strategies. What do you want from your partner in order to meet your need for understanding?" She faced her partner and said, "I'd like you to listen to me when I talk to you." "I do listen to you when you talk!," the partner retorted. It's not unusual, if someone tells us they'd like us to listen when they are talking, for us to hear accusations and thus feel some resentment.

> Action language requires the use of action verbs.

They went back and forth, with the partner repeating, "I do listen," and the woman countering, "No, you don't." They told me they'd had this "conversation" for twelve years, a situation that is typical in conflicts when parties use vague words like "listen" to express strategies. I suggest instead the use of action verbs to capture *something that we can see or hear happening—something that can be recorded with a video camera.* "Listening" occurs inside a person's head; another person cannot see whether it is happening or not. One way to determine that someone is actually listening is to have that person reflect back what had been said: we ask the person to take an action that we ourselves can see or hear. If the other party can tell us what was just said, we know that person heard and was indeed listening to us.

In another conflict between a husband and wife, the wife wanted to know that her husband respected her choices. Once she

第十一章 化解冲突，调和纷争

"不想要"的事物上。谈论我们"不想要"什么，很容易让对方感到困惑并引发抗拒心理。

所谓"行动语言"指的是代表某个行动的动词，要避免模糊不清或可能被他人视为有抨击意味的说法。举例来说，有位女士表示在伴侣关系中理解的需要一直没有得到满足。当她的伴侣能够准确听到她的需要并且复述给她后，我转向那位女士："现在让我们来讨论策略吧。你希望你的伴侣做些什么来满足你得到理解的需要呢？"她看着伴侣说："我希望在我对你说话时，你能聆听我。""我在听啊！"伴侣立刻反驳道。发生这样的状况并不稀奇——如果有人告诉我们，希望我们能注意听他们说话，我们很容易认为对方在指责我们没有聆听他们，因而愤愤不平。

这对夫妻就这样你一句我一句地杠上了。先生一再说："我真的听你说了！"太太则反驳道："不，你没有！"他们告诉我，这样的"对话"持续了12年。当冲突双方使用类似"聆听"这样模糊的词语来表达策略时，经常就会发生这种状况。我建议他们使用行动动词来传达他们具体看到或听到的是什么，就像那些能被摄影机所捕捉到的内容。一个人是否真的在"聆听"，只有自己知道，别人无法用肉眼看见。要确定某个人是否真的在听我们说话，有一个办法是，请他复述刚才我们所说的话。这样我们就是在请求对方采取一个可以看得见或听得着的行动。如果对方讲得出刚才我们说了什么，就能知道对方确实在听。

还有另外一对夫妻，太太希望先生能尊重她的选择。在她成功表达了需要后，接下来她就要搞清楚采取什么策略来满足她的需要，并且向先生提出请求。于是，她对先生说："我希望你让我自由地成长并且做我自己。""我就是这么做的啊！"先生回答道。随后他们就像之前那

expressed her need successfully, her next step was to get clear on her strategy for meeting that need and to make a request of the husband. She told him, "I want you to give me the freedom to grow and be myself." "I do," he replied, and just as with the other couple, this was followed by a fruitless volley of "Yes, I do," and "No, you don't."

Non-action language, such as "Give me the freedom to grow" often exacerbates conflict. In this instance, the husband heard himself being judged as domineering. I pointed out to the wife that it wasn't clear to her husband what she wanted: "Please tell him exactly what you'd like him to *do* to meet your need to have your choices respected."

"I want you to let me—," she began. I interrupted that "let" was too vague: "What do you really mean when you say you want somebody to 'let' you?"

After reflecting for a few seconds, she arrived at an important understanding. She acknowledged that what she really meant when she said things like "I want you to let me be" and "I want you to give me the freedom to grow" is for her husband to tell her that no matter what she did, it was okay.

> Maintaining respect is a key element in successful conflict resolution.

When she got clear as to what she was actually requesting—for him to *tell her something*—she recognized that what she wanted did not leave him much freedom to be himself and to have *his* choices respected. And maintaining respect is a key element in successful conflict resolution.

Translating "No"

When we express a request, it's very important to be respectful of the other person's reaction, whether or not they agree to our request. Many mediations I have witnessed consist of waiting for people to wear down to the point where they'll accept any compromise. This is very different from a resolution in which everyone's needs are met and nobody experiences loss.

对夫妻一样，一个说："我就是这么做的啊！"另一个说："不，你没有！"你来我往，反反复复，却徒劳无功。

类似"让我自由地成长"这样的非"行动语言"往往只会使冲突升级。在这个例子中，先生认为太太是在指责自己过于掌控她。我向那位太太说明，她的丈夫并不清楚她要什么："请你明确地告诉他，你希望他怎么做能够满足你被尊重的需要？"

"我希望你让我……"她一开口，我便立即打断了她，告诉她"让"这样的说法太模糊了："当你说你希望某人'让'你如何时，究竟是什么意思？"

沉思了几秒钟后，她终于恍然大悟。她发现，当她说"我希望你让我做自己"以及"我希望你让我自由地成长"之类的话时，她的意思其实是希望先生能够告诉她：不管你做什么，都是可以的。

当明白了自己的请求实际上是希望先生对她说那些话时，她便发现这样的诉求并没有给先生太多自由做他自己，也没有尊重他的选择。而相互尊重乃是成功化解冲突的关键要素。

翻译他人说的"不"

当我们提出一个请求时，要注意的是，无论对方是否同意，都要尊重他们的回应。我在许多传统调解中都看到人们如何被拖延战术消磨意志，直到接受妥协。与此非常不同的是，非暴力沟通冲突解决的目标是让每个人的需要都得到满足，没有一方是输家。

在第八章中，我们谈到了一个重要的话题：当听到别人说"不"

In Chapter 8, we discovered the importance of not hearing "no" as rejection. Listening carefully to the message behind the "no" helps us understand the other person's needs: *When they say "no," they're saying they have a need that keeps them from saying "yes" to what we are asking.* If we can hear the need behind a "no," we can continue the conflict resolution process—maintaining our focus on finding a way to meet everybody's needs—even if the other party says "no" to the particular strategy we presented them.

NVC and the Mediator Role

Although in this chapter I have offered examples from mediations I've facilitated between conflicting parties, the focus so far has been on how to apply these skills when resolving conflicts between ourselves and another person. There are, however, a few things to keep in mind at those times when we want to use our NVC tools to help two other parties reach a resolution and we take on the role of mediator.

Your Role, and Trust in the Process

When entering a conflict process as mediator, a good place to start might be to assure the people in conflict that we are not there to take sides, but to support them in hearing each other, and to help guide them to a solution that meets everyone's needs. Depending on the circumstances, we may also want to convey our confidence that, if the parties follow the steps of NVC, both of their needs will be met in the end.

Remember: It's Not About Us

At the beginning of the chapter, I emphasized that the objective is *not* to get the other person to do what we want them to do. This also applies to mediating someone else's conflict. Though we may have our own wishes for how the conflict is

> The objective is not to get the parties to do what we want them to do.

第十一章　化解冲突，调和纷争

时，我们无须认为这是对我们的"拒绝"。仔细聆听那个"不"背后所隐藏的信息，就能帮助我们理解对方的需要——当他们说"不"时，是出于什么样的需要而无法答应我们的请求呢？如果我们能听见"不"背后的需要，即使对方不同意我们提出的策略，我们依然能继续进行调解，将我们的注意力聚焦在找到办法满足所有人的需要上。

非暴力沟通与调解人的角色

到目前为止，除了少数几个我作为调解人化解冲突的案例，我在本章节主要谈论了如何用非暴力沟通的调解技术来化解自己和他人的冲突。然而，若想要作为第三方调解人来协助双方调停纷争，我们还要记住几件事。

1. 你的角色以及对非暴力沟通调解过程的信心

当作为调解人参与冲突解决时，我们最好开宗明义地告诉冲突双方——我们的工作不会偏袒任何一方，而是支持双方听见彼此的声音，引导他们找到满足各方需要的解决方案。视当下状况，我们也可以向人们传达我们的信心，告诉他们：你相信，只要双方都遵照非暴力沟通的步骤，最终，所有人的需要都能得到满足。

2. 谨记：冲突与我们无关

我曾在本章开头强调：用非暴力沟通化解冲突的目标并非要让对方按照我们的意愿去做。同样的原则也适用于调解他人的冲突。尽管我们

resolved—especially if the conflict is between family, friends, or co-workers—we need to remember that we are not here to accomplish our own goals. The mediator's role is to create an environment in which the parties can connect, express their needs, understand each other's needs, and arrive at strategies to meet those needs.

Emergency First-Aid Empathy

As mediator, I stress my intention for both parties to be fully and accurately understood. Despite that, as soon as I express empathy toward one side, it is not unusual for the other side to immediately accuse me of favoritism. At this time, what's called for is emergency first-aid empathy. This might sound like "So you're really annoyed, and you need some assurance that you're going to get your side on the table?"

Once the empathy has been expressed, I remind them that everyone will have the opportunity to be heard, and their turn will be next. It is then helpful to confirm they are in agreement with waiting by asking, for example, "Are you feeling reassured about that, or would you like more reassurance that your opportunity to be heard will come soon?"

We may need to do this repeatedly to keep the mediation on track.

Keep Track: Follow the Bouncing Ball

When we are mediating, we have to "keep score" by paying careful attention to what has been said, making sure both parties have the opportunity to express their needs, listen to the other person's needs, and make requests. We also need to "follow the bouncing ball": being conscious of where one party left off so we can return to what that party said after the other party has been heard.

This can be challenging, especially when things get heated. In such situations, I often find it helpful to use a white board or flip chart to capture the essence of what was spoken by the last speaker who had opportunity to express a feeling or need.

第十一章　化解冲突，调和纷争

可能对于要如何化解冲突有着自己的心愿，尤其是在家人、朋友和同事发生冲突时，但我们务必谨记：身为调解人，我们的工作不是为了实现自己的目标，而是要创造一个环境，让双方能够相互连结，表达各自的需要，理解彼此的需要，并找到策略来满足这些需要。

3. 急救式同理

作为调解人，我会强调我的目标是让双方都得到充分和准确的理解。但有时也不免发生这样的状况：当我同理了一方，另一方就会立刻控诉我在偏袒。这时，我们就要给予这一方一些"急救式同理"。我们也许可以说："你是不是很生气，想要确保你有机会陈述自己的立场？"

在同理了他们的心境后，我会提醒他们每一个人都有机会发声，并且接下来就会轮到他们。然后，为了确保他们真的同意等待，我可能还会询问他们："这样你是不是比较放心了，还是你希望能更确定很快就可以发言了？"

我们可能需要反复这样做，以确保调解过程顺利进行。

4. 掌握进度：追踪

在调解过程中，我们务必做好"追踪"进程的工作——仔细注意人们所说的话，确保双方都有机会表达自己的需要，聆听对方的需要并提出请求。此外，我们还要"追踪"——注意其中一方刚才说到哪里，以便在另一方说完后，回到前者所说的内容上。

要这样做并不容易，尤其在双方争执不下、情绪激动时。此时，如果能在白板或挂纸上将上一位讲话者所表述的要义（感受或需要）记录下来，会颇有帮助。

This form of visual tracking can also serve to reassure both parties that their needs will be addressed because so often before we have a chance to fully draw out one party's needs, the other will be jumping ahead to express themselves. Taking the time to note those needs in a way that is visible to everyone present can help the listener feel comfortable that their own needs will also be addressed. In this way, everyone can more easily offer their full attention to what is being expressed in the current moment.

Keep the Conversation in the Present

Another important quality to bring to mediation is awareness of the moment: who needs what right now? What are their present requests? Maintaining this awareness requires a lot of practice in being present in the moment, which is something most of us have never been taught to do.

As we move through the mediation process, it is likely that we will hear a lot of discussion about what happened in the past and what people want to happen differently in the future. However, conflict resolution can only happen right now, so now is where we need to focus.

Keep Things Moving

Another mediation task is to keep the conversation from getting bogged down; this can happen very easily, as people often think that if they just tell that same story *one more time*, they will finally be understood and the other person will do what they want.

To keep things moving, the mediator needs to ask effective questions, and when necessary, maintain or even speed up the pace. Once, when I was scheduled to lead a workshop in a small town, the event organizer asked if I would help him with a personal dispute related to the division of family property. I agreed to mediate, aware there was only a three-hour window in between workshops to do so.

The family dispute centered on a man who owned a large farm and was about to retire. His two sons were at war over how

用视觉的形式追踪进程也能让双方确保自己的需要会被听见。调解过程中经常会发生这样的状况：调解人还没来得及引导一方充分表达完自己的需要，另一方就抢着发言了。花一些时间记录下需要，并且让在场的每一个人都看得到，这会让聆听的一方感到踏实，相信自己的需要会得到处理。这样，每个人就都能更专心地听对方说话了。

5. 聚焦于当下

调解人需要为调解过程注入的另一个重要品质是——对当下的觉察：此刻谁需要什么？人们此刻的请求是什么？要保持这样的觉察，需要大量练习如何安住在当下，而我们大部分人从未受过这方面的训练。

在调解过程中，我们会听到人们有许多讨论，关于过去所发生的事件以及未来所期望的改变。但唯有把握此时此刻才能化解冲突，因此，当下才是我们需要关注的焦点。

6. 推动对话进程

调解人的另一项任务是避免对话陷入泥潭。人们往往认为只要把同样的话多说几遍，别人就能够理解并且按照他们的意思去做，因此，对话很容易陷入原地打转。

为了推动对话进程，调解人需要提出有效的问题，并且在必要时刻维持好对话的节奏，甚至加快步调。有一次，我受邀在一个小镇主持工作坊，主办方问我是否可以帮助他调和一桩家庭内财产分配纠纷。我答应了，同时也意识到我在课余只有3、4个小时的空档来做这件事。

这场纠纷的核心是，一个拥有一大片农场的男子即将退休，他的两

11 Conflict Resolution and Mediation

the property was to be divided. They hadn't spoken in eight years even though they lived close to each other at the same end of the farm. I met the brothers, their wives, and their sister, all of whom were involved in this set of complicated legal matters and eight years of pain.

In order to get things moving—and to stay on schedule—I had to speed up the mediation process. To keep them from spending time telling the same stories over and over, I asked one of the brothers if I could play his role; then I would switch and play the part of the other brother.

> Use role-play to speed up the mediation process.

As I was going through my role-play, I joked about wanting to see if I was playing the part right by asking if I could check in with my "director." Looking over at the brother whose part I had been playing, I saw something I wasn't prepared for: he had tears in his eyes. I guessed that he was experiencing deep empathy, both with himself from my playing his role, as well as for his brother's pain, which he had not seen until then. The next day, the father approached me, also with tearful eyes, to say that the night before the whole family had gone out to dinner for the first time in eight years. Though the conflict had persisted for years, with lawyers on both sides working unsuccessfully to come to agreement, it became simple to resolve once the brothers heard each other's pain and needs as revealed through the role-playing. If I had waited for both of them to tell their stories, the resolution would have taken much longer.

When relying on this method, I periodically turn to the person whose role I'm playing, addressing them as "my director" to see how I am doing. For a while I thought I had acting talent because of how often I find them crying and saying, "That's exactly what I've been trying to say!" However, when I started training others in role-playing, I now know that any of us can do it as long as we are in touch with our own needs. No matter what else is going on, we all have the same needs. Needs are universal.

I sometimes work with people who have been raped or tortured and where the perpetrator is absent, I would assume their role.

第十一章　化解冲突，调和纷争

个儿子为了财产分配陷入了剧烈争吵。两人虽然都住在农场的一端，彼此距离很近，但已经有8年不曾交谈了。我会见了这对兄弟以及他们的妻子和姐妹。8年来，所有人都卷入这桩复杂的法律纠纷，非常痛苦。

为了让调解工作取得进展，并且不耽误我的工作坊，我不得不加快调解的进程。为了不让他们再花时间重复同样的故事，我便问其中一位兄弟是否可以先来扮演他，然后我再来扮演另一位兄弟。

在角色扮演过程中，我开玩笑地问他们，是否可以请"导演"看看我演得对不对。出乎我的意料，我看见了那位我所扮演的兄弟已泪流满面。我猜我的角色扮演让他得以深深地同理自己，并且终于体会到兄弟的痛苦。第二天，他们的父亲双目含泪地告诉我，昨晚，他们全家一起出去吃了晚饭，这是8年来的第一次。这场纷争旷日持久，双方的律师都无法让彼此达成共识，但当两兄弟在角色扮演中真正听见彼此的苦痛与需要后，冲突终于迎刃而解。如果我当时任由他们各自讲述自己的立场，调解过程就会冗长得多。

我在进行角色扮演时，会时不时地转向我所扮演的人（我称他们为"导演"），看看他们认为我演得如何。我甚至一度认为我有表演天赋，因为我经常都会看见他们流泪，并对我说："这就是我一直想要说的话。"但后来，当我开始指导别人角色扮演后，便明白了只要能和自己的需要连结，任何人都可以做到。这是因为，无论具体发生的事情是什么，我们的需要是共通的。

有时我会辅导一些曾经被强暴或遭受过暴力折磨的人。当迫害者不在场时，我会扮演他们的角色。那些受害者时常会惊讶地听到我在角色扮演时说的话与迫害者说过的话不谋而合，他们会追问我："你是怎

Oftentimes the victim is surprised to hear me in the role-play saying the same thing they had heard from their perpetrator, and press me with the question, "But how did you know?" I believe the answer to that question is that I know because I am that person. And so are we all. As we apply a literacy of feelings and needs, we are not thinking about the issues, but simply putting ourselves in the other person's shoes, trying to be that person. "Getting the part right" is not in our thoughts, although from time to time we check in with the "director" because we don't always get it right. Nobody gets it right all the time, and that's fine. If we're off the mark, the person whom we are playing will let us know one way or another. We are thus offered another opportunity to make a closer guess.

> **Role-play is simply putting ourselves in the other person's shoes.**

Interrupting

Sometimes mediations get heated, with people shouting at or talking over one another. To keep the process on track under such circumstances, we need to get comfortable with interrupting. Once when I was mediating in Israel, and having a difficult time because my translator was too polite, I finally taught him to be nasty: "Shut them up!," I instructed. "Tell them to wait until we at least get the translation out before they go back to screaming at each other." So when both sides are screaming or talking at the same time, I insert myself: *"Excuse me, excuse me, excuse me!"* I repeat this as loudly and as often as necessary until I regain their attention.

When we are grabbing their attention, we have to be quick. If the person reacts with anger when we interrupt, we can sense that they are in too much pain to hear us. This is the time for emergency first-aid empathy. Here is what it might sound like, using an example from a business meeting.

Speaker: This happens all the time! They've already called three meetings, and each time there is some new rationale as to why it can't be done. Last time they

第十一章　化解冲突，调和纷争

么知道的？"我相信我之所以知道，是因为我就是那个迫害者——事实上，我们每一个人都是。在角色扮演时，我们不是去思考导致冲突的那些问题，而只是试着站在当事人所处的情景里，设身处地揣摩他们的感受和需要。尽管我们会时不时地与"导演"核实情况，我们并不一定总能把话说对，但我们的目的不在于"正确扮演角色"。没有人可以永远演得对，这并没有关系。如果演得有所偏离，角色扮演的对象会以某种方式让我们知道，我们也因此多了一个机会猜得更准确一些。

7. 打断

在调解过程中，当事人的情绪有时会变得十分激烈，彼此大声咆哮或抢着发言。在这种情况下，为了让调解过程得以顺利进行，我们必须勇于打断他们。有一次我在以色列做调解，我遇到的困难是，我的翻译太有礼貌了。后来我终于教会他如何说狠话："让他们住嘴！让他们至少等到你把我的话翻译完后再来对骂！"因此，每当他们相互叫嚣或在同一时间发言时，我就会打断他们："请听我说！请听我说！请听我说！"我会大声地说上几遍，直到我把他们的注意力拉回来。

一旦把他们的注意力拉回来，调解人就需要赶紧行动。如果一个人因为被打断而生气，我们也可以感受到那个人之所以无法听见我们，是因为内心带着太多痛苦。这时候就需要我们展开"急救式同理"。以下是在一场商务会议中进行这个过程的例子。

讲述者：每次都是这样！他们已经开了3次会，但每次都有新的理由来
　　　　解释他们为什么做不到。上回他们甚至还签署了协议！现在又

11 Conflict Resolution and Mediation

even signed an agreement! Now another promise and it will be just that: another promise! There's little point in working with people who . . .

Mediator: Excuse me, excuse me, EXCUSE ME! Could you tell me back what the other person said?

Speaker: *(realizing he had not listened to what had been said)* No!

Mediator: So you're feeling so full of distrust right now and really need some trust that people will do what they say?

Speaker: Well, of course but . . .

Mediator: So could you tell me what you heard them say? Let me repeat it for you. I hear the other side saying they have a real need for integrity. Could you just say it back so I'm sure we all understand each other?

Speaker: *(silence)*

Mediator: No? Then let me say it again.

And we say it again.

We might view our role as that of a translator—translating each party's message so as to be understood by the other. I ask them to get used to my interrupting for the sake of resolving the conflict. When I do interrupt, I also check that the speaker feels that I'm translating them accurately. I translate many messages even if I am only guessing, but the speaker is always the final authority on the accuracy of my translation.

> **The purpose of interrupting is to restore the process.**

It's important to remember that the purpose of interrupting and grabbing people's attention back in this way is to restore the process of making observations, identifying and expressing feelings, connecting feelings with needs, and making doable requests using clear, concrete, positive action language.

第十一章　化解冲突，调和纷争

提出了新的保证，事情还是老样子，然后再来做一个保证！和这些人一起工作实在没有任何意义……

调解者：请听我说，请听我说，请听我说（声音渐大）！你可不可以告诉我，对方说了什么？

讲述者：（意识到自己并没有注意对方说的话）不！

调解者：所以你现在是不是失去了信任，很希望能够相信他们会说话算话？

讲述者：那当然，可是……

调解者：那你可以告诉我你听到他们说了什么吗？我来和你重复一下。我听到对方说，他们希望坦诚相待。你可以告诉他们你听到的吗，以便我能确定你们理解了彼此？

讲述者：（默不作声）

调解者：不行吗？那我再说一遍。

我们再来说一遍。

作为调解人，我们可以将这个角色视为翻译者：翻译一方说的话让另一方得以理解。我还会告诉人们，为了化解冲突，我会打断他们的话，请他们接受这样的方式。当我打断讲话时，我会和讲述者确认是否把他们的意思准确"翻译"出来了。我会"翻译"许多信息，有时是通过揣测，但要判定我的翻译是否准确，只有讲述者本人才能说了算。

我们务必要记住，打断讲话以及拉回注意力的目的是让人们重新回到非暴力沟通的过程中：做出观察，辨识并表达出自己的感受，将感受和需要相连，并以明晰、具体、正向的行动语言来提出可行的请求。

When People Say "No" to Meeting Face to Face

I am optimistic about what can happen when we bring people together to express their needs and requests. However, one of the biggest problems I've encountered is simply getting access to both parties. Because it occasionally takes time for a party to become clear about its own needs, mediators require adequate access in order for both parties to express, and then receive each other's needs. Oftentimes, what we hear from someone in conflict is: "No, there's no use talking—they won't listen. I've tried to talk and it doesn't work."

To solve this problem I've sought strategies to resolve conflicts where people in conflict are unwilling to meet. One method that shows promising results relies on the use of an audio recorder. I work with each party separately while playing the role of the other side. If there are two people in our own lives who are in too much pain to be willing to meet, this would be an option for us to consider.

As an example, a woman was suffering heavily from a conflict with her husband, particularly from the way he was directing anger toward her. First, I listened in a way that supported her to clearly express her needs and to experience being received with respectful understanding. Then, I took on the role of her husband, and asked her to listen to me as I expressed what I guessed to be the husband's needs.

The needs of the conflicting parties having been clearly conveyed in this role-play, I asked the woman to share the recording with her husband for his reaction.

Because I had, in this case, been accurate in guessing the husband's needs, he experienced huge relief when listening to the recording. With the increased trust that came from hearing himself understood, he later agreed to come in so we could work together until the two of them found ways of meeting their needs in mutually respectful ways.

When the hardest thing about resolving a conflict is getting the parties together in the same room, the use of recorded role-plays may be the answer.

第十一章　化解冲突，调和纷争

当人们不愿意面对面对话

我相信，若能设法安排冲突双方会面，相互表达需要和请求，冲突解决便会有希望。然而，一大挑战就是让双方碰面。我们时常会听到冲突中的一方这样说："不，对话起不了作用，他们不会听的。我已经都试过了，根本没用！"因为有时人们需要好一段时间才能厘清自己的需要，调解人须在前期花很大力气接触当事人，让他们表达出自己的需要，并了解对方的需要。

为了解决这个问题，我想了一些办法，让不愿意会面的当事人也能化解他们之间的冲突。一个效果不错的方法是借助录音设备。我会分别与一方一起工作，在这个过程中我扮演另一方。如果两个人之间因为冲突带来的痛苦太大而避而不见，就可以采用这个方法。

例如，有位女士和丈夫之间发生了一次严重的冲突，尤其让她感到痛苦的是丈夫将自己的怒气发泄到她身上。我从聆听她的心声开始，鼓励她明确地表达自己的需要，并让她体会受到尊重和被听见。接着，我扮演她丈夫的角色，邀请她来聆听我，揣测他可能有什么需要。

当双方的需要在角色扮演中被明确表达出来后，我请这位女士把记录这个过程的录音分享给她丈夫，看他有何反应。

由于我准确猜出了先生的需要，他在聆听录音时如释重负，因此他对我的信任度有了很大的提升。于是他同意了会面，我们得以面对面一起沟通，直到夫妻两人以相互尊重的态度，找到了满足双方需要的解决方式。

Informal Mediation: Sticking Our Nose in Other People's Business

Informal mediation is a polite way to refer to mediating in situations where we've not been invited to do so. In so many words, we're sticking our nose in other people's business.

I was shopping in a grocery store one day when I saw a woman strike her toddler. She was about to do it again when I jumped in. She didn't ask, "Marshall, would you mediate between us?" Another time I was walking in the streets of Paris; a woman was walking alongside me when a rather inebriated man ran up from behind, turned her around, and slapped her in the face. As there wasn't time for me to talk with this man, I resorted to the protective use of force by restraining him just as he was about to strike her again. I inserted myself between the two, and stuck my nose in their business. On another occasion, during a business meeting, I watched two factions in a repetitious exchange, arguing back and forth over an age-old issue and again I stuck my nose in between them.

When we witness behaviors that raise concern in us—unless it is a situation that calls for the protective use of force as described in Chapter 12—the first thing we do is to empathize with the needs of the person who is behaving in the way we dislike. In the first situation, if we wanted to see *more* violence directed at the toddler, we could, instead of offering empathy to the mother, say something to imply that she was wrong to hit the child. Such a response on our part would only escalate the situation.

> We need to be well practiced at hearing the need in any message.

In order to be truly helpful to people in whose business we are sticking our nose we need to have developed an extensive literacy regarding needs, and be well practiced at hearing the need in any message, including the need underneath the act of slapping another person. And we need to be practiced in verbal empathy such that the people sense that we are connected with their need.

第十一章 化解冲突，调和纷争

要解决冲突却又很难让双方碰面的话，将角色扮演的过程录下来，或许可以解决问题。

多管闲事的非正式调解

我们有时会在未受邀的情况下径自为他人调解纠纷，含蓄的说法是"非正式调解"，说得直白一些，就是在管他人的闲事。

有一天我在一间杂货铺买东西，看到一位女士在打她一两岁大的孩子。正当她准备再次动手时，我插手了。还有一次，我走在巴黎的街上，突然有一个看起来喝得醉醺醺的男人从后面冲上来，一把抓住走在我旁边的女人，将她转过身，然后打了她一个耳光。那个瞬间，我并没有时间和这个男人说话，于是我使用了"保护性强制力"（详见第十二章），在他即将再度动手时制止了他。我将自己安插在他们俩中间，开始管起了他们的事。还有一次在一场商务会议中，看到两拨人为一件陈年旧事反复争论不休，我忍不住又管了一次人家的闲事。

当目睹那些引发我们担忧的行为时，除非是需要采取"保护性强制力"的特殊情况，我们首先要做的是去同理他们——倾听让我们不喜欢的行为背后有什么样的需要。第一个例子中，我们如果不去同理那位母亲，而是以言语暗示她"打孩子是不对的"，我们就有可能看到带着不满的母亲将更多的暴力施加给这个孩子。没有同理的回应只能使情况恶化。

为了在管闲事时能真正帮助到他人，我们有必要对当事人的需要有

11 Conflict Resolution and Mediation

We need to remember, when we choose to stick our nose in someone's business, it's not enough to simply support someone to get in touch with his or her own needs. We aim to practice all the other steps covered in this chapter. For example, after empathizing, we may tell the toddler's mother that we care about safety and have a need to protect people, and then request her willingness to try another strategy to meet her need with her child.

We refrain, however, from mentioning our own needs regarding the person's behavior until it is clear to them that we understand and care about *his or her* needs. Otherwise people will not care about our needs nor will they see that their needs and ours are one and the same. As expressed so beautifully by Alice Walker in *The Color Purple*: "One day when I was sitting quiet and feeling like a motherless child, which I was, it come to me: that feeling of being part of everything, not separate at all. I knew that if I cut a tree, my arm would bleed."

Unless we make sure that both sides are aware of their own as well as each other's needs, it will be hard for us to succeed when we stick our nose in other people's business. We are likely to get caught up in scarcity thinking—seeing only the importance of our own needs being met. When scarcity thinking then gets mixed with right-and-wrong thinking, any of us can become militant and violent, and blinded to even the most obvious solutions. At that point, the conflict seems unresolvable—and it will be if we don't connect with the other person by first offering empathy without focusing on our own needs.

Summary

The use of NVC to resolve conflict differs from traditional mediation methods; instead of deliberating over issues, strategies, and means of compromise, we concentrate foremost on identifying the needs of both parties, and only then seek strategies to fulfill those needs.

We start by forging a human connection between the parties in conflict. Then we ensure that both parties have the opportunity to fully express their needs, that they carefully

第十一章 化解冲突，调和纷争

充分的了解，并且娴熟地在任何信息背后听见需要，包括打别人耳光的行为。同时，我们要练习用语言表达同理心，让他人感受到我们明白他们的需要。

我们还要记住，若选择了去管他人闲事，仅仅帮助他们和自己的需要连结是不够的，还要用上本章所提到的所有步骤。比如，在同理了那个打小孩的妈妈后，可以告诉她，我们在意孩子的安全，希望孩子受到保护，然后再请问她是否愿意尝试其他的策略来满足她在管教孩子方面的需要。

另外，在对方尚未明白我们理解并在乎他们的需要前，我们要避免提及我们自己（与对方行为有关）的需要。因为，这时的他们并不会在乎我们的需要，也看不到他们和我们的需要是共通的。艾丽斯·沃克（Alice Walker）在《紫色姐妹花》一书中十分美妙地写道："有一天我静静地坐在那儿，感觉自己像是一个没妈的小孩——我的母亲确实已经过世了。我突然有一种感觉：我是万事万物的一部分，没有任何的分离。我知道，如果我砍了一棵树，我的手臂也将会流血。"

除非我们能确定冲突中的双方明白了自己和对方的需要，否则，我们的多管闲事就很难达到化解冲突的目标。因为我们很有可能陷入一种匮乏思维，只看得到满足我们自己的需要才是重要的。当匮乏思维和是非对错的思维绑在一起时，任何人都可能变得好勇斗狠，哪怕是最显而易见的解决方案也无法看见。至此，冲突似乎也会变得难以化解，除非我们能先同理对方，借此和对方建立连结，而不只是关注自己的需要。

listen to the other person's needs, and that once the needs have been heard, they clearly express doable action steps to meet those needs. We avoid judging or analyzing the conflict and instead remain focused on needs.

When one party is in too much pain to hear the needs of the other, we extend empathy, taking as long as necessary to ensure that the person knows their pain is heard. We do not hear "no" as a rejection but rather as an expression of the need that is keeping the person from saying "yes." Only after all needs have been mutually heard, do we progress to the solutions stage: making doable requests using positive, action language.

When we assume the role of mediating a conflict between two other parties, the same principles apply. In addition, we keep careful track of progress, extend empathy where needed, keep the conversation focused on the present, moving it forward, and interrupting where necessary to return to the process.

With these tools and understanding, we can practice and help others resolve even long-standing conflicts to their mutual satisfaction.

第十一章 化解冲突，调和纷争

小结

使用非暴力沟通来化解冲突与传统的调解方法不同。我们不去讨论事件本身、策略和妥协之道，而是首先集中注意力找到双方的需要，然后再寻求策略满足那些需要。

一开始，我们会先让冲突中的双方建立连结；然后确保双方都有机会充分表达自己的需要并且也能仔细聆听对方的需要；一旦人们听见彼此的需要，就让他们清楚地提出可行的步骤来满足那些需要。我们要避免对冲突做出判断或分析，而始终关注在需要上。

当有一方太过痛苦以至于无法聆听另一方的需要时，我们要花足够的时间同理他们，直到他们确认了自己的痛苦已经被听到。此外，当别人对我们的请求说"不"时，我们听到的不是对我们的拒绝，而是对方正在告诉我们——因为某个需要阻碍了他们对我们的请求说"是"。只有当双方充分聆听了彼此所有的需要后，我们才能进入解决方案阶段，引导双方使用正向的"行动语言"来提出可行的请求。

当我们为两个冲突的人群化解纠纷时，以上这些原则同样适用。此外，我们还要格外密切地追踪进程，在必要的时候给予同理，让对话聚焦于当下，推动对话的进程而不在原地打转，并适时打断讲述者的发言，以让人们回到调解的轨道上来。

有了这些方法和观念，我们就可以协助他人用非暴力沟通来化解冲突，即使是经年累月的冲突也能得以解决，直至皆大欢喜。

11 Conflict Resolution and Mediation

The key to fostering connection in the face of a "no" is always "yes" to something else and, as such, it is the beginning, not the end of a conversation. Hear the "Yes" behind the "No".

第十二章

为了保护使用强制力

The Protective Use of Force

When the Use of Force Is Unavoidable

When two disputing parties have each had an opportunity to fully express what they are observing, feeling, needing, and requesting—and each has empathized with the other—a resolution can usually be reached that meets the needs of both sides. At the very least, the two can agree, in goodwill, to disagree.

In some situations, however, the opportunity for such dialogue may not exist, and the use of force may be necessary to protect life or individual rights. For instance, the other party may be unwilling to communicate, or imminent danger may not allow time for communication. In these situations, we may need to resort to force. If we do, NVC requires us to differentiate between the protective and the punitive uses of force.

The Thinking Behind the Use of Force

The intention behind the protective use of force is to prevent injury or injustice. The intention behind the punitive use of force is to cause individuals to suffer for their perceived misdeeds. When we grab a child who is running into the street to prevent the child from being injured, we are applying protective force. The punitive use of force, on the other hand, might involve physical or psychological attack, such as spanking the child or saying, "How could you be so stupid! You should be ashamed of yourself!"

第十二章　为了保护使用强制力

当冲突双方充分表达了各自的观察、感受、需要和请求，并同理了对方，他们通常就能找到满足双方需要的解决方案。就算不认同对方，也保有善意和尊重。

然而，在有些情况下，双方没有机会进行这样的对话，例如，对方可能不愿意沟通，或是危险迫在眉睫来不及沟通。这时，为了保护生命或捍卫权益，我们就需要采取强制力。发生这样的情况时，务必区分使用强制力的目的是为了保护还是惩罚。

采取强制力背后的思考

采取"保护性强制力"的出发点是为了防止人们受伤或受到不公平的待遇，而采取"惩罚性强制力"则是为了让"做错事"的人吃苦头。例如，我们一把抓住正要冲向马路的孩子，以免孩子受伤，这就是采取"保护性强制力"。相反，如果我们动手打孩子或对孩子说"你怎么这么笨！你真是太丢脸了"，那就是在采取"惩罚性强制力"。

在采取"保护性强制力"时，我们关注的是对生命或权益的保护，

12 The Protective Use of Force

> The intention behind the protective use of force is only to protect, not to punish, blame, or condemn.

When we exercise the protective use of force, we are focusing on the life or rights we want to protect, without passing judgment on either the person or the behavior. We are not blaming or condemning the child who rushes into the street; our thinking is solely directed toward protecting the child from danger. (For application of this kind of force in social and political conflicts, see Robert Irwin's book, *Building a Peace System*.) The assumption behind the protective use of force is that people behave in ways injurious to themselves and others due to some form of ignorance. The corrective process is therefore one of education, not punishment. Ignorance includes (1) a lack of awareness of the consequences of our actions, (2) an inability to see how our needs may be met without injury to others, (3) the belief that we have the right to punish or hurt others because they "deserve" it, and (4) delusional thinking that involves, for example, hearing a voice that instructs us to kill someone.

Punitive action, on the other hand, is based on the assumption that people commit offenses because they are bad or evil, and to correct the situation, they need to be made to repent. Their "correction" is undertaken through punitive action designed to make them (1) suffer enough to see the error of their ways, (2) repent, and (3) change. In practice, however, punitive action, rather than evoking repentance and learning, is just as likely to generate resentment and hostility and to reinforce resistance to the very behavior we are seeking.

Types of Punitive Force

Physical punishment, such as spanking, is one punitive use of force. I have found the subject of corporal punishment to provoke strong sentiments among parents. Some adamantly defend the practice, referring to the Bible: "Spare the rod, spoil the child. It's because parents don't spank that delinquency is now rampant." They are persuaded that spanking our children shows that we

第十二章　为了保护使用强制力

而不论断他人及其行为。我们不会指责那个要冲上马路的孩子，而只是想保护他。采取"保护性强制力"背后的假设是，人们之所以做出伤害自己或他人的行为是出于无知。所谓的"无知"包括：（1）对行为的后果缺乏意识；（2）认识不到可以用不伤害他人的方式来满足自己的需要；（3）认为自己有权利惩罚或伤害他人，因为他们"罪有应得"；（4）妄想，例如，听到"某种声音"指示自己去杀人。对此，我们需要通过教育来纠正他们，而非惩罚。

相反，"惩罚性强制力"背后的假设是：人们做出不当行为是因为他们是坏的或邪恶的，为了纠正这种行为，必须通过惩罚使他们有所悔改，让他们：（1）吃足苦头，从而认清自己的过错；（2）对所作所为后悔；（3）改变行为。然而实际上，惩罚非但不能让人悔改和学习，反而会引发仇恨和敌意，并对他人所期待的改变心生抗拒。

惩罚性强制力的种类

体罚（例如打屁股）是常见的惩罚性强制力。我发现，家长们对此有截然不同的看法。有的家长坚决维护体罚，甚至引用《圣经》中的说法："不打不成才。父母不对孩子棍棒相加，会让世风日下。"他们相信体罚孩子、树立清晰的规则是爱孩子的表现。另一些家长则坚持，体罚是无爱和无效的，反而教会了孩子这样一种观念：当所有的方法都行不通时，可以诉诸肢体暴力来解决问题。

我的担忧是，孩子可能会因为害怕体罚而难以体会在父母要求背后的爱。家长们时常告诉我，他们"不得不"惩罚孩子，因为没有其他办

love them by setting clear boundaries. Other parents are equally insistent that spanking is unloving and ineffective because it teaches children that, when all else fails, we can always resort to physical violence.

My personal concern is that children's fear of corporal punishment may obscure their awareness of the compassion that underlies parental demands. Parents often tell me that they "have to" use punitive force because they see no other way to influence their children to do "what's good for them." They support their opinion with anecdotes of children expressing appreciation for "seeing the light" after having been punished. Having raised four children, I empathize deeply with parents regarding the daily challenges they face in educating children and keeping them safe. This does not, however, lessen my concern about the use of physical punishment.

> **Fear of corporal punishment obscures children's awareness of the compassion underlying their parents' demands.**

First, I wonder whether people who proclaim the successes of such punishment are aware of the countless instances of children who turn against what might be good for them simply because they choose to fight, rather than succumb, to coercion. Second, the apparent success of corporal punishment in influencing a child doesn't mean that other methods of influence wouldn't have worked equally well. Finally, I share the concerns of many parents about the social consequences of using physical punishment. When parents opt to use force, we may win the battle of getting children to do what we want, but, in the process, are we not perpetuating a social norm that justifies violence as a means of resolving differences?

In addition to the physical, other uses of force also qualify as punishment. One is the use of blame to discredit another person; for example, a parent may label a child as "wrong," "selfish," or "immature" when a child doesn't behave in a certain way. Another form of punitive force is the withholding

> **Punishment also includes judgmental labeling and the withholding of privileges.**

第十二章 为了保护使用强制力

法让他们去做家长们认为"对孩子有好处的事"。为了支持他们的观点，有的父母甚至提到有些孩子在受罚后终于"明白了道理"，因而对父母表示感激。身为4个孩子的父亲，我深深理解为人父母的不易，父母们每天都要面临如何教育孩子和保护孩子安全的挑战。即使这样，对于体罚，我也深感疑虑。

首先，有无数的孩子拒绝去做那些在大人看来对他们有益的事情，他们故意选择反抗，为的就是不想屈服于父母的胁迫。其次，即使体罚看上去达到了影响孩子的效果，却并不意味着其他方法不会同样有效。最后，和许多家长一样，我很担心体罚孩子所带来的社会影响。惩罚或许可以让孩子暂时听话，但这样的选择难道不是在延续一种社会规范，认可了用暴力来解决分歧吗？

除了体罚，还有心理上的惩罚，那就是通过指责来羞辱人。例如，孩子若没有照家长的话去做，就可能被贴上"犯错""自私"或"不成熟"的标签。另外一种惩罚方式是拒绝满足孩子，例如限制零花钱或取消做某些事的权利（诸如开车），父母用这样的方式拿走对孩子的关爱或尊重，可谓是最强有力的威胁。

惩罚的代价

如果纯粹为了免受惩罚而去做事情，我们就会关注如果不这样做会带来的后果上，并为此焦虑担忧，却忽略了事情本身的价值。如果员工为了担心处罚而工作，那么，即使任务完成了，士气也会受到影响，迟早，工作的效率也会下降。惩罚还会削弱人的自尊。假如孩子刷牙是因

of some means of gratification, such as parents' curtailing allowances or driving privileges. In this vein, the withdrawal of caring or respect is one of the most powerful threats of all.

The Costs of Punishment

When we submit to doing something solely for the purpose of avoiding punishment, our attention is distracted from the value of the action itself. Instead, we are focusing upon the consequences, on what might happen if we fail to take that action. If a worker's performance is prompted by fear of punishment, the job gets done, but morale suffers; sooner or later, productivity will decrease. Self-esteem is also diminished when punitive force is used. If children brush their teeth because they fear shame and ridicule, their oral health may improve but their self-respect will develop cavities. Furthermore, as we all know, punishment is costly in terms of goodwill. The more we are seen as agents of punishment, the harder it is for others to respond compassionately to our needs.

> When we fear punishment, we focus on consequences, not on our own values.
>
> Fear of punishment diminishes self-esteem and goodwill.

I was visiting a friend, a school principal, at his office when he noticed through the window a big child hitting a smaller one. "Excuse me," he said as he leapt up and rushed to the playground. Grabbing the larger child, he gave him a swat and scolded, "I'll teach you not to hit smaller people!" When the principal returned inside, I remarked, "I don't think you taught that child what you thought you were teaching him. I suspect what he learned instead was not to hit people smaller than he is when somebody bigger—like the principal—might be watching! If anything, it seems to me that you have reinforced the notion that the way to get what you want from somebody else is to hit them."

In such situations, I recommend first empathizing with the child who is behaving violently. For example, if I saw a child hit someone after being called a name, I might empathize,

第十二章　为了保护使用强制力

为担心丢脸或被嘲笑，那么，即使口腔健康了，自尊心却被蛀食。此外，惩罚还会磨灭善意，人们越是将我们视为惩罚者，就越难对我们的需要做出善意的回应。

有一次，我去拜访一位担任小学校长的朋友。在谈话时，他透过办公室的窗户看到一个大个子孩子正在打一个小个子孩子。立刻，他就跳起来，边对我说着"抱歉"边冲向操场。然后，他跑过去一把抓住那个大个子孩子，重重地推了他一下，训斥道："我要教会你不许欺负比你小的同学！"校长回到办公室后，我对他说："我不认为那个孩子会明白你想教他的道理。我猜他学到的是：在打比他弱小的人时，要注意是否会被比他强大的人（比如校长）看到。在我看来，你的做法在他心中强化了使用拳头来让人顺服的观念。"

在上述情形下，我建议首先同理那个动手的孩子。例如，如果看到一个孩子在遭到辱骂后动手打人，我可能会对这个孩子说："我知道你很生气，因为你希望得到尊重。"如果孩子肯定了我的猜测，我会接着表达我的感受、需要和请求，而不带任何的指责："我觉得有些难过，因为我希望我们既能得到尊重又不树敌。你是否愿意和我一起找到一些别的方法使你得到尊重呢？"

惩罚的局限

有两个提问可以帮助我们认识，为何惩罚无法让我们如愿地改变他人的行为。第一个提问是：我希望这个人在行为上做出什么样的改变？如果只问这个问题，惩罚看起来似乎是有效的，因为威胁或惩罚确实可

"I'm sensing that you're feeling angry because you'd like to be treated with more respect." If I guessed correctly, and the child acknowledges this to be true, I would then continue by expressing my own feelings, needs, and requests in the situation without insinuating blame: "I'm feeling sad because I want us to find ways to get respect that don't turn people into enemies. I'd like you to tell me if you'd be willing to explore with me some other ways to get the respect you're wanting."

Two Questions That Reveal the Limitations of Punishment

Two questions help us see why we are unlikely to get what we want by using punishment to change people's behavior. The first question is: *What do I want this person to do that's different from what he or she is currently doing?* If we ask only this first question, punishment may seem effective, because the threat or exercise of punitive force may well influence someone's behavior. However, with the second question, it becomes evident that punishment isn't likely to work: *What do I want this person's reasons to be for doing what I'm asking?*

We seldom address the latter question, but when we do, we soon realize that punishment and reward interfere with people's ability to do things motivated by the reasons we'd like them to have. I believe it is critical to be aware of the importance of people's reasons for behaving as we request. For example, blaming or punishing would obviously not be effective strategies if we want children to clean their rooms out of either a desire for order or a desire to contribute to their parents' enjoyment of order. Often children clean their rooms motivated by obedience to authority ("Because my Mom said so"), avoidance of punishment, or fear of upsetting or being rejected by parents. NVC, however, fosters a level of moral development based on autonomy and interdependence, whereby we acknowledge responsibility for our

> Question 1: What do I want this person to do?
>
> Question 2: What do I want this person's reasons to be for doing it?

第十二章　为了保护使用强制力

以对他人的行为产生影响。然而，通过第二个问题——这个人是因为什么原因才照着我的话去做，我们就可以清楚地看到惩罚的局限性了。

我们很少关注第二个问题，借助这个问题我们会意识到：奖励或惩罚让他人的行为背离了我们的初衷。例如，如果我们希望孩子是出于爱整洁或让父母轻松来打扫房间，指责或惩罚显然不是有效的策略。常见的情形是，孩子打扫房间是为了服从父母的权威（"因为妈妈叫我这么做"）、避免惩罚、不想惹爸妈生气或被他们冷落。然而，非暴力沟通所要培养的道德意识是建立在自主和人与人相互依存的基础上，我们既为自己的行为负责，也需要明白自己与他人的福祉是一体且无分别的。

在校园使用保护性强制力

接下来，我想讲述我是如何与一所体制外学校的学生们以保护性强制力恢复校园秩序的。这所学校专门收容那些从体制内的学校辍学或被开除的学生。校方和我希望能用非暴力沟通的方式和这些学生沟通。我的工作是培训教职员工，并担任顾问一年。由于只有4天时间来培训教师，我没有充分说明非暴力沟通和放任不管之间的区别。结果，在出现冲突和扰乱秩序的行为时，有些老师选择了回避，并未加以干预。校园秩序也因而越来越混乱，以致校方几乎要将学校关闭。

此时，我向校方提出请求，希望和那些带来最多麻烦的学生交谈。校长挑选了8位年龄在11至14岁间的男孩。以下是我和学生们会谈的摘录。

own actions and are aware that our own well-being and that of others are one and the same.

The Protective Use of Force in Schools

I'd like to describe how some students and I used protective force to bring order into a chaotic situation at an alternative school. This school was designed for students who had dropped out or been expelled from conventional classrooms. The administration and I hoped to demonstrate that a school based on the principles of NVC would be able to reach these students. My job was to train the faculty in NVC and serve as consultant over the year. With only four days to prepare the faculty, I was unable to sufficiently clarify the difference between NVC and permissiveness. As a result, some teachers were ignoring, rather than intervening in, situations of conflict and disturbing behavior. Besieged by increasing pandemonium, the administrators were nearly ready to shut down the school.

When I requested to talk with the students who had contributed most to the turbulence, the principal selected eight boys, ages eleven to fourteen, to meet with me. The following are excerpts from the dialogue I had with the students.

> MBR: *(expressing my feeling and needs without asking probing questions)* I'm very upset about the teachers' reports that things are getting out of hand in many of the classes. I want very much for this school to be successful. I'm hopeful that you can help me understand what the problems are and what can be done about them.
> Will: The teachers in this school—they fools, man!
> MBR: Are you saying, Will, that you are disgusted with the teachers and you want them to change some things they do?
> Will: No, man, they is fools because they just stand around and don't do nothin'.

第十二章　为了保护使用强制力

马歇尔：（单纯表达我的感受和需要，而不追问事情的始末）听到老师们说，许多班级的教学工作无法正常进行，我感到很不安。我非常希望学校能够继续办下去。希望你们可以帮助我了解学校中存在的问题以及应对的办法。

威　尔：这个学校的老师都太蠢了！

马歇尔：威尔，你的意思是你对老师们感到不满，希望他们改变做事的方式对吗？

威　尔：不，老兄，我说他们很蠢是因为他们就只是站在那里，什么都不做。

马歇尔：你的意思是你感到不满，因为你希望在出现问题时，他们能做些什么？（再次尝试体会他的感受和需要。）

威　尔：是的，老兄。不管谁做了什么事，他们就像白痴一样站在那里傻笑。

马歇尔：可以给我举个例子吗？

威　尔：这很容易。今天早上，有个家伙在裤子后面的口袋里装了一瓶威士忌酒，大摇大摆地走进了教室，所有人都看见了，老师也看见了，但她却装作什么也没发生。

马歇尔：听起来，你不想尊重那些不作为的老师，你希望他们能做点什么，是吗？（我继续尝试充分理解他。）

威　尔：正是！

马歇尔：我有些失望，因为我希望老师们能够和学生一起解决问题，但听上去我没能让他们明白我的意思。

接着，讨论转向了另一个迫切的问题：那些不想学习的学生干扰了

12 The Protective Use of Force

MBR: You mean you're disgusted because you want them to do more when problems happen. *(This is a second attempt to receive the feelings and wants.)*

Will: That's right, man. No matter what anybody do they just stand there smilin' like fools.

MBR: Would you be willing to give me an example of how the teachers do nothing?

Will: Easy. Just this morning a dude walks in wearin' a bottle of Wild Turkey on his hip pocket plain as day. Everybody seen it; the teacher, she seen it but she's lookin' the other way.

MBR: It sounds to me, then, that you don't have respect for the teachers when they stand around doing nothing. You'd like them to do something. *(This is a continued attempt to fully understand.)*

Will: Yeah.

MBR: I feel disappointed because I want them to be able to work things out with students, but it sounds like I wasn't able to show them what I meant.

The discussion then turned to one particularly pressing problem: that of students who didn't want to work disturbing those who did.

MBR: I'm anxious to try to solve this problem because the teachers tell me it's the one that bothers them the most. I would appreciate your sharing whatever ideas you have with me.

Joe: The teacher got to get a rattan *(a stick covered with leather that was carried by some principals in St. Louis to administer corporal punishment)*.

MBR: So you're saying, Joe, that you want the teachers to hit students when they bother others.

Joe: That's the only way students gonna stop playing the fool.

MBR: *(still trying to receive Joe's feelings)* So you doubt that any other way would work.

第十二章 为了保护使用强制力

想要学习的学生。

马歇尔:我迫切地想要解决这个问题,老师们告诉我这是最让他们头疼的问题。我非常希望你能和我分享一些建议。

乔:老师应该带根棍子。(圣路易市的一些校长会随身携带绑有皮带的棍子,用来体罚学生。)

马歇尔:乔,你的意思是,如果有人干扰别人学习,老师就给他一棍子?

乔:只有这样,学生们才会停止胡闹。

马歇尔:(仍然试着体会乔的感受)所以你不相信有其他的解决办法?

乔:(点头表示同意)

马歇尔:如果这是唯一的方式,我会觉得很灰心。我希望我们能找到别的解决办法。

艾 德:为什么?

马歇尔:有几个原因。假如我用棍子教训你们不许在学校胡闹,请你告诉我,被我打过的几个学生会在我下班回家时怎么对付我?

艾 德:(笑)那你最好带根大点的棍子。

马歇尔:(确信双方已相互理解,我不再复述他的话,而是继续表达)这正是我的意思。我希望你能看到,用这样的方式来解决问题让我不安。我不会总是记得要带一根大棍子,就算我记得,我也不想用它来打任何人。

艾 德:那就把他们踢出去。

马歇尔:艾德,你的意思是希望学校让那些学生们停课或开除他们?

艾 德:是的!

12 The Protective Use of Force

Joe: *(nods agreement)*

MBR: I'm discouraged if that's the only way. I hate that way of settling things and want to learn other ways.

Ed: Why?

MBR: Several reasons. Like if I get you to stop horsing around in school by using the rattan, I'd like you to tell me what happens if three or four of you that I've hit in class are out by my car when I go home.

Ed: *(smiling)* Then you better have a big stick, man!

MBR: *(Feeling certain I understood Ed's message and certain he knew I understood, I continue without paraphrasing it.)* That's what I mean. I'd like you to see I'm bothered about that way of settling things. I'm too absentminded to always remember to carry a big stick, and even if I remembered, I would hate to hit someone with it.

Ed: You could kick the cat out of school.

MBR: You're suggesting, Ed, that you would like us to suspend or expel kids from the school?

Ed: Yeah.

MBR: I'm discouraged with that idea, too. I want to show that there are other ways of solving differences in school without kicking people out. I'd feel like a failure if that was the best we could do.

Will: If a dude ain't doin' nothin', how come you can't put him in a do-nothin' room?

MBR: Are you suggesting, Will, that you would like to have a room to send people to if they bother other students?

Will: That's right. No use they bein' in class if they ain't doin' nothin'.

MBR: I'm very interested in that idea. I'd like to hear how you think such a room might work.

Will: Sometimes you come to school and just feel evil: you don't want to do nothin'. So we just have a room students go to till they feel like doin' somethin'.

第十二章　为了保护使用强制力

马歇尔：我对这个想法也感到灰心。我希望有别的方式来解决冲突，而不用让任何一位同学离开。如果这是我们能想到的最佳方案，我会认为自己很失败。

威　尔：如果有谁不想学习，不如就让他待在一间可以什么都不做的教室。

马歇尔：威尔，你是说，我们能腾出一间教室，让不想学习的人有个去处，是吗？

威　尔：没错。既然他们不想学习，呆在教室里也没用啊。

马歇尔：我对这个点子很感兴趣。具体怎么操作呢？

威　尔：有的时候，你到了学校却心情糟糕，什么也不想做。这时，你就可以先去这个房间。直到你想上课了再回到自己班级。

马歇尔：我明白你的意思了。不过，老师们可能会担心，同学们是否会自愿去那个房间。

威　尔：（自信地说）他们会去的。

　　我对他们说，如果我们可以让同学们明白设置这个房间的目的不是为了惩罚，而是给暂时不想学习的同学提供一个去处，同时让愿意学习的同学专心上课，那这个计划就能行得通。我还建议让大家知道这个点子是学生们头脑风暴的结果，而非校方的规定，那这个方案会更加有可能取得成功。

　　于是，学校设置了这样一间教室，那些心情不好、不想上课或会影响其他人学习的学生们就可以去那里。有时，有的学生会主动去那里，有时老师会请学生过去。我们为这个教室安排了一位熟练掌握非暴力沟通的老师来管理。她和来这里的学生们开展了一些卓有成效的对话。这

MBR: I understand what you are saying, but I'm anticipating that the teacher will be concerned about whether the students will go willingly to the do-nothing room.

Will: *(confidently)* They'll go.

I said I thought the plan might work if we could show that the purpose was not to punish, but to provide a place to go for those who weren't ready to study, and simultaneously a chance to study for those who wanted to study. I also suggested that a do-nothing room would be more likely to succeed if it was known to be a product of student brainstorming rather than staff decree.

A do-nothing room was set up for students who were upset and didn't feel like doing schoolwork or whose behavior kept others from learning. Sometimes students asked to go; sometimes teachers asked students to go. We placed the teacher who had best mastered NVC in the do-nothing room, where she had some very productive talks with the children who came in. This set-up was an immense success in restoring order to the school because the students who devised it made its purpose clear to their peers: to protect the rights of students who wanted to learn. We used the dialogue with the students to demonstrate to the teachers that there were other means of resolving conflicts besides withdrawal from the conflict or using punitive force.

Summary

In situations where there is no opportunity for communication, such as in instances of imminent danger, we may need to resort to the protective use of force. The intention behind the protective use of force is to prevent injury or injustice, never to punish or to cause individuals to suffer, repent, or change. The punitive use of force tends to generate hostility and to reinforce resistance to the very behavior we are seeking. Punishment damages goodwill and self-esteem, and shifts our attention from the intrinsic value of an action to external consequences. Blaming and punishing fail to contribute to the motivations we would like to inspire in others.

第十二章 为了保护使用强制力

样的安排大大改善了学校的秩序，那些曾参加讨论的学生们向他们的同学表明了这个教室的目的是维护学习者的权益。我们也借由这件事向教师们展现了，除了回避冲突和实施处罚，还有别的方式来化解冲突。

小结

在有些没有机会沟通（例如危险迫在眉睫）的情况下，我们需要采取保护性强制力。这样做的目的是防止人们受到伤害或不公待遇，而不是为了惩罚他人或让他人难受、忏悔或改变。惩罚性强制力会让人产生敌意和抵触心理。惩罚还会伤害他人的善意和自尊，也会让我们只注意行为的外在后果，而忽视行为本身的价值。惩罚和指责也无法让他人按照我们所期望的理由来行动。

12 The Protective Use of Force

*Humanity
has been sleeping
—and still sleeps—
lulled within the
narrowly confining
joys of its
closed loves.*

—Pierre Teilhard de Chardin,
theologian and scientist

第十三章

解放自我,协助他人

> 人类以小爱为足,
> 沉睡在那有限的欢愉中,
> 至今仍未清醒。
> ——皮埃尔·特拉德,神学家、科学家

13

Liberating Ourselves and Counseling Others

Freeing Ourselves From Old Programming

We've all learned things that limit us as human beings, whether from well-intentioned parents, teachers, clergy, or others. Passed down through generations, even centuries, much of this destructive cultural learning is so ingrained in our lives that we are no longer conscious of it. In one of his routines, comedian Buddy Hackett, raised on his mother's rich cooking, claimed that he never realized it was possible to leave the table without feeling heartburn until he was in the army. In the same way, pain engendered by damaging cultural conditioning is such an integral part of our lives that we can no longer distinguish its presence. It takes tremendous energy and awareness to recognize this destructive learning and to transform it into thoughts and behaviors that are of value and of service to life.

This transformation requires a literacy of needs and the ability to get in touch with ourselves, both of which are difficult for people in our culture. Not only have we never been educated about our needs, we are often exposed to cultural training that actively blocks our consciousness of them. As mentioned earlier, we have inherited a language that served kings and powerful elites in domination societies. The masses, discouraged from developing awareness of their own needs, have instead been educated to be

第十三章　解放自我，协助他人

摆脱旧有模式的束缚

在成长过程中，我们从家长、老师、神职人员或其他人那里，或多或少习得了一些限制我们生命的教导，尽管他们是心怀好意。千百年来，这些有害的教导代代相传，许多已经根深蒂固，让人无从察觉。喜剧演员巴迪·哈克特在一次节目中谈到，他从小吃母亲烹饪的油腻食物长大，直到参军后才发现，原来吃完饭后肠胃还是可以保持轻松的。同样的，对于那些伤害性文化制约所带来的痛苦，我们也仿佛习以为常，甚至感觉不到痛苦的存在。要认清有害的习惯并将它们转化成对生命有益的认知和行为，需要我们投入巨大的努力和觉知。

要实现这样的转变，我们就要熟悉"需要"，并且有能力与自己的内心建立连结。在我们的文化中，要做到这两点是困难的。我们不仅从来没有学过"需要"的知识，我们的文化也往往不鼓励我们觉察需要，而是把"需要"看作消极、有害的。一个人有需要会被认为不够好或不成熟。当人们表达自己的需要时，很容易被贴上"自私""索取太多"的标签。

docile and subservient to authority. Our culture implies that needs are negative and destructive; the word *needy* applied to a person suggests inadequacy or immaturity. When people express their needs, they are often labeled selfish, and the use of the personal pronoun *I* is at times equated with selfishness or neediness.

By encouraging us to separate observation and evaluation, to acknowledge the thoughts or needs shaping our feelings, and to express our requests in clear action language, NVC heightens our awareness of the cultural conditioning influencing us at any given moment. And drawing this conditioning into the light of consciousness is a key step in breaking its hold on us.

> We can liberate ourselves from cultural conditioning.

Resolving Internal Conflicts

We can apply NVC to resolve the internal conflicts that often result in depression. In his book *The Revolution in Psychiatry*, Ernest Becker attributes depression to "cognitively arrested alternatives." This means that when we have a judgmental dialogue going on within, we become alienated from what we are needing and cannot then act to meet those needs. Depression is indicative of a state of alienation from our own needs.

A woman studying NVC was suffering a profound bout of depression. She was asked to identify the voices within her when she felt the most depressed and to write them down in dialogue form as though they were speaking to each other. These were the first two lines of her dialogue:

Voice 1 ("career woman"): *I should do something more with my life. I'm wasting my education and talents.*

Voice 2 ("responsible mother"): *You're being unrealistic. You're a mother of two children and can't handle that responsibility, so how can you handle anything else?*

Notice how these inner messages are infested with judgmental terms and phrases such as *should, wasting my education and talents,* and *can't handle*. Variations of this dialogue had been

第十三章 解放自我，协助他人

因此，通过区分观察与评判、认识感受背后的想法或需要，并以清晰的行动语言提出请求，非暴力沟通让我们更有能力在每一个当下觉察那些加诸我们身上的文化制约。若要摆脱这些制约对我们的束缚，最关键的一步便是看清它们。

化解内在冲突

内在冲突往往会让人陷入抑郁状态，而我们可以用非暴力沟通来化解这些冲突。在《精神病学的革命》一书中，厄内斯特·贝克（Ernest Becker）将抑郁症归因为"无法认知到自己有选择"。当我们评判自己时，便是在远离自己的需要，更无法采取行动来满足那些需要。因此我们感到抑郁，就是说，我们和自己的需要失去了连结。

有位饱受抑郁折磨的女士来学习非暴力沟通。我请她找到自己在极度抑郁时内在出现的不同声音，并将它们以对话的形式写下来，就好像这些声音彼此在交谈一样。以下是她写下的前两句对话：

声音1（作为职业女性）：我的人生应该有更大的作为，我这是在浪费我所受的教育和才华。

声音2（作为有责任感的母亲）：你太不现实了。作为两个小孩的妈妈，你连他们都照顾不好，还妄谈做其他事情？

我们看到，这些内在声音充满了评判和指责，比如"应该""浪费我所受的教育和才华""照顾不好"，等等。类似这样的对话已经在她的

running in this woman's head for months. She was asked to imagine the "career woman" voice taking an "NVC pill" in order to restate its message in the following form: "When *a*, I feel *b*, because I am needing *c*. Therefore I now would like *d*."

She subsequently translated "I should do something with my life. I'm wasting my education and talents" into: "*When* I spend as much time at home with the children as I do without practicing my profession, *I feel* depressed and discouraged *because I am needing* the fulfillment I once had in my profession. *Therefore, I now would like* to find part-time work in my profession."

Then it was the turn of her "responsible mother" voice to undergo the same process of translation. These lines, "You're being unrealistic. You're a mother of two children and can't handle *that* responsibility, so how can you handle anything else?" were transformed into: "*When* I imagine going to work, *I feel* scared *because I'm needing* reassurance that the children will be well taken care of. *Therefore, I now would like* to plan how to provide high-quality child care while I work and how to find sufficient time to be with the children when I am not tired."

This woman felt great relief as soon as she translated her inner messages into NVC. She was able to get beneath the alienating messages she was repeating to herself and offer herself empathy. Although she still faced practical challenges, such as securing quality child care and her husband's support, she was no longer subject to the judgmental internal dialogue that kept her from being aware of her own needs.

> The ability to hear our own feelings and needs and empathize with them can free us from depression.

Caring for Our Inner Environment

When we are entangled in critical, blaming, or angry thoughts, it is difficult to establish a healthy internal environment for ourselves. NVC helps us create a more peaceful state of mind by encouraging us to focus on what we are truly wanting rather than on what is wrong with others or ourselves.

第十三章　解放自我，协助他人

头脑中持续了好几个月。接着，我请她想象那个"职业女性"服下了"非暴力沟通药丸"，然后用以下句式重新表达："当……，我感到……，因为我有……的需要，因此我想要……"

于是她将"我的人生应该有更大的作为，我这是在浪费我所受的教育和才华"转换为："当我放弃工作、待在家里花很多时间照顾孩子们时，我感到压抑和挫败，因为我很需要在工作中获得的成就感。所以，现在我想在我的老本行里找一份兼职。"

接下来轮到"有责任感的母亲"用同样的方式来重新表达。她将"你太不现实了。作为两个小孩的妈妈，你连他们都照顾不好，还妄谈做其他事情"转换为："当我想到要去上班，我感到害怕，因为我需要确保孩子们被好好照顾。因此，我想计划一下如何在我工作时为他们提供妥善的安排，并且在我不那么累时有足够的时间陪伴孩子们。"

这位女士用非暴力沟通的语言表达了内在的声音后，顿时如释重负。因为她得以明白那些不断重复、撕扯她的想法背后所隐藏的感受和需要，并同理自己的处境。尽管她依然要面对现实中的挑战，例如：为孩子们寻求好的照顾、获得先生的支持……但她已经明白了自己的需要，而不再一味地自我评判了。

呵护我们的心灵环境

当我们陷在批判、指责或愤怒中时，很难为自己建立一个健康的内在环境。非暴力沟通鼓励我们关注什么是自己真正想要的，而不是自己

13 Liberating Ourselves and Counseling Others

A participant once reported a profound personal breakthrough during a three-day training. One of her goals for the workshop was to take better care of herself, but she woke at dawn the second morning with the worst headache in recent memory. "Normally, the first thing I'd do would be to analyze what I had done wrong. Did I eat the wrong food? Did I let myself get stressed-out? Did I do this; did I not do that? But, since I had been working on using NVC to take better care of myself, I asked instead, 'What do I need to do for myself right now with this headache?'

> Focus on what we want to do rather than what went wrong.

"I sat up and did a lot of really slow neck rolls, then got up and walked around, and did other things to take care of myself right then instead of beating up on myself. My headache relaxed to the point where I was able to go through the day's workshop. This was a major, major breakthrough for me. What I understood, when I empathized with the headache, was that I hadn't given myself enough attention the day before, and the headache was a way to say to myself, 'I need more attention.' I ended up giving myself the attention I needed and was then able to make it through the workshop. I've had headaches all my life, and this was a very remarkable turning point for me."

At another workshop a participant asked how NVC might be used to free us from anger-provoking messages when we are driving on the freeway. This was a familiar topic for me! For years my work involved traveling by car across the country, and I was worn and frazzled by the violence-provoking messages racing through my brain. Everybody who wasn't driving by my standards was an archenemy, a villain. Thoughts spewed through my head: "What the hell is the matter with that guy!? Doesn't he even watch where he's driving?" In that state of mind, all I wanted was to punish the other drivers, and since I couldn't do that, the anger lodged in my body and exacted its toll.

Eventually I learned to translate my judgments into feelings and needs and to give myself empathy: "Boy, I am petrified

第十三章　解放自我，协助他人

或他人有什么问题。

一位学员分享了她在一场 3 天的培训中收获的巨大突破。她提到自己来上课的一个目标是学习如何更好地照顾自己，但在第 2 天早晨醒来时，她却头疼欲裂。"在过去，我的第一反应是去检讨自己哪里做错了。是不是吃了什么不该吃的食物？是不是让自己压力过度？是因为自己做了这个，还是因为自己没有做那个？但这一次，因为学习了如何用非暴力沟通来照顾自己，我转而问自己：'我现在需要做什么来缓解头痛？'"

"我坐起来，慢慢舒展了脖子，走动了一下，又做了些别的事情让自己舒服些。我不再责罚自己。很快，头痛缓解了，我得以参加一整天的学习。对我来说，这是一个非常重大的突破。当我尝试同理我的头疼时，我发现在前一天没有把足够的注意力放在自己身上，而身体通过头痛来告诉我：'我需要得到更多的关注。'当我这样去做，我的身体也支持我完成了学习。我一辈子都在与头痛打交道，这一次的经历成了我人生的转折点。"

在另外一场工作坊上，有位学员询问我如何在开车时保持良好心态。这可是我非常熟悉的话题！因为工作的缘故，我有好几年的时间经常要开车到美国各地出差。每次行驶在路上，我的脑海中便不断冒出一个个具有暴力意味的念头："该死的，那个男的在干什么？他开车都不看路吗？"任何不以我的标准来开车的人都是敌人、恶人。这些念头让我疲惫不堪，它们驱使我想要惩罚那些司机，可实际上又不可能这样做，愤怒便积存在我的体内，也对我的身心造成了伤害。

于是，我尝试将评判转换为感受和需要来同理自己："老天，看到他们那样子开车，我简直吓坏了，我真希望他们能明白那样做有多危险。"天哪！我惊讶地发现，只是把注意力放在自己的感受和需要上，

when people drive like that; I really wish they would see the danger in what they are doing!" Whew! I was amazed how I could create a less stressful situation for myself by simply becoming aware of what I was feeling and needing rather than blaming others.

> Defuse stress by hearing our own feelings and needs.

Later I decided to practice empathy toward other drivers and was rewarded with a gratifying first experience. I was stuck behind a car going far below the speed limit and slowing down at every intersection. Fuming and grumbling, "That's no way to drive," I noticed the stress I was causing myself and shifted my thinking instead to what the other driver might be feeling and needing. I sensed that the person was lost, feeling confused, and wishing for some patience from those of us following. When the road widened enough for me to pass, I saw that the driver was a woman who looked to be in her eighties with an expression of terror on her face. I was pleased that my attempt at empathy had kept me from honking the horn or engaging in my customary tactics of displaying displeasure toward people whose driving bothered me.

> Defuse stress by empathizing with others.

Replacing Diagnosis With NVC

Many years ago, after having just invested nine years of my life in the training and diplomas necessary to qualify as a psychotherapist, I came across a dialogue between the Israeli philosopher Martin Buber and the American psychologist Carl Rogers in which Buber questions whether anyone can do psychotherapy in the role of a psychotherapist. Buber was visiting the United States at the time and had been invited, along with Carl Rogers, to a discussion at a mental hospital in front of a group of mental health professionals.

In this dialogue Buber posits that human growth occurs through a meeting between two individuals who express themselves vulnerably and authentically in what he termed an "I-Thou"

第十三章　解放自我，协助他人

我的压力便减轻了不少。

后来，我又决定去尝试同理那些驾驶人。第一次的尝试就让我十分满足。那次我行驶在一辆车后面，它的速度不仅远低于限速，还会在每一个交叉口减速。我火冒三丈，一直在心里抱怨："哪有人这样开车的。"注意到我已经给自己造成了一些压力，我开始体会那位司机可能会有的感受和需要。我猜那人可能迷路了，有点不知所措，希望跟在后面的司机多一些耐心。当道路变宽，我超车前进，发现那位司机是位看上去已经80来岁的女士，她的脸上满是惶恐。我很庆幸，由于同理了她，我没有对她大声按喇叭，也没有做出一些表达不满的举动。

用非暴力沟通取代诊断

许多年前，在完成长达9年的临床心理学课程训练后，我获得了博士学位并取得了心理治疗师的资质。毕业后不久，我有幸旁听了以色列哲学家马丁·布伯（Martin Buber）与美国心理学家卡尔·罗杰斯（Carl Rogers）的一场对话。那时，布伯正在访问美国，他受邀来到一所精神病院，在一群精神科医生面前和卡尔·罗杰斯对谈。

布伯的观点是，人的成长发生在两个个体相遇时以脆弱而坦诚的方式表达自己的过程中，他称这是"我与你"的关系。他认为，这样的坦诚无法存在于心理治疗师和来访者的角色之间。罗杰斯同意布伯的看法，认为坦诚是个人成长的先决条件，不过他也主张，开明的心理治疗师能够超越自己的角色，与来访者坦诚相见。

对此，布伯则表示怀疑。他认为，即使心理治疗师努力和来访者建

relationship. He did not believe that this type of authenticity was likely to exist when people meet in the roles of psychotherapist and client. Rogers agreed that authenticity was a prerequisite to growth. He maintained, however, that enlightened psychotherapists could choose to transcend their own role and encounter their clients authentically.

Buber was skeptical. He was of the opinion that even if psychotherapists were committed and able to relate to their clients in an authentic fashion, such encounters would be impossible as long as clients continued to view themselves as clients and their psychotherapists as psychotherapists. He observed how the very process of making appointments to see someone at their office, and paying fees to be "fixed," dimmed the likelihood of an authentic relationship developing between two persons.

This dialogue clarified my own long-standing ambivalence toward clinical detachment—a sacrosanct rule in the psychoanalytic psychotherapy I was taught. To bring one's own feelings and needs into the psychotherapy was typically viewed as a sign of pathology on the part of the therapist. Competent psychotherapists were to stay out of the therapy process and to function as a mirror onto which clients projected their transferences, which were then worked through with the psychotherapist's help. I understood the theory behind keeping the psychotherapist's inner process out of psychotherapy and guarding against the danger of addressing internal conflicts at the client's expense. However, I had always been uncomfortable maintaining the requisite emotional distance, and furthermore believed in the advantages of bringing myself into the process.

I thus began to experiment by replacing clinical language with the language of NVC. Instead of interpreting what my clients were saying in line with the personality theories I had studied, I made myself present to their words and listened empathically. Instead of diagnosing them, I revealed what was going on within myself. At first, this was frightening. I worried about how colleagues would react to the authenticity with which I was entering into dialogue with clients. However, the

第十三章 解放自我，协助他人

立坦诚的关系，但只要来访者依然以"来访者"自居，把对方视为"心理治疗师"，这样的相遇便不可能发生。他指出，来访者预约就诊、前往诊疗室以及付费"被治疗"的全过程都阻碍着两个人之间发展出坦诚的关系。

这场对话厘清了我长久以来的困惑。在我所接受的精神分析和心理治疗领域的教育中，心理医生在治疗中抽离自己可谓是金科玉律。如果治疗师把自己的感受和需要带到治疗过程中，通常被视为一种异常行为。专业的心理治疗师该在治疗过程中保持超然，让自己成为来访者投射想法和情感的一面镜子，再设法帮助病人解决问题。心理治疗师不在治疗中袒露内心，避免在处理内心冲突时损及病人的利益，这背后的理论和道理我十分理解。然而，对于要和来访者保持必要的心理距离，我总是感到不太舒服。不仅如此，我坚信将自己带到治疗过程中是有益的。

于是，我开始试着用非暴力沟通的语言来替代医疗术语。我不再用我所学到的人格理论来分析来访者，而是全然地和他们同在，并且同理他们说的话；我不再诊断他们得了什么病症，而是袒露这个过程中我的内心。刚开始，我颇有些胆战心惊，不知道同事们对此会有什么样的看法。然而，这样做的效果却令来访者和我都很满意，很快我便放下了自己的顾虑。35 年后的今天，将自己完全地投入咨访关系，这样的概念早已不再被视为离经叛道。记得在刚开始时，经常有心理治疗团体邀请我去演讲，并以现场示范来证明效果。

有一次，我受邀去一所州立精神病医院，向一大群精神病学领域的专业人士演示如何用非暴力沟通帮助精神极度痛苦的人。讲解了一

13 Liberating Ourselves and Counseling Others

results were so gratifying to both my clients and myself that I soon overcame any hesitation. Today, thirty-five years later, the concept of bringing oneself fully into the client-therapist relationship is no

> I empathized with clients instead of interpreting them; I revealed myself instead of diagnosing them.

longer heretical, but when I began practicing this way, I was often invited to speak to groups of psychotherapists who would challenge me to demonstrate this new role.

Once I was asked, by a large gathering of mental health professionals at a state mental hospital, to show how NVC might serve in counseling distressed people. After my one-hour presentation, I was requested to interview a patient in order to produce an evaluation and recommendation for treatment. I talked with the twenty-nine-year-old mother of three children for about half an hour. After she left the room, the staff responsible for her care posed their questions. "Dr. Rosenberg," her psychiatrist began, "please make a differential diagnosis. In your opinion, is this woman manifesting a schizophrenic reaction or is this a case of drug-induced psychosis?"

I said that I was uncomfortable with such questions. Even when I worked in a mental hospital during my training, I was never sure how to fit people into the diagnostic classifications. Since then I had read research indicating a lack of agreement among psychiatrists and psychologists regarding these terms. The reports concluded that diagnoses of patients in mental hospitals depended more upon the school the psychiatrist had attended than the characteristics of the patients themselves.

I would be reluctant, I continued, to apply these terms even if consistent usage did exist, because I failed to see how they benefited patients. In physical medicine, pinpointing the disease process that has created the illness often gives clear direction to its treatment, but I did not perceive this relationship in the field we call mental illness. In my experience of case conferences at hospitals, the staff would spend most of its time deliberating

第十三章　解放自我，协助他人

小时后，他们请我会见一位病人，评估她的病情并给出治疗建议。那是一位有着3个孩子的29岁母亲，我们谈了约半小时。在她离开房间后，负责治疗她的医生便向我提问："卢森堡博士，请您做出一个鉴别诊断。在您看来，这位女士表现的是精神分裂症状还是由毒品引起的精神错乱？"

我回答说，对于这类问题，我感到不舒服。即使是在精神病医院实习时，我也不太知道该如何对病人做出诊断分类。后来我读到的研究报告让我发现，精神病医生与心理学专家对诊断分类其实也没有一致的意见。那些报告的结论是，精神病医生会对病人做出什么诊断，主要取决于他们所属的学派，而不是病人本身的特质。

接着，我告诉他们，就算精神病医生对这些术语的运用具有共识，我也不太想用它们，因为我看不出这样对病人有什么好处。在物理医学领域，医师如果能了解疾病形成的原因，往往就能确定治疗的方向；但在精神疾病领域，情况并非如此。根据我的经历，在医院的病例讨论会上，医生们用大部分时间来讨论病人属于哪种精神病类型。到了会议必须结束时，主治医生可能会请其他人帮忙确立一个治疗方案，由于医生们大多更加热衷于对诊断的争论，这类请求通常会被忽略。

我向提问的这位医生解释：非暴力沟通让我不再去探讨病人有什么问题，而是转而关注这样一些方面："他（她）现在的感受是什么？他（她）需要什么？面对他（她），我有什么感受呢？我的感受反映了我怎样的需要呢？我想请求他（她）采取什么行动或做出什么行动，使他（她）过得更幸福呢？"由于对这些问题的回答透露出我们的内心世界和我们的价值观，因而，相较于只是对他人做出诊断，我们会感到更加

over a diagnosis. As the allotted hour threatened to run out, the psychiatrist in charge of the case might appeal to the others for help in setting up a treatment plan. Often this request would be ignored in favor of continued wrangling over the diagnosis.

I explained to the psychiatrist that NVC urges me to ask myself the following questions rather than think in terms of what is wrong with a patient: "What is this person feeling? What is she or he needing? How am I feeling in response to this person, and what needs of mine are behind my feelings? What action or decision would I request this person to take in the belief that it would enable them to live more happily?" Because our responses to these questions would reveal a lot about ourselves and our values, we would feel far more vulnerable than if we were to simply diagnose the other person.

On another occasion, I was called to demonstrate how NVC could be taught to people diagnosed as chronic schizophrenics. With about eighty psychologists, psychiatrists, social workers, and nurses watching, fifteen patients who had been thus diagnosed were assembled on the stage for me. As I introduced myself and explained the purpose of NVC, one of the patients expressed a reaction that seemed irrelevant to what I was saying. Aware that he'd been diagnosed as a chronic schizophrenic, I succumbed to clinical thinking by assuming that my failure to understand him was due to his confusion. "You seem to have trouble following what I'm saying," I remarked.

At this, another patient interjected, "I understand what he's saying," and proceeded to explain the relevance of the first patient's words in the context of my introduction. Recognizing that the man was not confused, but that I had simply not grasped the connection between our thoughts, I was dismayed by the ease with which I had attributed responsibility for the breakdown in communication to him. I would have liked to have owned my own feelings by saying, for example, "I'm confused. I'd like to see the connection between what I said and your response, but I don't. Would you be willing to explain how your words relate to what I said?"

第十三章　解放自我，协助他人

脆弱。

　　在另一次活动中，我受邀示范如何向那些被诊断为慢性精神分裂的人教授非暴力沟通。在大约 80 名心理学家、心理治疗师、社工和护工的围观下，15 位病人被请到台上。我开始介绍自己，讲解非暴力沟通的目的，忽然一位病人做了一个看似与我所述无关的回应。由于依然带着他被确诊为慢性精神分裂的临床思维，我下意识地认定，自己无法理解他讲的话是因为他头脑混乱，于是我对他说："你看上去不太明白我说的话。"

　　此时，另一位病人插话道："我懂他在说什么。"紧接着他解释了那位病人先前的话与我之前的介绍有什么关联。当我发现并非那个男人神智不清，而是我自己没有领悟其中的关联时，我惊愕地看到自己如此轻易就把沟通障碍归咎于他。我真希望为自己的感受负起责任，但愿说出口的话是："我感到困惑，我想理解我的话与你的回答之间的关联，但我并不知道，你愿意向我说明一下吗？"

　　除了这一片刻我跌入了临床诊断思维，余下的时间里，我与病人顺畅地交流。那些病人的反应让医生惊讶。他们问我是否认为这是一群特别合作的病人。我回答说：当我不再试图诊断、分析人，而是把我的内心世界与他们的内心世界连结时，人们通常都会给予积极的回应。

　　后来，一位工作人员请求我再进行一轮相似的交流，让心理学家和治疗师参与其中。于是，台上的几位病人与观众席的志愿者交换了位置。与工作人员一起工作时，我艰难地试图向其中一位心理学家澄清，"头脑的理解"与"非暴力沟通的同理"有何不同。每当组里有人表达感受，他便会从心理学的角度阐述自己的分析，而不是同理那些

With the exception of this brief departure into clinical thinking, the session with the patients went successfully. The staff, impressed with the patients' responses, wondered whether I considered them to be an unusually cooperative group of patients. I answered that when I avoided diagnosing people and instead stayed connected to the life going on in them and in myself, people usually responded positively.

A staff member then requested a similar session be conducted, as a learning experience, with some of the psychologists and psychiatrists as participants. At this, the patients who had been on stage exchanged seats with several volunteers in the audience. In working with the staff, I had a difficult time clarifying to one psychiatrist the difference between intellectual understanding and the empathy of NVC. Whenever someone in the group expressed feelings, he would offer his understanding of the psychological dynamics behind their feelings rather than empathize with the feelings. When this happened for the third time, one of the patients in the audience burst out, "Can't you see you're doing it again? You're interpreting what she's saying rather than empathizing with her feelings!"

By adopting the skills and consciousness of NVC, we can counsel others in encounters that are genuine, open, and mutual, rather than resort to professional relationships characterized by emotional distance, diagnosis, and hierarchy.

Summary

NVC enhances inner communication by helping us translate negative internal messages into feelings and needs. Our ability to distinguish our own feelings and needs and to empathize with them can free us from depression. By showing us how to focus on what we truly want rather than on what is wrong with others or ourselves, NVC gives us the tools and understanding to create a more peaceful state of mind. Professionals in counseling and psychotherapy may also use NVC to engender mutual and authentic relationships with their clients.

感受。当他第3次做出这样的表达时,一位观众席上的病人大声喊道:"你看不到自己又在分析了吗?你在解释她说的话,而不是在同理她的感受!"

用非暴力沟通的方法和意识来辅导他人时,我们和对方创造的是真诚、坦率和双向的关系,而不是和对方保持情感上的距离,也不是在诊断对方,或是摆出一副高高在上的专业辅导者姿态。

小结

非暴力沟通可以帮助我们将内心的负面信息转化成感受和需要,从而改善和自己的沟通。如果有能力做到同理自身的感受和需要,我们就可以转化抑郁情绪。非暴力沟通教导我们如何专注在自己及他人心底真正的渴望上,摆脱在自己或他人身上纠错的习惯,从而创造更加平和的心境。心理辅导与治疗的专业人士也可以用非暴力沟通与来访者建立真诚的关系。

13 Liberating Ourselves and Counseling Others

NVC in Action

Dealing With Resentment and Self-Judgment

A student of Nonviolent Communication shares the following story.

I had just returned from my first residential training in NVC. A friend whom I hadn't seen for two years was waiting for me at home. I first met Iris, who had been a school librarian for twenty-five years, during an intense two-week heartwork and wilderness journey that culminated in a three-day solo fast in the Rockies. After she listened to my enthusiastic description of NVC, Iris revealed that she was still hurting from what one of the wilderness leaders in Colorado had said to her six years before. I had a clear memory of that person: wild-woman Leav, her palms, gouged with rope cuts, holding steady a belayed body dangling against the mountain face; she read animal droppings, howled in the dark, danced her joy, cried her truth, and mooned our bus as we waved good-bye for the last time. What Iris had heard Leav say during one of the personal feedback sessions was this:

"Iris, I can't stand people like you, always and everywhere being so damn nice and sweet, constantly the meek little librarian that you are. Why don't you just drop it and get on with it?"

For six years Iris had been listening to Leav's voice in her head, and for six years she'd been answering Leav in her head. We were both eager to explore how a consciousness of NVC could have affected the situation. I role-played Leav and repeated her statement to Iris.

Iris: *(forgetting about NVC and hearing criticism and put-down)* You have no right to say that to me. You don't know who I am, or what kind of librarian I am! I take my profession seriously, and for your information,

第十三章 解放自我,协助他人

非暴力沟通实践案例

化解怨气和自我批评

以下是一个非暴力沟通学习者的故事:

有一次,我结束了非暴力沟通的集训回到家,发现两年没见的朋友艾瑞斯正在等我。25年来,她一直在一所小学担任图书管理员。6年前,我们在科罗拉多一个为期两周的荒野探寻活动中相识,这是一个极富挑战性的训练营,其中最后一个环节是在落基山独自断食3天。一见面,我就迫不及待地和她分享非暴力沟通课程的情况。这时,艾瑞斯告诉我,虽然已经过了6年,但只要一想起那次活动的野外领队对她说的话,她还是会感到愤愤不平。我知道她说的是莉芙,一位令人印象深刻的豪放女子。我记得她的手掌布满了被麻绳割开的痕迹;攀岩时,她稳稳地将自己悬挂在悬崖上;她能辨识动物的粪便,会在黑暗中长嚎;开心时,她会舞蹈,不快时,她会直率地说出心里话。最后一天,我们在巴士上向她挥手告别时,她甚至朝着我们撅起了屁股。

而让艾瑞斯耿耿于怀的是莉芙在一次个人反馈环节中对她说的话:

"艾瑞斯,我真受不了像你这样的人,不管什么时候、在什么地方,你都甜得腻死人,总是一副温顺的小图书管理员样儿。你为什么不能丢

I consider myself to be an educator, just like any teacher . . .

Me: *(with NVC consciousness, listening empathically, as if I were Leav)* It sounds to me like you're angry because you want me to know and recognize who you really are before criticizing you. Is that so?

Iris: That's right! You have simply no idea how much it took for me to even sign up for this trek. Look! Here I am: I finished, didn't I? I took on all the challenges these fourteen days and overcame them all!

Me: Am I hearing that you feel hurt and would have liked some recognition and appreciation for all your courage and hard work?

A few more exchanges followed, whereupon Iris showed a shift; these shifts, when a person feels "heard" to his or her satisfaction, can often be observed bodily. For instance, a person may relax and take a deeper breath. This often indicates that the person has received adequate empathy and is now able to shift attention to something other than the pain they have been expressing. Sometimes they are ready to hear another person's feelings and needs. Or sometimes another round of empathy is needed to attend to another area of pain. In this situation with Iris, I could see that another piece needed attention before she would be able to hear Leav. This is because Iris had had six years of opportunities to put herself down for not having produced an honorable comeback on the spot. After the subtle shift, she immediately went on:

Iris: Darn, I should have said all this stuff to her six years ago!

Me: *(as myself, an empathic friend)* You're frustrated because you wish you could have articulated yourself better at the time?

第十三章　解放自我，协助他人

下这些包袱，直率些呢？"

6年来，艾瑞斯时不时地想起莉芙这些话，并在心里不断驳斥她。于是，我们决定看看如何用非暴力沟通处理这个情形。

于是，我首先扮演莉芙的角色，对艾瑞斯再次说了当年的那些话。

艾瑞斯：（暂不考虑非暴力沟通，认为莉芙在批评和羞辱她）你没有权利这样对我说话。你根本不了解我，你也不知道我是什么样的图书管理员！我很认真地对待我的工作，并且我认为自己是一名教育工作者，和其他老师并没有什么不同……

我：（扮演莉芙的角色，带着非暴力沟通的意识，同理艾瑞斯）听起来你很生气，因为你希望我在评价你之前了解你真正的样子，是这样吗？

艾瑞斯：没错！你根本不知道我鼓起多大的勇气才报名参加了这场野外活动……你看！我不是完成了吗？这14天里，我接受了所有的挑战，并且——克服了它们！

我：（继续扮演莉芙）你是不是觉得很委屈，希望你的勇气和努力能够得到肯定和欣赏，是这样吗？

经过一番对话后，艾瑞斯有了一些转变。如果一个人感觉被充分聆听了，我们能从他（她）身上观察到相应的变化。比如，他（她）可能会放松下来并且深呼一口气。这样的举动往往意味着这个人获得了足够的同理，因而，内心释放了更多的空间去关注其他的事情；或许，这个

13 Liberating Ourselves and Counseling Others

> **Iris:** I feel like such an idiot! I knew I wasn't a "meek little librarian," but why didn't I say that to her?
> **Me:** So you wish you had been enough in touch with yourself to say that?
> **Iris:** Yes. And I'm also mad at myself! I wish I hadn't let her push me around.
> **Me:** You'd like to have been more assertive than you were?
> **Iris:** Exactly. I need to remember I have a right to stand up for who I am.
>
> Iris was quiet for a few seconds. She expressed readiness to practice NVC and hear what Leav said to her in a different way.
>
> **Me:** *(as Leav)* Iris, I can't stand people like you, always so nice and sweet, being forever the meek little librarian. Why don't you just drop it and get on with it?
> **Iris:** *(listening for Leav's feelings, needs, and requests)* Oh, Leav, it sounds to me like you're really frustrated . . . frustrated because . . . because I . . .
>
> Here Iris catches herself at a common mistake. By using the word I, she attributes Leav's feeling to Iris herself, rather than to some desire on Leav's own part that generates the feeling. That is, not "You're frustrated because I am a certain way," but "You're frustrated because you wanted something different from me."
>
> **Iris:** *(trying again)* Okay, Leav, it sounds like you're really frustrated because you are wanting . . . um . . . you're wanting . . .

第十三章　解放自我，协助他人

人甚至能够开始聆听别人的感受和需要。但有时，若有其他痛苦浮现出来，他们便需要继续被同理。我注意到，艾瑞斯还流露出有心事的样子，需要多一些聆听。毕竟，6年来她都一直为自己当时没能反驳莉芙而自责懊恼，果然她紧接着说：

艾瑞斯：该死的！6年前，我就该和她说这番话！
　　我：（我作为我自己，一个充满同理心的友人）你是不是觉得很挫败，因为你希望当初能够说得清楚一些，是吗？
艾瑞斯：我觉得自己就是一个白痴！我知道自己不是那种"温顺的小图书管理员"，但我为什么没有反驳她呢？
　　我：你希望那时候有足够的勇气表达自己？
艾瑞斯：是的。我对自己很生气！真希望我当时没有任她摆布。
　　我：你希望能够更加主动地表达自己？
艾瑞斯：正是！我要记住这一点，我有权为自己挺身而出。

艾瑞斯沉默了片刻后表示，她准备好了，愿意用非暴力沟通的方式来聆听莉芙所说的话。

　　我：（扮演莉芙）艾瑞斯，我真受不了像你这样的人。不管什么时候、在什么地方，你都甜得腻死人，总是一副温顺的小图书管理员样儿。你为什么不能丢下这些包袱，直率一些呢？
艾瑞斯：（试着聆听莉芙的感受、需要和请求）哦，莉芙，听起来，你好像有些恼火，你很恼火因为我……因为我……

13 Liberating Ourselves and Counseling Others

As I tried in my role-play to earnestly identify with Leav, I felt a sudden flash of awareness of what I *(as Leav)* was yearning for:

Me: *(as Leav)* Connection! . . . That's what I am wanting! I want to feel connected . . . with you, Iris! And I am so frustrated with all the sweetness and niceness that stand in the way that I just want to tear it all down so I can truly touch you!

We both sat a bit stunned after this outburst, and then Iris said, "If I had known that's what she had wanted, if she could have told me that it was genuine connection with me she was after . . . Gosh, I mean, that feels almost loving." While she never did find the real Leav to verify the insight, after this practice session in NVC, Iris achieved an internal resolution about this nagging conflict and found it easier to hear with a new awareness when people around her said things to her that she might previously have interpreted as "put-downs."

第十三章　解放自我，协助他人

艾瑞斯意识到自己犯了一个常见错误。当用到"因为我"时，她将莉芙的感受归咎到了自己身上，而不是去体会莉芙的感受源于莉芙自己的需要。也就是说，莉芙感到恼火不是因为艾瑞斯做了什么，而是因为她期望艾瑞斯能够有所不同。

艾瑞斯：（再次尝试）好，莉芙，听起来你非常恼火，因为你希望……呃……你希望……

当我在角色扮演过程中认真体会莉芙时，我突然意识到莉芙的渴望是什么了！

我：（作为莉芙）和你连结！……这是我想要的！艾瑞斯，我想和你有更多的连结！但你总是表现得那么乖巧可人，我不知道要如何与你连结。所以我想要把你的这个面具扯下来，让我能真正触碰到你的心！

当我说出这番话后，我们两人都愣了一下，接着艾瑞斯说："如果当时我能知道她渴望的是这个，如果她能告诉我她想和我建立真正的连结……天啊，这些话听起来是如此充满爱意。"虽然艾瑞斯并未找到莉芙来证实这番猜测，但经过这次非暴力沟通的对话练习，艾瑞斯终于打开了心结。之后，当身边的人再对她说一些从前可能会被她当成"贬低"的话时，她也能够带着更多觉察来聆听对方真正的渴望了。

13 Liberating Ourselves and Counseling Others

. . . the more you become a connoisseur of gratitude, the less you are a victim of resentment, depression, and despair. Gratitude will act as an elixir that will gradually dissolve the hard shell of your ego—your need to possess and control—and transform you into a generous being. The sense of gratitude produces true spiritual alchemy, makes us magnanimous—large souled.

—Sam Keen, philosopher

第十四章

用非暴力沟通表达感激与赞赏

"你愈懂得感谢,就愈不会为仇恨、压抑与绝望所苦。感恩是灵丹妙药,能消融小我占有和掌控的硬壳,让你成为一个胸怀坦荡的人。感恩之心是真正的灵性炼金术,让我们成为宽厚仁慈的灵魂。"

—— 桑姆·基恩 (Sam Keen),哲人

Expressing Appreciation in Nonviolent Communication

The Intention Behind the Appreciation

"You did a good job on that report."
"You are a very sensitive person."
"It was kind of you to offer me a ride home last evening."

Such statements are typically uttered as expressions of appreciation in life-alienating communication. Perhaps you are surprised that I regard praise and compliments to be life-alienating. Notice, however, that appreciation expressed in this form reveals little of what's going on in the speaker; it establishes the speaker as someone who sits in judgment. I define judgments—both positive and negative—as life-alienating communication.

> Compliments are often judgments—however positive—of others.

In corporate trainings, I often encounter managers who defend the practice of praising and complimenting by claiming that "it works." "Research shows," they assert, "that if a manager compliments employees, they work harder. And the same goes for schools: if teachers praise students, they study harder." I have reviewed this research, and my belief is that recipients of such praise do work harder, but only initially. Once they sense the manipulation behind the appreciation, their productivity drops.

第十四章　用非暴力沟通表达感激与赞赏

感激背后的意图

"你这份报告做得真好。"
"你是一个非常体贴的人。"
"你昨天晚上开车送我回家，真是太暖心了。"

在我看来，以上这些我们常常用来表达赞赏和感激的话却是一种疏离生命的沟通方式。你也许会感到惊讶，我竟然将夸奖与恭维视为疏离生命的沟通！请注意，说话人以这样的形式表达赞赏时，并未传递其内心，而是以裁判者自居。也就是说，我将所有评判——无论是正向的还是负向的——都定义为疏离生命的沟通。

在为企业开展培训时，我经常遇到管理者捍卫表扬与赞美的语言，称这样的表达是"管用的"。他们坚持的理由是："研究表明，如果管理人员表扬员工，员工会更努力工作；在学校也是一样，受到老师表扬的学生会更努力学习。"我阅读过这类研究，我认为受到赞美的人虽然会因此更努力，但效果却并不长久。一旦人们发现表扬是为了控制，他们

14 Expressing Appreciation in Nonviolent Communication

What is most disturbing for me, however, is that the beauty of appreciation is spoiled when people begin to notice the lurking intent to get something out of them.

Furthermore, when we use positive feedback as a means to influence others, it may not be clear how they are receiving the message. There is a cartoon where one Native American remarks to another, "Watch me use modern psychology on my horse!" He then leads his friend to where the horse can overhear their conversation and exclaims, "I have the fastest, most courageous horse in all the West!" The horse looks sad and says to itself, "How do you like that? He's gone and bought himself another horse."

When we use NVC to express appreciation, it is purely to celebrate, not to get something in return. Our sole intention is to celebrate the way our lives have been enriched by others.

> Express appreciation to celebrate, not to manipulate.

The Three Components of Appreciation

NVC clearly distinguishes three components in the expression of appreciation:

1. the actions that have contributed to our well-being
2. the particular needs of ours that have been fulfilled
3. the pleasureful feelings engendered by the fulfillment of those needs

The sequence of these ingredients may vary; sometimes all three can be conveyed by a smile or a simple "Thank you." However, if we want to ensure that our appreciation has been fully received, it is valuable to develop the eloquence to express all three components verbally. The following dialogue illustrates how praise may be transformed into an appreciation that embraces all three components.

> Saying "thank you" in NVC: "This is what you did; this is what I feel; this is the need of mine that was met."

的生产力就会下滑。最让我感到不安的是，一旦人们发现隐藏在赞赏背后的意图是为了从他们身上索取回报，人们便不会再看到赞赏的美好所在。

此外，当我们试图用正向的反馈来影响他人时，并不能确定对方会有什么反应。记得一则漫画这样描绘：一位北美原住民对同伴说："看我怎么把现代心理学用在我的马上！"接着他将朋友带到马匹可以听见他们说话的地方，大声喊道："我有一匹全西部跑得最快、最勇敢的马！"这时，只见那匹马露出了悲伤的神情，它自言自语道："真是的！他又买了匹新马！"

当我们用非暴力沟通来表达赞赏和感激时，纯粹是为了庆祝生命，不为获取任何回报。我们唯一的意图就是去庆祝他人的作为如何使我们的生命变得更加丰盛。

表达感激的三个要素

在使用非暴力沟通表达感激时，我们会清楚地包含以下三个要素：

- 他人做了什么增进了我们的福祉。
- 我们有哪些需要因此得到了满足。
- 因为这些需要得到了满足，引起了我们什么样的愉悦感受。

表达这三个要素时，并不一定要遵照以上的顺序。有时哪怕是一个微笑或一句简单的"谢谢你"就足以传递这一切。不过，如果我们想

Participant: *(approaching me after a workshop)* Marshall, you're brilliant!

MBR: I'm not able to get as much out of your appreciation as I would like.

Participant: Why, what do you mean?

MBR: In my lifetime I've been called a multitude of names, yet I can't recall seriously learning anything by being told what I am. I'd like to learn from your appreciation and enjoy it, but I would need more information.

Participant: Like what?

MBR: First, I'd like to know what I said or did that made life more wonderful for you.

Participant: Well, you're so intelligent.

MBR: I'm afraid you've just given me another judgment that still leaves me wondering what I did that made life more wonderful for you.

Participant: *(thinks for a while, then points to notes she had taken during the workshop)* Look at these two places. It was these two things you said.

MBR: Ah, so it's my saying those two things that you appreciate.

Participant: Yes.

MBR: Next, I'd like to know how you feel in conjunction to my having said those two things.

Participant: Hopeful and relieved.

MBR: And now I'd like to know what needs of yours were fulfilled by my saying those two things.

Participant: I have this eighteen-year-old son whom I haven't been able to communicate with. I'd been desperately searching for some direction that might help me to relate with him in a more loving manner, and those two things you said provide the direction I was looking for.

第十四章　用非暴力沟通表达感激与赞赏

要确保对方能够充分收到我们的心意，用语言完整地表达这三个要素是有意义的。在下文的对话中，大家可以看到如何用这三个要素来表达"赞赏"。

学　　员：（在工作坊结束后来找我）马歇尔，你太棒了！

马歇尔：我好像不太理解你为什么要这么称赞我。

学　　员：为什么？你的意思是？

马歇尔：人们给过我无数的头衔，但我却完全无法从这些表述中学到什么。我想从你对我的赞赏中有所学习，并且因此感到喜悦，但我需要你再多说一些。

学　　员：比如说？

马歇尔：首先，我想知道我说了什么或者做了什么让你的生命变得更加美好。

学　　员：嗯，你很有智慧。

马歇尔：恐怕你刚刚又给了我另一个评判。我依然想知道我做了什么让你的生命更美好。

学　　员：（思索了一会儿后，她指着自己在工作坊上写下的笔记）看这两处，就是你说的这两点。

马歇尔：噢，所以你赞赏的是我说的这两点？

学　　员：是的。

马歇尔：接下来，我想要知道这些话带给你的感受。

学　　员：感到充满希望，并且释然。

马歇尔：那么现在我想知道，我说了这两点满足了你哪些需要。

学　　员：我一直无法和我18岁的儿子沟通，一直在努力寻找一种更加

Hearing all three pieces of information—what I did, how she felt, and what needs of hers were fulfilled—I could then celebrate the appreciation with her. Had she initially expressed her appreciation in NVC, it might have sounded like this: "Marshall, when you said these two things (showing me her notes), I felt very hopeful and relieved, because I've been searching for a way to make a connection with my son, and these gave me the direction I was looking for."

Receiving Appreciation

For many of us, it is difficult to receive appreciation gracefully. We fret over whether we deserve it. We worry about what's being expected of us—especially if we have teachers or managers who use appreciation as a means to spur productivity. Or we're nervous about living up to the appreciation. Accustomed to a culture where buying, earning, and deserving are the standard modes of interchange, we are often uncomfortable with simple giving and receiving.

NVC encourages us to receive appreciation with the same quality of empathy we express when listening to other messages. We hear what we have done that has contributed to others' well-being; we hear their feelings and the needs that were fulfilled. We take into our hearts the joyous reality that we can each enhance the quality of others' lives.

I was taught to receive appreciation with grace by my friend Nafez Assailey. He was a member of a Palestinian team whom I had invited to Switzerland for training in NVC at a time when security precautions made training of mixed groups of Palestinians and Israelis impossible in either of their own countries. At the end of the workshop, Nafez came up to me. "This training will be very valuable for us in working for peace in our country," he acknowledged. "I would like to thank you in a way that we Sufi Muslims do when we want to express special appreciation for something." Locking his thumb onto mine, he looked me in the eye and said, "I kiss the God in you that allows you to give us what you did." He then kissed my hand.

情意相通的方式和他相处,你说的这两点让我找到了方向。

听到这三个要素的内容(我做了什么、她有何感受以及满足了她哪些需要)后,我就能真正和她一起享受这份赞赏。如果一开始就用非暴力沟通的方式来表达,她可以说:"马歇尔,当你说这两点时(向我展示她的笔记),我感到充满了希望并且释然,因为我一直在寻找方法和儿子连结,你的这些话给了我方向。"

接受来自他人的感激

对于许多人来说,得体地接受别人的赞赏和感激并非易事。我们会担心自己是否值得他人的感激;也会担心感激背后的期待,特别当我们的老师或上司用感激作为激励我们的手段时;我们还会因为不想辜负感激而感到焦虑。在当今的文化中,人们已经习惯了基于买卖、有偿或者估值来运作的关系,以至于对于纯粹的施与受,我们多半会感到不适。

非暴力沟通鼓励我们带着同理心来接受感激,就像我们同理他人那样。我们聆听自己做了什么增进了他人的福祉,由此满足了他人什么样的需要以及引发的感受。因为能为彼此的生命做出贡献,我们从心底为之喜悦。

我的朋友那菲兹·阿萨黎教会了我如何优雅地接受感激。他是我邀请前来瑞士参加非暴力沟通培训的巴勒斯坦小组成员之一。当时,巴勒斯坦和以色列两国局势紧张,基于安全考虑,无论是在以色列或巴勒斯坦都无法让双方的学员一起参加培训。工作坊结束那一天,那菲

14 Expressing Appreciation in Nonviolent Communication

Nafez's expression of gratitude showed me a different way to receive appreciation. Usually it is received from one of two polar positions. At one end is egotism, believing ourselves to be superior because we've been appreciated. At the other extreme is false humility, denying the importance of the appreciation by shrugging it off: "Oh, it was nothing." Nafez showed me that I could receive appreciation joyfully, in the awareness that God has given everyone the power to enrich the lives of others. If I am aware that it is this power of God working through me that gives me the power to enrich life for others, then I may avoid both the ego trap and the false humility.

> **Receive appreciation without feelings of superiority or false humility.**

Golda Meir, when she was the Israeli prime minister, once chided one of her ministers: "Don't be so humble, you're not that great." The following lines, attributed to contemporary writer Marianne Williamson, serve as another reminder for me to avoid the pitfall of false humility:

> Our deepest fear is not that we are inadequate. Our deepest fear is that we are powerful beyond measure.
>
> It is our light, not our darkness, that frightens us. You are a child of God. Your playing small doesn't serve the world.
>
> There's nothing enlightened about shrinking so that other people won't feel insecure around you.
>
> We were born to make manifest the glory of God that is within us. It's not just in some of us, it is in everyone.
>
> And as we let our own light shine, we unconsciously give other people permission to do the same.
>
> As we are liberated from our fear, our presence automatically liberates others.

第十四章　用非暴力沟通表达感激与赞赏

兹来到我跟前对我说："这个培训对于我们以后在国内推动和平工作太有价值了。我想以我们苏菲穆斯林信徒赞美神的方式来向你表达感激。"于是，他用大拇指紧扣着我的大拇指，并注视着我的眼睛说："我亲吻你内心那位让你为我们带来这一切的神明。"接着，他亲吻了我的手。

那菲兹向我展示了我们可以用不同的方式接受来自他人的赞赏和感激。通常，人们在听见对自己的赞赏时会有两种极端的反应——一种是自负，因为得到了赞美而认为自己高人一等；另一种是故作谦虚，满不在乎地否认赞赏："哦，那没什么。"那菲兹让我明白，记得是神给了我们每个人丰盈他人生命的力量，我就能充满喜悦地接受感激，而不会掉入自负和故作谦虚的陷阱。

以色列前总理梅厄夫人曾经训斥她的一位内阁大臣："别这么谦虚，你没有那么伟大。"下面这段文字来自当代作家玛丽安娜·威廉姆斯（Marianne Williamson），也提醒着我们不要掉入故作谦虚的陷阱。

我们最深的恐惧不是自己不够好，
而是我们无比强大。
让我们恐惧的不是自身的幽暗，而是我们的光芒。
你是神的孩子。你的退缩对这个世界并无益处。
为了让身边的人不受威胁而缩小自己，决不会带来任何启迪。
我们生来就是为了彰显内在的荣光。
那不仅存在于某些人，而是存在于每个人之中。
当我们容许自己的光芒闪耀，也就默许了他人一同绽放。

14 Expressing Appreciation in Nonviolent Communication

The Hunger for Appreciation

Paradoxically, despite our unease in receiving appreciation, most of us yearn to be genuinely recognized and appreciated. During a surprise party for me, a twelve-year-old friend of mine suggested a party game to help introduce the guests to each other. We were to write down a question, drop it in a box, and then take turns, each person drawing out a question and responding to it out loud.

Having recently consulted with various social service agencies and industrial organizations, I was feeling struck by how often people expressed a hunger for appreciation on the job. "No matter how hard you work," they would sigh, "you never hear a good word from anyone. But make one mistake and there's always someone jumping all over you." So for the game, I wrote this question: "What appreciation might someone give you that would leave you jumping for joy?"

A woman drew that question out of the box, read it, and started to cry. As director of a shelter for battered women, she would put considerable energy each month into creating a schedule to please as many people as possible. Yet each time the schedule was presented, at least a couple of individuals would complain. She couldn't remember ever receiving appreciation for her efforts to design a fair schedule. All this had flashed through her mind as she read my question, and the hunger for appreciation brought tears to her eyes.

Upon hearing the woman's story, another friend of mine said that he, too, would like to answer the question. Everyone else then requested a turn; as they responded to the question, several people wept.

While the craving for appreciation—as opposed to manipulative "strokes"—is particularly evident in the workplace, it affects family life as well. One evening when I pointed out his failure to perform a house chore, my son Brett retorted, "Dad, are you aware how often you bring up what's gone wrong but almost never bring up what's gone right?" His observation stayed with me. I realized how I was continually searching

> We tend to notice what's wrong rather than what's right.

第十四章 用非暴力沟通表达感激与赞赏

当我们挣脱了自己的恐惧，我们的存在也会让他人得到解放。

对赞赏和感激的渴望

说来矛盾，尽管我们在接受赞赏和感激时会感到不自在，但大多数人依然渴望得到真诚的肯定与欣赏。在一次为我举办的惊喜派对中，一位我认识了12年之久的朋友提议大家玩一个游戏让彼此熟悉。他让每个人在纸上写下一个问题后，投入一个盒子里，接着让每人轮流抽出一个问题，抽到什么问题就要当众回答。

由于那段时间我为许多不同的社会服务机构和商业机构做咨询，我惊讶地发现人们时常提及自己有多么渴望在工作中得到赞赏。他们会叹着气说："不管你工作多么努力，都没有人说你一句好话。可如果你犯了一个错误，一定会有人立马来训斥你。"于是，我在这个游戏中写下了这样一个问题："什么样的赞赏会让你在听到后欢欣雀跃呢？"

一位女士抽到了这个问题，念完问题后她便哭了起来。她说，自己是一名受虐女性庇护中心的主任，为了尽可能让大家都满意，每个月她都要投入大量精力设计各种活动。然而每次公布安排表时，总有几个人会表示不满，却没有谁曾感谢她所做的努力。当她在念这个问题时，脑海中便浮现出这些事情，又想到自己是多么渴望得到赞赏，此情此景她不禁落泪。

听完这位女士的故事，另一位朋友说他也想来回答这个问题。接着，所有人都纷纷要来回答，好几个人在这个过程中流下了眼泪。

for improvements, while barely stopping to celebrate things that were going well. I had just completed a workshop with more than a hundred participants, all of whom had evaluated it very highly, with the exception of one person. However, what lingered in my mind was that one person's dissatisfaction.

That evening I wrote a song that began like this:
If I'm ninety-eight percent perfect
in anything I do,
it's the two percent I've messed up
I'll remember when I'm through.

It occurred to me that I had a choice to adopt instead the outlook of a teacher I knew. One of her students, having neglected to study for an exam, had resigned himself to turning in a blank piece of paper with his name at the top. He was surprised when she later returned the test to him with a grade of 14 percent. "What did I get 14 percent for?" he asked incredulously. "Neatness," she replied. Ever since hearing my son Brett's wake-up call, I've tried to be more aware of what others around me are doing that enriches my life, and to hone my skills in expressing this appreciation.

Overcoming the Reluctance to Express Appreciation

I was deeply touched by a passage in John Powell's book *The Secret of Staying in Love*, in which Powell describes his sadness over having been unable, during his father's lifetime, to express the appreciation he felt for his father *to* his father. How grievous it seemed to me to miss the chance of appreciating the people who have been the greatest positive influences in our lives!

Immediately an uncle of mine, Julius Fox, came to mind. When I was a boy, he came daily to offer nursing care to my grandmother, who was totally paralyzed. While he cared for my grandmother, he always had a warm and loving smile on his face. No matter how unpleasant the task may have appeared to my boyish eyes, he treated her as if she were doing him the greatest favor in the

第十四章　用非暴力沟通表达感激与赞赏

人们渴望在工作中得到赞赏（真诚而非操控式的），在家庭中也未尝不是这样。一天晚上，当我提醒儿子布莱特忘了做一件家务活儿时，他回嘴道："爸，你有没有注意到，你常常说我哪里做得不好，却几乎从没有说过我哪里做得好！"我一直谨记他的这番话。他让我意识到自己总是在试图寻找哪里可以做得更好，却很少停下来去为那些做得好的地方庆祝。例如，我刚带领完一场参与人数过百的工作坊，除了一个人，所有参加者都给予了极高的评价。然而，让我念念不忘的仍是那一个人的不满。

当天晚上我写下了一首歌，是这样开头的：

无论做什么，就算我有百分之九十八做得很好，
但事后我记得的，却是那让我不满的百分之二。

这也启发了我向我认识的一位老师学习。她的一位学生由于没有准备考试，只写了名字便交了白卷。当学生拿到批改好的卷子时，十分吃惊地发现自己竟然得了 14 分。他满腹怀疑地问老师："我做了什么可以拿到这 14 分呢？" "你的考卷很整洁。"老师回答他。自从我的儿子给了我当头一棒后，我便开始更多地觉察别人做了什么让我的生命更加美好，同时不断地练习表达感激。

当你不愿表达感激时

约翰·鲍威尔（John Powell）在他的《爱的秘密》一书中有一段

world by letting him care for her. This provided a wonderful model of masculine strength for me—one that I've often called upon in the years since.

I realized that I had never expressed my appreciation for my uncle, who himself was now ill and near death. I considered doing so, but sensed my own resistance: "I'm sure he already knows how much he means to me, I don't need to express it out loud; besides, it might embarrass him if I put it into words." As soon as these thoughts entered my head, I already knew they weren't true. Too often I had assumed that others knew the intensity of my appreciation for them, only to discover otherwise. And even when people were embarrassed, they still wanted to hear appreciation verbalized.

Still hesitant, I told myself that words couldn't do justice to the depth of what I wished to communicate. I quickly saw through that one, though: yes, words may be poor vehicles in conveying our heartfelt realities, but as I have learned, "Anything that is worth doing is worth doing poorly!"

As it happened, I soon found myself seated next to Uncle Julius at a family gathering, and the words simply flowed out of me. He took them in joyfully, without embarrassment. Brimming over with feelings from the evening, I went home, composed a poem and sent it to him. I was later told that each day until he died three weeks later, my uncle had asked that the poem be read to him.

Summary

Conventional compliments often take the form of judgments, however positive, and are sometimes intended to manipulate the behavior of others. NVC encourages the expression of appreciation solely for celebration. We state (1) the action that has contributed to our well-being, (2) the particular need of ours that has been fulfilled, and (3) the feelings of pleasure engendered as a result.

When we receive appreciation expressed in this way, we can do so without any feeling of superiority or false humility—instead we can celebrate along with the person who is offering the appreciation.

第十四章　用非暴力沟通表达感激与赞赏

文字深深打动了我。他描述了父亲在世时，自己从来没有向他表达过感激，为此他深感悲伤。我想如果错失了机会向那些对我们很重要的人表达谢意，实在是令人遗憾的。

这使我想到了我的舅舅朱利亚斯·福克斯。当我还小的时候，他每天会到我们家照顾我那位已经全身瘫痪的祖母。我记得当他在照顾祖母时，脸上总是挂着温暖又充满爱的笑容。无论那些活儿在年少的我眼中是多么不堪，他却好像视照顾祖母为莫大的恩惠。他的亲身示范教会了我何为男性的力量，所有这些，我在往后的岁月里时常都会忆起。

直至舅舅病危，我才发现自己从未向他表达过感激。每当我想要这么做时，总感到自己有些抗拒："我相信他已经知道他对我有多重要，所以没必要说出来吧。如果我真的说出来了，可能反而会让他觉得尴尬吧。"当脑海中浮现出这些想法时，我马上知道这并不是真的。我经常以为别人知道我有多感激他们，后来却发现事实并非如此。而即使人们听见感激的话时会感到尴尬，却依然希望能从别人那里听到对自己的感激。

可我还是有些犹豫，我对自己说：语言并不足以表达我对他的感激之情。好在很快我就醒悟了：是的，尽管语言不足以充分传递我们的心意，但我已经知道"一件值得做的事情，即使我们做得不怎么样也值得去做！"

在不久后的一次家庭聚会中，当我坐在朱利亚斯舅舅身旁时，感激的话便从我心里涌了出来。舅舅听了非常高兴，没有丝毫尴尬。当晚，激动不已的我回到家后写下了一首诗寄给他。3个星期后，他便过世了。我后来得知，舅舅在去世前，每天都请人把那首诗念给他听。

14 Expressing Appreciation in Nonviolent Communication

Praise and reward create a system of extrinsic motivations for behavior. Children (and adults) end up taking action in order to receive the praise or rewards.

第十四章 用非暴力沟通表达感激与赞赏

小结

我们惯常的赞美方式往往带有评判,哪怕是正向的,有时甚至被用来操纵他人的行为。非暴力沟通所鼓励的是,向他人表达感激时,庆祝是我们唯一的意图。我们表达的内容包括:(1)对方做了什么对我们的福祉做出了贡献;(2)我们有哪些需要得到了满足;(3)我们因此产生了什么样的愉悦感受。

当我们接收这样的赞赏和感谢时,我们也能免于自负或是假谦虚,而是和对方一起庆祝。

14 Expressing Appreciation in Nonviolent Communication

Social change involves helping people see new options for making life wonderful that are less costly to get needs met.

后记

　　有一次，我问舅舅朱利亚斯，他何以做到如此由衷地给予。对于我的提问，他似乎颇引以为荣，他思索了一会儿后答道："那是因为我很幸运地遇到了好老师。"我问他老师是谁，他说："你的祖母是我最好的老师。你和她一起住的时候她已经生病了，所以你并没有见识到她真正的样子。在大萧条时期，一位裁缝和他的老婆、两个孩子丢了房子和生意后，你的祖母把他们接到我们家，同住了3年。你的妈妈告诉过你吗？"我对这个故事记忆深刻。母亲第一次告诉我时，我清晰地记得当时我完全无法想象，养育9个孩子的祖母是如何在她那幢不算大的房子里腾出空间给裁缝一家人的。

　　朱利亚斯舅舅又回忆了一些奶奶的善行，那些都是我小时候听过的故事，接着他问我："你妈妈一定和你说过有关耶稣的故事吧？"

　　"谁的故事？"

　　"耶稣。"

　　"没有，她从来没有告诉过我关于耶稣的故事。"

　　有关耶稣的故事是舅舅临终前送给我最后的珍贵礼物。一次，一个男人来到祖母家的后门向她乞求食物。这样的事并不罕见。尽管祖母很穷，所有的邻里都知道只要有人上门来要饭，她一定会给他们东西吃。这个男人留着胡子，有一头乱蓬蓬的黑发，衣衫褴褛，脖子上挂着一串木枝做的十字架。祖母请他进厨房，在他吃东西的时候问起他的名字。

Epilogue

I once asked my uncle Julius how he had developed such a remarkable capacity to give compassionately. He seemed honored by my question, which he pondered before replying, "I've been blessed with good teachers." When I asked who these were, he recalled, "Your grandmother was the best teacher I had. You lived with her when she was already ill, so you didn't know what she was really like. For example, did your mother ever tell you about the time during the Depression when your grandmother brought a tailor and his wife and two children to live with her for three years, after he lost his house and business?" I remembered the story well. It had left a deep impression when my mother first told it to me because I could never figure out where grandmother had found space for the tailor's family when she was raising nine children of her own in a modest-sized house!

Uncle Julius recollected my grandmother's compassion in a few more anecdotes, all of which I had heard as a child. Then he asked, "Surely your mother told you about Jesus."

"About who?"

"Jesus."

"No, she never told me about Jesus."

The story about Jesus was the final precious gift I received from my uncle before he died. It's a true story of a time when a man came to my grandmother's back door asking for some food. This wasn't unusual. Although grandmother was very poor, the entire neighborhood knew that she would feed anyone who showed up at her door. This man had a beard and wild, scraggly black hair; his clothes were ragged, and he wore a cross around his neck fashioned out of branches tied with rope. My grandmother invited him into her kitchen for some food, and while he was eating she asked his name.

后记

"我叫耶稣。"他答道。

"那你姓什么?"她询问着。

"我叫主耶稣。"(祖母的英语不是太好。另外一位舅舅艾西多后来告诉我,那天男子在用餐时,他正好进了厨房,祖母向他介绍这位陌生人,说他是"主先生"。)

接着,祖母又问他住哪儿。

"我没有住处。"

"那,今晚你住在哪里呢?外面很冷呀。"

"我不知道。"

"你要住在这里吗?"她问。

之后,他一住就是7年。

说到非暴力沟通,我的祖母是个天生的能手。她没有去想这个男人是什么样的人,否则她可能会把这个人当作疯子而打发走。不,祖母所想的是他人的感受和需要。如果有人饿了,她就拿吃的给他们;如果有人无家可归,她就给他们一处地方睡觉。

祖母热爱跳舞,我的母亲记得祖母经常说:"若你能跳舞就永远不要走路。"因此,我想以一首关于祖母的歌来作为这本书的结尾,因为她终其一生都说着非暴力沟通的语言,都活出了非暴力沟通的精神。

"My name is Jesus," he replied.

"Do you have a last name?" she inquired.

"I am Jesus the Lord." (My grandmother's English wasn't too good. Another uncle, Isidor, later told me he had come into the kitchen while the man was still eating, and grandmother had introduced the stranger as Mr. Thelord.)

As the man continued to eat, my grandmother asked where he lived.

"I don't have a home."

"Well, where are you going to stay tonight? It's cold."

"I don't know."

"Would you like to stay here?" she offered.

He stayed seven years.

When it came to communicating nonviolently, my grandmother was a natural. She didn't think of what this man "was." If she had, she probably would have judged him as crazy and gotten rid of him. No, she thought in terms of what people feel and what they need. If they're hungry, feed them. If they're without a roof over their head, give them a place to sleep.

My grandmother loved to dance, and my mother remembers her saying often, "Never walk when you can dance." And thus I end this book on a language of compassion with a song about my grandmother, who spoke and lived the language of Nonviolent Communication.

> *One day a man named Jesus*
> *came around to my grandmother's door.*
> *He asked for a little food,*
> *she gave him more.*
>
> *He said he was Jesus the Lord;*
> *she didn't check him out with Rome.*
> *He stayed for several years,*
> *as did many without a home.*
>
> *It was in her Jewish way,*
> *she taught me what Jesus had to say.*

后记

一天，一个名叫耶稣的男人
徘徊到祖母家门口。
他要了一点吃的，
但她给得更多。
他说他叫主耶稣；
她没有向教廷核实他的身份。
他一住便是许多年，
与许多无家可归的人一样。
正是以犹太人的方式，
她教导了我耶稣的箴言。
如此珍贵，
铭记耶稣的教导：
"为饥饿的人喂食，为生病的人治疗，
然后得以安息。
若你能跳舞就别走路；
将家筑成一个温暖的巢。"
正是以犹太人的方式，
她教导了我耶稣的箴言。
如此珍贵，
让我铭记耶稣的教导。
——《祖母与耶稣》马歇尔·卢森堡

Epilogue

In that precious way,
she taught me what Jesus had to say.
And that's: "Feed the hungry, heal the sick,
then take a rest.
Never walk when you can dance;
make your home a cozy nest."

It was in her Jewish way,
she taught me what Jesus had to say.
In her precious way,
she taught me what Jesus had to say.

—"Grandma and Jesus" by Marshall B. Rosenberg

资源

非暴力沟通四要素

非暴力沟通四要素	
清晰地，不带指责或批评地表达自己	带着同理心倾听对方，而不解读为指责或批评
观察	
1. 我所观察到的(看到的、听到的、记忆里的、想象的、不带自己的评价) 是否为我的幸福做出了贡献： "当我(看，听)……"	1. 你所观察到的(看到的、听到的、记忆里的、想象的、而不是你所评价的) 是否为你的幸福做出了贡献： "当你(看、听)……" (有时会以静默的方式同理倾听)
感受	
2. 与我的观察相关联，我的感受(情绪、知觉而非想法)： "我感到……"	2. 与你的观察相关联，你的感受(情绪、知觉而不是想法)： "你感到……"
需要	
3. 引发我感受的根源是我所需要或看重的(而不是偏好或特定的行为)： "……因为我需要/看重……"	3. 引发你感受的根源是你所需要或看重的(而不是偏好或特定的行为)： "……因为你需要/看重……"
请求	
为了服务我的生命需要，清晰地表达请求而不是要求。	同理倾听什么请求能服务你的生命需要，而不是听到任何要求。
4. 我想采取的具体行动是： "你愿意试试……吗？"	4.. 你想采取的具体行动是： "你愿意试试……吗？" (有时会以静默的方式同理倾听)

The Four-Part Nonviolent Communication Process

Clearly expressing
how **I am**
without blaming
or criticizing

Empathically receiving
how **you are**
without hearing
blame or criticism

OBSERVATIONS

1. What I observe *(see, hear, remember, imagine, free from my evaluations)* that does or does not contribute to my well-being:

   "When I (see, hear) . . . "

1. What you observe *(see, hear, remember, imagine, free from your evaluations)* that does or does not contribute to your well-being:

   "When you see/hear . . . "
   (Sometimes unspoken when offering empathy)

FEELINGS

2. How I feel *(emotion or sensation rather than thought)* in relation to what I observe:

   "I feel . . . "

2. How you feel *(emotion or sensation rather than thought)* in relation to what you observe:

   "You feel . . ."

NEEDS

3. What I need or value *(rather than a preference, or a specific action)* that causes my feelings:

   " . . . because I need/value . . . "

3. What you need or value *(rather than a preference, or a specific action)* that causes your feelings:

   " . . . because you need/value . . ."

Clearly requesting that
which would enrich **my**
life without demanding

Empathically receiving that
which would enrich **your** life
without hearing any demand

REQUESTS

4. The concrete actions I would like taken:

   "Would you be willing to . . . ?"

4. The concrete actions you would like taken:

   "Would you like . . . ?"
   (Sometimes unspoken when offering empathy)

© Marshall B. Rosenberg. For more information about Marshall B. Rosenberg
or the Center for Nonviolent Communication, please visit www.CNVC.org.

人类共有的一些基本感受

需要得到满足时的感受

- 惊叹
- 舒适
- 自信
- 期待
- 精力充沛

- 满足
- 开心
- 满怀希望
- 受启发
- 好奇

- 愉快
- 感动
- 乐观
- 自豪
- 放心

- 兴奋
- 惊喜
- 感激
- 触动
- 信赖

需要未得到满足时的感受

- 生气
- 烦闷
- 担心
- 困惑
- 失望

- 灰心
- 苦恼
- 尴尬
- 挫败
- 无助

- 无望
- 不耐烦
- 恼火
- 孤单
- 紧张

- 不堪重负
- 迷茫
- 犹豫
- 难过
- 不适

Some Basic Feelings We All Have

Feelings when needs are fulfilled
- Amazed
- Comfortable
- Confident
- Eager
- Energetic
- Fulfilled
- Glad
- Hopeful
- Inspired
- Intrigued
- Joyous
- Moved
- Optimistic
- Proud
- Relieved
- Stimulated
- Surprised
- Thankful
- Touched
- Trustful

Feelings when needs are not fulfilled
- Angry
- Annoyed
- Concerned
- Confused
- Disappointed
- Discouraged
- Distressed
- Embarrassed
- Frustrated
- Helpless
- Hopeless
- Impatient
- Irritated
- Lonely
- Nervous
- Overwhelmed
- Puzzled
- Reluctant
- Sad
- Uncomfortable

Some Basic Needs We All Have

Autonomy
- Choosing dreams/goals/values
- Choosing plans for fulfilling one's dreams, goals, values

Celebration
- Celebrating the creation of life and dreams fulfilled
- Celebrating losses: loved ones, dreams, etc. (mourning)

Integrity
- Authenticity • Creativity
- Meaning • Self-worth

Interdependence
- Acceptance • Appreciation
- Closeness • Community
- Consideration
- Contribution to the enrichment of life
- Emotional Safety • Empathy

Physical Nurturance
- Air • Food
- Movement, exercise
- Protection from life-threatening forms of life: viruses, bacteria, insects, predatory animals
- Rest • Sexual Expression
- Shelter • Touch • Water

Play
- Fun • Laughter

Spiritual Communion
- Beauty • Harmony
- Inspiration • Order • Peace
- Honesty (the empowering honesty that enables us to learn from our limitations)
- Love • Reassurance
- Respect • Support
- Trust • Understanding

©CNVC. Please visit www.CNVC.org to learn more.

资源

人类共有的一些基本需要

自主选择 · 选择梦想、目标和价值 · 选择实现梦想、目标和价值的方法	**精神交融** · 美 · 和谐 · 启迪 · 秩序 · 和平
内外一致 · 真实 · 创造力 · 意义 · 自我价值	**玩耍** · 乐趣 · 欢笑
庆祝/哀悼 · 庆祝人生的创造和梦想的实现 · 哀悼失去：亲人离世、梦想破灭，等等	**滋养身体** · 空气 · 食物 · 运动，锻炼 · 保护（免受病毒、细菌、昆虫及食肉动物的威胁） · 休息 · 性表达 · 住所 · 触摸 · 水
相互依存 · 接纳 · 欣赏 · 亲近 · 社群 · 体谅 · 服务生命 · 心理安全 · 同理 · 诚实（有力量的诚实，可以让我们从自身的局限中得以学习） · 爱 · 确认 · 尊重 · 支持 · 信任 · 理解 · 温暖	

 About Nonviolent Communication

Nonviolent Communication has flourished for more than four decades across sixty countries selling more than 3,000,000 books in over thirty-five languages for one simple reason: it works.

From the bedroom to the boardroom, from the classroom to the war zone, Nonviolent Communication (NVC) is changing lives every day. NVC provides an easy-to-grasp, effective method to get to the root of violence and pain peacefully. By examining the unmet needs behind what we do and say, NVC helps reduce hostility, heal pain, and strengthen professional and personal relationships. NVC is now being taught in corporations, classrooms, prisons, and mediation centers worldwide. And it is affecting cultural shifts as institutions, corporations, and governments integrate NVC consciousness into their organizational structures and their approach to leadership.

Most of us are hungry for skills that can improve the quality of our relationships, to deepen our sense of personal empowerment or simply help us communicate more effectively. Unfortunately, most of us have been educated from birth to compete, judge, demand, and diagnose; to think and communicate in terms of what is "right" and "wrong" with people. At best, the habitual ways we think and speak hinder communication and create misunderstanding or frustration. And still worse, they can cause anger and pain, and may lead to violence. Without wanting to, even people with the best of intentions generate needless conflict.

NVC helps us reach beneath the surface and discover what is alive and vital within us, and how all of our actions are based on human needs that we are seeking to meet. We learn to develop a vocabulary of feelings and needs that helps us more clearly express what is going on in us at any given moment. When we understand and acknowledge our needs, we develop a shared foundation for much more satisfying relationships. Join the thousands of people worldwide who have improved their relationships and their lives with this simple yet revolutionary process.

有关非暴力沟通的更多信息，请联系国际非暴力沟通中心，地址如下：
Center for Nonviolent Communication (CNVC)
9301 Indian School Rd., NE, Suite 204Albuquerque NM 87112-2861 USA
Ph: 505-244-4041
US Only: 800-255-7696
Fax: 505-247-0414
Email: cnvc@CNVC.org
Website: www.CNVC.org

About the Center for Nonviolent Communication

The Center for Nonviolent Communication (CNVC) is an international nonprofit peacemaking organization whose vision is a world where everyone's needs are met peacefully. CNVC is devoted to supporting the spread of Nonviolent Communication (NVC) around the world.

Founded in 1984 by Dr. Marshall B. Rosenberg, CNVC has been contributing to a vast social transformation in thinking, speaking and acting—showing people how to connect in ways that inspire compassionate results. NVC is now being taught around the globe in communities, schools, prisons, mediation centers, churches, businesses, professional conferences, and more. Hundreds of certified trainers and hundreds more supporters teach NVC to tens of thousands of people each year in more than sixty countries.

CNVC believes that NVC training is a crucial step to continue building a compassionate, peaceful society. Your tax-deductible donation will help CNVC continue to provide training in some of the most impoverished, violent corners of the world. It will also support the development and continuation of organized projects aimed at bringing NVC training to high-need geographic regions and populations.

To make a tax-deductible donation or to learn more about the valuable resources described below, visit the CNVC website at www.CNVC.org:

- **Training and Certification**—Find local, national, and international training opportunities, access trainer certification information, connect to local NVC communities, trainers, and more.
- **CNVC Bookstore**—Find mail or phone order information for a complete selection of NVC books, booklets, audio, and video materials at the CNVC website.
- **CNVC Projects**—Participate in one of the several regional and theme-based projects that provide focus and leadership for teaching NVC in a particular application or geographic region.

For more information, please contact CNVC at:
Ph: 505-244-4041 • US Only: 800-255-7696 • Fax: 505-247-0414
Email: cnvc@CNVC.org • Website: www.CNVC.org

Bibliography

Alinsky, Saul D. *Rules for Radicals: A Pragmatic Primer for Realistic Radicals.* New York: Random House, 1971.

Arendt, Hannah. *Eichmann in Jerusalem: A Report on the Banality of Evil.* New York: Viking Press, 1963.

Becker, Ernest. *The Birth and Death of Meaning: An Interdisciplinary Perspective on the Problem of Man.* New York: Free Press, 1971.

———. *The Revolution in Psychiatry: The New Understanding of Man.* New York: Free Press, 1964.

Benedict, Ruth. "Synergy—Patterns of the Good Culture." *Psychology Today* 4 (June 1970): 53–77.

Boserup, Anders, and Andrew Mack. *War Without Weapons: Non-Violence in National Defence.* New York: Schocken Books, 1975.

Bowles, Samuel, and Herbert Gintis. *Schooling in Capitalist America: Educational Reform and the Contradictions of Economic Life.* New York: Basic Books, 1976.

Buber, Martin. *I and Thou.* Translated by Ronald Gregor Smith. New York: Scribner, 1958.

Craig, James, and Marguerite Craig. *Synergic Power Beyond Domination and Permissiveness.* Berkeley, CA: Proactive Press, 1974.

Dass, Ram. *The Only Dance There Is.* New York: Jason Aronson, 1985.

Dass, Ram, and Mirabai Bush. *Compassion in Action: Setting Out on the Path of Service.* New York: Bell Tower, 1992.

Dass, Ram, and Paul Gorman. *How Can I Help? Stories and Reflections on Service.* New York: Knopf, 1985.

Domhoff, William G. *The Higher Circles: The Governing Class in America.* New York: Vintage Books, 1971.

Ellis, Albert, and Robert A. Harper. *A Guide to Rational Living.* Englewood Cliffs, NJ: Prentice-Hall, 1961.

Freire, Paulo. *Pedagogy of the Oppressed.* Translated by Myra Bergman Ramos. New York: Herder and Herder, 1970.

Fromm, Erich. *Escape from Freedom.* New York: Farrar & Rinehart, Inc., 1941.

Fromm, Erich. *The Art of Loving.* New York: Harper & Row, 1956.

Gardner, Herb. *A Thousand Clowns,* in *The Collected Plays.* New York: Applause Books, 2000.

Gendlin, Eugene. *Focusing.* New York: Everest House, 1978.

Glenn, Michael, and Richard Kunnes. *Repression or Revolution? Therapy in the United States Today.* New York: Harper and Row, 1973.

Greenburg, Dan, and Marcia Jacobs. *How to Make Yourself Miserable for the Rest of the Century: Another Vital Training Manual.* New York: Vintage Books, 1987.

Harvey, O.J. *Conceptual Systems and Personality Organization.* New York: Wiley, 1961.

Hillesum, Etty. *Etty: A Diary, 1941-1943.* Introduced by J. G. Gaarlandt; translated by Arnold J. Pomerans. London: Jonathan Cape, 1983

Holt, John. *How Children Fail.* New York: Pitman, 1964.

Humphreys, Christmas. *The Way of Action: A Working Philosophy for Western Life.* New York: MacMillan, 1960.

Irwin, Robert. *Building a Peace System: Exploratory Project on the Conditions of Peace.* Expro Press, 1989.

Johnson, Wendell. *Living with Change: The Semantics of Coping.* New York: Harper and Row, 1972.

Katz, Michael B. *Class, Bureaucracy and Schools: The Illusion of Educational Change in America.* New York: Frederick A. Praeger, Inc., 1975.

Katz, Michael B., ed. *School Reform: Past and Present.* Boston: Little, Brown & Co., 1971.

Kaufmann, Walter. *Without Guilt and Justice: From Decidophobia to Autonomy.* New York: P.H. Wyden, 1973.

Keen, Sam. *Hymns to an Unknown God: Awakening the Spirit in Everyday Life.* New York: Bantam Books, 1994.

———. *To a Dancing God.* New York: Harper and Row, 1970.

Kelly, George A. *The Psychology of Personal Constructs.* 2 vols. New York: Norton, 1955.

Kornfield, Jack. *A Path with Heart: A Guide Through the Perils and Promises of Spiritual Life.* New York: Bantam Books, 1993.

Kozol, Jonathan. *The Night Is Dark and I Am Far from Home.* Boston: Houghton-Mifflin Co., 1975.

Kurtz, Ernest, and Katherine Ketcham. *The Spirituality of Imperfection: Modern Wisdom from Classic Stories.* New York: Bantam Books, 1992.

Lyons, Gracie. *Constructive Criticism: A Handbook.* Oakland, CA: IRT Press, 1976.

Mager, Robert. *Preparing Instructional Objectives.* Belmont, CA: Fearon-Pitman Pub., 1975.

Maslow, Abraham. *Eupsychian Management.* Homewood, IL: Richard D. Irwin, 1965.

———. *Toward a Psychology of Being.* Princeton, NJ: Van Nostrand, 1962.
McLaughlin, Corinne, and Gordon Davidson. *Spiritual Politics: Changing the World from the Inside Out.* New York: Ballantine Books, 1994.
Milgram, Stanley. *Obedience to Authority: An Experimental View.* New York: Harper and Row, 1974.
Postman, Neil, and Charles Weingartner. *The Soft Revolution: A Student Handbook for Turning Schools Around.* New York: Delacorte Press, 1971.
———. *Teaching as a Subversive Activity.* New York: Delacorte Press, 1969.
Powell, John. *The Secret of Staying in Love.* Niles, IL: Argus Communications, 1974.
———. *Why Am I Afraid to Tell You Who I Am?* Chicago: Argus Communications, 1969.
Putney, Snell. *The Conquest of Society: Sociological Observations for the Autonomous Revolt against the Autosystems Which Turn Humanity into Servo-Men.* Belmont, CA: Wadsworth, 1972.
Robben, John. *Coming to My Senses.* New York: Thomas Crowell, 1973.
Rogers, Carl. *A Way of Being.* New York: Houghton Mifflin Books, 1980, p. 12.
———. *Carl Rogers on Personal Power.* New York: Delacorte Press, 1977.
———. *Freedom to Learn: A View of What Education Might Become.* Columbus, OH: Charles E. Merrill, 1969.
———. "Some Elements of Effective Interpersonal Communication." Mimeographed paper from speech given at California Institute of Technology, Pasadena, CA, Nov. 9, 1964.
A Way of Being. New York: Houghton Mifflin Books, 1980, p. 12.
Rosenberg, Marshall. *Mutual Education: Toward Autonomy and Interdependence.* Seattle: Special Child Publications, 1972.
Ryan, William. *Blaming the Victim.* New York: Vintage Books, 1976.
Scheff, Thomas J., ed. *Labeling Madness.* Englewood Cliffs, NJ: Prentice-Hall, 1975.
Schmookler, Andrew Bard. *Out of Weakness: Healing the Wounds That Drive Us to War.* New York: Bantam Books, 1988.
Sharp, Gene. *Social Power and Political Freedom.* Boston: Porter Sargent, 1980.
Steiner, Claude. *Scripts People Live: Transactional Analysis of Life Scripts.* New York: Grove Press, 1974.
Szasz, Thomas S. *Ideology and Insanity: Essays on the Psychiatric Dehumanization of Man.* New York: M. Boyars, 1983.
Tagore, Rabindranath. *Sadhana: The Realization of Life.* Tucson: Omen Press, 1972.

About the Author

Photo by Beth Banning

Marshall B. Rosenberg, PhD (1934–2015) founded and was for many years the Director of Educational Services for the Center for Nonviolent Communication, an international peacemaking organization.

During his life he authored fifteen books, including the bestselling *Nonviolent Communication: A Language of Life* (PuddleDancer Press), which has sold more than three million copies worldwide and has been translated into more than thirty-five languages, with more translations in the works.

Dr. Rosenberg has received a number of awards for his Nonviolent Communication work including:

2014: Champion of Forgiveness Award from the Worldwide Forgiveness Alliance
2006: Bridge of Peace Nonviolence Award from the Global Village Foundation
2005: Light of God Expressing in Society Award from the Association of Unity Churches
2004: Religious Science International Golden Works Award
2004: International Peace Prayer Day Man of Peace Award by the Healthy, Happy Holy (3HO) Organization
2002: Princess Anne of England and Chief of Police Restorative Justice Appreciation Award
2000: International Listening Association Listener of the Year Award

Dr. Rosenberg first used the NVC process in federally funded school integration projects to provide mediation and communication skills training during the 1960s. The Center for Nonviolent Communication, which he founded in 1984, now has hundreds of certified NVC trainers and supporters teaching NVC in more than sixty countries around the globe.

A sought-after presenter, peacemaker and visionary leader, Dr. Rosenberg led NVC workshops and international intensive trainings for tens of thousands of people in more than sixty countries around the world and provided training and initiated peace programs in many war-torn areas including Nigeria, Sierra Leone, and the Middle East. He worked tirelessly with educators, managers, health care providers, lawyers, military officers, prisoners, police and prison officials, government officials, and individual families. With guitar and puppets in hand and a spiritual energy that filled a room, Marshall showed us how to create a more peaceful and satisfying world.

图书在版编目（CIP）数据

非暴力沟通：汉英对照版/（美）马歇尔·卢森堡（Marshall B. Rosenberg）著；刘轶译. — 北京：华夏出版社有限公司, 2021.10（2025.3 重印）

书名原文：Nonviolent Communication: A Language of Life 3rd Edition

ISBN 978-7-5222-0181-8

Ⅰ. ①非… Ⅱ. ①马… ②刘… Ⅲ. ①心理交往－通俗读物－汉、英 Ⅳ. ①C912.11-49

中国版本图书馆 CIP 数据核字（2021）第 205450 号

Translated from the book Nonviolent Communication 3rd Edition and ISBN 9781892005281 by Marshall Rosenberg.
Copyright © September 2015, published by PuddleDancer Press. Used with permission.
For further information about Nonviolent Communication (TM) please visit the Center for Nonviolent Communication on the Web at: www.cnvc.org.
Simplified Chinese copyright © Huaxia Publishing House Co., Ltd.
All rights reserved.

版权所有 翻印必究

北京市版权局著作权合同登记号：图字 01-2016-2253 号

非暴力沟通：汉英对照版

著　　者	[美] 马歇尔·卢森堡	
译　　者	刘　轶	
策划编辑	朱　悦　　卢莎莎	
责任编辑	朱　悦　　卢莎莎	
责任印制	刘　洋	
出版发行	华夏出版社有限公司	
经　　销	新华书店	
印　　刷	三河市万龙印装有限公司	
装　　订	三河市万龙印装有限公司	
版　　次	2021 年 10 月北京第 1 版　　2025 年 3 月北京第 3 次印刷	
开　　本	710×1000　　1/16 开	
印　　张	31	
字　　数	290 千字	
定　　价	139.00 元	

华夏出版社有限公司　地址：北京市东直门外香河园北里 4 号　邮编：100028
网址：www.hxph.com.cn　电话：(010) 64663331（转）
若发现本版图书有印装质量问题，请与我社营销中心联系调换。